The Making of Israel

# Supplements
# to
# Vetus Testamentum

*Editor-in-Chief*

Christl M. Maier

*Editorial Board*

VOLUME 162

The titles published in this series are listed at *brill.com/vts*

# The Making of Israel

*By*

C.L. Crouch

BRILL

LEIDEN | BOSTON

Library of Congress Cataloging-in-Publication Data

Crouch, Carly L. (Carly Lorraine), 1982– author.
  The making of Israel / by C.L. Crouch.
    pages cm. — (Vetus Testamentum, Supplements ; 162)
  In The Making of Israel C.L. Crouch presents the southern Levant during the seventh century BCE as
a major period for the formation of Israelite ethnic identity, challenging scholarship which dates biblical
texts with identity concerns to the exilic and post-exilic periods as well as scholarship which limits
pre-exilic identity concerns to Josianic nationalism. The argument analyses the archaeological material
from the southern Levant during Iron Age II, then draws on anthropological research to argue for an ethnic
response to the economic, political and cultural change of this period. The volume concludes with an
investigation into identity issues in Deuteronomy, highlighting centralisation and exclusive Yahwism as part
of the deuteronomic formulation of Israelite ethnic identity—Supplied by publisher.
  ISBN 978-90-04-27467-9 (hardback : alk. paper) — ISBN 978-90-04-27469-3 (e-book) 1. Jews—
History—1200–953 B.C. 2. Jews—Palestine—Identity—History. 3. Ethnology in the Bible. 4. Ethnology—
Palestine. 5. Sociology, Biblical. 6. Bible. Deuteronomy—Criticism, interpretation, etc. 7. Bible.
Old Testament—Antiquities. [1. Palestine—Antiquities.] I. Title.

  DS121.55.C76 2014
  933'.02—dc23

                                                                                          2014011781

This publication has been typeset in the multilingual 'Brill' typeface. With over 5,100 characters covering
Latin, IPA, Greek, and Cyrillic, this typeface is especially suitable for use in the humanities.
For more information, please see brill.com/brill-typeface.

ISSN 0083-5889
ISBN 978 90 04 27467 9 (hardback)
ISBN 978 90 04 27469 3 (e-book)

PRINTED BY DRUKKERIJ WILCO B.V. - AMERSFOORT, THE NETHERLANDS

*for my parents*

*I love you forever / I like you for always*

⁞

# Contents

# Acknowledgements

The origins of the following may be traced to a paper delivered at the first Interdisciplinary Approaches to the Biblical World Conference, at Trinity College, Dublin, in 2007. Though a comparison of that paper to what follows will reveal the nearly wholesale alteration of my approach in the interim, I am grateful to the organisers of the conference—Jason Silverman, Lidia Matassa and Killian McAleese—for turning my mind to the identity concerns of the pre-exilic period. Versions of more recent material have been heard by the biblical studies seminars at Durham, Sheffield, and Edinburgh and in San Francisco and Chicago by the members of the Theology of the Hebrew Scriptures, Israelite Religion in Its West Asian Environment and Assyriology and the Bible program units of the Society of Biblical Literature; thanks are due to the chairs—Walter Moberly, Hugh Pyper, Alison Jack, Esther Hamori, Simi Chavel and Peter Machinist—for their invitations and to the audiences of those sessions for their critical feedback and suggestions.

Funding for conference travel has been provided by the Faculty of Theology of the University of Oxford (now the Faculty of Theology and Religion); the Bethune-Baker Trust Fund of the Faculty of Divinity of the University of Cambridge; the Rice Research Fund of Fitzwilliam College, Cambridge; the School of Humanities of the University of Nottingham; and the British Academy; funding for books and excavation costs came from the E.O. James Bequest of All Souls College, Oxford. Research fellowships at Keble College, Oxford and Fitzwilliam College, Cambridge supported the research and early writing stages of the project; the support of colleagues at the University of Nottingham since my arrival in 2011, including and especially Karen Kilby and Simon Oliver as Heads of Department, has been essential to its completion. Funding from the Deichmann Foundation, generously extended by Roland Deines, supported the employment of Cat Quine as research assistant; her efforts with the footnotes have been much appreciated.

Numerous colleagues have given of their time and energy to read parts or the entirety of the manuscript. Foremost among these are Hans Barstad, Ido Koch, Jonathan Stökl and Casey Strine. The argument, in all its details, has been improved by their critical attentions; its errors and eccentricities remain mine. The staff of the excavations at Ramat Rahel and Tel Azekah—Oded Lipschits, Manfred Oeming, Yuval Gadot, Benjamin Arubas, Omer Sergi, Boaz Gross and especially Ido Koch—have endured broken bones, missing visas and incessant interrogation in order to induct me into the archaeological fraternity. The support of the Oxford mafia in life both personal and professional has been, as always, received with gratitude.

Last but not least: my husband, whom I have met, loved and married in the time it has taken to see this book to completion; his family, who have welcomed me and my family with open arms; my sister, who keeps me in baked goods and out of the madhouse; my grandmother, whose commitment to higher education has profoundly affected the opportunities available to me; and my parents, who have supported me—quite literally—to the ends of the earth. This one is for them.

*Nottingham*
*February 2014*

# Abbreviations

The volume uses the following abbreviations, in addition to those detailed in the *SBL Handbook of Style*:

| | |
|---|---|
| ANESupS | Ancient Near Eastern Studies Supplement Series |
| *ARA* | *Annual Review of Anthropology* |
| BAMA | British Academy Monographs in Archaeology |
| CHANE | Culture and History of the Ancient Near East |
| *CSSH* | *Comparative Studies in Society and History* |
| HBS | Herders Biblische Studien |
| *JHS* | *Journal of Hebrew Scriptures* |
| LHBOTS | Library of Hebrew Bible/Old Testament Studies |
| MSIA | Monograph Series of the Institute of Archaeology |
| OikSAW | Oikumene: Studien zur antiken Weltgeschichte |
| OTM | Oxford Theological Monographs |
| *OTS* | *Old Testament Studies* |
| PIA | Publications of the Institute of Archaeology of Tel Aviv University |
| RINAP | The Royal Inscriptions of the Neo-Assyrian Period |
| SAHL | Studies in the Archaeology and History of the Levant |

# Introduction

Discussions of Israelite identity focus overwhelmingly on two periods: the emergence of Israel sometime around the tenth century and the experience of Babylonian exile in the sixth century. Scholarly histories of Israel and Judah all but ignore the question of Israelite identity in the intervening four hundred years. There are a few exceptions to the rule, but especially with regard to textual analysis there is a propensity to read passages which express an interest in or concern for identity issues as responding to the circumstances of Babylonian exile. Lang reflects the majority opinion when he declares that 'isolation from foreigners or xenophobia does not appear in Israel during the monarchy but is first documented in the period of early Judaism, when the people were living under foreign domination and were concerned for their identity'.[1] The present

---

1  B. Lang, '*nkr; nēkār; nokrî*', *TDOT* 9:426. Rare exceptions to this rule include Machinist's discussion of the confrontation with Assyrian representatives at Jerusalem in 2 Kings 18 // Isaiah 36 (P. Machinist, 'The Rab Saqeh at the Wall of Jerusalem: Israelite Identity in the Face of the Assyrian "Other"', *HS* 41 [2000], 151–168); a section on Deuteronomy in Sparks' well-known *Prolegomena* (K.L. Sparks, *Ethnicity and Identity in Ancient Israel: Prolegomena to the Study of Ethnic Sentiments and Their Expression in the Hebrew Bible* [Winona Lake, Ind., Eisenbrauns, 1998], 222–284); and part of Nestor's application of cognitive approaches to identity to the Hebrew Bible, articulated mainly in terms of covenant theology (D.A. Nestor, *Cognitive Perspectives on Israelite Identity* [LHBOTS 519, London, T&T Clark, 2010], 192–215, although this latter is not focused on chronology and covers a wide range of texts and [implicit] chronology). The one widespread exception concerns a supposed surge in nationalist sentiments under Josiah. The basis of this phenomenon in the text of 2 Kings, however, has been generally acknowledged as deeply problematic, at least for the purposes of historical reconstruction of events during the reigns of the seventh century kings (F. Stavrakopoulou, *King Manasseh and Child Sacrifice: Biblical Distortions of Historical Realities* [BZAW 338, Berlin, de Gruyter, 2004]; E. Ben Zvi, 'Prelude to a Reconstruction of Historical Manassic Judah', *BN* 81 [1996], 31–44; E.A. Knauf, 'The Glorious Days of Manasseh', *Good Kings and Bad Kings: The Kingdom of Judah in the Seventh Century B.C.E.* [ed. L.L. Grabbe, LHBOTS 393, London, T&T Clark, 2005], 164–188; R.H. Lowery, *The Reforming Kings: Cults and Society in First Temple Judah* [JSOTSup 210, Sheffield, JSOT, 1991]; L.A.S. Monroe, *Josiah's Reform and the Dynamics of Defilement: Israelite Rites of Violence and the Making of a Biblical Text* [Oxford, Oxford University Press, 2011]; P.R. Davies, 'Josiah and the Law Book', *Good Kings and Bad Kings: The Kingdom of Judah in the Seventh Century B.C.E.* [ed. L.L. Grabbe, LHBOTS 393, London, T&T Clark, 2005], 65–77). Combined with the discrediting of assumptions of imposed Neo-Assyrian religious practices as forming a political background for Josiah's cult purge, the foundations of a nationalist project under Josiah are extremely weak (see variously M.D. Cogan, *Imperialism and Religion: Assyria, Judah and Israel in the Eighth and Seventh Centuries B.C.E.* [SBLMS 19, Missoula, Mont., Scholars, 1974]; M.D. Cogan, 'Judah under Assyrian Hegemony: A Reexamination of

study intends to attract attention to this scholarly blind spot, focusing on the southern Levant from the late eighth century to the early sixth century and arguing that this period is a prime candidate for Israelite identity issues.

During this period, referred to here as the long seventh century, the southern Levant witnessed significant political, economic and social change. This upheaval was spurred primarily by the advent of the Assyrian empire as the dominant power in the west, beginning in the middle of the eighth century and accelerating through the latter part of the century with the empire-building of Tiglath-pileser III, Sargon II and Sennacherib, before continuing into the major part of the seventh century with Esarhaddon and Assurbanipal. In the first instance the impact of the Assyrians' arrival took the form of military campaigns and exertions of political strength, but as time went on their presence in the southern Levant was increasingly characterised by a more or less peaceful exertion of power and the development of economic interests, especially through the fostering of prosperous commercial trade routes in this region. The focus of this volume is on the cultural and ideological impact of this period on the population of the southern Levant and on the population of Judah in particular.

Its objectives are threefold. First, it presents extensive archaeological material to argue that political, social and economic changes arising from the *pax Assyriaca* made the long seventh century a period of increased cultural interaction in the southern Levant. Second, it employs anthropological material to argue that this increase in exposure to different cultures provoked a heightened awareness of cultural difference among existing southern Levantine groups, resulting in the reinforcement of existing group boundaries and the formation of new ones. Bringing these together, it argues that the social, economic and political changes of the long seventh century provoked significant ethnic identity concerns among the populations of the southern Levant, including the population of Judah. Thirdly, it explores the implications of this conclusion by examining Deuteronomy with this period of heightened concern about group identity in mind, considering whether the identity concerns which pervade

Imperialism and Religion', *JBL* 112 [1993], 403–412; S.W. Holloway, *Aššur is King! Aššur is King!: Religion in the Exercise of Power in the Neo-Assyrian Empire* [CHANE 10, Leiden, Brill, 2001]; D.R. Miller, 'The Shadow of the Overlord: Revisiting the Question of Neo-Assyrian Imposition on the Judaean Cult during the Eighth–Seventh Centuries BCE', *From Babel to Babylon: Essays on Biblical History and Literature in Honor of Brian Peckham* [ed. J.R. Wood, J.E. Harvey and M. Leuchter, LHBOTS 455, London, T&T Clark, 2006], 146–168; A.M. Bagg, 'Palestine under Assyrian Rule: A New Look at Assyrian Policy in the West', *JAOS* 133 [2013], 119–144).

the book may be understood as deriving from this context. The argument itself is undertaken in three parts, corresponding to these three objectives.

Chapter One addresses the history and archaeology of the southern Levant during the long seventh century. The chapter discusses the major powers of Assyria and Egypt, paying attention to the broad effects of the former's political and economic policies on the region in particular, before considering the manifestation of these effects in the smaller southern Levantine states. Anticipating the latter half of the volume, this chapter culminates with a discussion of the territories of Judah. The focus throughout this chapter is on relevant archaeological material and on its capacity to witness to the widespread movements of persons during this period. The broader trends of the region and the distribution of the most diverse material tends to suggest that much of this movement may be linked to an increase in trading activities during this period. Relating these material culture remains to specific ideological identity associations is difficult; nevertheless, the diversity of the remains and the evidence for increased diversity warrant the interpretation of these remains as reflecting a political, social and economic climate in which the populations of the region were exposed at a much greater frequency to persons whose cultural identities were differentiable from their own. The chapter concludes that the long seventh century in the southern Levant was a period of increased interaction among diverse cultural groups, both those local to the region as well as those from further afield.

The significance of the introduction of cultural difference is explored on the theoretical level in Chapter Two with a discussion of identity as an anthropological phenomenon. The focus is on anthropological theories of ethnic identity formation which emphasise the generative impact of the introduction of cultural alternatives, as these theories offer both a convincing understanding of identity phenomena in general as well as significant explanatory potential for understanding the effects of the major changes in the southern Levantine experience identified in Chapter One.

Key to these studies is the idea that consciousness of an identity or group affiliation arises usually in response to experience of or interaction with a person or group whose cultural—broadly understood—practices are recognisably different from the subject's own. Exposure to different cultural practices heightens awareness of the possibility of pursuing an alternative set of practices and leads to defensiveness regarding the native cultural set. Interpretation of the seventh century increase in material diversity in light of these theories of identity formation is argued to favour an understanding of the long seventh century in the southern Levant as an environment in which social, political and economic conditions were of the kind likely to provoke increased consciousness of ethnic identity. Judah specifically witnessed the convergence of decreased political autonomy arising from its subordination as an Assyrian vassal state, increased involvement in a booming, *pax Assyriaca*-fuelled economic network and, as a result of Sennacherib's campaign in 701, significantly narrowed geo-political borders and the reassignment of large sections of Judah's southwestern agricultural territory elsewhere; all of these factors combined to introduce the population of Judah to outsiders and their unfamiliar cultural *accoutrements* on a previously unknown scale. In the conditions of the long seventh century, in other words, it is reasonable to expect the kind of identity formation phenomena in Judah which has been observed by anthropological studies of similar circumstances elsewhere.

Anticipating the textual exploration to follow, the section concludes by noting a number of ways in which identity formation phenomena manifest, including the differentiation and homogenisation of group practice, efforts to establish the spatial proximity of members, emphases on common historical and genealogical origins and various means by which the identity group is isolated physically and ideologically from outsiders.

The implications of this emphasis on identity concerns in the long seventh century for biblical scholarship is the focus of Chapter Three, which examines a number of passages in the book of Deuteronomy in light of this suggestion. The chapter focuses on the material which may be attributed to a deuteronomic version of the book, arguing that the identity concerns expressed by these texts may be understood as a phenomenon of Israelite identity formation occurring against the historical backdrop described in Chapter One. Texts are analysed in terms of their interest in differentiating and defending a distinctive Israelite practice, noting especially the way in which they manifest the kinds of identity formation phenomena observed by anthropological studies. Deuteronomic Israel is defined as a community brought together spatially around a single cult site, as a community with common origins which may be traced to Egypt and as a community characterised by a distinctively Israelite praxis, exclusive Yahwism being the foremost feature of the latter. The deuteronomic text undertakes to protect this Israelite community by minimising its interactions with non-Israelites. Some protective mechanisms are focused on the family, such as the prohibitions against exogamy; others are designed to isolate the community as a whole, avoiding non-Israelites when possible and distinguishing the treatment of non-Israelites from Israelites when not. The deuteronomic text is thus understood as a project of Israelite cultural identity, working to define what it is to be Israelite and to defend that identity once established.

As the foregoing already anticipates, the following refers consistently to 'Israelites' and 'non-Israelites'. This demands discussion of the purview of these terms. What is an 'Israelite'? This is the question at stake in the long seventh century, in which the battle over Israelite identity is focused in the southern Levant and on the diverse inhabitants of Judah.[2]

As is all but universally acknowledged, the people living in the land of Judah are largely indistinguishable from their neighbours until an extremely late stage in history; to use the classical language, the people who become 'Israelites' are essentially 'Canaanites' in origin. Indeed, many of the practices which the deuteronomic text rejects are well attested in Judah even in the long seventh century. The question thus arises: when and why does 'Israel' differentiate itself from this southern Levantine cultural mass? Much ink has been spilt concerning the very early stages of this process, but this is not the period which interests us here. Rather the following is concerned with the late eighth and the seventh centuries, in which political and economic developments converge to produce a social world in the southern Levant conducive to the accentuation of identity concerns. This is the period in which recognisable differences in material culture appear in the southern Levant.[3]

According to the deuteronomic material examined in Chapter Three, 'Israel' is defined according to a specific set of cultural characteristics, exclusive Yahwistic worship centralised at a single Yahwistic site foremost among them. The answer the deuteronomic text provides to the question of what defines an Israelite, however, is only one possible answer. Indeed, the very emphasis with which the deuteronomic text expresses itself is a witness to the lack of agreement over the definition of an Israelite among those with claim to the title; the most virulent rhetoric about identity occurs between those competing for the same identity, even more so than the rhetoric between competing identities: 'the most elaborate and extreme forms of ethnic "othering" are more likely to occur in relationships that are in some sense close, rather than in distant ones'.[4] Similarly, 'ethnic groups may sometimes conceive themselves as in

---

2   C.L. Crouch, 'The Threat to Israel's Identity in Deuteronomy: Mesopotamian or Levantine?', *ZAW* 124 (2012), 541–554.

3   L.G. Herr, 'Archaeological Sources for the History of Palestine: The Iron Age II Period: Emerging Nations', *BA* 60 (1997), 114–183.

4   S. Harrison, 'Cultural Difference as Denied Resemblance: Reconsidering Nationalism and Ethnicity', *CSSH* 45 (2003), 345.

conflict not so much because they have irreconcilably different identities, but rather because they have irreconcilable claims or aspirations to
the *same* identities'.[5] The virulence of the deuteronomic text reflects an
intense debate over rightful claims to Israelite identity. In the deuteronomic text as well as the historical context it reflects, 'Israel' is an identity
in the process of formation. Although the deuteronomic definition of
Israel was ultimately extremely successful, with many of its emphases
becoming key features of later definitions of Israel, Yahwism and, ultimately, Judaism, this was not inevitable. In its own moment the deuteronomic text is engaged in a battle—literally unto death—over what it
means to be an Israelite.

It must also be held in mind throughout the following that identities in
contention—including the Israelite one on which this study is focused—
reside as much in the intellect as they reside in actual practice.[6] The
Israelite identity delineated by the deuteronomic text, whose peculiarities will be explored in Chapter Three, has no absolute relationship with
historical reality. This is an idea of Israel—an ideal of Israel, even—which
has been formulated in a context perceived as threatening the very existence of such an idea. This is far from saying that the characteristics of
this idea(l)ised Israel were manifest in its author's reality.[7] Indeed, were
they already manifest, there is no motivation to define or defend them.[8]

This returns us to the question of terms. The observant reader will note
that 'Israel' and 'Israelite' (as well as the latter's counterpart, 'non-Israelite') are entirely avoided in Chapter One, in which the material witnesses
to the southern Levant are discussed; only the terminology of 'Judah' and
'Judahite' is used there. 'Israelite' and 'non-Israelite' are brought in only in
the shift toward the discussion of ideas which begins in Chapter Two.[9]

---

5  S. Harrison, 'Identity as a Scarce Resource', *Social Anthropology* 7 (1999), 239.

6  For an extended exposition of this point see Nestor, *Cognitive Perspectives*.

7  The use of the singular 'author' here is a matter of convenience, not contention.

8  It is indeed a fine line between idea and reality in a project of this kind; there may be
   principles—ideals—which the author chooses to articulate despite awareness that they are
   not, or may never be, reality. The idea of an 'Englishman' may include the consumption of
   fish and chips every Friday lunchtime, but the reality of the Englishman may prefer chicken
   korma or profess a devout vegetarianism. We must therefore be wary of attempts to draw
   conclusions about Israelite realities from the ideas about 'Israel' set out in an imagining and
   imaginative text.

9  Why at least some, if not all, of the inhabitants of Judah call themselves 'Israel' is a matter of much discussion and one to which I hope to return elsewhere. In the interim, see
   the various explanations offered by I. Finkelstein and N.A. Silberman, 'Temple and Dynasty:

This distinction reflects the fact that the 'Israel' and 'not Israel' do not relate directly to two (or more) established and clearly distinct entities in the long seventh century: this is an intellectual differentiation undertaken by the deuteronomic text. Though the deuteronomic Israel may have its roots in the land of Judah, its reality was slow to come to fruition. Some elements of this identity, such as the absolute and exclusive association between Israel and Yhwh, became a fundamental part of definitions of Israel ever after; others, such as the annihilation of all non-Israelites, never came to pass.

Hezekiah, the Remaking of Judah and the Rise of the Pan-Israelite Ideology', *JSOT* 30 (2006), 259–285; N. Na'aman, 'The Israelite-Judahite Struggle for the Patrimony of Ancient Israel', *Bib* 91 (2010), 1–23; N.P. Lemche, *Ancient Israel* (Sheffield, JSOT, 1988); P.R. Davies, *In Search of 'Ancient Israel'* (2nd edn., JSOTSup 148, Sheffield, Sheffield Academic, 1992); R.G. Kratz, *Die Komposition der erzählenden Bücher des Alten Testaments* (Göttingen, Vandenhoeck & Ruprecht, 2000).

# The History and Archaeology of the Southern Levant during the Long Seventh Century

## 1    Introduction

The discussion of pre-exilic identity formation begins in the long seventh century: the decades spanning the Neo-Assyrian empire's arrival in the southern Levant in the late eighth century and its domination through much of the seventh; its ultimate collapse in the last third of the latter and the turbulent final decades of conflict between the rival empires of Egypt and Neo-Babylonia. The territorial and economic expansion of the Neo-Assyrian (hereafter Assyrian) empire forms the most significant single influence on the historical, political, economic and social background to Judah's existence during this long century, with ramifications at every level.[1]

## 2    The Empires of the Long Seventh Century

The southern Levant was dominated by three major states between the middle of the eighth century and the beginning of the sixth century: the Assyrian empire, beginning with Tiglath-pileser III (745–727) and climaxing with the reign of Assurbanipal (668–626), whereafter it sank into an irrecoverable decline; a short-lived period of Egyptian imperial ambition, in which it assumed control over the region as the Assyrians withdrew; and the Neo-Babylonian (hereafter Babylonian) empire, whose control over Assyria's former western territories was reasonably secure by the turn of the sixth century. The first of these is undoubtedly the most important for the pre-exilic history of Judah as well as the present discussion, with its influence on the region both foremost among the three as well as enduring the longest. The Egyptians have generally been neglected in discussions of the southern Levant's transition between the Mesopotamian powers; their influence was necessarily short-lived. The effects

---

1    Accessible overviews of this period may be found in A. Kuhrt, *The Ancient Near East: c.3000–330 B.C.* (2nd edn., vol. 2., Routledge History of the Ancient World, London, Routledge, 1997), 473–546 and M. Van De Mieroop, *A History of the Ancient Near East: ca. 3000–323 BC* (2nd edn., Oxford, Blackwell, 2007), 247–269.

© KONINKLIJKE BRILL NV, LEIDEN, 2014 | DOI 10.1163/9789004274693_003

of the Babylonians are too well known to require rehearsing and are largely outside the purview of the present study.

## 2.1    *Assyria*

The Assyrian empire began its westward expansion in the middle of the eighth century, with the effect of Assyrian ambition in the west felt most acutely, in its early stages, in the northern territories of Aram and Israel. During the early decades of Assyrian imperial expansion, Judah's more southern location, along with the position of Israel as a buffer state, meant that Judah was largely shielded from direct influence of Assyrian power. Assyria's impact on Judah became much more direct with the defeat and destruction of Samaria and its territories by Shalmaneser V/Sargon II in 721.[2] Before the fall of Samaria Judah had accepted Assyrian vassalage, formally subordinating itself to Assyrian power and interests, but in the wake of the northern kingdom's dissolution the new provincial territory of Samaria was directly on Judah's doorstep, mere miles from Jerusalem.[3] A series of rebellions among the coastal states prompted another Assyrian campaign to the region and the formation of the province of Ashdod in 712, bringing the provinces closer also on Judah's western flank. Judahite political uncertainty during this period is probably reflected in parts of the material attributed to Isaiah of Jerusalem, as the political elites sought to align themselves with the ultimate victors while preserving local autonomy.

---

2   The attribution of the destruction of Samaria varies by source; 2 Kings 17 attributes the act to Shalmaneser, but Sargon also claims to have been the one to defeat the city.

3   Note, among the varied witnesses to the changes in population demographics in the former northern kingdom, the Assyrian centres at Gezer and Hazor as well as the textual reminders of Assyrian deportation policies (R. Reich, 'The Persian Building at Ayyelet ha-Shaḥar: The Assyrian Palace at Hazor?', *IEJ* 25 (1975), 233–237; R. Reich, and B. Brandl, 'Gezer under Assyrian Rule', *PEQ* 117 (1985), 41–54; O. Lipschits, 'The Date of the "Assyrian Residence" at Ayyelet ha-Shaḥar', *TA* 17 (1990), 96–99; N. Na'aman and R. Zadok, 'Assyrian Deportations to the Province of Samerina in the Light of Two Cuneiform Tablets from Tel Hadid', *TA* 27 (2000), 159–188; B. Becking, *The Fall of Samaria: An Historical and Archaeological Study* (SHANE 2, Leiden, Brill, 1992), 95–118; I. Finkelstein, 'Gezer Revisited and Revised', *TA* 29 (2002), 286–287. At Gezer, for example, sale contracts from the middle of the seventh century reflect an international population: 20 of the 21 completely legible names are unlikely to be descendants of the native inhabitants, with a dozen Akkadians (mostly Babylonian), one Egyptian and five from other West Semitic speaking areas (N. Na'aman, 'Population Changes in Palestine following Assyrian Deportations', *Ancient Israel and Its Neighbors: Interaction and Counteraction* [Winona Lake, Ind., Eisenbrauns, 2005], 213); note also the assyrianizing seal in T. Ornan, 'A Rediscovered Lost Seal from Gezer', *PEQ* 145 (2013), 53–60.

Assyria's assertions of its authority over the southern Levant in the latter half of the eighth century continued into the seventh. Assyrian domination continued with the reigns of Esarhaddon and Assurbanipal and was thus a presence unabated for most of the seventh century. The phrase *pax Assyriaca* is often applied to this period, intended as a description of the relative stabilisation in the relationships between Assyria and its western vassals and the overall reduction in the political and military tumult of the region. This stability derived in no small part from the minimisation of military conflict: as the majority of the Levant came under the greater or lesser control of the Assyrian empire, conflict among vassal states was discouraged and outright rebellion dealt with as quickly as possible. Assyrian control was largely solidified by the turn of the seventh century. Between 745 and 705, Tiglath-pileser, Shalmaneser and Sargon had conducted six campaigns aimed at consolidating their power in the west. In the subsequent decades military activity in the region reduced dramatically: there were only three western campaigns of any magnitude in the 60 years after 705.[4] Kuhrt observes that,

> in spite of problems of control, particularly in frontier areas (and what imperial power does not experience these?), the Assyrian kings in the period between *c.* 700 and *c.* 630 exercised control over a very large territory with singular success and relative ease: it is not totally inappropriate to describe this period as the *pax Assyriaca*.[5]

---

4 K.L. Younger, Jr., 'Assyrian Involvement in the Southern Levant at the End of the Eighth Century B.C.E.', *Jerusalem in Bible and Archaeology: The First Temple Period* (ed. A.G. Vaughn and A.E. Killebrew, SBLSymS, Leiden, Brill, 2003), 245–246. Younger, Jr. identifies the three subsequent campaigns as those of 701, 677 (Esarhaddon's campaign against Sidon) and 673–663 (Esarhaddon and Assurbanipal's sorties against Egypt). This last might be justifiably considered more than one campaign but, as far as the southern Levant itself was concerned, it was an exercise in collective vassal support for, rather than rebellion against, the imperial overlord, with a number of southern Levantine states sending troops to fight alongside the Assyrian regulars (Prism E 10, 13–21 and Prism C II 37–67, in R. Borger, with A. Fuchs, *Beiträge zum Inschriftenwerk Assurbanipals: Die Prismenklassen A, B, C = K, D, E, F, G, H, J und T sowie andere Inschriften* [Wiesbaden, Harrassowitz, 1996]). The Egyptian campaigns, in other words, did not constitute a period of violent upheaval of southern Levantine life in the manner of the previous campaigns to the west.

5 Kuhrt, *The Ancient Near East*, 500–501. This is contra Rainey, who argues that the entire concept of a *pax Assyriaca* was derived solely from the dating of Tel 'Ira pottery which suggested a rebuilding of the Negev and Beersheba valley sites during the middle of the seventh century, subsequently developed by Na'aman to argue that Manasseh benefitted from a *pax Assyriaca* economy (A.F. Rainey, 'Manasseh, King of Judah, in the Whirlpool of the Seventh Century B.C.E.', *Kinattūtu ša dārâti: Raphael Kutscher Memorial Volume* [ed. A.F. Rainey, Tel

The strong Assyrian grasp on the region created an imperial sphere of influence in which concerns about political subordination could largely give way to other matters. Despite occasional rumbling, usually in conjunction with the death of an Assyrian king, the upper hand in the southern Levant was clearly Assyrian.

The source of the region's authority became murky only as the Assyrian empire began to retract toward the latter third of the century. The Assyrian records more or less disappear after the death of Assurbanipal, a reflection of weakening Assyrian power both at home and abroad. A widespread awareness of Assyria's political and military vulnerability at this time was no doubt responsible for the efforts of several of the western territories to reassert their independence in connection with the fall of Nineveh in 612. After a few years of Egyptian control over the region such efforts ultimately failed in the face of Babylonian military superiority.[6]

### Assyrians in the Southern Levant

Throughout its tenure as imperial overlord of the southern Levant, Assyria's principal interests in the western territories were twofold, with both economic and military policy aimed toward the exertion of more or less direct control

---

Aviv Occasional Publications 1, Tel Aviv, Tel Aviv University, 1993], 151–152). Discussion may be found in, among others, S. Gitin, 'Tel Miqne-Ekron in the 7th Century B.C.E.: The Impact of Economic Innovation and Foreign Cultural Influences on a Neo-Assyrian Vassal City-State', *Recent Excavations in Israel: A View to the West* (ed. S. Gitin, Archaeological Institute of America, Colloquia and Conference Papers 1, Dubuque, Ia., Kendall/Hunt, 1995), 61–79; S. Gitin, 'The Neo-Assyrian Empire and its Western Periphery: The Levant, with a Focus on Philistine Ekron', *Assyria 1995* (ed. S. Parpola and R.M. Whiting, Helsinki, Neo-Assyrian Text Corpus Project, 1997), 77–103; N. Na'aman, 'Sennacherib's Campaign to Judah and the Date of the *lmlk* Stamps', *VT* 29 (1979), 61–86; N. Na'aman, 'The Debated Historicity of Hezekiah's Reform in the Light of Historical and Archaeological Research', *ZAW* 107 (1995), 179–195; N. Na'aman, 'Ekron under the Assyrian and Egyptian Empires', *BASOR* 332 (2003), 81–91; S. Bunimovitz, and Z. Lederman, 'The Final Destruction of Beth-Shemesh and the Pax Assyriaca in the Judean Shephelah', *TA* 30 (2003), 1–26; A. Fantalkin, 'The Final Destruction of Beth-Shemesh and the *Pax Assyriaca* in the Judean Shephelah: An Alternative View', *TA* 31 (2004), 245–261; F.M. Fales, *Guerre et paix en Assyrie: Religion et impérialisme* (Paris, Editions du CERF, 2010), 219–228.

6 Van De Mieroop, *A History of the Ancient Near East*, 266–269; Kuhrt, *The Ancient Near East*, 540–546; also, among many others, O. Lipschits, *The Fall and Rise of Jerusalem: Judah under Babylonian Rule* (Winona Lake, Ind., Eisenbrauns, 2005). Note that the Babylonians apparently had a rather different approach to the economics of conquered territories (see A. Fantalkin, 'Meẓad Ḥashavyahu: Its Material Culture and Historical Background', *TA* 28 [2001], 131, with further references).

over the lucrative Philistine port cities and the passageway to Egypt.[7] On the one hand, Assyrian activity was focused on ensuring the stability of the region by expanding the Assyrian sphere of influence and actively quelling rebellions against imperial authority. As is noted in the discussion of Egypt to follow, Egypt remained a more or less compelling alternative power in the southern Levant through much of this period and Assyria was frequently obliged to contend with challenges directly from, or inspired by, that quarter. A major role of the southern Levantine vassals in this regard was to act as buffer states between the Assyrian heartland and Egypt.[8] It is unsurprising, therefore, to find remains of a number of Assyrian settlements in the southern Levantine-Egyptian border region and Assyrian military-administrative centres operating in numerous locations across the southern 'Levant during this period, including Tel Abu-Salima, Tel Jemmeh, Tel Sera', Tel Haror, Ashdod-Yam, Tel Qudadi, 'En Haseva, Tel el-Kheleifah, Buseirah and Ramat Rahel.[9] Among the more

---

7   N. Na'aman, 'Sennacherib's "Letter to God" on his Campaign to Judah', *Ancient Israel and Its Neighbors: Interaction and Counteraction* (Winona Lake, Ind., Eisenbrauns, 2005), 143. For further discussions of the nature of Assyrian policies on the Philistine coast see I. Finkelstein, 'Horvat Qitmīt and the Southern Trade in the Late Iron Age II', *ZDPV* 108 (1992), 160; Na'aman, 'Ekron under the Assyrian and Egyptian Empires'; A. Faust and E. Weiss, 'Judah, Philistia, and the Mediterranean World: Reconstructing the Economic System of the Seventh Century BCE', *BASOR* 338 (2005), 71–92.

8   B. Otzen, 'Israel under the Assyrians', *Power and Propaganda: A Symposium on Ancient Empires* (ed. M.T. Larsen, Mesopotamia 7, Copenhagen, Akademisk Forlag, 1979), 251–261.

9   See P. Bienkowski and E. Van der Steen, 'Tribes, Trade, and Towns: A New Framework for the Late Iron Age in Southern Jordan and the Negev', *BASOR* 323 (2001), 39; I. Finkelstein, *Living on the Fringe: The Archaeology and History of the Negev, Sinai and Neighbouring Regions in the Bronze and Iron Ages* (Monographs in Mediterranean Archaeology 6, Sheffield, Sheffield Academic Press, 1995), 147; L.G. Herr, 'Archaeological Sources for the History of Palestine: The Iron Age II Period: Emerging Nations', *BA* 60 (1997), 167–168; A. Fantalkin, and O. Tal, 'Re-Discovering the Iron Age Fortress at Tell Qudadi in the Context of Neo-Assyrian Imperialistic Policies', *PEQ* 141 (2009), 188–206; N. Na'aman, 'An Assyrian Residence at Ramat Rahel?', *TA* 28 (2001), 260–280; C.M. Bennett, 'Some Reflections on Neo-Assyrian Influence in Transjordan', *Archaeology in the Levant: Essays for Kathleen Kenyon* (ed. R. Moorey and P. Parr, Warminster, Aris & Phillips, 1978), 164–171; C.M. Bennett, 'Neo-Assyrian Influence in Transjordan', *Studies in the History and Archaeology of Jordan I* (ed. A. Hadidi, Amman, Department of Antiquities, 1982), 181–187. Inside the Assyrian provincial system, similarly Hazor and Gezer (Reich, 'The Persian Building', 1975; Reich and Brandl, 'Gezer under Assyrian Rule'; Lipschits, 'The Date of the "Assyrian Residence"'). Note that agreement is not universal with regard to all of these sites (thus P. Bienkowski, 'Architecture of Edom', *Studies in the History and Archaeology of Jordan V* [ed. K. 'Amr, F. Zayadine and M. Zaghloul, Amman, Department of Antiquities, 1995], 135, 149–141, regarding Buseirah, while Finkelstein, 'Gezer

prominent of these is Tel Jemmeh, whose architecture and material remains suggest a site built to serve as the seat of an Assyrian military governor or a residence for the Assyrian king; the site probably also served as a staging point (perhaps one among several) for the campaigns against Egypt.[10] In addition,

> direct Assyrian habitation probably occurred at military garrisons in for-
> tresses such as Hazor III, Chinneret I, Megiddo III-II, and Abu Salima G,
> and at trading centers like Jemmeh. Other, smaller sites in their neigh-
> bourhood most likely comprised supporters of the Assyrian administra-
> tion or groups controlled by it (Qiri, Qashish, and Yin'am).[11]

This Assyrian presence in the southern Levant was not, however, purely mil-
itary in intent. Rather, it was equally caught up in the encouragement and exploitation of economic development in the region, whose proceeds bene-
fitted Assyria in the form of abundant tribute payments as well as by the more usual commercial means.[12] As Na'aman notes, 'the flourishing and economic success of its vassal states was in Assyria's interest, since rich countries were able to pay heavier tributes'; he notes that 'Assyria might have encouraged the economic development of these states, provided it did not clash with its own interests.'[13]

The eventual reduction of active military campaigns which these permanent outposts reflected did not mean a reduction in Assyrian presence or

---

Revisited', 287 raises uncertainties about Gezer), but the evidence is sufficiently widespread for the overall trend to be clear.

10    G.W. Van Beek, 'Digging up Tell Jemmeh: Smithsonian Archaeologists Unlock a Mound's Secrets', *Archaeology* 36 (1983), 12–19; G.W. Van Beek, 'Jemmeh, Tell', *The New Encyclopedia of Archaeological Excavations in the Holy Land* (ed. E. Stern, Jerusalem, Israel Exploration Society, 1993), 667–674; N. Na'aman and R. Zadok, 'Sargon II's Deportations to Israel and Philistia (716–708 B.C.)', *JCS* 40 (1988), 36–42. In the present context it is also worth noting the evidence that, as part of their occupation, the Assyrians brought various other population groups into the southern Levant; see Na'aman and Zadok, 'Sargon II', 37–40; cf. Na'aman and Zadok, 'Assyrian Deportations'.

11    Herr, 'Archaeological Sources', 167.

12    S. Frankenstein, 'The Phoenicians in the Far West: A Function of Neo-Assyrian Imperialism', *Power and Propaganda: A Symposium on Ancient Empires* (ed. M.T. Larsen, Mesopotamia 7, Copenhagen, Akademisk Forlag, 1979), 263–293; on the ideological background of this movement see also M. Liverani, 'The Ideology of the Assyrian Empire', *Power and Propaganda: A Symposium on Ancient Empires* (ed. M.T. Larsen, Mesopotamia 7, Copenhagen, Akademisk Forlag, 1979), 297–318; M. Liverani, 'Memorandum on the Approach to Historiographic Texts', *Or* 42 (1973), 178–194.

13    Na'aman, 'Ekron under the Assyrian and Egyptian Empires', 87.

influence, as a number of the sites used or constructed by the Assyrians appear to have been doing double duty, ensuring the area's political stability while funnelling trading activities from Egypt and Arabia through the Philistine port cities to Phoenicia, Assyria and beyond.[14] Radiating out from these centres, the influence of Assyria on the southern Levant extended to most aspects of life in provincial and vassal territories, from the national political level down to the material goods used in the home on a daily basis, although these latter were often mediated through one or the other of the southern Levantine states.

Under the influence of the Assyrian presence in the region, many of the trade routes in the region flourished, with many of the southern Levantine territories on the east-west routes (to the Philistine coastal ports, from the Arabian peninsula and the Transjordanian highlands through the Beersheba and Arad valleys) experiencing demographic increases during the seventh century which may be understood as a result of their role in the region's economic system.[15] Bienkowski and van der Steen likewise interpret a number of these sites 'as Assyrian administrative centers located precisely at the end of the Arabian trade route in order to guarantee Assyrian involvement.'[16] Tel er-Ruqeish is one particularly noteworthy site in this regard, founded in the late eighth century in conjunction with extensive building works in southern Philistia and the western Negev and developed further in the seventh century as a maritime commercial centre.[17] Indeed, a major factor influencing the

---

14    Whether the Assyrians were actively involved in encouraging the southern Levant's economic development or were merely passive beneficiaries of it is disputed; see the discussion below and variously Na'aman, 'Ekron under the Assyrian and Egyptian Empires'; Bienkowski and van der Steen, 'Tribes, Trade, and Towns'; A. Faust, 'The Interests of the Assyrian Empire in the West: Olive Oil Production as a Test-Case', *JESHO* 54 (2011), 62–86. On the role of the Phoenicians in this system see Frankenstein, 'The Phoenicians'; cf. D.M. Master, 'Trade and Politics: Ashkelon's Balancing Act in the Seventh Century B.C.E.', *BASOR* 330 (2003), 47–64; Faust and Weiss, 'Judah, Philistia, and the Mediterranean World'.

15    I. Finkelstein, 'The Archaeology of the Days of Manasseh', *Scripture and Other Artifacts: Essays on the Bible and Archaeology in Honor of Philip J. King* (ed. M.D. Coogan, J.C. Exum and L.E. Stager, Louisville, Ky., Westminster John Knox, 1994), 178; also I. Finkelstein, 'Khirbet en-Nahas, Edom and Biblical History', *TA* 32 (2005), 119–125 and Na'aman, 'The Debated Historicity', 113–114 regarding related population increases in the Transjordanian states.

16    Bienkowski and van der Steen, 'Tribes, Trade, and Towns', 40; they note in connection Sargon's deportation of Arab tribes to this area.

17    Similarly, Tel Haror, Tel Sera', Ḥorvat Hoga, Tel Abu Seleimeh; Na'aman, 'Population Changes in Palestine', 208; Na'aman, 'Sennacherib's Campaign', 80–85; Na'aman, 'The Debated Historicity', 111–112.

Assyrian desire for control over the southern Levant was the lucrative nature of the trade routes running through the region, especially those bringing luxury goods from the Arabian peninsula to the Mediterranean coast. Archaeological finds from Edom to Philistia indicate that Assyrians, Arabians, Phoenicians, Edomites and Judahites were all involved to some degree or another in this Assyrian-generated commercial activity.[18] The effect of these activities will be discussed in its particulars throughout the material which follows but, as only one small example of the wide-scale commercial networks of this period, 'several of the jewelry objects found in the Ketef Hinnom tombs . . . were imported from as far afield as Assyria, Babylon, and Urartu.'[19]

Whether or not Assyria's effect on the region's economic development involved its direct intervention in commercial ventures, however, is a matter of debate. As the particular focus of these debates has been the Philistine city of Ekron, this point will be revisited below. Here it may suffice to note that, while it is appropriate to concede a certain economic momentum to the tides of history, it seems preferable to understand the exceptional economic prosperity of much of the southern Levant during the *pax Assyriaca* as arising from at least a certain degree of deliberation and involvement on the part of the Assyrians, given the relationship which these economic developments had with the population shifts and building works in which the Assyrians were also directly involved.[20]

Given the presence of Assyrians in both military and commercial capacities in the southern Levant it is hardly surprising that elements of Assyrian material culture appear throughout the region, with areas under direct Assyrian control or influence naturally exhibiting these in greater quantity. Assyrian palace ware or local imitations of it, for example, are found in almost every late Iron Age II site in the region, from the Edomite highlands and the southern Negev to the trade routes through the Beersheba and Arad valleys and the commercial cities on the coast. Mesopotamian iconographic influences are recognisable

---

18   Finkelstein, 'Ḥorvat Qitmīt'; Finkelstein, 'The Archaeology of the Days of Manasseh', 179. On the mechanics of the system see L. Singer-Avitz, 'Beersheba—A Gateway Community in Southern Arabian Long-Distance Trade in the Eighth Century B.C.E.', *TA* 26 (1999), 3–75; N. Na'aman and Y. Thareani-Sussely, 'Dating the Appearance of Imitations of Assyrian Ware in Southern Palestine', *TA* 33 (2006), 61–82; L. Singer-Avitz, 'On Pottery in Assyrian Style: A Rejoinder', *TA* 34 (2007), 182–203.

19   Herr, 'Archaeological Sources', 159.

20   Note also that even those whose argue against Assyrian interest in the agricultural component of the region's trade allow for its interest in the region's luxury goods (including, for example, Faust, 'The Interests of the Assyrian Empire', 72).

across the southern Levant.[21] However, there is an on-going debate over the directness of Assyrian influence, on pottery as well as other aspects of material culture. Bienkowski and van der Steen, for example, argue that

> the so-called assyrianizing pottery in Edom and the Negev is not true Assyrian palace ware, but a local imitation. Individual objects occasionally show traces of Assyrian influence, but in many cases the influence could be indirect, from elsewhere in the Levant. None of these examples implies an Assyrian presence in Edom or the Negev, and they are more likely selective borrowings.[22]

There have been similar disagreements regarding the ceramic tradition in the Beersheba and Arad valleys.[23] Nevertheless, whether direct or indirect, the influence of Assyrian material culture is recognisably present in most sites of the southern Levant during the long seventh century.

The ultimate effects of the Assyrian empire on the kingdoms and cultures of the southern Levant, however, went far beyond an influence on material culture: in forging an empire across the ancient Near East, the Assyrians created the political and economic framework for the interactions and influences which will be discussed throughout what follows. As a result of Assyria's policies, all of the inhabitants of the southern Levant experienced an increase in their contacts with their more immediate neighbours. This is aptly summed up by Na'aman; concluding a discussion of population changes in the south-

---

21    The extent of this varies: it is fairly frequent in Aramaic and Transjordanian seals and notably less so in Hebrew ones (T. Ornan, 'The Mesopotamian Influence on West Semitic Inscribed Seals: A Preference for the Depiction of Mortals', *Studies in the Iconography of Northwest Semitic Inscribed Seals* [ed. B. Sass and C. Uehlinger, OBO 125, Freiburg, Universität Freiburg, 1993], 52–73). Keel and Uehlinger observe that, of those Hebrew seals which do contain some iconographic element, those from the ninth and eighth centuries tend to reflect Egyptian-Phoenician influences, whereas the later eighth and seventh century seals reflect stronger Assyrian and Syrian influences (O. Keel and C. Uehlinger, *Gods, Goddesses, and Images of God in Ancient Israel* [transl. T.H. Trapp, Minneapolis, Minn., Fortress, 1998], 177–372; also B. Sass, 'The Pre-Exilic Hebrew Seals: Iconism vs. Aniconism', *Studies in the Iconography of Northwest Semitic Inscribed Seals* [ed. B. Sass and C. Uehlinger, OBO 125, Freiburg, Universität Freiburg, 1993], 199).

22    On the Edomite material, Bienkowski and van der Steen, 'Tribes, Trade, and Towns', 39, contra Finkelstein, 'Ḥorvat Qitmīt', 161; Finkelstein, *Living on the Fringe*, 147; on Assyrian influence more generally, Herr, 'Archaeological Sources', 167–168.

23    On the Beersheba-Arad valley repertoire, Singer-Avitz, 'Beersheba'; Na'aman and Thareani-Sussely, 'Dating the Appearance'; Singer-Avitz, 'On Pottery'.

ern Levant during the long seventh century he describes how, 'following the *pax Assyriaca*, the borders between kingdoms were open' and how the development of international and local trade under the auspices of the Assyrian empire led to an increase in contacts among the cultures of the region during this period, noting especially the strong contrast between this period and the preceding. Speaking of Judah in particular, he observes that the material culture of Judah during the eighth century indicates that its borders were effectively closed to outsiders, whether by accident or by design, while in the seventh century Judah's 'contacts with neighboring regions are manifold'.[24] Perhaps the most significant impact of the Assyrian presence in and around Judah may not have been the Assyrians themselves but the manifold populations they brought into greater contact as a result of their policies. The impact of the Assyrian empire on the southern Levant is undeniable and, as many of the discussions in this section will indicate, the Assyrian presence and involvement in its western territories constituted a major influence on the economic, political and social developments in these areas.

### Assyria and Judah

Before progressing to these, a brief note regarding Assyria's particular relationship with Judah is in order. Judah's direct interaction with Assyrian military outposts during the seventh century is indicated by, among other things, the inclusion of a Judahite troop contingent among the lists of troops provided by the southern Levantine vassal states for Assurbanipal's Egyptian campaigns, implying the participation of Judahite military contingents on the battlefield alongside those from Assyria and elsewhere in the empire.[25] Manasseh is mentioned several times in the inscriptions, indicating relatively direct interaction

---

24    Na'aman, 'Population Changes in Palestine', 215. Elsewhere: 'It appears that, in the eighth century BCE, the borders of Judah were largely closed, and contacts with neighboring states to the east and west were limited. On the other hand, in the seventh century, following the *pax Assyriaca*, the borders were opened, and the available evidence of material culture attests to manifold contacts with various regions within the Assyrian empire' (N. Na'aman, 'The Kingdom of Judah under Josiah', *Ancient Israel and Its Neighbors: Interaction and Counteraction* [Winona Lake, Ind., Eisenbrauns, 2005], 331, referring especially to O. Zimhoni, 'Two Ceramic Assemblages from Lachish Levels III and II', *TA* 17 [1990], 47–49).

25    E.A. Knauf, 'The Glorious Days of Manasseh', *Good Kings and Bad Kings: The Kingdom of Judah in the Seventh Century B.C.E.* (ed. L.L. Grabbe, LHBOTS 393, London, T&T Clark, 2005), 168–169, referring to Prism E 10, 13–21 and Prism C II 37–67 in Borger, *Beiträge zum Inschriftenwerk Assurbanipals*.

between the Judahite vassal state and its Mesopotamian master.[26] The possibility of direct experience of Assyria, in Assyria, by at least a few members of
the Judahite court circle is raised by some passages from the royal inscriptions;
in his Great Summary Inscription Sargon claims that when he finished the
construction of Dur Sharrukin in 706 he summoned all the western kings to
attend its dedication. Though not named explicitly, it is possible that Hezekiah
was among those present on the occasion.[27] Similarly, tribute payment from
Manasseh's Judah, intended as a contribution for the palace at Nineveh, is
explicitly mentioned in Esarhaddon's inscriptions; it is at least possible that
representatives from Judah took the items involved all the way to Nineveh, and
certainly probable that they took them at least as far as Lebanon.[28] Hezekiah
also appears in the accounts of Sennacherib's 701 campaign.[29] The recent excavators of Ramat Raḥel, four kilometres outside Jerusalem, have argued that the
site served as an imperial centre.[30] Various literary influences on the Hebrew
Bible from Assyrian sources have also been proposed, most notably on Isaiah
and on Deuteronomy.[31]

---

26    RINAP 4 1 v 54–vi 1; 5 vi 7', among others.

27    A. Fuchs, *Die Inschriften Sargons II. aus Khorsabad* (Göttingen, Cuvillier, 1994), 355;
      Younger, Jr., 'Assyrian Involvement', 244.

28    RINAP 4 1 v 54–vi 1; 5 vi 7'; Knauf, '"The Glorious Days of Manasseh"', 168.

29    RINAP 3/1 4 39–58 *passim*; see also Na'aman, 'Sennacherib's "Letter to God"'; and the essays
      in L.L. Grabbe, ed., *'Like a Bird in a Cage': The Invasion of Sennacherib in 701 BCE* (JSOTSup
      363/European Seminar in Historical Methodology 4, London: Sheffield Academic, 2003).

30    O. Lipschits, Y. Gadot, B. Arubas and M. Oeming, 'Palace and Village, Paradise and
      Oblivion: Unraveling the Riddles of Ramat Raḥel', *Near Eastern Archaeology* 74 (2011),
      2–49; already N. Na'aman, 'An Assyrian Residence at Ramat Raḥel?', *TA* 28 (2001), 260–280.

31    P. Machinist, 'Assyria and Its Image in the First Isaiah', *JAOS* 103 (1983), 719–737; P.E. Dion,
      'Deuteronomy 13: The Suppression of Alien Religious Propaganda in Israel during the
      Late Monarchical Era', *Law and Ideology in Monarchic Israel* (ed. B. Halpern and D.W.
      Hobson, JSOTSup 124, Sheffield, JSOT, 1991), 147–216; R. Frankena, 'The Vassal-Treaties of
      Esarhaddon and the Dating of Deuteronomy', *OTS* 14 (1965), 122–154; B.M. Levinson, *'The
      Right Chorale': Studies in Biblical Law and Interpretation* (Winona Lake, Ind., Eisenbrauns,
      2011); B.M. Levinson, 'The Reconceptualization of Kingship in Deuteronomy and the
      Deuteronomistic History's Transformation of Torah', *VT* 51 (2001), 511–534; H.U. Steymans,
      'Eine assyrische Vorlage für Deuteronomium 28:20–44', *Bundesdokument und Gesetz:
      Studien zum Deuteronomium* (ed. G. Braulik, HBS 4, Freiburg, Herder, 1995), 119–141; H.U.
      Steymans, *Deuteronomium 28 und die Adê zur Thronfolgeregelung Asarhaddons: Segen
      und Fluch im Alten Orient und in Israel* (OBO 145, Göttingen, Vandenhoeck & Ruprecht,
      1995); M. Weinfeld, 'Traces of Assyrian Treaty Formulae in Deuteronomy', *Bib* 46 (1965),
      417–427; E. Otto, 'Treueid und Gesetz: Die Ursprünge des Deuteronomiums im Horizont
      neuassyrischen Vertragsrechts', *ZABR* 2 (1996), 1–52; C. Koch, *Vertrag, Treueid und Bund:*

## 2.2    *Egypt*

During the heyday of Assyrian dominance Egypt was, although still a power with which the Assyrians were obliged to contend, clearly the second empire of the ancient Near East; the southern Levant was more or less firmly under Assyrian control during the majority of the long seventh century and, despite the persistence of political manoeuvring between Egypt and Assyria by the small Levantine states (resulting in the several western campaigns at the beginning of the period and bleeding into the Egyptian-Babylonian conflict at the end), remained so from the last two decades of the eighth century through the second third of the seventh.[32] The influence of Egypt in the southern Levant over many centuries is often forgotten or discounted in the shadow of the Assyrian empire's role in the fall of Samaria and its dominance in the west through most of the long seventh century, but Egypt's ongoing involvement in the southern Levant, in trade and in politics, is witnessed in a variety of aspects of the material culture found there.

Complicating matters somewhat is the varying relationship between Egypt and Assyria during this period. As with the rest of the western states, Assyrian interest in Egypt was largely economic—the Nile kingdoms were a major source for luxury items such as gold, papyrus and linen—but also sometimes motivated by Egypt's role in fomenting rebellions among Assyria's Levantine vassals.[33]

---

*Studien zur Rezeption des altorientalischen Vertragsrechts im Deuteronomium und zur Ausbildung der Bundestheologie im alten Testament* (BZAW 383, Berlin, de Gruyter, 2008). As I am dealing with these questions in a forthcoming monograph, I will not discuss them extensively here.

32    M. Elat, 'The Economic Relations of the Neo-Assyrian Empire with Egypt', *JAOS* 98 (1978), 34; see also J.K. Hoffmeier, 'Egypt's Role in the Events of 701 B.C. in Jerusalem', *Jerusalem in Bible and Archaeology: The First Temple Period* (ed. A.G. Vaughn and A.E. Killebrew, SBLSymS, Leiden, Brill, 2003), 219–234; J.J.M. Roberts, 'Egypt, Assyria, Isaiah, and the Ashdod Affair: An Alternative Proposal', *Jerusalem in Bible and Archaeology: The First Temple Period* (ed. A.G. Vaughn and A.E. Killebrew, SBLSymS, Leiden, Brill, 2003), 265–283; J.K. Hoffmeier, 'Egypt's Role in the Events of 701 B.C.: A Rejoinder to J.J.M. Roberts', *Jerusalem in Bible and Archaeology: The First Temple Period* (ed. A.G. Vaughn and A.E. Killebrew, SBLSymS, Leiden, Brill, 2003), 285–289.

33    Determined to control the Egyptian trade, Sargon famously declared that he 'opened the sealed h[arb]our of Egypt, mingled Assyrians and Egyptians together and made them trade with each other' (Fuchs, *Die Inschriften Sargons II*, 1994: 88, ll. 1–18; note also the establishment of a trading harbour by Tiglath-pileser at Gaza [E. Frahm, 'Rezensionen. H. Tadmor, The Inscriptions of Tiglath-pileser III, King of Assyria', *AfO* 44–45 (1997/1998), 403; for discussion see Na'aman, 'An Assyrian Residence', 260–261]). The practice was apparently designed to control and exploit trade by extracting a form of tax on the goods

Given Egypt's wealth it is hardly surprising that Assyria eventually attempted to gain direct authority over the Nile kingdoms. Though Esarhaddon's campaign in 671 brought them briefly under Assyrian power, Assyrian control over the region was never wholly convincing; the Assyrian sources do not mention it, but the Babylonian chronicles report that the victory in 671 occurred only after an earlier, failed campaign in 673.[34] In fact, although considered a success, the 671 campaign involved only a relatively low-level imposition of Assyrian authority, consisting of the ejection of the existing southern (Nubian) rulers and the installation of an Assyrian administration, alongside which the rule of the local Egyptian kings was allowed to continue.[35] Another campaign, aimed at quelling rebellion and establishing a stronger Assyrian presence, was already necessary for Assurbanipal in 667. These attempts to bring Egypt into Assyria's purview are often viewed as an overextension whose drain on Assyria's military resources likely contributed to the empire's eventual decline.[36]

Assyria's nominal control over Egypt lasted little more than a decade: the resurgence of Egyptian power began under Psammeticus I, who stopped paying tribute to the Assyrians in 656/655 and began to increase the degree of Egyptian involvement in the southern Levant around the same time.[37] Katzenstein includes the assassination of the pro-Assyrian Amon among these activities, although he contends that there was no real Egyptian dominance in the region until as late as 610, around the same time as the second Egyptian

---

transported; the tribute and tax lists from Philistia include a number of goods of Egyptian provenance, including papyrus and linen (Elat, 'Economic Relations', 27, 30–31). Elat also suggests that Assyria's effective dependence on the Philistine and Arabian trade routes to obtain Egyptian goods allowed these two entities particularly privileged status within the empire and produced a higher degree of tolerance for rebellions than is evidenced elsewhere (Elat, 'Economic Relations', 34).

34   Babylonian Chronicle 1 iv 16–18; see A. Spalinger, 'Esarhaddon and Egypt: An Analysis of the First Invasion of Egypt', *Or* 13 (1976), 300–301 and D. Kahn, 'The Assyrian Invasions of Egypt (673–663 B.C.) and the Final Expulsion of the Kushites', *Studien zur Altägyptischen Kultur* 34 (2006), 252. On the chronicles, A.K. Grayson, *Assyrian and Babylonian Chronicles* (Texts from Cuneiform Sources 5, Locust Valley, N.Y., Augustin, 1975) and, most recently, J.-J. Glassner, *Mesopotamian Chronicles* (SBLWAW 19, Atlanta, Ga., Society of Biblical Literature, 2004). On Esarhaddon's campaigns also A. Spalinger, 'Assurbanipal and Egypt: A Source Study', *JAOS* 94 (1974), 316–328.

35   Spalinger, 'Esarhaddon and Egypt', 302–315.

36   On issues surrounding the fall of Assyria see Kuhrt, *The Ancient Near East*, 540–546.

37   H.J. Katzenstein, *The History of Tyre: From the Beginning of the Second Millennium B.C.E. until the Fall of the Neo-Babylonian Empire in 538 B.C.E.* (Jerusalem, The Schocken Institute for Jewish Research of the Jewish Theological Seminary of America, 1973), 294; B.U. Schipper, 'Egypt and the Kingdom of Judah under Josiah and Jehoiakim', *TA* 37 (2010), 202.

campaign to aid in Assyria's defence against the Babylonians.[38] Schipper dates
the ascent of the Egyptians in the southern Levant slightly earlier, from the
first campaign to Assyria, in 616.[39] Regardless of the exact date, the end of the
seventh century saw the southern Levant briefly under the control of Egypt, as
Assyria withdrew from the region in order to better contend with the increasingly powerful Babylonians in Mesopotamia. In the interim between the
decline of the century of Assyrian dominance in the southern Levant, beginning around the death of Assurbanipal, and the rise of their Mesopotamian
successor, the Babylonians, the southern Levant came under the sway of its
neighbour to the south. In the final decade and a half of the seventh century
and the first decade of the sixth, Egyptian power and presence in the southern
Levant was a real possibility with which the small states of the region were
obliged to calculate.[40] At the height of this period, between about 616 and 605,
Schipper postulates an effective, Egyptian-controlled system of vassal states
in the region, complete with taxes and a corvée system which included Judah
among its number.[41] This Egyptian control over the southern Levant was not
long uncontested, however, and a series of battles between the Egyptians
and the Babylonians between 609 and 605 ultimately settled in favour of the

---

38  Katzenstein, *History of Tyre*, 294, 297. Katzenstein also suggests that Amon might have
    been named after the Egyptian god (Katzenstein, *History of Tyre*, 292).

39  Schipper, 'Egypt', 200.

40  Malamat calculates no less than six major shifts in Judah's foreign policy in these two
    decades: Josiah's rejection of Neco in 609, resulting in his death; Judahite (return to
    and?) persistence in loyalty to Egypt in the midst of Egypt's 605 defeat at Carchemish,
    leading to Judah's subjugation by Babylon in about 603 (this may make better sense if
    Josiah's encounter with Neco was not a rejection of Egyptian sovereignty; see R.D. Nelson,
    'Realpolitik in Judah (687–609 BCE)', *Scripture in Context II: More Essays on the Comparative
    Method* [ed. W.W. Hallo, J.C. Moyer and L.G. Perdue, Winona Lake, Ind., Eisenbrauns,
    1983], 177–189 and Na'aman, 'The Kingdom of Judah', 381–382; contrast especially the
    older scholarship in the tradition of F.M. Cross and D.N. Freedman, 'Josiah's Revolt
    against Assyria', *JNES* 12 [1953], 56–58; A. Malamat, 'Josiah's Bid for Armageddon: The
    Background of the Judean-Egyptian Encounter in 609 B.C.', *JANESCU* 5 [1973], 267–279);
    a rebellion by Jehoiakim in 601/600 in connection with the failure of the Babylonians'
    Egyptian campaign in 601, leading to the first siege of Jerusalem in 598/597; an anti-
    Babylonian conference in Jerusalem convened by Zedekiah around 594/593 (this is the
    rebellion which Katzenstein associates with the change of pharaoh in Egypt); and the
    final reaction of Nebuchadnezzar in the second siege of Jerusalem beginning in 589/588
    (A. Malamat, 'The Kingdom of Judah between Egypt and Babylon: A Small State within
    a Great Power Confrontation', *Text and Context: Old Testament and Semitic Studies for
    F.C. Fensham* [ed. W. Classen, JSOTSup 48, Sheffield, JSOT, 1988], 120–127).

41  Schipper, 'Egypt', 200, 212–213, 220; so also Na'aman, 'The Kingdom of Judah', 368.

latter.[42] After a brief period of quiet, the death of Psammeticus II and the ascent of Hophra in 588 signalled renewed conflict, as Hophra reasserted Egyptian claims to the coastal territories; it was in the midst of this that the final end of Judah came about.[43]

## Egypt and Judah

The inclusion of Judah in an Egyptian imperial system in the southern Levant already before the death of Josiah in 609 is, Schipper confirms, difficult to ascertain; there are no written sources available to either confirm or deny the hypothesised extent of Egyptian control.[44] He contends, however, that the archaeological record strongly suggests Egyptian influence in the southern Levant and in Judah itself already from the earliest days of Assyria's decline, around 630, marked by a rise in both the quantity and the quality of artefacts dating from the Twenty-sixth Dynasty.[45] These include 'an astounding concentration of Egyptian objects' at Ashkelon, mirrored at Ekron and elsewhere in the coastal plain and the Shephelah and extending eventually further inland.[46] The transfer appears to have been essentially peaceful; there are no destruction levels associated with this shift, suggesting that the withdrawal of the Assyrians from the area was more or less seamlessly followed by the appearance of the Egyptians.[47] In the picture drawn by Schipper, this brief period at

---

42    Katzenstein, *History of Tyre*, 305–306; Schipper, 'Egypt', 203.

43    Katzenstein, *History of Tyre*, 317–319; cf. Lipschits, *The Fall and Rise of Jerusalem*, 1–35. In the interim the death of Neco II and the ascent of Psammeticus II around 594 seem to have triggered some low-level rumblings, if the politicking between Judah, Edom, Moab, Ammon, Sidon and Tyre reported in Jeremiah 27 relate to this transfer of power (Katzenstein, *History of Tyre*, 315).

44    Schipper, 'Egypt', 203–204. Note, however, that the attribution of Jehoahaz's deportation and Jehoachim's installation to Egyptian whims, both on the heels of the execution of Josiah, all seem to suggest a significant degree of Egyptian involvement in Judahite affairs at this time (see, among others, Na'aman, 'The Kingdom of Judah', 381–382; Nelson, 'Realpolitik in Judah').

45    Schipper, 'Egypt', 204.

46    Schipper, 'Egypt', 206–208; cf. Na'aman, 'The Kingdom of Judah'; E.D. Oren, 'Ethnicity and Regional Archaeology: The Western Negev under Assyrian Rule', *Biblical Archaeology Today 1990* (ed. A. Biran and J. Aviram, Jerusalem, Israel Exploration Society, 1993), 102–105; A. Fantalkin, 'Why Did Nebuchadnezzar II Destroy Ashkelon in Kislev 604 B.C.E.?', *The Fire Signals of Lachish: Studies in the Archaeology and History of Israel in the Late Bronze Age, Iron Age, and Persian Period in Honor of David Ussishkin* (ed. I. Finkelstein and N. Na'aman, Winona Lake, Ind., Eisenbrauns, 2011), 98–101.

47    Schipper, 'Egypt', 207–208. Na'aman observes that the transition to Egyptian control over the southern Levant appears to have occurred as part of the Assyrian retreat rather than

the end of the seventh century saw the coastal plain, the Shephelah and parts of the Negev under Egyptian control, subject to varying degrees of Egyptian cultural influence.[48]

One of the more intriguing sites involved in this debate is Mesad Hashavyahu, a fortress founded in the last two decades of the century and abandoned around 600, probably in connection with the Babylonian invasion.[49] This coastal site near Ashdod revealed a significant mix of material culture remains, most significantly including the combination of East Greek pottery—some of which was manufactured locally—as well as Hebrew ostraca mentioning individuals possessed of Yahwistic names.[50] The Greek materials may indicate a settlement of persons of Greek extraction sometime in the last third of the seventh century.[51] The Hebrew ostraca, according to Naveh's initial analysis, 'indicate clearly that the site was under the rule of Judah'.[52] On the basis of the presence of Greek mercenaries in the Egyptian army, combined with the military character of the site, Naveh concluded that the site was home to a contingent of Greek mercenaries, now under Judahite control, most likely during the reign of Josiah (on the basis of the improbability that any of his successors controlled the Mediterranean coast).[53] More recent consideration of the

through active military engagements between the Egyptians and the southern Levantine states (Na'aman, 'The Kingdom of Judah', 367).

48    Schipper, 'Egypt', 212. Schipper suggests that Egypt's interest was mainly with the coast, with neither the political nor cultural reach of Egypt extending significantly into the main territory of Judah (Schipper, 'Egypt', 212; see also Na'aman, 'The Kingdom of Judah', 368). He suggests that this was in part due to Judah's political insignificance; as the kings of Judah were not powerful enough to pose a threat to the Egyptian pharaoh, Egypt's interest was driven only by Judah's control over the trade routes through the Negev (Schipper, 'Egypt', 214).

49    Fantalkin, 'Meẓad Ḥashavyahu', 128–136. The excavator's preliminary report appears as J. Naveh, 'The Excavations of Meṣad Ḥashavyahu: Preliminary Report', *IEJ* 12 (1962), 89–113; with a full publication undertaken in Fantalkin, 'Meẓad Ḥashavyahu'.

50    J. Naveh, 'A Hebrew Letter from the Seventh Century B.C.', *IEJ* 10 (1960), 129–139; J. Naveh, 'More Hebrew Inscriptions from Meṣad Ḥashavyahu', *IEJ* 12 (1962), 27–32; Naveh, 'The Excavations', 96–97; more recently, Fantalkin, 'Meẓad Ḥashavyahu', 3–165; Schipper, 'Egypt', with further references.

51    Fantalkin, 'Meẓad Ḥashavyahu', 137–144; see also A. Fantalkin, 'Identity in the Making: Greeks in the Eastern Mediterranean during the Iron Age', *Naukratis: Greek Diversity in Egypt: Studies on East Greek Pottery and Exchange in the Eastern Mediterranean* (ed. A. Villing and U. Schlotzhauer, The British Museum Research Publication Number 162, London, The British Museum, 2006), 202–203.

52    Naveh, 'The Excavations', 97–98.

53    Naveh, 'The Excavations', 98–99; see also Katzenstein, *History of Tyre*, 296.

international political situation in the late seventh century, however, has suggested that the theory of a Josianic expansion to the Mediterranean is untenable, the area having been clearly under Egyptian control.[54] The presence of Greek pottery continues to suggest a contingent of Greek mercenaries, but the foundation of the site is most plausibly connected to the Egyptian takeover of the southern Levant in the late seventh century; the Greek population arrived as mercenaries of the Egyptian army.[55] In a related case, Fantalkin has argued for a similar Egyptian garrison at Ashkelon.[56]

Mesad Hashavyahu may also be understood as part of a more general type of close relationship between Egypt and Judah in the late seventh century. The Egyptian weight system, including the use of hieratic numerals on weights appears to have become much more widespread at this time. Although the analysis of the Judahite weight system is fraught with difficulty and disagreement, Scott already argued that the *shekel* weight with which the hieratic markings are associated constituted the 'establishment for the purposes of international trade of a fixed relationship between the new standard shekel and the Egyptian "deben" weight unit', and he located this in the late seventh century, under Josiah.[57] Similarly, Aharoni suggested that 'it becomes most plausible that this was selected, probably by Josiah, as an exact equivalent to that most common weight in international commerce'; thus he too dated the use of such weights relatively late in Judah's history and tied them directly (if implicitly) to the resurgence of Egyptian dominance in the southern Levant.[58] The more recent variant of this hypothesis has been to suggest that the adoption of an essentially Egyptian weight system was motivated not merely by the exigencies of trade but by the strength of Egyptian political power in the region; not imposed, perhaps, but deemed highly favourable in light of the prevailing political winds.[59] Kletter, however, has argued that the introduc-

---

54  Schipper, 'Egypt', 208; note also R. Kletter, 'Clay Figurines: Human and Animal Clay Figurines', *Tel 'Ira: A Stronghold in the Biblical Negev* (ed. I. Beit-Arieh, MSIA 15, Tel Aviv, Tel Aviv University, 1999), 342 who concludes that a Judahite presence at the site is much more likely due to the conditions of Judah's vassalage to Egypt than to independent Judahite control over the site, likewise Fantalkin, 'Meẓad Ḥashavyahu', 144–146.

55  Fantalkin, 'Meẓad Ḥashavyahu', 137–144; Schipper, 'Egypt', 209.

56  Fantalkin, 'Why Did Nebuchadnezzar II Destroy Ashkelon', 98–101.

57  R.B.Y. Scott, 'The N-Ṣ-P Weights from Judah', *BASOR* 200 (1970), 62–66; R.B.Y. Scott, 'Weights from Jerusalem', *Excavations in Jerusalem 1961–1967* (ed. A.D. Tushingham, Toronto, Royal Ontario Museum, 1985), 62–64.

58  Y. Aharoni, 'The Use of Hieratic Numerals in Hebrew Ostraca and the Shekel Weights', *BASOR* 184 (1966), 18; cf. Scott, 'The N-Ṣ-P Weights', 62.

59  Schipper, 'Egypt', 210–212.

tion of Judahite weights calibrated to an Egyptian standard occurred already at the end of the eighth century, suggesting Judah's growing trade contacts with Egypt at that time as a possible reason.[60] If Kletter is correct, the persistence of the Egyptian system through the long seventh century, despite formal Assyrian authority, suggests that Egypt's influence never fully retreated from the southern Levant.

The reader will observe that Egyptian political presence in the southern Levant is most overtly of interest to the study of Judah in its final three to four decades; although the possibility of Egyptian aid in throwing off the Assyrian yoke is a recurring theme at the beginning of the long seventh century, the Assyrians dominate the period to an almost overwhelming degree. Given the pivotal role of the Assyrian empire in bringing Judah into a world of imperial scope, the relatively brief period during which Egypt held sway in the region and the volatility of the area during the years before and after, it is perhaps unsurprising that the influence of Egyptian culture in the Judahite heartland is often overlooked. Yet Egypt should not be forgotten; influence from and interaction with people from the south will be persistently evident in much of what follows.

## 3      The Southern Levant

Despite the fundamental role played by the Assyrian empire in bringing about major political, economic and cultural changes in the southern Levant during the long seventh century, these changes did not involve the Assyrians alone and, although imperial policies were a driving force behind dramatic changes in southern Levantine life during this period, the face of these changes was not necessarily Assyrian. The top-level decisions of the empire had significant effects on southern Levantine economic and commercial activities and much of the movement across and around the Levant occasioned by these imperial

---

60    R. Kletter, 'The Inscribed Weights of the Kingdom of Judah', *TA* 18 (1991), 121–163; also Kletter, 'Clay Figurines', 32–34. It is not entirely clear quite how Kletter sees the origins and purpose of the inscribed weights: on the one hand he attributes their relationship to the Egyptian system to a royal impetus in the late eighth century and to trading needs (Kletter, 'The Inscribed Weights', 137) while on the other he observes that they were found primarily in domestic loci and not on international trade routes (Kletter, 'Clay Figurines', 34). In the next breath, however, he contends that the weights found outside the heartland of Judah—in Israel and the Transjordan—probably got there via trade and asserts that there were probably also royal weights, differing in shape or material.

policies involved the local populations of the southern Levant more than it involved the Assyrians themselves. In what follows the various territories of the southern Levant will be discussed in terms of the changes which each community experienced during the time in question. In each case the material record of these populations, as witnessed by one or more archaeological sites, is discussed with particular attention to the evidence for increased interaction with both their immediate and their more distant neighbours, all but ubiquitous in the southern Levantine sites of this period. Given the focus of the present study special attention is given to interaction with Judah; each section finishes with a discussion of the evidence for this. As Chapter One concludes with a discussion of the material record of Judah itself *vis-à-vis* these changes, this section begins with the populations at the greatest distance from Judah and moves progressively inward, culminating with those bordering directly on Judah.

### 3.1    *Phoenicia*

Phoenicia comprises the coastal territory north of Philistia; not usually unified, the area's principal cities included the major port cities of Byblos, Sidon and Tyre, which flourished during the *pax Assyriaca*.[61] West of the kingdom centred on Samaria, the close contacts between these cities and that kingdom while it still existed are well attested and are indeed nicely summed up in the account of marriage between the Tyrian Jezebel and the Omride Ahab, whatever the narrative's reliability.[62]

The reach of the Phoenician trading empire, however, extended well beyond its immediate eastern neighbour. The prosperity and enormous economic potential of the Phoenician mercantile cities attracted the attention of the Assyrians already from the time of Tiglath-pileser, whose policy of involvement in the western periphery's economic activities was continued and expanded by his successors, though the relationship between the Phoenician cities and the Assyrians was not always smooth.[63] Tyre, which had resisted Sargon, was

---

61    Gitin, 'The Neo-Assyrian Empire', 79; M.E. Aubet, *The Phoenicians and the West: Politics, Colonies, and Trade* (2nd edn., Cambridge, Cambridge University Press, 2001); Katzenstein, *History of Tyre*, 8.

62    Katzenstein, *History of Tyre*, 172.

63    On the role of Phoenicia in the southern Levantine economic system see Aubet, *The Phoenicians and the West*, 92–95; M. Elat, 'Phoenician Overland Trade within the Mesopotamian Empire', *Ah, Assyria ... Studies in Assyrian History and Ancient Near Eastern Historiography Presented to Hayim Tadmor* (ed. M. Cogan and I. Eph'al, ScrHier 23,

subordinated to Assyrian power by Sennacherib, who favoured Sidon in its stead.[64] This campaign marked the beginning of a period of a more direct expression of Assyrian interests in the west; under Esarhaddon and Assurbanipal almost all of the Phoenician territories were annexed to Assyria.[65] A subsequent treaty between Baal of Tyre and Esarhaddon installed an Assyrian administrator to supervise the Tyrian's activities.[66] Worth note, however, are the relatively favourable trading conditions granted in the same treaty to the Tyrian king, who was allowed access to all the Assyrian ports of trade along the eastern Mediterranean as well as gaining territory previously under the purview of Sidon.[67] While the island of Tyre resisted outsiders' control until the arrival of Alexander, the mainland city was provincialised under Assurbanipal during his 667 campaign to Egypt (during which the city had again revolted).[68] After destroying Sidon, Esarhaddon established Kar Esarhaddon 'to function as the focal point of Assyrian trade in Phoenicia by eliminating the intermediaries, the Phoenician mercantile cities'.[69] The region is last mentioned in Assyrian texts in the eponym lists for the 640s and 630s (the precise dates are broken off), as the western parts of the empire attempt to reassert their independence.[70]

Jerusalem, Magnes, 1991), 21–35; Faust and Weiss, 'Judah, Philistia, and the Mediterranean World', 85–86; Master, 'Trade and Politics'; Fantalkin, 'Identity in the Making', 200–201; Frankenstein, 'The Phoenicians', 269–273; Katzenstein, *History of Tyre*, 242; Herr, 'Archaeological Sources', 164; B. Oded, 'The Phoenician Cities and the Assyrian Empire in the Time of Tiglath-pileser III', *ZDPV* 90 (1974), 38–49.

64    Aubet, *The Phoenicians and the West*, 94; J. Elayi, 'Les relations entre les cités phéniciennes et l'empire Assyrien sous le règne de Sennachérib', *Semitica* 35 (1985), 23–26.

65    Na'aman, 'The Kingdom of Judah', 197.

66    The treaty appears in SAA 2 5; for discussion see also Aubet, *The Phoenicians and the West*, 59, 93; Katzenstein, *History of Tyre*, 267–271. Note that the exact date of the treaty is disputed.

67    Na'aman, 'The Kingdom of Judah', 194–195. On the economic leverage wielded by the Phoenicians in their relations with the Assyrians see Frankenstein, 'The Phoenicians', 269–273. Whether the role of the Assyrian administrator was continued into the reign of Assurbanipal is unknown; if so, he is not mentioned in any known inscription (Katzenstein, *History of Tyre*, 287).

68    Katzenstein, *History of Tyre*, 287–293.

69    H. Tadmor, 'Philistia under Assyrian Rule', *BA* 29 (1966), 98.

70    Katzenstein, *History of Tyre*, 294.

Phoenicia and Judah

Trade relations between Phoenicia and Judah, possibly indirect, are attested by the Phoenician storage jars which appear at Judahite sites.[71] Singer-Avitz has analysed a number of these storage jars from Tel Beersheba III and II, drawing conclusions regarding the city's trade relationships during the late eighth century; she observes that a number of the Tel Beersheba jars were manufactured on the Phoenician coast, not locally, and probably indicate the existence of trade relations with Phoenicia (rather than a contingent of Phoenicians settled at the site).[72] Intriguingly, however, this appears to have occurred only during the late eighth century and, in fact, Stratum II is distinguished from Stratum III specifically by the presence of vessels associated with the Phoenician coastal area. Singer-Avitz dates the end of Stratum III and the beginning of Stratum II somewhere between 720 and 715, locating the beginning of Stratum II, in which the connection to Phoenicia is attested, at the beginning of the long seventh century.[73] She suggests that the change is related to Sargon having opened the 'sealed harbour of Egypt'—a trade network which significantly involved the Phoenicians—as well as Sargon's more general encouragement of trade among the western vassals and their neighbours which the Egyptian case reflects.[74] She concludes that 'during the last two decades of the eighth century BCE, some kind of connection was established' between Phoenicia and Judah, arguing that '[t]he Phoenician pottery vessels and the cedar beams found in Stratum II at Beersheba are evidence of the existence of a trade network by which the products arrived from the Lebanese coast to sites in Judah'.[75] She notes, however, that this network probably routed via the ports of Philistia and the trade caravans running from the western ports inland through the Beersheba Valley; influence from Phoenicia on Judah, therefore, may well have

---

71    Noting that the Phoenician cities were largely independent, Peckham suggests that Tyre dealt with Judah while Sidon concerned itself more with the territory to the north (B. Peckham, 'Phoenicians and Aramaeans: The Literary and Epigraphic Evidence', *The World of the Arameans: Studies in Language and Literature in Honour of Paul-Eugéne Dion* [ed. P.M.M. Daviau, J.W. Wevers and M. Weigl, JSOTSup 324, Sheffield, Sheffield Academic, 2001], 20, 23).

72    L. Singer-Avitz, 'A Group of Phoenician Vessels from Tel Beersheba', *TA* 37 (2010), 188–199.

73    Singer-Avitz, 'A Group of Phoenician Vessels', 195.

74    Sargon's policy was a change from that of Tiglath-pileser, who sought to prevent trade between Phoenicia and its southern neighbours; Singer-Avitz, 'A Group of Phoenician Vessels', 188, 194–196. On the beginning of this phenomenon in the eighth century see Thareani-Sussely, 'The "Archaeology of the Days of Manasseh"', who credits Tiglath-pileser with at least its early impetus.

75    Singer-Avitz, 'A Group of Phoenician Vessels', 195.

been more indirect than direct.[76] It seems likely that Judahites would have been aware of the Phoenician origin of the goods transported in the vessels and of the immense (and growing) trading power wielded by the Phoenicians, but whether they ever experienced it directly is uncertain. That said, the fact that some of the jars exhibiting Phoenician characteristics were manufactured in the Shephelah (which in the last decades of the eighth century remained under Judahite control), under the influence of the native Phoenician types, perhaps suggests some more significant interaction, either in the form of Judahite imitation of exotic foreign forms or the presence of Phoenicians in Judah, recreating familiar forms from local clay.[77]

In sum, the Phoenician cities were probably not a direct trading partner for Judah during the long seventh century and few if any Phoenicians were likely resident or regularly present in Judah itself. The major role of these cities in the Assyrian economic policies of the long seventh century, however, combined with the more particular Judahite evidence for an increased volume of Phoenicia-derived material traffic at the same time, contributes to a developing picture of a Judah exposed to outside influences in the long seventh century in a more sustained and significant way than previously experienced.

## 3.2    *Philistia*

Mention Philistia and identity in the same sentence in the presence of a biblical scholar and the conversation most likely to result will concern the consumption or non-consumption of pig products.[78] That differentiation, if such it was, was long over by the long seventh century, when the importance of Philistia is its ascent as a commercial power, fuelled by imperial economic interests.[79]

---

76    Phoenician goods, influences and actual presence are attested among Judah's Philistine neighbours at Ashkelon and Ekron (Master, 'Trade and Politics', 52–59; Gitin, 'Tel Miqne-Ekron in the 7th Century B.C.E.', 71–73).

77    Singer-Avitz, 'A Group of Phoenician Vessels', 194.

78    Among others, B. Hesse, 'Animal Use at Tel Miqne-Ekron in the Bronze Age and Iron Age', *BASOR* 264 (1986), 17–27; B. Hesse, 'Pig Lovers and Pig Haters: Patterns of Palestinian Pork Production', *Journal of Ethnobiology* 10 (1990), 195–225; B. Hesse and P. Wapnish, 'Can Pig Bones Be Used for Ethnic Diagnosis in the Ancient Near East?', *The Archaeology of Israel: Constructing the Past, Interpreting the Present* (ed. N.A. Silberman and D. Small, JSOTSup 237, Sheffield, Sheffield Academic, 1997), 238–270.

79    Herr has discussed Philistine material culture in the context of a discussion of widespread material culture differentiation in the southern Levant in the long seventh century and observed that the material culture across the region is 'very similar from site to site, suggesting close connections' among the Philistine cities (Herr, 'Archaeological Sources', 162–164). The exact nature of the political relationship between the Philistine cities is

As the preceding discussions of Assyria, Egypt and Phoenicia have already indicated, the Philistine city-states were at the crossroads of nearly every economic and political move in the southern Levant. All of Assyria's dealings with Egypt were obliged to pass through Philistia; geographic expediency also seems to have resulted in most of Assyria's interactions with Judah progressing via Philistia. Economically, Assyrian access to Egypt, to the Shephelah and the Negev, to the Transjordan and to Arabia all ran through this handful of cities on the southern Mediterranean coast. The Philistine cities were the main intermediaries between Egypt and Phoenicia—whence to Assyria—as well as the primary outlets for the lucrative Arabian trade.[80] Assyrian interest in Philistia was thus spurred by economic factors, a priority overtly expressed in Tiglath-pileser's establishment of a trading harbour at Gaza and Sargon's boast of having opened trade with Egypt via Philistia.[81] These actions were focused on controlling the trade in luxury goods from the Arabian peninsula and the trade with Egypt, although later Assyrian interest came to encompass a military aspect as imperial ambitions extended to the Nile.[82]

A number of changes occurred in Philistia as part of Assyrian interests. These included the installation of Assyrian governors (which at times seem to have co-existed with native rulers) and the construction of new towns and cities to facilitate commercial activities as well as the development of existing ones.[83] Tel Jemmeh, flanked by Tel el-Ajjul and Tel el-Farah on the Wadi Besor,

---

fortunately tangential to the culture issue at hand; for discussions see I. Finkelstein, 'Is the Philistine Paradigm Still Viable?', *The Synchronisation of Civilisations in the Eastern Mediterranean in the Second Millennium B.C. III: Proceedings of the SCIEM 2000—2nd EuroConference, Vienna, 28th of May—1st of June 2003* (ed. M. Bietak and H. Hunger, Contributions to the Chronology of the Eastern Mediterranean 9, Vienna, Österreichische Akademie der Wissenschaften, 2007), 520–521, with further references.

80    Tadmor, 'Philistia under Assyrian Rule', 87. 'Ashkelon . . . was probably the gate through which many imported goods reached the entire region' (Faust and Weiss, 'Judah, Philistia, and the Mediterranean World', 80).

81    Frahm, 'Rezensionen', 403 (for discussion see Na'aman, 'An Assyrian Residence', 260–261); Fuchs, *Die Inschriften Sargons II*, 88, ll. 1–18; J.J.M. Roberts, 'Egypt, Assyria, Isaiah, and the Ashdod Affair', 268. On the date of the latter see Roberts, with further references. On Assyrian interest in the Phoenician end of the trading economy, see 3.1. Phoenicia.

82    Tadmor, 'Philistia under Assyrian Rule', 98–101; Faust and Weiss, 'Judah, Philistia, and the Mediterranean World', 71–73; for further discussion, see 2.1. Assyria. As Na'aman notes, 'whoever ruled Philistia ruled the approaches to Egypt' (Na'aman, 'The Kingdom of Judah', 143) (note the similar sentiment regarding the importance of the Phoenician cities, voiced by B. Oded, 'The Phoenician Cities', 39).

83    See Tadmor, 'Philistia under Assyrian Rule', 95; Na'aman, 'Population Changes in Palestine', 204–208; Faust and Weiss, 'Judah, Philistia, and the Mediterranean World', 72.

ten kilometres south of Gaza, is a major example of this phenomenon.[84] The Assyrians also affected the population of the region through the practice of two-way deportation, resulting in mixed or largely non-native populations in many of these cities; Tel Jemmeh, for example, seems on the basis of onomastics to have been populated largely by persons of Iranian or Kassite descent.[85] It is possible that northern Israelites were deported to Ekron.[86] In addition to the presence of Assyrians in the area to supervise the enhanced economic efforts of the region, therefore, the Philistine territories bordering on Judah experienced an influx of new cultural groups, especially at the beginning of the long seventh century but continuing into the seventh century proper. Overall demographic patterns also reflect the increasing economic importance of Philistia, attesting to significant population and settlement growth on the coastal plain.[87]

A number of the architectural and material cultural influences of the Assyrians on these Philistine cities have already been noted above. Petrographic analysis of the seventh century assemblage at Ashkelon indicates contacts with

---

84    Na'aman, 'Population Changes in Palestine', 204–205, 208; Van Beek, 'Digging up Tell Jemmeh', 17.

85    Na'aman, 'Population Changes in Palestine', 204–205; on the Assyrian deportations in general see B. Oded, *Mass Deportations and Deportees in the Neo-Assyrian Empire* (Weisbaden, Reichert, 1979). In two ostraca found at Tel Jemmeh only five names—and none of the 11 patronymics—are West Semitic in origin. Naveh argued for their identification as Anatolian or Greek mercenaries, but Na'aman and Zadok point out that the use of such mercenaries by the Assyrians is nowhere else attested and link the people to deportees mentioned by Sargon as being settled by him near the Brook of Egypt (which some identify as the Wadi Besor, near Tel Jemmeh), suggesting a population with origins in the Zagros mountains (Na'aman and Zadok, 'Sargon II', 36–40). The repopulation of Ashdod after 712 may have been with people from the same area (Na'aman and Zadok, 'Sargon II', 43–44).

86    S. Gitin, 'Seventh Century B.C.E. Cultic Elements at Ekron', *Biblical Archaeology Today 1990* (ed. A. Biran and J. Aviram, Jerusalem, Israel Exploration Society, 1993), 250, 255–256 n. 21; S. Gitin, 'Tel Miqne-Ekron: A Type Site for the Inner Coastal Plain in the Iron Age II Period', *Recent Excavations in Israel: Studies in Iron Age Archaeology* (ed. S. Gitin and W.G. Dever, AASOR 49, Winona Lake, Ind., Eisenbrauns, 1989), 49; see also C.S. Ehrlich, *The Philistines in Transition: A History from ca. 1000–730 BCE* (SHANE 10, Leiden, Brill, 1996), 15. It is not entirely clear whether deportations to the southern Levant continued in the reigns of Esarhaddon and Assurbanipal; while none are mentioned in the inscriptions, this may be due to changes in scribal habits. See Na'aman, 'Population Changes in Palestine', 212, who elsewhere argues that Esarhaddon revived the policy (Na'aman and Zadok, 'Sargon II', 46). Deportation is mentioned in Ezek. 4:1–2, but the reliability of this report is unknown.

87    Faust and Weiss, 'Judah, Philistia, and the Mediterranean World', 72–73.

cultures as far-flung as Cyprus, northern Syria and the Aegean, in addition to the city's nearer neighbours in Phoenicia, the Shephelah and the Negev.[88] The ceramic repertoire at Ashdod indicates increasing Assyrian influence in conjunction with the destruction of Stratum VIII in 712 by Sargon.[89] At Ekron, the Philistine city nearest to Judah, evidence for trading exchange ranges from the use of building materials likely sourced from the Shephelah to the presence of notable percentages of Judahite forms in the ceramic assemblage, alongside vessels of Assyrian and Phoenician types.[90] In addition to Assyrian palace ware and local imitations thereof, the site's ceramic assemblage contains Judahite, East Greek and Transjordanian forms, while the architectural elements include the Assyrian-type open courtyard and a temple complex based on Assyrian design.[91] Also intriguing is the discovery of a number of four-horned altars, found otherwise only in the territory of the northern kingdom and supposed by some to indicate the presence of former inhabitants of the northern kingdom in Ekron as skilled deportees.[92] Miscellaneous votive objects have also been excavated, including figurines displaying varied Judahite, Egyptian and Phoenician influences.[93] Two dedicatory inscriptions in Phoenician script mention Asherat, probably referring to a local form of the goddess Asherah or her cult, while the titulary of the city's female deity may suggest contacts

---

88    Master, 'Trade and Politics', 52–55. For varying arguments regarding Ashkelon's relative status *vis-à-vis* the other Philistine cities in the seventh century see Faust and Weiss, 'Judah, Philistia, and the Mediterranean World'; Fantalkin, 'Why Did Nebuchadnezzar II Destroy Ashkelon', 89–93.

89    M. Dothan and D. Ben-Schlomo, eds., *Ashdod VI: The Excavations of Areas H and K (1968–1969)* (IAA Reports 24, Jerusalem, Israel Antiquities Authority, 2005), 7, 222, 232; D. Ben-Schlomo, 'Material Culture', *Ashdod VI: The Excavations of Areas H and K (1968–1969)* (ed. M. Dothan and D. Ben-Schlomo, IAA Reports 24, Jerusalem, Israel Antiquities Authority, 2005), 217–235.

90    Gitin, 'Tel Miqne-Ekron', 50–51; S. Gitin, T.K. Dothan and J. Naveh, 'A Royal Dedicatory Inscription from Ekron', *IEJ* 47 (1997), 8.

91    Gitin, 'The Neo-Assyrian Empire', 92; S. Gitin, 'Israelite and Philistine Culture and the Archaeological Record in Iron Age II: The "Smoking Gun" Phenomenon', *Symbiosis, Symbolism, and the Power of the Past: Canaan, Ancient Israel, and Their Neighbors From the Late Bronze Age through Roman Palaestina* (ed. W.G. Dever and S. Gitin, Winona Lake, Ind., Eisenbrauns, 2003), 284–286.

92    Gitin, 'Seventh Century B.C.E. Cultic Elements at Ekron', 250, 255–256 n. 21; Gitin, 'Tel Miqne-Ekron', 49; also Ehrlich, *Philistines in Transition*, 15.

93    Gitin, 'Seventh Century B.C.E. Cultic Elements at Ekron', 254; Gitin, Dothan and Naveh, 'A Royal Dedicatory Inscription', 7–8.

between Byblos and Ekron.[94] A silver cache in the upper city produced jewellery depicting Ishtar on a lion and the excavators suggest that the city's temple complex reflects Assyrian design.[95] Musical instruments familiar from the Egyptian cult have also been discovered at the site, as have a number of other Egyptian objects.[96] Speaking in reference to the four-horned, 'Israelite' altars, Gitin noted that there are 'many indications which point to a multicultural impact on Ekron in the 7th century, one of the results of its new status as an international industrial center within the Neo-Assyrian empire'.[97] He suggests that the diversity is 'a direct result of Ekron's status as a border city . . . a reflex of the nature of its population, given that the city would have needed a large labor force for the oil industry, which may have been composed of multiple ethnic groups.[98]

As mentioned above, with regard to Philistia in particular there is an ongoing debate between those who see Philistine economic development during this period as a consequence but not necessarily an object of Assyrian imperialism and those who see a more overt involvement by the Assyrians.[99] In the former category, Na'aman concludes that 'the prosperity of certain western vassals arose from the stability produced by the *pax Assyriaca* and from the new economic opportunities created by the empire—rather than the result

---

94    Gitin, 'Seventh Century B.C.E. Cultic Elements at Ekron', 250–252; Gitin, 'Tel Miqne-Ekron in the 7th Century B.C.E.', 72; Gitin, 'The Neo-Assyrian Empire', 98; C. Schäfer-Lichtenberger, 'The Goddess of Ekron and the Religious-Cultural Background of the Philistines', *IEJ* 50 (2000), 85–86.

95    Gitin, 'Tel Miqne-Ekron in the 7th Century B.C.E.', 69–70; Gitin, 'The Neo-Assyrian Empire', 93; Gitin, Dothan and Naveh, 'A Royal Dedicatory Inscription', 3. Gitin observes that the silver caches are also 'consistent with the increased use of silver as currency which was initiated in the Neo-Assyrian period and may be related to the commerce and trade generated by the olive oil and textile industries' (Gitin, 'The Neo-Assyrian Empire', 93).

96    Gitin, 'Seventh Century B.C.E. Cultic Elements at Ekron', 254; Gitin, 'The Neo-Assyrian Empire', 98–101. These appear especially in the last phases of the buildings destroyed by Nebuchadnezzar in 603 (per Gitin), contributing to the argument that the withdrawal of the Assyrians from the region was accompanied by an expansion of Egyptian control (Gitin, 'The Neo-Assyrian Empire', 98–100, including discussion).

97    Gitin, 'The Neo-Assyrian Empire', 91; cf. Gitin, 'Seventh Century B.C.E. Cultic Elements at Ekron', 254.

98    Gitin, 'Seventh Century B.C.E. Cultic Elements at Ekron', 254.

99    That the argument has focused on Ekron seems most likely attributable to Gitin's involvement in the excavations there, rather than any real historical peculiarity attributable to Ekron itself.

of a deliberate imperial policy of economic development of these states'.[100] In other words, the Assyrians may have created a favourable climate for Philistine economic success, but they were not actively engaged in ensuring it. In specific terms Na'aman is willing to concede no more than a short-term favouritism regarding Ekron in the lead-up and aftermath of 701, as part of an Assyrian effort to weaken Judah, whereafter the city became independently prosperous.[101] Gitin, by contrast, is inclined to see a more deliberate Assyrian policy at work, concluding that 'Ekron was apparently chosen as a focus of Assyrian economic activity'.[102] Furthermore, while Na'aman's aversion to deliberate Assyrian policy in the development of Ekron in particular and Philistia in general should be noted, Finkelstein and Na'aman elsewhere suggest that Sennacherib's targeting of the Shephelah in 701 was related to an Assyrian attempt to exert more control over the region's oil industry; they note that sites in the Shephelah which were not related to the Judahite oil industry exhibit evidence of an uninterrupted habitation through the long seventh century.[103] The strategic destruction of specific sites and the reassignment of most of the Shephelah to Philistine control are understood by Na'aman and Finkelstein as a deliberate refocusing of the region's economic activities around a site firmly under Assyrian control.

Elsewhere in the region, Faust and Weiss have reconstructed the south-western Levant's economic network as a concentric system focused on Ashkelon, as an enormous port city trading with Phoenicia, Egypt and beyond.[104] They contend that Assyria would not have been interested in the productivity of

---

100    Na'aman, 'Ekron under the Assyrian and Egyptian Empires', 87; cf. Faust, 'The Interests of the Assyrian Empire'.

101    Na'aman, 'Ekron under the Assyrian and Egyptian Empires', 87.

102    Gitin, 'Tel Miqne-Ekron in the 7th Century B.C.E.', 63; see also Gitin, 'The Neo-Assyrian Empire', with further references, especially Oded, 'The Phoenician Cities'; Elat, 'Economic Relations'; J.N. Postgate, 'The Economic Structure of the Assyrian Empire', *The Land of Assur and the Yoke of Assur: Studies on Assyria 1971–2005* (Oxford, Oxbow, 2007), 71–100.

103    I. Finkelstein and N. Na'aman, 'The Judahite Shephelah in the Late 8th and Early 7th Centuries BCE', *TA* 31 (2004), 75. In other words, Sennacherib intended to undermine the Judahite oil industry and transfer its focus to Philistia, and was accordingly disinterested in destroying sites critical to this industry.

104    Faust and Weiss, 'Judah, Philistia, and the Mediterranean World', 71–73; see also Master, 'Trade and Politics'; Gitin, 'The Neo-Assyrian Empire', 84; Ehrlich, *Philistines in Transition*, 18. The site preserves weights corresponding to multiple scale systems, probably corresponding to diverse clientele; fish bones from Egypt; Greek ceramics as well as Transjordanian ceramics; and grain from Judah (L.E. Stager, D.M. Master and J.D. Schloen, *Ashkelon 3: The Seventh Century B.C.* [Winona Lake, Ind., Eisenbrauns, 2011], 737–739).

the region for its own sake, because transport of the perishable proceeds to Assyria would not have been practicable and, in lieu of the Assyrians as the driving force of this system, they point to a Phoenician trading empire extending across the Mediterranean and a growing population in Egypt; they suggest that these provided the impetus for the region's economic growth. Their analysis suggests that 'while there is no doubt that the Assyrians *enabled* the prosperity and *greatly benefited* from it, the economic driving force behind it was located elsewhere'.[105] More recently, however, Fantalkin has argued that this identification of Ashkelon as the major hub of the southern Levantine economy during the long seventh century is disproportionately influenced by data relating only to the very end of this period.[106] As already discussed, the decline of the Assyrian empire in the last third of the seventh century led to a reorientation of the southern Levant toward Egypt. According to Fantalkin, it is therefore more appropriate to take a broader view of the Philistine economic picture during the Assyrian period:

---

105   Faust and Weiss, 'Judah, Philistia, and the Mediterranean World', 86. The excavators observed no artefacts at the site indicating direct interaction with Assyria (Stager, Master and Schloen, *Ashkelon 3*, 740); note also L.E. Stager, 'Farming in the Judean Desert during the Iron Age', *BASOR* 221 (1976), 145–158, in which he contends that it was Egypt's late seventh century resurgence which fuelled the Ekron oil industry; Gitin, 'Israelite and Philistine Culture', counters this proposal on the basis of the timing of both Ekron's and Ashekelon's periods of maximum growth. In a related argument Faust, 'The Interests of the Assyrian Empire', depicts an Assyrian tendency to destroy the economic potential of its provincialised territories and cites this as eliminating the possibility of Assyrian economic interests in its vassal territories. However, Faust neglects to take the political and military rationale for provincialisation into account when discussing the associated economic demolition; the destruction of olive oil production centres around Samaria on which Faust focuses, for example, should be seen in connection with the larger punitive objectives of the provincialisation process itself, rather than as a self-standing economic policy. Note Bienkowski's observation that 'all the evidence suggests that turning an independent state into a province incurred substantial military and administrative expenditure, so presumably it was in Assyria's interests to leave it as a tributary state if at all possible'; P. Bienkowski, 'Transjordan and Assyria', *The Archaeology of Jordan and Beyond: Essays in Honor of James A. Sauer* (ed. M.D. Coogan, J.A. Greene and L.E. Stager, SAHL 5, Winona Lake, Ind., Eisenbrauns, 2000), 45. Economic expenditure should probably also be added to this list. Similarly, the economic development observable in the vassal states should be understood in the context of loyal vassalhood.

106   Fantalkin, 'Why Did Nebuchadnezzar II Destroy Ashkelon'; cf. Gitin, 'Israelite and Philistine Culture'.

There is little doubt that during the period of Neo-Assyrian domination, Ashkelon was an important city, serving Phoenician trade and mediating in supplying Egyptian goods to the Assyrians for the benefit of all parties involved. However, to single out Ashkelon as the trading hub of the southern Levant does little justice to other Palestinian-coast port powers, such as Gaza, Dor, or Acco.[107]

Supporting a broad view of the region's incorporation into wider economic networks during this period is that a number of the Philistine cities appear to have undergone a similar process of specialisation during this period. 'Gaza was turned into a commercial center... Ashdod became a center for pottery production... Ashkelon prospered as a great emporium, probably exporting Philistia's oil and wine and importing fish and grain from Egypt'.[108] To this we should also add the development of Ekron as the largest centre of olive oil production known from the ancient Near East.[109] This process of broad economic development is convincingly understood as a move encouraged by the Assyrians in the interests of the Assyrian economic system, facilitated by the period of relative political stability of the southern Levant under Assyrian power, the *pax Assyriaca*.[110]

---

107  Fantalkin, 'Why Did Nebuchadnezzar II Destroy Ashkelon', 93. Similarly, with regard to Ashkelon, Stager writes that '[t]he Assyrians did not directly determine these outcomes but they certainly created the conditions in which others changed their economic behavior to take advantage of the new economic situation that had been created' (Stager, Master and Schloen, *Ashkelon 3*, 740).

108  Gitin, 'The Neo-Assyrian Empire', 84; cf. Ehrlich, *Philistines in Transition*, 18; Stager, Master and Schloen, *Ashkelon 3*, 737–740.

109  This site is an excellent example of the degree of change which occurred between the eighth century and the seventh: in the ninth-eighth century there is no evidence of oil production, whereas by the seventh century the city had become the largest centre for oil manufacture known in the ancient Near East (Na'aman, 'Ekron under the Assyrian and Egyptian Empires', 81; Gitin, 'Tel Miqne-Ekron', 23–24; Gitin, 'The Neo-Assyrian Empire', 84, 87). Note the probable use of the oil installations in the off-season(s) for textile production (Gitin, 'The Neo-Assyrian Empire', 87, 90; Ehrlich, *Philistines in Transition*, 18; O. Shamir, 'Loomweights and Textile Production at Tel Miqne-Ekron: A Prelimary Report', *'Up to the Gates of Ekron': Essays on the Archaeology and History of the Eastern Mediterranean in Honor of Seymour Gitin* [ed. S.W. Crawford, A. Ben-Tor, J.P. Dessel, W.G. Dever, A. Mazar and J. Aviram, Jerusalem, W.F. Albright Institute of Archaeological Research and Israel Exploration Society, 2007], 43–49).

110  Gitin, 'Tel Miqne-Ekron', 48; cf. Faust and Weiss, 'Judah, Philistia, and the Mediterranean World', 72. For an attempt to amalgamate the agricultural emphasis of Faust and Weiss with the Arabian trade emphasis of Finkelstein and others see J.M. Tebes, 'Trade and

### Philistia and Judah

Both the politics and economics of the southern Levant as well as the imme-diate proximity of Philistia and Judah render the Philistine territories one of the two neighbours with whom Judah's relations were both most intimate and best-attested (the other is Edom, to which we turn next). An important element of the interaction between Judah and Philistia during the long seventh century is the changes wrought to the economic-agricultural system of the area by the advent of the Assyrian empire. Already in the late eighth century Judah would have been conscious of the increasing power of Assyria in the Philistine west as well as the increasing economic activities—frequently involving transit across Judah—which Assyrian support for Philistia occasioned. The presence of Judahite ceramic forms in the eighth century Stratum VIII at Ashdod, one of the coastal termini for the east-west trade routes (prior to its destruction in 712), attests the involvement of Judahites in these routes already at this early point in the period.[111]

After 701, the burgeoning Philistine economy also moved geographically closer to the heartland of Judah, as whatever control Hezekiah and Judah had previously exerted over the Shephelah was undermined by the assignment of this region to Philistine control. Especially prominent in this reorientation of the lowlands was the city of Ekron, which became a major focus of the agricul-tural and economic activities deriving from the Shephelah. Located in the bor-der area between the Philistine and Judahite heartlands, Ekron seems to have changed hands fairly frequently during its 'dark ages' (between the tenth and seventh centuries), apparently at some stage residing under Judahite influ-ence.[112] Although the exact degree of Judahite and Philistine authority in the period immediately preceding the arrival of the Assyrians is murky, Judahite involvement in the city's affairs is evident still in the reign of Hezekiah, noted in the Assyrian texts as complicit in the city's rebellion against its Assyrian masters.[113] Sennacherib's punitive campaign culminated in the significant loss

---

Nomads: The Commercial Relations between the Negev, Edom, and the Mediterranean in the Late Iron Age', *Journal of the Serbian Archaeological Society* 22 (2006), 45–62.

111   Singer-Avitz, 'Beersheba', 13, who estimates the Judahite forms at Ashdod to be in the region of five percent of the total.

112   Gitin, 'Tel Miqne-Ekron', 41.

113   RINAP 3/1 4 39–58. For discussions of this episode see S. Mittmann, 'Hiskia und die Philister', *JNSL* 16 (1991), 91–106; Gitin, 'Tel Miqne-Ekron', 26; Gitin, 'Seventh Century B.C.E. Cultic Elements at Ekron', 255–256 n. 21; Roberts, 'Egypt, Assyria, Isaiah, and the Ashdod Affair', 271–272; Hoffmeier, 'Egypt's Role in the Events of 701', 219; Hoffmeier, 'Egypt's Role in the Events of 701 B.C.: A Rejoinder', 287–288; Younger, Jr., 'Assyrian Involvement', 245–262. The city may have been under Judahite political control during the middle of

of Judahite territory in the neighbouring Shephelah and its reassignment to Philistia, primarily Ekron, drawing the final line under any Judahite stage in Ekron's political history.[114] This reassignment marked the beginning of a major surge in Ekron's prominence, with the site becoming the largest in Philistia's inner coastal plain.[115]

As far as Judah was concerned, Finkelstein's conclusion that 'Sennacherib's campaign altered the economic and political systems in the region: the Judahite centers in the eastern Shephelah were destroyed and Judah was forced to ship its produce to a new center in the western Shephelah [Ekron], close to the

------

the eighth century; the involvement of Hezekiah in the Padi affair, while not necessarily indicative of Judahite control over the city, suggests a close relationship between the two neighbours around this time (for discussion and reconstructions see Gitin, 'Tel Miqne-Ekron', 41; Gitin, 'The Neo-Assyrian Empire', 86–87; Na'aman, 'Ekron under the Assyrian and Egyptian Empires'). If the city was at an earlier stage considered part of Judah, it is noteworthy the extent to which its material culture is clearly orientated towards the coastal cities in the long seventh century, as well as the dramatic increase in its size and wealth during the same period. What might have been a Judahite backwater in the eighth century became during the seventh century a major Philistine economic power, one whose influence would have been keenly felt in whatever territory remained under Judahite control, as their produce was channelled to the west for processing and further export.

114   Gitin, 'Tel Miqne-Ekron', 43; see also N. Na'aman, 'Two Notes on the History of Ashkelon and Ekron in the Late Eighth-Seventh Centuries BCE', *Ancient Israel and Its Neighbors: Interaction and Counteraction* (Winona Lake, Ind., Eisenbrauns, 2005), 68–75. Na'aman elsewhere suggests that 'the aim of [Sennacherib's] campaign against Hezekiah, the leader of the anti-Assyrian coalition, was to break and weaken Judah, the strongest kingdom that remained near the Egyptian border' (Na'aman, 'Population Changes in Palestine', 209). Ashdod and Gaza are also said to have profited from Judah's punishment, as is, in one version of the annals, Ashkelon (Tadmor, 'Philistia under Assyrian Rule', 97).

115   Gitin, 'Tel Miqne-Ekron', 23. Both Ussishkin and Na'aman contend that expansion into the lower city, clearly evident in the seventh century proper, had begun already in the second half of the eighth century, following the Assyrians' arrival on the scene (Na'aman, 'Ekron under the Assyrian and Egyptian Empires', 85; N. Na'aman, 'When and How did Jerusalem Become a Great City? The Rise of Jerusalem as Judah's Premier City in the Eighth-Seventh Centuries B.C.E.', *BASOR* 347 [2007], 26–27; see also D. Ussishkin, 'The Fortifications of Philistine Ekron', *IEJ* 55 [2005], 35–65). Gitin, 'Seventh Century B.C.E. Cultic Elements at Ekron', 255–256 n. 21 apparently attributes the Judahite ceramic forms from the late eighth century stratum to refugees from the northern kingdom; compare Na'aman's suggestion that refugees from the Shephelah might have fled to Ekron after 701 and that this would have been permitted by the Assyrians as in keeping with their attempt, through the 701 campaign, to reduce Judahite power (Na'aman, 'When and How did Jerusalem Become a Great City', 27; also Na'aman, 'Population Changes in Palestine', 209).

gateway communities of the coast' is surely correct.[116] Physical evidence to this effect may be seen in Ekron's pottery record at the time of the city's destruction in the last years of the seventh or the early sixth century, in which a significant percentage of the assemblage reflects Judahite forms.[117] This may be attributed at least in part to the sourcing of the olives used as raw material in the Ekron olive presses from inland, much of which was formerly or currently under Judahite control.[118] Indeed, Gitin writes that '[t]he very presence of the oil industry at Ekron is a strong indicator that there must have been a long-term economic interrelation between the Coastal Plain and Inland Judah during the seventh century B.C.'[119] Economic contact is further indicated by the presence in Ekron and Tel Batash of inscribed stone weights, typical of the

---

116   Finkelstein, 'The Archaeology of the Days of Manasseh', 180; Finkelstein and Na'aman, 'The Judahite Shephelah', 74–75.

117   T.K. Dothan and S. Gitin, 'Tell Miqne, 1985', *IEJ* 36 (1986), 106; Gitin, 'Tel Miqne-Ekron', 50–51; Gitin, 'The Neo-Assyrian Empire', 90–91. In the industrial zone in the lower city the ceramics contain 83.5% coastal forms and seven percent Judahite forms; a further 9% are non-specific southern forms while a few (0.5%) are classed as northern—supporting, perhaps, the possibility raised by the discovery of distinctive four-horned altars in the zone: that some part of the population in Ekron was composed of deported craftspeople from the former northern kingdom (Gitin, 'Tel Miqne-Ekron', 49–51; Gitin, 'Seventh Century B.C.E. Cultic Elements at Ekron', 249–250). The proportion of Judahite ceramic forms appears to increase in the inner city living quarters (Gitin notes this as a 'tentative conclusion'), suggesting perhaps an even larger Judahite presence in and interaction with the city (Gitin, 'Tel Miqne-Ekron', 51).

The destruction of this phase is dated by the excavators to Nebuchadnezzar's Philistine campaign in 603 (see Dothan and Gitin, 'Tell Miqne 1985', 106–107; T.K. Dothan and S. Gitin, 'Tell Miqne, 1984', *IEJ* 35 [1985], 71; Gitin, 'The Neo-Assyrian Empire', 98; see also A. Malamat, 'The Twilight of Judah: In the Egyptian-Babylonian Maelstrom', *Congress Volume: Edinburgh 1974* [ed. J. Emerton, VTSup 28, Leiden, Brill, 1975], 123–145; A. Malamat, 'The Last Years of the Kingdom of Judah', *The Age of the Monarchies: Political History* [vol. 4 of *A World History of the Jewish People*, ed. A. Malamat, Jerusalem, Massada, 1979], 205–221; though this is disputed by N. Na'aman, 'Nebuchadrezzar's Campaign in the Year 603 BCE', *Ancient Israel and Its Neighbors: Interaction and Counteraction* [Winona Lake, Ind., Eisenbrauns, 2005], 399–402). It also, therefore, reflects the intimate economic relationship between the Judahite Shephelah and Ekron as the Assyrian empire was on the wane, although there is no reason to believe that this was not a continuation of a relationship established much earlier. Note, for comparison, the case for dating the development of the Beersheba and Arad valleys region to the latter half of the eighth century, that is, in response to the *pax Assyriaca* (Thareani-Sussely, '"Archaeology of the Days of Manasseh"').

118   Herr, 'Archaeological Sources', 163; also Knauf, '"The Glorious Days of Manasseh"', 171.

119   Gitin, 'Tel Miqne-Ekron', 50.

kind used in Judah at this time; a similar weight was also found at a Philistine site about eight kilometres east of Gaza, near Kibbutz Mefalsim.[120] Towards the end of the period, when Lachish had recovered somewhat from the devastation wrought upon it by Sennacherib, the script on a storage jar found at that site also 'seems to indicate that there were commercial relations between Lachish and a Philistine city, probably Gaza'.[121]

Reflecting the same reorientation toward the coast and the area's greater integration into the wider economic system, the town at Tel Batash, a few miles east of Ekron, reveals already some local imitations of Assyrian palace wares in the eighth century stratum (Stratum III) but substantially more in the strata from the seventh (II) and sixth (IIA) centuries.[122] Stratum II turned up a clay mould figurine with Phoenician or Philistine affinities and Phoenician, Transjordanian, coastal and Judahite pottery types are also present at the site.[123] Although the percentage of Judahite types is about the same in Stratum III and Stratum II, reflecting only a small decrease from about 29% to about 26%, the representation of coastal types more than doubles, from 25% to 54%. Assyrian forms likewise increase, from one to six percent, as do Phoenician forms, from 0.1% to three percent.[124] The four stone weights found in Stratum II—all

120    R. Kletter, *Economic Keystones: The Weight System of the Kingdom of Judah* (JSOTSup 276, Sheffield, Sheffield Academic Press, 1998), 57–58; Gitin, 'Tel Miqne-Ekron', 51; J. Naveh, 'Writing and Scripts in Seventh-Century BCE Philistia: The New Evidence from Tell Jemmeh', *IEJ* 35 (1985), 21 n. 39.

121    Naveh, 'Writing and Scripts', 17, 21; A. Lemaire, 'Ostraca and Incised Inscriptions', *The Iron Age and Post-Iron Age Pottery and Artefacts* (vol. 4 of *The Renewed Archaeological Excavations at Lachish (1973–1994)*, ed. D. Ussishkin, PIA 22, Tel Aviv, Emery and Claire Yass Publications in Archaeology, 2004), 2099–2132. The certainty of this link turns on the epigraphic debate over the inscription; its sole evidence would provide a very poor basis for interaction between Philistia and Judah, but as part of a larger body of evidence may contribute to the argument. Lemaire contends that 'the script is clearly not Hebrew' and that 'the storage jar indicates affinities to vessels from the Philistine coast', concluding that the script is 'neo-Philistine' or 'Philistian' (Lemaire, 'Ostraca', 2127–2128).

122    A. Mazar and N. Panitz-Cohen, eds., *The Finds from the First Millennium BCE: Text* (vol. 2 of *Timnah (Tel Batash) Final Reports*, Qedem 42, Jerusalem, Hebrew University of Jerusalem, 2001), 42–43.

123    G.L. Kelm and A. Mazar, *Timnah: A Biblical City in the Sorek Valley* (Winona Lake, Ind., Eisenbrauns, 1995), 164–168; Mazar and Panitz-Cohen, *Finds from the First Millennium*, 10–195, 205–206. Neutron activation analysis of vessels from both strata indicates vessel origins in Ashdod, the Shephelah around Lachish and Ekron (Mazar and Panitz-Cohen, *Finds from the First Millennium*, 452).

124    Mazar and Panitz-Cohen, *Finds from the First Millennium*, 157–162. Stratum II also includes some East Greek forms (J. Magness, 'Early Archaic Greek Pottery', *The Finds from the*

already according to Mesopotamian standards—multiply to 18 in Stratum II (plus a likely seven additional weights); these latter 'illustrate the complex and eclectic stock of weights used during the 7th century in the Shephelah' and include marked Judahite weights, five calibrated using Mesopotamian *shekel* standards, four using the Egyptian *deben* and four using Phoenician standards.[125] A Phoenician scaraboid, an amulet of the Egyptian Bastet and a bulla with Egyptian imagery mediated perhaps by the Phoenicians all also attest to 'the economic and cultural connections of Timnah with the Phoenician coast and Egypt'.[126]

All of this was occurring directly on the doorstep of Judah, in territory to which there persisted at least some sense of a Judahite claim. Whether by deliberate Assyrian policy or natural economic effect, the economies and populations of Philistia and Judah were closely intertwined during the long seventh century.

### 3.3      *Edom*

The Edomites are one of the several Levantine polities which came into their own in the seventh century. They appear in a tribal sense already in the eighth century Assyrian inscriptions of Adad-nirari III and appear to have sent envoys to Nimrud during the reign of Sargon II, but the archaeological record indicates a limited range of distinctive characteristics for the territory or its inhabitants until the long seventh century and minimal indications of a settled population until around the same time.[127] The notable lack of destruction

---

*First Millennium BCE: Text* [vol. 2 of *Timnah (Tel Batash) Final Reports*, ed. A. Mazar and N. Panitz-Cohen, Qedem 42, Jerusalem, Hebrew University of Jerusalem, 2001], 141–144). Notably, two thirds of the cooking pots in Stratum II are Judahite forms, suggesting that this increased ceramic diversity in the seventh and sixth centuries was occurring over the top of a population which was still largely Judahite in origin.

125   A. Eran, 'Stone Weights', *The Finds from the First Millennium BCE: Text* [vol. 2 of *Timnah (Tel Batash) Final Reports*, ed. A. Mazar and N. Panitz-Cohen, Qedem 42, Jerusalem, Hebrew University of Jerusalem, 2001), 238–243.

126   B. Brandl, 'A Scarab, a Bulla and an Amulet from Stratum II', *The Finds from the First Millennium BCE: Text* (vol. 2 of *Timnah (Tel Batash) Final Reports*, ed. A. Mazar and N. Panitz-Cohen, Qedem 42, Jerusalem, Hebrew University of Jerusalem, 2001), 266–272; all of these were imported.

127   M. Weippert, 'The Relations of the States East of the Jordan with the Mesopotamian Powers During the First Millennium BC', *Studies in the History and Archaeology of Jordan III* (ed. A. Hadidi, Amman, Department of Antiquities, 1987), 100; S. Hart, 'The Edom Survey Project 1984–85: The Iron Age', *Studies in the History and Archaeology of Jordan III* (ed. A. Hadidi, Amman, Department of Antiquities, 1987), 287; Bienkowski and van

layers in the Transjordan means that this date is reached by means of an inscribed royal seal ('Qos-gabr, king of Edom') whose owner is mentioned twice in the Assyrian royal inscriptions: once in Esarhaddon's Prism B, dated around 673–672, and once in the first campaign of Assurbanipal, dated 667.[128] While some entity called Edom may have existed in the area previously, all the evidence at present indicates that Edom as a materially identifiable entity dates to the long seventh century. As with other such entities, their identifying characteristics revolve around pottery and script as well as a particular deity, called Qaus (also Qôs, both renderings of *qws*).[129]

The broader historical context suggests that the development of an Edomite state was also connected to the advent of Assyrian interests in the southern Levant: the late eighth and first half of the seventh century marked the height of Assyrian power and the extent of its control in the region, and in Edom it is convincing to see the construction of a political state as directly prompted by the economic and political interests of the empire in this region.[130] Unlike

der Steen, 'Tribes, Trade, and Towns', 23; Finkelstein, 'Khirbet en-Nahas'; I. Finkelstein and L. Singer-Avitz, 'The Pottery of Edom: A Correction', *Antiguo Oriente* 6 (2008), 13–24; Herr, 'Archaeological Sources'. For an earlier date see T.E. Levy, R.B. Adams, M. Najjar, A. Hauptmann, J.D. Anderson, B. Brandl, M.A. Robinson and T. Higham, 'Reassessing the Chronology of Biblical Edom: New Excavations and 14C Dates from Khirbat en-Nahas (Jordan)', *Antiquity* 78 (2004), 865–879; but note the critique of E. Van Der Steen and P. Bienkowski, 'Radiocarbon Dates from Khirbat en-Nahas: A Methodological Critique', *Antiquity* 80 (2006), n.p.; and T.E. Levy, T. Higham and M. Najjar, 'Response to van der Steen & Bienkowski', *Antiquity* 80 (2006), n.p.

128  P. Bienkowski, 'The Edomites: The Archaeological Evidence from Transjordan', *You Shall Not Abhor an Edomite for He Is Your Brother: Edom and Seir in History and Tradition* (ed. D.V. Edelman, Archaeological and Biblical Studies 3, Atlanta, Ga., Scholars, 1995), 44.

129  I. Beit-Arieh, 'The Edomites in Cisjordan', *You Shall Not Abhor an Edomite for He Is Your Brother: Edom and Seir in History and Tradition* (ed. D.V. Edelman, SBLABS 3, Atlanta, Ga., Scholars, 1995), 33. Curiously, *qws* appears as a theophoric among the names in the lists of returnees in Ezra and Nehemiah (Ez. 2:53; Neh. 7:55) (Beit-Arieh, *Ḥorvat Qitmit*, 306). On the theory that *qws* and YHWH were at one time considered the same deity see J. Kelley, 'Toward a New Synthesis of the God of Edom and Yahweh', *Antiguo Oriente* 7 (2009), 255–280 and N. Amzallag, 'Yahweh, the Canaanite God of Metallurgy?', *JSOT* 33 (2009), 387–404, although this suggestion has not been widely adopted. A. Ofer, '"All the Hill Country of Judah": From A Settlement Fringe to a Prosperous Monarchy', *From Nomadism to Monarchy: Archaeological and Historical Aspects of Early Israel* (ed. I. Finkelstein and N. Na'aman, Jerusalem, Israel Exploration Society, 1994), 114–116 has also argued that approximately a third of the family names in onomastic material in the Hebrew Bible occur in both Edom and Judah, suggesting a close relationship of some kind.

130  Na'aman, 'Population Changes in Palestine', 214–215; Gitin, 'The Neo-Assyrian Empire', 79–82; Bienkowski, 'Architecture', 135, among others. This largely external impetus seems

the Philistine case, this is generally agreed: Knauf has argued cogently that the rise of an Edomite state was directly the consequence of Assyrian involvement in the west, while elsewhere he and Lenzen suggest that '[b]oth economic activities, copper production and agriculture, might have been stimulated by the Assyrians, who were interested in a well-organised Edom because major trade routes were in this area and because they were interested in its economic resources.'[131] Taking the point for granted, Bienkowski concludes that 'there is much to suggest that statehood—and by implication central control—was fairly superficial' and that it quickly dissipated with the disappearance of the Assyrian overlords who had prompted it.[132] Although noting that it is not proved, he and van der Steen suggest that Edomite state formation occurring alongside Assyrian expansion is unlikely to have been a coincidence—that the Assyrians were most likely interested in the copper mines in the region as well as the existing network of trade in Arabian luxury goods—while Gitin notes the apparent relation of much of the new development to trading activities, both on the north-south route and in the northeastern Negev: 'All of these settlements seem to have been the result of secondary state formation, as the fate of Edom was dependent on economic developments and political decisions made in Assyria'.[133]

---

to explain the relatively limited time frame in which an identifiable (political) 'Edom' persisted.

131    E.A. Knauf, 'The Cultural Impact of Secondary State Formation: The Cases of the Edomites and the Moabites', *Early Edom and Moab: The Beginning of the Iron Age in Southern Jordan* (ed. P. Bienkowski, Sheffield Archaeological Monographs 7, Sheffield, Collis, 1992), 47–54; E.A. Knauf and C.J. Lenzen, 'Edomite Copper Industry', *Studies in the History and Archaeology of Jordan III* (ed. A. Hadidi, Amman, Department of Antiquities, 1987), 86; Bienkowski, 'Architecture', 135. Whether the Assyrians were themselves present in the Transjordan is unresolved (although, if they were, it would have been unlikely to have been in large numbers); see Bienkowski and Van Der Steen, 'Tribes, Trade, and Towns', 39–40; Bennett, 'Neo-Assyrian Influence'; Bienkowski, 'The Edomites', 58–59; Bienkowski, 'Architecture', 135, 139–142; A. Millard, 'Assyrian Involvement in Edom', *Early Edom and Moab: The Beginning of the Iron Age in Southern Jordan* (ed. P. Bienkowski, Sheffield Archaeological Monographs 7, Sheffield, Collis, 1992), 36–37.

132    Bienkowski, 'The Edomites', 56; note also his discussion regarding the nature of Assyrian presence in the Transjordan in Bienkowski, 'Transjordan and Assyria'.

133    Bienkowski and van der Steen, 'Tribes, Trade, and Towns', 23–24, 40–41; Gitin, 'The Neo-Assyrian Empire', 79–82, here 81. Similarly, Bienkowski, 'Architecture', 135; Na'aman, 'Population Changes in Palestine', 214–215; N. Na'aman, 'Province System and Settlement Pattern in Southern Syria and Palestine in the Neo-Assyrian Period', *Neo-Assyrian Geography* (ed. M. Liverani, Quaderni di geografia storica 5, Rome, University of Rome, 1995), 103–115; Herr, 'Archaeological Sources', 151; B. Oded, 'Observations on Methods of Assyrian Rule in Transjordan after the Palestinian Campaigns of Tiglath-pileser III',

Increasing numbers of commercial travellers moved along the road to the coast in the long seventh century as a result of the Assyrian economic impetus, with some staying at sites alongside for extended periods of time. As will be detailed below, the material culture of the Negev experienced a significant period of diversification over the course of the long seventh century and a significant proportion of the remains reflect traditions from east of the Jordan.

As the problematic relationship between archaeological finds and the identity concepts of their ancient manufacturers has been especially hotly debated in the context of discussions about Edom, it is useful here to consider this issue in a little more detail. The underlying difficulty is the fact that there is no direct line between material culture and the more abstract phenomenon of group identity.[134] In Jones's warning

*JNES* 29 (1970), 177–186; Bennett, 'Neo-Assyrian Influence'; Knauf, 'The Cultural Impact'; Finkelstein, *Living on the Fringe*, 139–154; Finkelstein, 'Khirbet en-Nahas'; Finkelstein and Singer-Avitz, 'The Pottery of Edom'.

134   The literature on this issue is substantial. For more extensive discussions of the problematic relationship between cultural difference and cultural identity than may be undertaken here see S. Shennan, 'Introduction: Archaeological Approaches to Cultural Identity', *Archaeological Approaches to Cultural Identity* (ed. S. Shennan, London, Routledge, 1994), 1–32; the essays in M.T. Stark, ed., *The Archaeology of Social Boundaries* (London, Smithsonian Institute, 1998); also I. Hodder, 'Social Organisation and Human Interaction: The Development of Some Tentative Hypotheses in Terms of Material Culture', *The Spatial Organisation of Culture* (ed. I. Hodder, London, Duckworth, 1978), 199–269; I. Hodder, 'Economic and Social Stress and Material Culture Patterning', *American Antiquity* 44 (1979), 446–454; I. Hodder, *Symbols in Action: Ethnoarchaeological Studies of Material Culture* (New Studies in Archaeology, Cambridge, Cambridge University Press, 1982); I. Hodder, *Reading the Past: Current Approaches to Interpretation in Archaeology* (2nd edn., Cambridge, Cambridge University Press, 1991); G. Emberling, 'Ethnicity in Complex Societies: Archaeological Perspectives', *Journal of Archaeological Research* 5 (1997), 295–344; L.M. Meskell, 'The Intersections of Identity and Politics in Archaeology', *ARA* 31 (2002), 279–301; A. Wylie, *Thinking from Things: Essays in the Philosophy of Archaeology* (Berkeley, Ca., University of California Press, 2002); S. Jones, *Archaeology of Ethnicity: Constructing Identities in the Past and Present* (London, Routledge, 1997). With regard to the southern Levant in particular see, for example, Kletter, 'Clay Figurines'; Herr, 'Archaeological Sources'; A.H. Joffe, 'The Rise of Secondary States in the Iron Age Levant', *JESHO* 45 (2002), 425–467; Y. Thareani, 'The Spirit of Clay: "Edomite Pottery" and Social Awareness in the Late Iron Age', *BASOR* 359 (2010), 35–56; I.D. Wilson, 'Judean Pillar Figurines and Ethnic Identity in the Shadow of Assyria', *JSOT* 36 (2012), 259–278; Oren, 'Ethnicity and Regional Archaeology'; K.A. Kamp and N. Yoffee, 'Ethnicity in Ancient Western Asia: Archaeological Assessments and Ethnoarchaeological Prospectives', *BASOR* 237 (1980), 85–104; D.A. Nestor, *Cognitive Perspectives on Israelite Identity* (LHBOTS

words, 'it cannot be assumed *a priori* that similarity in material culture reflects the presence of a particular group of people in the past, an index of social interaction, or a shared normative framework'.[135] Such caution arises from a long-standing tendency, particularly in the earlier decades of the discipline, to equate material culture with ethnic groups—that is, to assume that material culture and ethnic identity were coterminous: similarity and difference in the content and style of material assemblages were taken to reflect similarity or difference in ethnic identity.[136]

From the mid-twentieth century archaeologists began to question the directness of this association, often focusing on the functional aspect of material cultural phenomena. Hodder, for example, plays on instrumentalist theories of ethnic identity in his theorisation, arguing that 'the material culture differences between tribes can only be understood if material culture is seen as a language, expressing within-group cohesion in competition over scarce resources'.[137] Recognising that not all aspects of material culture are communicative in this sense, he suggests that 'the archaeologist cannot hope to identify all the tribes or ethnic groups that existed in the past, but he can identify ethnicity if by this is meant ... the mechanism by which interest groups use culture to symbolize their within-group organization in opposition to and in competition with other interest groups'. [138]

Even if a relationship between material culture and identity is thus allowed in theory, recognising it in practice remains difficult. Part of the issue is that there is rarely a neat, one-to-one correlation between material culture and ethnic groups, reflecting the fact that only a few, specific elements are required to act as identity markers; other elements of

---

519, London, T&T Clark, 2010), 46–76, 126–191; G. Emberling and N. Yoffee, 'Thinking about Ethnicity in Mesopotamian Archaeology and History', *Fluchtpunkt Uruk: Archaeologische Einheit aus Methodologischer Vielfalt: Schriften für Hans J. Nissen* (ed. H. Kuehne, R. Bernbeck and K. Bartl, Rahden, Marie Leidorf Verlag, 1999), 272–281; A.E. Killebrew, *Biblical Peoples and Ethnicity: An Archaeological Study of Egyptians, Canaanites, Philistines, and Early Israel, 1300–1100 B.C.E.* (Archaeology and Biblical Studies 9, Leiden, Brill, 2005).

135    Jones, *Archaeology of Ethnicity*, 126.

136    For a history of the discipline see Jones, *Archaeology of Ethnicity*; Nestor, *Cognitive Perspectives*.

137    Hodder, 'Economic and Social Stress', 447.

138    Hodder, 'Economic and Social Stress', 452.

material culture may be shared by more than one ethnic group.[139] These common cultural traits are not obliged to bear the weight of ethnic meaning and may thus be common without causing concern. Similarly, some elements of a group's material culture may diversify within the group without causing problems for the identification of the group because those practices are not relevant symbols of ethnic identity. In both directions, therefore, an uninformed outsider may struggle to discern the boundaries of ethnic demarcation, as a group may both share cultural traits with outsiders and accommodate diversity within its ranks. The crux is in the location of meaning; Jones warns that,

> whether or not spatially and temporally bounded distributions of material culture are the product of a similar enculturative milieu, or a common *habitus*, they *do not necessarily 'map' the extent and boundaries of self-conscious ethnic groups in the past*. Ethnicity must be distinguished from mere spatial continuity and discontinuity in that it refers to self-conscious identification with a particular group of people.[140]

The complexity thus derives from the fact that not all cultural practices are meaningful in signalling identity affiliations. '[W]hether a particular artefact does or does not express the boundary of an ethnic group', writes Hodder, 'depends on the ideas people in that society have about different artifacts and what is an appropriate artifact for ethnic group marking'; there is 'no direct, universal cross-cultural relationship between behaviour and material culture'.[141] Scholars cannot, therefore, simply assume that any specific material object is relevant for identifying its owner as a member of a certain identity group. Everything except the body itself is transformable.[142] 'The problem for archaeologists', as Emberling writes,

---

139 Thus Hodder, *Symbols in Action*; also F. Barth, 'Introduction', *Ethnic Groups and Boundaries: The Social Organization of Cultural Difference* (ed. F. Barth, London, George Allen & Unwin, 1969), 14.

140 Jones, *Archaeology of Ethnicity*, 122–123; italics original.

141 Hodder, *Reading the Past*, 3, 14. Also Barth, 'Introduction', 14: 'one cannot predict from first principles which [cultural] features will be emphasized and made organizationally relevant by the actors'; and similarly M. Dietler and I. Herbich, 'Habitus, Techniques, Style: An Integrated Approach to the Social Understanding of Material Culture and Boundaries', *The Archaeology of Social Boundaries* (ed. M.T. Stark, London, Smithsonian Institute, 1998), 256–260.

142 H.R. Isaacs, 'Basic Group Identity: The Idols of the Tribe', *Ethnicity: Theory and Experience* (ed. N. Glazer and D.P. Moynihan, London, Harvard University Press, 1975), 36. Isaacs

'is to identify which characteristics would have been socially meaningful in a particular social situation, and which were unimportant.'[143]

There have been numerous attempts to determine which aspects of material culture are most likely to mark identity affiliations; Kamp and Yoffee offer three 'behavioural constellations': behaviours concerned with symbolising ethnic identity, the goal of which are communicative and for which differences and distinctions should be pronounced; behaviours which are learnt as part of the socialisation process of the group, such as manufacturing techniques and stylistic preferences, although these may become less important in situations of market exchange or large territorial diffusion; and behaviours reflecting economic or political strategy.[144] Emberling includes in this category elements of household structure, 'because of its close, meaningful relationship with daily life', aspects of ritual practice, including mortuary rituals, and cuisine.[145] Hegmon highlights a number of aspects of material culture which 'seem to relate to certain aspects of society and culture', including complex technologies and decorations which cross-cut a number of media. Also, any material object which is 'used in and that structures every day domestic life may be particularly relevant to the concept of *habitus*; that is, such material plays an important role in defining who people are socially'.[146] The particularly frequent mention of cultic paraphernalia and variables in the ceramic repertoire—especially cooking pots—reflect these and similar suggestions.

Ultimately, there is no decisive means of determining which aspects of a material culture act as signifiers of differentiation in group identity affiliations. Nevertheless, most archaeologists are willing to recognise that group identity is reflected in some way in the material record, even if they are unable to agree on exactly how this reflection can now be identified. Fortunate for the current purposes is the sheer volume of material

---

observes that '[b]ecause the body is the most primordial of all features of basic group identity, extraordinarily powerful taboos and sanctions have been attached in many groups to exogamous unions or marriages that threaten their physical sameness, their "racial purity"' (Isaacs, 'Basic Group Identity', 40).

143   Emberling, 'Ethnicity in Complex Societies', 311; cf. Shennan, 'Introduction', 13.

144   Kamp and Yoffee, 'Ethnicity in Ancient Western Asia', 96; cf. Hodder, *Symbols in Action*, 187.

145   Emberling, 'Ethnicity in Complex Societies', 325, 318.

146   M. Hegmon, 'Technology, Style, and Social Practices: Archaeological Approaches', *The Archaeology of Social Boundaries* (ed. M.T. Stark, London, Smithsonian Institute, 1998), 277.

difference evident in the southern Levant during the long seventh century, which by its abundance provides some confidence that at least some
of this diversity signals more than merely differences in technical production and reflects differentiation also in the identity affiliations of the persons who created these materials.

The ability of scholars to recognise ideological identity correlates in material culture has been especially hotly debated in discussions regarding the
Edomites as a result of arguments over the political and military history of
the Transjordan and the Negev. Thus Bienkowski and van der Steen rightly
sound a warning note regarding the identification of 'Edomite' pottery with
actual 'Edomite' people, noting especially that there are significant variations
within the assemblages in the Negev which have been identified as Edomite or
Judahite.[147] Beit-Arieh, more extremely, contends that '[t]here is insufficient
evidence to indicate that this pottery was confined to a specific ethnic group,
rather than being the standard Iron II ... painted pottery of an area extending beyond Edom proper'; he accordingly prefers the terminology of 'Buseirah'
(also 'Busayra') ware.[148] Bienkowski also points out that the primary identity
affiliation for members of the loose political coalition known as Edom was
likely always to the smaller kinship group rather than to an abstract state called
'Edom', calling into question the accuracy of such terminology in references to
the people behind the material culture; variations among the 'Edomite' assemblages at various southern Levantine sites point towards these smaller groups,
while at the same time they indicate a degree of overarching cultural continuity in these Transjordanian traditions; whether the smaller degrees of differentiation would have been identifiable by outsiders is unknown.[149]

Though recognising and emphasising a tribally-based identity framework
underlying this material, Bienkowski and van der Steen reject the use of 'ethnicity' as a relevant category for discussions about 'Edomites':

> this pottery and its distribution are a geographic and cultural product,
> probably of tribal groups, which has no connection at all to our modern
> concept of ethnicity or to 'the Edomite state' ... such pottery was probably

---

147   Bienkowski and van der Steen, 'Tribes, Trade, and Towns', 26.

148   Bienkowski, 'The Edomites', 51; similarly Bienkowski and van der Steen, 'Tribes, Trade, and
      Towns', 26.

149   P. Bienkowski, '"Tribalism" and "Segmentary Society" in Iron Age Transjordan', *Studies on
      Iron Age Moab and Neighbouring Areas in Honour of Michèle Daviau* [ANESupS 29, Leuven,
      Peeters, 2009], 7–26; also Bienkowski and van der Steen, 'Tribes, Trade, and Towns', 26–36.

produced by people who regarded themselves as members of particular tribes, and not as 'Edomites'; and it was produced over a wide area, which was not necessarily contiguous with the (changing) borders of the state of Edom.[150]

Similarly, Thareani-Sussely denies the possibility of identifying Edomites at Tel 'Aroer on the grounds that the evidence for Transjordanian material culture at this and other sites in the Negev does not amount to an ethnic consciousness among the users of these materials identifiable using modern terminology of ethnic identity:

> the geographic distribution of the 'Edomite' material culture has no con-nection with the modern concept of ethnicity or with the borders of the Edomite kingdom. Rather, the 'Edomite' assemblage appeared with tribal groups of an Edomite cultural orientation that resided in the Judaean Negev toward the end of the Iron Age.[151]

As already noted, it is frequently very difficult—if not impossible—to iden-tify which (if any) elements of the material culture repertoire are ideologically meaningful for identity; caution in drawing connections between material cul-ture and identity must therefore inevitably be the case in all discussions of material culture.

---

150    Bienkowski and van der Steen, 'Tribes, Trade, and Towns', 39.

151    Thareani, 'The Spirit of Clay', 51, referring to Finkelstein, 'Ḥorvat Qitmīt'; N. Na'aman, 'No Anthropomorphic Graven Image? Notes on the Assumed Anthropomorphic Cult Statues in the Temples of YHWH in the Pre-exilic Period', UF 31 (1999), 391–415; Bienkowski and van der Steen, 'Tribes, Trade, and Towns'. Thareani's use of the latter is obvious; Bienkowski and van der Steen wrote that 'this pottery and its distribution are a geographic and cultural product, probably of tribal groups, which has no connection at all to our modern concept of ethnicity or to "the Edomite state" ... such pottery was probably produced by people who regarded themselves as members of particular tribes, and not as "Edomites"; and it was produced over a wide area, which was not necessarily contiguous with the (changing) borders of the state of Edom' (Bienkowski and van der Steen, 'Tribes, Trade, and Towns', 39). Finkelstein is also cautious about the terminology employed to describe the users of distinctive material culture remains. He declares that the 'Edomite' pottery is best seen 'as a geographical-cultural occurrence, rather than as an ethnic phenomenon' (Finkelstein, 'Ḥorvat Qitmīt', 157–158). In neither, however, does the issue appear to be the acknowledgment of a distinctive cultural phenomenon and its presence at the site(s) in question, but rather an attempt to avoid equating the presence of Transjordanian cultural elements in the Negev with Edomite political domination.

Yet, despite the apparent rejection of ethnic identity as a relevant category for discussions of the Transjordan, the Negev and beyond, a closer inspection of the point of contention is in order. Both Thareani-Sussely and Bienkowski and van der Steen explicitly focus on the relationship between the material culture in question and a political and territorial entity based in the Transjordan: Bienkowski and van der Steen speak of an 'Edomite state' and 'the state of Edom', while Thareani-Sussely refers to an 'Edomite kingdom'. Their rejection of an 'ethnic' meaning for the 'Edomite' objects in the Cisjordan is not really a rejection of their significance for cultural and identity affiliation, as much as it is a rejection of these objects' significance for the debate about the extent of Edomite political control in the Negev.[152] The differentiations in material culture phenomena which these scholars are attempting to describe using the language of 'tribes' coincides with the particular emphasis in discussions of ethnic identity on distinguishable material culture; both Thareani-Sussely and Bienkowski and van der Steen describe these finds as 'cultural product . . . probably produced by people who regarded themselves as members of particular tribes' or as produced by 'tribal groups of an Edomite cultural orientation'.[153] The real issue here has to do with conceptions of Transjordanian political history; because Bienkowski, van der Steen and Thareani-Sussely are debating a tradition which has defined Edomite ethnic identity in terms of its relationship to an Edomite state—an Edomite ethnic identity which is indistinguishable from an Edomite nationalist identity—they are loathe to concede the possibility of an Edomite 'ethnicity'.[154] Such frustration is justifiable; there is a

---

152    Note the preference, in an attempt to circumvent associations with statehood, for the language of 'tribe' to express the 'shared cultural logic' of these groups (see especially the sustained definition of a tribe in Bienkowski, '"Tribalism" and "Segmentary Society"', 17–18, which includes a significant number of characteristics typical also of ethnic identity). Also picking up on the problems created by the conflation of cultural and political identities is C. Uehlinger, 'Arad, Qiṭmīt—Judahite Aniconism vs. Edomite Iconic Cult?', *Text, Artifact, and Image: Revealing Ancient Israelite Religion* (ed. G.M. Beckman and T.J. Lewis, BJS 346, Providence, Brown Judaic Studies, 2006), 80–112.

153    Bienkowski and van der Steen, 'Tribes, Trade, and Towns', 39; Thareani, 'The Spirit of Clay', 51. Note also Y. Thareani-Sussely, 'Desert Outsiders: Extramural Neighborhoods in the Iron Age Negev', *Bene Israel: Studies in the Archaeology of the Israel and the Levant during the Bronze and Iron Ages in Honour of Israel Finkelstein* (ed. A. Fantalkin and A. Yasur-Landau, CHANE 31, Leiden, Brill, 2008), 197–212, 288–302, in which Thareani-Sussely interprets the ceramic repertoire at 'Tel Aroer as expressing and fostering group identity among the (Edomite) tribal members resident at the site.

154    That these constitute part of the problem for Thareani and Bienkowski and van der Steen is suggested by the statements in both articles that the Edomite material has 'no

worthwhile distinction to be made between these phenomena and this kind of situation is an excellent example: the presence of Transjordanian cultural elements in the Negev, combined with the facile conflation of ethnic identity and nationalist identity, has produced assumptions about political and military incursions into the Negev by an Edomite state based in the Transjordan which are increasingly recognised as problematic. Indeed, most of the discussions which revolve around the presence of Edomites in the Negev are not really about whether people with cultural roots in the southern Transjordan were present in the southern Cisjordan during the long seventh century; the material cultural is sufficiently widespread and of a nature to indicate that they were. The issue is whether these people considered themselves to be members of and loyal to a Transjordanian political entity called Edom. Given the fragility of the Transjordanian Edomite state and the recent suggestions that the population of that state never really transitioned from a tribally-based identity system to a state-based one, it seems reasonable to suppose that people in the Cisjordan probably did not identify themselves as 'Edomite' in this sense (the name has to have come from somewhere, of course, so it is perfectly possible that some contingent of the political Edom consisted of a tribally-identifying group called Edom, but this is incidental to the larger point). The rejection of a political significance to Transjordanians' presence in the Negev, however, need not amount to the rejection of the cultural significance of their presence. The owners and producers of the culturally distinctive items in the Negev— however attached, or unattached, to the idea of a Transjordanian political state—could nonetheless view themselves as affiliated to a meaningful cultural entity which was different from others in the area.[155] As will become

---

connection at all to our modern concept of ethnicity' (Bienkowski and van der Steen, 'Tribes, Trade, and Towns', 39) and 'no connection with the modern concept of ethnicity' (Thareani, 'The Spirit of Clay', 51). For a fuller discussion of ethnic and nationalist identity see Chapter Two.

155  In fact, both Thareani-Sussely and Bienkowski and van der Steen acknowledge that the producers and users of the Edomite material probably viewed themselves as distinct from others. Bienkowski and van der Steen write that 'such pottery was probably produced by people who regarded themselves as members of particular tribes', while Thareani-Sussely refers to 'tribal groups of an Edomite cultural orientation', 'a concentration of "Edomite" ethnic activities' and 'a sharpening of tribal identity' (Bienkowski and van der Steen, 'Tribes, Trade, and Towns', 39; Thareani, 'The Spirit of Clay', 51–52). While these scholars are clearly at pains to emphasise the priority of the tribal rather than the state affiliation for these groups, they have no apparent issue with viewing the material distinctiveness attested in the archaeological record as most likely reflecting an associated and consciously distinctive group identity.

clear in Chapter Two, ultimately the vital point for the anthropological issue in the long seventh century is the matter of differentiation.

### Edom and Judah

Evidence for Transjordanians outside of the Transjordan is largely concentrated in the eastern Negev, primarily in the long seventh century.[156] This Transjordanian presence in the Negev is generally acknowledged; its nature is subject to debate regarding whether it reflects military, commercial or some other intent. The military interpretation holds the status of tradition, playing particularly on the portrayal of the Edomites in biblical texts where they are accused of expanding into Judahite territory by a number of the exilic writers (e.g., Lam. 4:21–22; Ezek. 25:12–14; Obadiah). One of the ostraca found at Tel 'Arad may be interpreted as urging fortification against a coming Edomite attack on Judah's frontier settlements, perhaps in conjunction with the defeat of Judah by the Babylonians, and this appears to be corroborated by fortification in the eastern Negev at this time; the primary excavator of Horvat Qitmit holds to this view.[157] The theory, however, traces back to Glueck's extrapolations from a handful of sites, which multiple scholars have acknowledged to be problematic.[158] Others have accordingly suggested that the pottery and ostraca linking a percentage of the Negev population to the material culture of the Transjordan are evidence for a flourishing trade network, from Arabia through Edom to the Beersheba Valley and finally Gaza; this route is thought to have developed in the late eighth century and continued into the seventh

---

156   See Singer-Avitz, 'Beersheba'; Thareani-Sussely, '"Archaeology of the Days of Manasseh"'. The nature of the relationship between the Transjordan and the eastern Negev in the long seventh century means that the discussion here should be read in conjunction with the discussion of the Negev in 3.5. Judah.

157   Beit-Arieh, 'The Edomites'; I. Beit-Arieh, ed., *Horvat Qitmit: An Edomite Shrine in the Biblical Negev* (MSIA 11, Tel Aviv, Tel Aviv University, 1995); I. Beit-Arieh, 'New Data on the Relationship between Judah and Edom toward the End of the Iron Age', *Recent Excavations in Israel: Studies in Iron Age Archaeology* (ed. S. Gitin and W.G. Dever, AASOR 49, Winona Lake, Ind., Eisenbrauns, 1989), 125–131; I. Beit-Arieh and B. Cresson, 'An Edomite Ostracon from Horvat 'Uza', *TA* 12 (1985), 96–101.

158   Bienkowski, 'The Edomites', 55; note also Knauf and Lenzen, 'Edomite Copper Industry', 85 who point out Glueck's equally problematic dating of pottery in the area. In short, the fortresses theory ought to be taken as unproven, requiring, if followed, an entirely revised system of evidence. See, perhaps, E. Van Der Steen, 'Nelson Glueck's "String of Fortresses" Revisited', *Studies on Iron Age Moab and Neighbouring Areas in Honour of Michèle Daviau* (ed. P. Bienkowski, ANESupS 29, Leuven, Peeters, 2009), 117–128.

before suffering from widespread destruction, most likely associated with the Babylonians, in the late seventh or early sixth century.[159]

The chronology of Transjordanians in the Cisjordan also works against a military reconstruction; ceramic ware of Transjordanian extraction appears in its unpainted form already in the late eighth century strata at Tel Beersheba, Tel 'Arad and Tel 'Ira.[160] Thus, while Beit-Arieh argues that the substantial increase in an identifiably Transjordanian population in the Negev is linked to the decline of the Assyrian empire and the rise of the Babylonians, signs of their presence in the Negev are already evident earlier in the period.[161] Singer-Avitz has argued that cultural interaction between Edom and Judah was occurring on some scale as early as the late eighth century; Thareani-Sussely has expanded the case for this to include the entirety of the Beersheba and Arad valleys.[162] Tel Beersheba, Tel 'Arad and Tel 'Ira are on the trade route which runs through the Beersheba valley to the coast and are therefore unsurprising in being among the earliest sites to display Transjordanian influences. That the source of the influence may even have been resident at these sites is suggested by the fact that much of this pottery—like the later sherds found across a wider expanse of the southern desert—was manufactured locally, rather than imported.[163] An existing route appears to have combined with the heightened Assyrian interest in Edom's economic activities in the long seventh century to create a well-trodden thoroughfare.

While reiterating that the Transjordanian entities were probably only just beginning to form a political state by the name of Edom and that the population of that state likely never really shifted away from tribal affiliations in favour of state affiliation—in other words, that we may be observing the remains of Transjordanian immigrants who were identifiably distinct in material culture and practice, whether calling themselves 'Edomite' or by some other tribal affiliation—this makes good sense. Assyrian interest in the southern Levant and the coastal ports was motivated in part by the access to Arabian luxury items these ports afforded; this indicates that the trade systems which brought these items to the southern coast were already in existence, albeit on a

---

159　Bienkowski and van der Steen, 'Tribes, Trade, and Towns', 24–26. Note also Uehlinger's suggestion of a spectrum of cultural affiliations in the Negev, with ambiguous relationships to both the Judahite and Edomite states (Uehlinger, 'Arad, Qiṭmīt').

160　L. Singer-Avitz, '"Busayra Painted Ware" at Tel Beersheba', *TA* 31 (2004), 84.

161　Beit-Arieh, *Ḥorvat Qitmit*, 313–315.

162　Singer-Avitz, 'Beersheba', 9; Thareani-Sussely, '"Archaeology of the Days of Manasseh"'.

163　Singer-Avitz, '"Busayra Painted Ware"', 85; cf. Singer-Avitz, 'Beersheba', 37–38; Bienkowski and van der Steen, 'Tribes, Trade, and Towns', 36–37.

smaller scale, and were developed as the century progressed to form a notable part of the material culture of the Negev territories.[164] Locating the beginning of Edomite cultural and commercial development in the earlier part of the seventh century or in the late eighth century is in keeping with the Assyrian economic interests in the region as well as the archaeological indications that the Assyrians were more or less directly involved in ensuring their success.

Perhaps the most well-known site to reflect Transjordanian influence in the Negev is Horvat Qitmit, where a large number of culinary and cultic objects identified as Edomite were excavated in and around two cultic complexes.[165] Petrographic analysis of the pottery indicates that the cooking pots originated in the Transjordan, while cultic objects and painted ware were made of local materials in the eastern Negev.[166] The latter indicates a permanent settlement of some kind, rather than items brought in via trade, although the excavator concluded, more cautiously, that '[a]t most, it can be concluded that it [Horvat Qitmit] served as an Edomite station for Edomite caravans on their way to the port of Gaza.'[167] Finkelstein has argued for a more mixed population at the site (akin to that of 'En Haseva in the characterisation of Bienkowski and van der Steen), emphasising its character as a site on the trade route from Arabia and the Transjordan region through the Beersheba Valley to the Mediterranean ports.[168] He argues that '[t]he special cultural *mélange* of *Ḥorvat Qitmit*

---

164     Singer-Avitz observes that the success of the routes would have depended on normal relations between Judah and Edom, suggesting that (significant) antagonism between them probably did not occur during this period (either by their own inclination or by the probable threat of Assyrian involvement in cases of backwater infighting posing a threat to their economic interests).

165     Beit-Arieh, *Ḥorvat Qitmit*.

166     Beit-Arieh, 'The Edomites', 35–36. The destruction-level pottery forms reflect the later seventh and early sixth centuries, fitting with the idea of an increase in trade initially spurred by a *pax Assyriaca*; Finkelstein suggests the site originated under a *pax Assyriaca* and continued under Egyptian control before widespread Babylonian destruction brought it to an end (Finkelstein, 'Ḥorvat Qitmīt', 164–166). Interestingly, he suggests that the Egyptians entrusted the southern trade routes to Judah, thereby accounting for the construction of Judahite forts at Kadesh Barnea and 'En Haseva as well as the use of Egyptian hieratic numerals, the presence of Judahites at Mesad Hashavyahu and the enigmatic Kittim at Arad (Finkelstein, 'Ḥorvat Qitmīt', 165).

167     Beit-Arieh, 'The Edomites', 36; cf. P. Beck, 'Ḥorvat Qitmit Revisited via 'En Ḥaseva', *TA* 23 (1996), 102–112.

168     Finkelstein, *Living on the Fringe*, 139–144; Finkelstein, 'Ḥorvat Qitmīt', 159–160; note Bienkowski and van der Steen, 'Tribes, Trade, and Towns', 28 with regard to Horvat Qitmit, 'En Haseva and Tel el-Kheleifeh as trade route sites, with the latter possibly a gateway town akin to Beersheba.

represents the culture of the different people who were active on the southern routes'.[169]

Evidence for the presence of Transjordanians in the eastern Negev, however, is not limited to Horvat Qitmit; it is attested by significant finds at a number of other sites. Horvat 'Uza revealed an ostracon in Edomite script recording a communication between two Edomite functionaries, which Beit-Arieh and Cresson conclude 'constitutes significant evidence in favour of an Edomite presence, in one guise or another, at this Judean fortress, which seems to have fallen into the hands of the Edomites around the time of the Babylonian conquest of Judah' and which may be the first clear evidence for an 'Edomite incursion' into the Negev.[170] Whether an ostracon which mentions grain and possibly the cult constitutes evidence for an Edomite military presence or not is debatable, but the blessing, which is 'by *qws*', and the ostracon's script attest to at least two persons in the region whom these cultural identifiers associate with the Transjordan, regardless of whether their presences were for political, religious, commercial or other reasons.[171] Elsewhere, Tel 'Aroer turned up a seal, several ostraca fragments and pottery, and excavations at Tel Malhata produced a significant proportion of Edomite ware as well as figurines stylistically similar enough to those at Horvat Qitmit to suggest that it was a site with significant Transjordanian influences in the seventh century (the excavators suggest a close association between the two).[172] Ostraca with Transjordanian names (identifiable principally by the use of *qws* as theophoric) have been found at several sites in the Negev, including Horvat Qitmit, Tel 'Aroer, Horvat 'Uza and possibly Tel 'Arad.[173] Transjordanian ceramic material in lesser quantity has been found also at Kadesh Barnea as well as at 'En Haseva, where the vessels and figurines found in the cultic structure 'closely resemble' those from

169   Finkelstein, 'Ḥorvat Qitmīt', 162 (italics original).

170   Beit-Arieh and Cresson, 'An Edomite Ostracon', 100; cf. Beit-Arieh, 'New Data', 125–126.

171   On the extent to which *qws* should be identified as 'the' god of Edom see Bienkowski, '"Tribalism" and "Segmentary Society"', 13. On the differentiation between Edomite and Hebrew see D. Vanderhooft, 'The Edomite Dialect and Script: A Review of Evidence', *You Shall Not Abhor an Edomite for He Is Your Brother: Edom and Seir in History and Tradition* (ed. D.V. Edelman, SBLABS 3, Atlanta, Ga., Scholars, 1995), 137–158. On language as an identity marker, variously S. Schwartz, 'Language, Power and Identity in Ancient Palestine', *Past and Present* 148 (1995), 3–47; S.L. Sanders, *The Invention of Hebrew* (Traditions, Chicago, Ill., University of Illinois, 2011).

172   Thareani, 'The Spirit of Clay', 41–52; Beck, 'Ḥorvat Qitmit Revisited'; Beit-Arieh, 'The Edomites', 36–37; Beit-Arieh, *Ḥorvat Qitmit*, 310.

173   Finkelstein, 'Ḥorvat Qitmīt', 158.

Horvat Qitmit.[174] Characteristic pottery also appears at other late Iron Age Negev sites including Tel 'Ira, Tel 'Arad and Tel Masos.[175] The pottery has also been found at Tel Sera' and Tel Haror in the Nahal Gerar and at Tel Jemmeh on the coast, again supporting the suggestion that the terminus for the east-west trade route from the Transjordan through the Negev was the coastal port cities.[176] Pottery subjected to neutron activation analysis (to identify the origins of the clay used in its production) at these sites revealed that 'all groups, with the exception of the originally Edomite cooking-pots, were found to have been manufactured locally, rather than in Edom'.[177] This petrographic analysis indicates that the majority of these items were not imported via trade but were made by inheritors of a Transjordanian ceramic tradition on-site in these various towns and forts. This in turn suggests more than merely passing traders, who might have brought their ceramic supplies with them but were unlikely to have stayed stationary long enough to make additional vessels. The creation of vessels on-site, from local clays, indicates a population with some degree of ongoing attachment to these settlements, who could not readily replace lost or broken items on their next trip to the Transjordan.[178] At the same time, the appearance of cooking pots originating in the Transjordan, alongside the persistence of vessels whose forms are clearly Transjordanian in origin, indicates continuity with the Transjordanian cultural tradition.[179]

It is clear that the long seventh century saw not only the appearance of distinctively Transjordanian cultural materials in significant portions of the Negev but also the development of the Transjordanian material culture itself into a distinctive and identifiable phenomenon, such that the presence of this cultural tradition in the Negev is identifiable in the archaeological record. At

---

174  Beit-Arieh, 'The Edomites', 37–38; Beit-Arieh and Cresson, 'An Edomite Ostracon', 100; Singer-Avitz, 'Busayra Painted Ware', 84; Beck, 'Ḥorvat Qitmit Revisited'. Note that at 'En Haseva that there is a mix of Edomite, Judahite, Qurayya, Negev and Cypro-Phoenician pottery and that a similar range appears at Horvat Qitmit (Bienkowski and van der Steen, 'Tribes, Trade, and Towns', 28; Beck, 'Ḥorvat Qitmit Revisited', 112).

175  Beit-Arieh and Cresson, 'An Edomite Ostracon', 100; Singer-Avitz, 'Busayra Painted Ware', 84. On the complexity of the assemblages at these sites see Bienkowski and van der Steen, 'Tribes, Trade, and Towns', 26–28.

176  Singer-Avitz, 'Busayra Painted Ware', 84.

177  Singer-Avitz, 'Busayra Painted Ware', 84.

178  That persons with ancestors from or themselves originating in the Transjordan might choose to migrate westward ought not to be surprising; the southern Transjordan and the Negev form 'part of the same environmental, cultural, and socio-economic system' (Bienkowski and van der Steen, 'Tribes, Trade, and Towns', 21).

179  Bienkowski and van der Steen, 'Tribes, Trade, and Towns', 37–38.

a rate and to a degree unfamiliar from the past, Judah's residents found culturally distinctive individuals and groups traipsing through, even resident in, their own backyard. All of these sites strongly indicate a mixed population, whose variability and difference from 'Judahite' culture would have been difficult to miss.

### 3.4    *Arabia*

The foregoing discussion of Assyrian policies in the southern Levant during the *pax Assyriaca* has already hinted at the role of the Arabian trade in much of the economic and commercial activities of this period. Unfortunately for comparative purposes, archaeological excavations in the Arabian peninsula are in their early days, making the chronological and contextual analysis of finds difficult. Nonetheless, and despite the as-yet-small number of published reports from the region, it has already been possible to identify Edomite and Judahite ceramic elements from the long seventh century in the excavated repertoire, including such classic examples as a Judahite hole-mouth jar, found at a site five miles northwest of Teima.[180] Although not yet extensive, these finds from the Arabian end of the trade routes affirm the finds in the southern Levant which attest to a strong and developing trade network between Arabia—source of incense, spices and other luxury items—and the populations of the southern Levant (and beyond) in the late Iron Age.[181]

In the Levant itself, various features of the material record attest to Arabian involvement in trade at this time and, notably, suggest a significant increase in the long seventh century. In particular, camels—strongly identifiable with Arabia—are generally very poorly represented in the southern Levant before the long seventh century. The evidence for them increases dramatically at this time, affirming the other indications in favour of an increase in traffic on the Arabia-Mediterranean trade routes, most likely in response to Assyrian interests in that quarter. The Tel Jemmeh faunal assemblage, for example, indicates the increased use of camels in the regional trading network.[182] Additionally,

180   Singer-Avitz, 'Beersheba', 47–48.

181   Singer-Avitz, 'Beersheba'; also Finkelstein, 'Ḥorvat Qitmīt', 161.

182   At Tel Jemmeh 40 bone fragments were recovered from the sample dated 675–600, compared to eight bones identified in the occupation debris of 800–700; this 'coincide[s] with the inception of a large-scale Assyrian occupation' (P. Wapnish, 'Camel Caravans and Camel Pastoralists at Tell Jemmeh', *JANESCU* 13 [1981], 102); cf. P. Wapnish, 'The Dromedary and Bactrian Camel in Levantine Historical Settings: The Evidence from Tell Jemmeh', *Animals and Archaeology* (ed. J. Clutton-Brock and C. Grigson, BAR International Series 202, Oxford, BAR, 1984), 171, 174. In her analysis of these remains Wapnish also suggests that the use of camels by the Assyrians in their campaigns against Egypt may provide an

a few textual witnesses attest to an Arabian presence in the southern Levant; inscriptions in Old South Arabian have been identified at Tel Jemmeh, Tel el-Kheleifeh, Ghrareh (in Edom), Tel ʿAroer and Jerusalem.[183]

### Arabia and Judah

Judah's involvement in the trade routes originating in Arabia is indicated by a number of features of the material record, foremost being the appearance of camels at sites in Judah.[184] The use of camels at Lachish, for example, was recorded by Sennacherib's relief of the city's destruction, as well as being more directly attested by the discovery of camel bones in the excavation of Lachish III; they are also mentioned as booty appropriated by Sennacherib in the course of his campaign against Hezekiah.[185] Camels are also attested at Tel Beersheba by bones found in Stratum II.[186]

As already mentioned, a few textual witnesses attest to Arabians' presence in Judah. The major trade route from Arabia ran east to west, through the Transjordan and the Beersheba and Arad valleys to the Philistine coast, skimming along the southern edge of Judahite territory, and it is along this route that two sherds with signs in Old South Arabian are noted at Tel ʿAroer.[187] A secondary avenue ran north via Jerusalem. That some of the Arabian purveyors of traded goods passed through Jerusalem and that a few might even have settled in the city has been suggested by the discovery of three brief inscriptions, interpreted by Shiloh as South Arabian names, written in Old South Arabian

---

additional partial explanation for the spike in their presence during the Assyrian period (Wapnish, 'Camel Caravans', 115–117, cf. 108–109).

183   Finkelstein, 'The Archaeology of the Days of Manasseh', 179; Thareani-Sussely, 'Desert Outsiders', 207–208, 302.

184   Some time ago, McKay suggested that Manasseh had married an Arabian woman, perhaps with a mind toward strengthening Judah's commercial interests (J.W. McKay, *Religion in Judah under the Assyrians, 732–609 B.C.* [SBT 26, London, SCM, 1973], 23–24). Aside from the uncertainty of such an assertion on a historical level, it ought also to be noted that the Arabian population was at the time still tribally-based and a marriage alliance with a woman from one tribe would have had limited effect on the wider picture.

185   M. Elat, 'Monarchy and Development of Trade in Ancient Israel', *State and Temple Economy in the Ancient Near East II: Proceedings of the International Conference Organized by the Katholieke Universiteit Leuven from the 10th to the 14th of April 1978* (ed. E. Lipiński, OLA 6, Leuven, Departement Oriëntalistiek, 1979), 537; RINAP 3/1 4 51 *passim*.

186   Singer-Avitz, 'Beersheba', 52 n. 15.

187   Thareani-Sussely, 'Desert Outsiders', 207–208, 302. Thareani-Sussely also refers, without further details, to 'various artifacts' at the site which attest to its involvement on the trade route (Thareani-Sussely, 'Desert Outsiders', 208).

letters but inscribed in Jerusalem (on the basis of the method of writing, namely, incision). The vessels on which the names are inscribed he deemed 'undoubtedly locally made'.[188]

Two of the three inscriptions were located in the destruction layer associated with 586 (Stratum 10); the third was a surface find. Shiloh concluded that they are certainly no earlier than the eighth century (Stratum 12) and reached a probable chronological determination in the seventh century.[189] He noted that the individuals named may have been in Jerusalem as part of the incense trade or may have been resident expatriates; he pointed to the discovery of *Tridacna squamosa* shells as further evidence of relations between Judah and the area around the Red Sea, either directly or via Egypt and Phoenicia (perhaps both).[190] He concluded that all of the above 'suggests a strengthening of Arabic elements in the area of Palestine at the end of the Iron Age'.[191] Subsequently Sass argued that two of the inscriptions could be interpreted as Greek rather than Old South Arabian, noting that biblical, extra-biblical and archaeological sources all testify to the presence of Greeks in late Iron Age Judah (see also on Egypt).[192] If Sass is correct about either inscription it would be the first Greek text(s) of pre-exilic date discovered in the southern Levant.[193] The third inscription, on a cooking pot, he agreed was either North or South Arabian.

Whether all the inscriptions from Jerusalem should be understood as Old South Arabian or only some, various indicators attest to the presence of Arabians in Judahite territories during the long seventh century, most likely as a consequence of their involvement in trading activities en route to the port cities on the coast.

## 3.5 *Judah*

Like the rest of the region, Judah experienced a series of major social, demographic and cultural shifts during the long seventh century, prompted by the geographic and political changes wrought in the wake of Assyrian campaigns and the economic effects of Assyrian dominance. Politically and geographically its territory was significantly reduced in the wake of the Sennacherib campaign, with the Shephelah largely lost and (re-)assigned to Philistine

---

188   Y. Shiloh, 'South Arabian Inscriptions from the City of David, Jerusalem', *PEQ* 119 (1987), 14.

189   Shiloh, 'South Arabian Inscriptions', 14.

190   Shiloh, 'South Arabian Inscriptions', 16–17.

191   Shiloh, 'South Arabian Inscriptions', 17.

192   B. Sass, 'Arabs and Greeks in Late First Temple Jerusalem', *PEQ* 122 (1990), 59; note also Fantalkin, 'Identity in the Making', 202–204.

193   Sass, 'Arabs and Greeks', 59.

control. Probably partly in response to this loss, Judahite settlement patterns during the long seventh century changed dramatically, expanding into previously sparsely inhabited territories, especially the Judean desert and the Beersheba and Arad valleys, while the capital city of Jerusalem experienced a period of population growth and physical expansion around the same time.[194] Assyrian involvement in Judah's economic affairs appears to have been less direct than that experienced by its neighbours (Philistia and Edom especially), but its influence over the local economies of these neighbours and the economy of the region as a whole meant that its effects were keenly felt in Judah as well.[195] In particular, it is worth recalling Judah's location, surrounded by and dependent on the economic networks described above, whether these involved the transport of its agricultural products to Philistia, Phoenicia and Assyria or participation in the heavily-trafficked trade routes from Arabia and

194   For summaries and discussion see Faust and Weiss, 'Judah, Philistia, and the Mediterranean World', 74–75 and Finkelstein, 'The Archaeology of the Days of Manasseh', with further references. The precise timings and causes of these population shifts are variously explained; see Thareani-Sussely, '"Archaeology of the Days of Manasseh"'; Stager, 'Farming in the Judean Desert'; Beit-Arieh, Ḥorvat Qitmit; I. Beit-Arieh, 'The Dead Sea Region: An Archaeological Perspective', The Dead Sea, The Lake and Its Setting (ed. T.M. Niemi, Z. Ben-Avraham and J.R. Gat, Oxford, Oxford University Press, 1997), 249–251; I. Beit-Arieh, 'Settlement in the Eastern Negev', Tel 'Ira: A Stronghold in the Biblical Negev (ed. I. Beit-Arieh, MSIA 15, Tel Aviv, Tel Aviv University, 1999), 1–8; Finkelstein, Living on the Fringe, 139–154; Finkelstein and Na'aman, 'The Judahite Shephelah'; I. Finkelstein, 'The Settlement History of Jerusalem in the Eighth and Seventh Century BCE', RB 115 (2008), 499–515; Na'aman, 'When and How did Jerusalem Become a Great City'; M. Broshi, 'The Expansion of Jerusalem in the Reigns of Hezekiah and Manasseh', IEJ 24 (1974), 21–26; A. Faust, 'The Settlement of Jerusalem's Western Hill and the City's Status in Iron Age II Revisited', ZDPV 121 (2005), 97–118; A. Faust, 'Settlement and Demography in Seventh Century Judah and the Extent and Intensity of Sennacherib's Campaign', PEQ 140 (2008), 168–194; R. Reich, 'On the Assyrian Presence at Ramat Raḥel', TA 30 (2003), 124–129; H.J. Franken and M.L. Steiner, eds., The Iron Age Extramural Quarter on the South-East Hill (vol. 2 of Excavations in Jerusalem 1961–1967, BAMA 2, London, Oxford University Press, 1990); and the various essays in A.G. Vaughn and A.E. Killebrew, eds., Jerusalem in Bible and Archaeology: The First Temple Period (Atlanta, Ga., SBL, 2003).

195   'These drastic changes in occupation patterns and in the demographic balance of Jerusalem and its adjacent territory demonstrate the indirect impact on Judah of Assyrian imperial economic policy' (Gitin, 'The Neo-Assyrian Empire', 83–84). On Judah's integration into the regional economy see Faust and Weiss, 'Judah, Philistia, and the Mediterranean World'; E. Weiss and M.E. Kislev, 'Plant Remains as Indicators of Economic Activity: A Case Study from Iron Age Ashkelon', Journal of Archaeological Science 31 (2004), 1–13; Finkelstein, 'The Archaeology of the Days of Manasseh'; Finkelstein and Na'aman, 'The Judahite Shephelah'; Na'aman, 'Province System'; Master, 'Trade and Politics'.

the Transjordan, whether transversing Judah's southern territories, especially the Beersheba and Arad valleys, en route toward the coast, or running north via Jerusalem and the Judahite heartland.

In addition to the extensive evidence attesting to Judahite contacts with and travel outside of Judah, which has already been discussed, archaeological material found in Judah provides further details of the intensification of trade with the surrounding territories during the long seventh century. As one small example, the discovery of fish bones in Jerusalem 'indicate[s] everyday, ordinary trade with the Mediterranean'.[196] In return for these edibles, Judah supplied oil and grain to the southern Levant and beyond. Internal witness for Judah's new-found interactions with its neighbours has been found in each of its regions: the Negev, the Shephelah and the hill country of Jerusalem and its environs.

### The Negev

Most of the Negev was peripheral to the central Judahite territory during the long seventh century. As the foregoing discussion of several Negevite sites in the context of the Edomite presence in the Negev reflects, at least parts of this region experienced a strong Transjordanian presence and influence during this period; formal control over the area is often difficult to determine. Judahite control was focused on the Beersheba and Arad valleys, and it is there that the following discussion of Judah's interactions with its neighbours will focus. A few brief notes regarding sites in the Negev proper ('En Haseva, Kadesh Barnea) and in the adjacent Nahal Gerar (Tel Haror, Tel Sera') will be noted in conclusion.

The Beersheba and Arad valleys were a major thoroughfare for the trade routes running from Arabia to the Philistine coast, a point which has already arisen in the discussions of Philistia and Edom. A number of the sites which have appeared in the preceding discussions may be located here, including Tel Beersheba and Horvat Qitmit. Several new sites are founded along this

---

196    H. Lernau and O. Lernau, 'Fish Bone Remains', *Excavations in the South of the Temple Mount: The Ophel of Biblical Jerusalem* (ed. E. Mazar and B. Mazar, Qedem 29, Jerusalem, Institute of Archaeology, Hebrew University of Jerusalem, 1989), 155–161; H. Lernau and O. Lernau, 'Fish Remains', *Stratigraphical, Environmental, and Other Reports* (vol. 3 of *Excavations in the City of David 1978–1985 Directed by Yigal Shiloh*, ed. A. De Groot and D.T. Ariel, Qedem 33, Jerusalem, Hebrew University of Jerusalem, 1992), 131–148; on molluscs see H.K. Mienes, 'Molluscs', *Stratigraphical, Environmental, and Other Reports* (vol. 3 of *Excavations at the City of David 1978–1985 Directed by Yigal Shiloh*, ed. A. De Groot and D.T. Ariel, Qedem 33, Jerusalem, Hebrew University of Jerusalem, 1992), 129.

route in the late eighth or first half of the seventh century, while existing sites exhibit notable growth around the same time.[197] According to Finkelstein and Na'aman, this 'represents the late 8th century incorporation of the Judahite economy into the Assyrian regional system, with its newly established administrative centres and ports in the coastal plain.'[198] Both valleys feed into the Nahal Gerar and together this region provided the major east-west transit corridor for a longstanding trading network between Arabia and the coast. Beginning in the late eighth century, however, this older route experienced a major increase in the volume of trading traffic and a concomitant increase in population which may most likely be attributed to some combination of the intensification in trade and the changing economic demands on Judah in connection with changes in the wider southern Levantine economic system.

The development of this trading network was surely related to the appearance of the Assyrian empire in the west and its interest in the economic potential of the southern Levantine trade routes with Arabia and with Egypt. Similarly, the construction of a series of fortified settlements along the southern coast from the middle of the eighth century constituted a form of—direct or indirect—encouragement of economic development in the Transjordan.[199] In concluding a study of the chronology of this development in the Beersheba valley, Thareani-Sussely writes that

> the development of the settlement growth and the economic prosperity in the Negev were stimulated by the Assyrian occupation of the Levant during the days of Tiglath-Pileser III . . . the significant growth in the scope of settlement and the economic potential of the Judean Negev was not an isolated phenomenon but an integral factor in the settlement and economic developments in a large geographic region . . . the developments in Judah during this time should be understood as an outcome of the *pax Assyriaca* and new economic opportunities created in the second half of the 8th century.[200]

Particularly worth note is that Thareani-Sussely sees the Judahite government as closely involved in this Assyria-driven development, especially in

---

197  Singer-Avitz, 'Beersheba', 11, 56; Thareani-Sussely, '"Archaeology of the Days of Manasseh"', 71–74.

198  Finkelstein and Na'aman, 'The Judahite Shephelah', 74. On the date of this see especially Thareani-Sussely, '"Archaeology of the Days of Manasseh"'.

199  Singer-Avitz, 'Beersheba', 8.

200  Thareani-Sussely, '"Archaeology of the Days of Manasseh"', 74.

the common architectural planning of Tel 'Ira, Tel 'Aroer and Tel Malhata and the administrative centre at Tel Beersheba, as well as in the unusually large assemblage of written materials from the area.[201] This was not, in other words, an isolated phenomenon with which the Judahite government had little to do but a development project in which the central administrative structures of the country were intimately involved. Unsurprisingly, the material culture in this area strongly attests to the high degree of regional involvement in the trading network.

The current survey of the material culture of this region begins at Tel Beersheba. In the late eighth century, the destruction layer associated with 701 (Stratum II) indicates that the transition from the cultural isolation of the eighth century proper toward the internationalism of the long seventh century had begun already in the late eighth century.[202] Specifically, Beersheba II revealed a ceramic repertoire dominated by typically Judahite pottery but also containing a significant number of vessels characteristic of the southern coastal plain, as well as a small number whose origins may be traced to Egypt, Edom and the territories between Phoenicia and the former northern kingdom.[203] A number of the jars were manufactured on the Phoenician coast, probably indicating the existence of trade relations with Phoenicia during the late eighth century—possibly in connection to Sargon's encouragement of trade between Phoenicia and Egypt—rather than a contingent of Phoenicians settled at the site; cedar beams in the same stratum offer further evidence for such a relationship, also probably mediated by Philistia.[204] It at least seems likely that Judahites would have been aware of the Phoenician origin of these goods; also, some of the jars exhibiting Phoenician characteristics

201  Thareani-Sussely, '"Archaeology of the Days of Manasseh"', 71, 75–76; cf., on Tel 'Uza, L. Tatum, 'King Manasseh and the Royal Fortress at Horvat 'Uza', *BA* 54 (1991), 136, 141. On the relevance of the *lmlk* stamp impressions to studies of the borders of Judah see O. Lipschits, O. Sergi and I. Koch, 'Royal Judahite Jar Handles: Reconsidering the Chronology of the *lmlk* Stamp Impressions', *TA* 37 (2010), 3–32, with further references.

202  Tel Beersheba was founded in the last third of the eighth century and destroyed in 701 and is therefore also significant for the insight it provides into the speed with which the absorption of outside influences can occur (Singer-Avitz, 'Beersheba', 57–58).

203  The coastal forms in this assemblage comprised 12.5% of the total; the majority are Judahite (84%) with the rest (3.5%) of various Edomite, Assyrian, Egyptian and northern styles. This contrasts with 96.5% Judahite forms, 2.9% coastal and 0.5% other in Lachish III (Singer-Avitz, 'Beersheba', 3, 12).

204  Singer-Avitz, 'A Group of Phoenician Vessels', 188, 194–196; see also Master, 'Trade and Politics', 52–59; Gitin, 'Tel Miqne-Ekron in the 7th Century B.C.E.', 71–73.

were manufactured in the Shephelah, perhaps suggesting some more significant interaction with these outside traditions.[205]

Also reflecting the site's connections further afield are items which suggest
contact with Assyria and Egypt, either directly or indirectly. A cylinder seal
dedicated to the god Apil-Adad is probably a provincial product, but indicative
of creeping Assyrian influence, while Egyptian pottery (in this case petrograph-
ically as well as stylistically Egyptian), a Nephthys inscription, an unidentified
figurine, an ear stud and a pendant all indicate links with Nilotic culture.[206] A
figurine of the goddess Hathor suggests the local adoption of some elements
of this culture (or the immigration of an Egyptian or two): it is also made of
Judahite clay. Particularly intriguing is that the figurine is not hand-modelled
but made using a mould—hinting at a greater number of such items in antiquity than have survived to be discovered in the present.[207]

As observed with regard to Edomite forms elsewhere, the coastal forms in
the Tel Beersheba pottery assemblage were revealed through petrographic
analysis to have been made using local and other Judahite clays.[208] In contrast
to the majority of the Phoenician forms, this suggests either the presence of
Philistine cultural groups in the settlement or the assimilation of Philistine
cultural production techniques by a Judahite population (or some combination thereof). The site's 'Edomite-Assyrian' ceramics (largely Edomite, but
with notable Assyrian influences) are similar, all being made of Judahite clay.[209]
As with the coastal forms, this suggests either the continuous presence of
non-Judahite groups at the site (Transjordanian, in this case), the extensive
assimilation of Transjordanian cultural influences by the Judahite population,
or both phenomena occurring simultaneously.

Interestingly, however, Singer-Avitz downplays the extent to which the
Judahite inhabitants of Tel Beersheba would have been exposed to any of
these non-Judahite populations. The Arabian traders, she contends, 'were the
agents distributing vessels in the settlements they visited, which precludes the
need for any direct contact between the inhabitants of Beersheba, Edom and
Assyria.'[210] Thus minimising Judah's direct contact with the east, Singer-Avitz
turns to the west:

---

205   Singer-Avitz, 'A Group of Phoenician Vessels', 194.
206   Singer-Avitz, 'Beersheba', 40–41, 44.
207   Singer-Avitz, 'Beersheba', 46.
208   Singer-Avitz, 'Busayra Painted Ware', 84; Singer-Avitz, 'A Group of Phoenician Vessels', 194;
      Singer-Avitz, 'Beersheba', 30.
209   Singer-Avitz, 'Beersheba', 37–38.
210   Singer-Avitz, 'Beersheba', 53.

Between Beersheba and Philistia there may have existed a local trading system, as part of the international system. But, it is equally likely that the 'coastal' group [of pottery] was formed as a result of the passage of traders, without any need for direct contacts between the inhabitants of Philistia and the Beersheba Valley.[211]

While the long-distance, camel-driven Arabian trade was clearly a major part of the *raison d'être* of the east-west trade routes, agricultural and other products of the Transjordan and Negev were also in transit along the same routes. There is no particular reason to suppose that the transport of these goods was relegated into the hands of the Arabian traders rather than undertaken by Judahite, Philistine and Transjordanian merchants. While it is not necessary, as such, that merchants from these other regions undertook to transport their own goods, the pottery repertoire and material record throughout the entire region as well as in the Beersheba and Arad valleys in particular suggests a more significant and more meaningful level of cultural contact than that which might be expected from bits and pieces picked up and abandoned along the way by itinerant Arabian traders.[212]

With this in mind the thrust of Singer-Avitz's conclusions remains valid. The beginning of the Assyrian economic involvement in the southern Levant in the late eighth century provided the impetus for a level of cultural interaction in the Beersheba and Arad valleys which went well beyond that previously known in the region. As she writes,

> The developing international trade engendered prosperity in the region and increased cooperation between the elements participating in the trade. Under the aegis of Assyrian hegemony, Judahites on the Beersheba-Arad valley trade routes likely came to be acquainted with cultures with which they had not previously been in contact. Therefore, rather than being 'closed' social systems, the various cultures/states in the region were exposed to foreign influences. There is archaeological evidence for

---

211  Singer-Avitz, 'Beersheba', 54.

212  It is worth noting in this respect that none of the pottery forms imitated in local clays at Beersheba have been identified as derivatives of Arabian forms (and indicators of assimilation of other elements of Arabian material culture are equally slim). If Arabian traders were able to acquire and transport vessels at other points along the trade route one would expect at least a few examples of their own ware to have left their mark in the ceramic repertoire. None have yet been found or identified.

Interaction between all peoples of the region, with each entity displaying foreign elements gleaned from neighboring cultures.[213]

We turn next to Tel 'Aroer. Thareani-Sussely has characterised this site as a Judahite caravanserai, with a diverse population comprising both local tribes from the environs of the settlement as well as Edomites, Arabs and others.[214] Its material culture is extremely mixed, much like other sites in the Negev. As already discussed, there is some dispute regarding the appropriate terminology with which to describe the wide range of material cultures preserved at the site; that such diversity is present is not under debate.

In the site's Iron Age IIB–C strata there is an abundance of the 'Edomite' ceramics, especially in the extramural neighbourhood excavated outside the town, which Thareani-Sussely has associated with the site's commercial functions.[215] Drawing on anthropological studies about frontier sites (especially Cohen's work on the Hausa and Yoruba, to which we will return in Chapter Two), Thareani-Sussely has constructed a picture of Tel 'Aroer as 'a zone of interaction and hybridization that maintains more complex relationship with the outside world' than the average heartland site. Like other sites along the trade routes, Tel 'Aroer represents a point of contact between native and non-native cultural influences and the place at which this contact provokes a definition of the cultural boundary between the interacting cultures.[216] Specifically, Thareani-Sussely attributes the appearance of decorative markings on the Edomite ware during this period to this phenomenon; the same ware occurs in the eighth century without the decoration, and its appearance now 'reflects a sharpening of tribal identity'.[217] This would be in keeping with the cultural trends of the long seventh century in the southern Levant.[218] Aside from the diverse ceramic assemblage, Tel 'Aroer has also produced ostraca with names using a *qws* theophoric, a seal, a painted Edomite incense burner and two sherds with south Arabian signs.[219] All of these contribute to the picture of a site with a diverse variety of inhabitants, both permanent and temporary.

Like the other sites in the Beersheba and Arad valleys which pre-date the seventh century, Tel Malhata reached a settlement peak in the seventh

---

213    Singer-Avitz, 'Beersheba', 55.
214    Thareani, 'The Spirit of Clay', 52.
215    Thareani, 'The Spirit of Clay', 41, 52; Thareani-Sussely, 'Desert Outsiders', 202–205.
216    Thareani, 'The Spirit of Clay', 49.
217    Thareani, 'The Spirit of Clay', 52.
218    See Herr, 'Archaeological Sources'.
219    Finkelstein, 'Ḥorvat Qitmīt', 158; Beit-Arieh, 'The Edomites', 37; Finkelstein, 'The Archaeology of the Days of Manasseh', 179; Thareani-Sussely, 'Desert Outsiders', 207–208, 302.

century, before its destruction at the beginning of the sixth century.[220] It is noteworthy especially because of the high percentage of its pottery which exhibits Transjordanian (Edomite) affinities, including as many as 85% of the cooking pots.[221] This is very similar to the ceramic assemblage found at Horvat Qitmit; the current excavator has even suggested that some of the ceramic objects at the site were made at the same workshop as some of those found at Horvat Qitmit, perhaps even by the same artisan.[222] The site, in the Arad valley toward the eastern end of the trade route, thus contains a remarkable mixture of Judahite and Transjordanian cultural elements.[223] In addition to the extensive pottery assemblage, ostraca indicating the presence of Transjordanians also attest to the confluence of multiple cultural traditions.[224] The latest tally of ostraca from the site includes eight fragments of Edomite ostraca, one Aramaic ostracon and four Hebrew inscriptions.[225] Among the small finds are multiple Egyptian scarabs.[226]

---

220   I. Beit-Arieh, 'Excavations at Tel Malḥata: An Interim Report', *The Fire Signals of Lachish: Studies in the Archaeology and History of Israel in the Late Bronze Age, Iron Age, and Persian Period in Honor of David Ussishkin* (ed. I. Finkelstein and N. Na'aman, Winona Lake, Ind., Eisenbrauns, 2011), 17–32; M. Kochavi, 'Malḥata, Tel', *Encyclopedia of Archaeological Excavations in the Holy Land* (ed. M. Avi-Yonah and E. Stern, Oxford, Oxford University Press, 1977), 771–775.

221   Beit-Arieh, 'Excavations at Tel Malḥata', 24–25; also Zimhoni, 'Two Ceramic Assemblages', 48; Thareani, 'The Spirit of Clay', 41–52; Beck, 'Ḥorvat Qitmit Revisited', 102–112; Beit-Arieh, 'The Edomites', 36–37; Beit-Arieh, *Ḥorvat Qitmit*, 310.

222   Beit-Arieh, 'Excavations at Tel Malḥata', 28. The interpretation of the presence of large numbers of Transjordanians in these valleys is variably understood; the latest interim report from the site's most recent excavations suggests the wave of fortifications (at Tel Malhata, Horvat 'Uza, Horvat Radum, Horvat Tov and Horvat Anim) in the seventh century should be attributed to defensive manoeuvres against Edomite incursions (Beit-Arieh, 'Excavations at Tel Malḥata', 30). However, a recent study of the extramural neighbourhoods at several of these sites observes that '[t]he appearance of extramural constructions outside the forts supports the hypothesis that the Late Iron Age was generally peaceful and that people felt secure enough to live and interact outside the walls'; Thareani-Sussely concludes that '[s]trong Assyrian imperial rule made marketplaces and commercial activities available at sites that were situated along trade routes . . . the extramural remains at the Beersheba Valley sites could have served as marketplaces, merchants' quarters, or other trade-related institutions as well as for domestic functions' (Thareani-Sussely, 'Desert Outsiders', 208, 209).

223   Beit-Arieh, *Ḥorvat Qitmit*; Beit-Arieh, 'The Edomites'.

224   Finkelstein, 'Ḥorvat Qitmīt', 158.

225   Beit-Arieh, 'Excavations at Tel Malḥata', 28; the Aramaic ostracon was noted already by Kochavi, 'Malḥata, Tel', 771–775.

226   Beit-Arieh, 'Excavations at Tel Malḥata', 27.

The late eighth and seventh century strata at Tel 'Ira are similarly diverse. They reveal a dominance of Judahite forms as well as Transjordanian forms, on which neutron activation analysis has not yet been performed but which the excavator suspects to be mostly Negev-made, as at Qitmit; there are also small jars which may have come from the coast as well as jugs and bottles with their nearest parallels at Ekron and Tel Batash.[227] A Cypro-Phoenician juglet and Cypriot jug, as well as sherds of other Cypro-Phoenician vessels, appear in Stratum VII (late eighth century); a Cypriot amphora, sherds of coastal and Transjordanian cooking pots and handleless jars—usually attributed to Assyrian influence but common in the Transjordan, where they are known as Ammonite pottery—appear in Stratum VI (latter half of the seventh and early sixth centuries).[228] Kletter notes probable Transjordanian influences on the figurines found at the site, including a bird figurine and a hermaphrodite figurine; Beck's study of the latter notes its nearest parallels in two figurines from the Transjordan which, in turn, are noted in connection with possible Phoenician influences there.[229] A scarab from the site—a surface find—has been dated to the seventh century.[230]

Horvat 'Uza was built in the midst of a seventh century construction boom; Tatum associates this with a process of governmental and religious centralisation and Finkelstein attributes to a desire to defend the east-west trade route, possibly with Assyrian encouragement.[231] The site boasts the ostracon in Edomite script and referencing Qaus, noted above.[232] An inscribed, non-Hebrew seal may be likewise Transjordanian in origin, as may be a scaraboid bull depicting a striding bull typical of Ammonite iconography.[233] A bulla found

---

227    L. Freud, 'Pottery: Iron Age', *Tel 'Ira: A Stronghold in the Biblical Negev* (ed. I. Beit-Arieh, MSIA 15, Tel Aviv, Tel Aviv University, 1999), 189–203.

228    Freud, 'Pottery: Iron Age', 215–223.

229    Kletter, 'Clay Figurines', 381–385; P. Beck, 'Human Figurine with Tambourine', *Tel 'Ira: A Stronghold in the Biblical Negev* (ed. I. Beit-Arieh, MSIA 15, Tel Aviv, Tel Aviv University, 1999), 386–394.

230    B. Brandl, 'A Seventh Century B.C.E. Scarab', *Tel 'Ira: A Stronghold in the Biblical Negev* (ed. I. Beit-Arieh, MSIA 15, Tel Aviv, Tel Aviv University, 1999), 414–420.

231    Tatum, 'King Manasseh', 136, 141; I. Finkelstein, 'Kadesh Barnea: A Reevaluation of Its Archaeology and History', *TA* 37 (2010), 121–122.

232    Beit-Arieh and Cresson, 'An Edomite Ostracon', 100; Finkelstein, 'Ḥorvat Qitmīt', 158; I. Beit-Arieh, 'Epigraphic Finds', *Ḥorvat 'Uza and Ḥorvat Radum: Two Fortresses in the Biblical Negev* (ed. I. Beit-Arieh, MSIA 25, Tel Aviv, Tel Aviv University, 2007), 122.

233    Beit-Arieh, 'Epigraphic Finds', 128; I. Ziffer, 'Stamps and Stamp Seals: I. The Iron Age', *Ḥorvat 'Uza and Ḥorvat Radum: Two Fortresses in the Biblical Negev* (ed. I. Beit-Arieh, MSIA 25, Tel Aviv, Tel Aviv University, 2007), 197–200.

nearby reflects a mixture of eastern and western elements, while another seal, in technique and symbolism, appears to 'indicate the diffusion in the Syria-Palestine of the Neo-Assyrian repertory during the 8th and 7th centuries BCE'.[234] Remains of Mediterranean fish and a couple of sea shells indicate connections to the coast.[235]

Tel 'Arad is the final site to mention in the valleys. The site is fascinating, yet deeply problematic.[236] The usual focus of interest is the sanctuary, the relationship of which to any process—or lack thereof—of centralisation has been variably construed.[237] With regard to the present concern, the site appears to have undergone a period of notable growth during the long seventh century, apparently reflective of the wider economic and demographic trends in the southern Levant at this time.[238] An Assyrian lion weight in Stratum VIII (currently agreed to culminate with Sennacherib's campaign in 701) contributes to this picture of Tel 'Arad during the *pax Assyriaca*, as does a cylinder seal.[239] Cedars indicate trade with the Lebanon region.[240] Typical of other sites in the Beersheba and Arad valleys, Edomite ware appears in its unpainted form already in the late eighth century strata, though the overall quantity of Transjordanian forms at the site suggest that it probably was not directly on

234 P. Beck, 'A Neo-Assyrian Bulla', *Ḥorvat 'Uza and Ḥorvat Radum: Two Fortresses in the Biblical Negev* (ed. I. Beit-Arieh, MSIA 25, Tel Aviv, Tel Aviv University, 2007), 194–196; Ziffer, 'Stamps and Stamp Seals', 197.

235 M. Sade, 'Faunal Remains', *Ḥorvat 'Uza and Ḥorvat Radum: Two Fortresses in the Biblical Negev* (ed. I. Beit-Arieh, MSIA 25, Tel Aviv, Tel Aviv University, 2007), 289–297.

236 The stratigraphy of the site is so disputed that the value of its finds for any historical discussion is dubious. It is included here because it remains a prominent site in discussions of the period; at best, the finds may be seen as providing a general affirmation of the phenomenon occurring elsewhere, but the impossibility of establishing a reliable stratigraphic and dating scheme makes more precise speculation all but worthless.

237 See Z. Herzog, M. Aharoni, A.F. Rainey and S. Moshkovitz, 'The Israelite Fortress at Arad', *BASOR* 254 (1984), 1–34; D. Ussishkin, 'The Date of the Judean Shrine at Arad', *IEJ* 38 (1988), 142–157; Na'aman, 'No Anthropomorphic Graven Image?'; Z. Herzog, 'The Fortress Mound at Tel Arad: An Interim Report', *TA* 29 (2002), 3–109; Z. Herzog, 'Perspectives on Southern Israel's Cult Centralization: Arad and Beer-scheba', *One God—One Cult—One Nation: Archaeological and Biblical Perspectives* (ed. R.G. Kratz and H. Spieckermann in collaboration with B. Corzilius and T. Pilger, BZAW 405, Berlin, de Gruyter, 2010), 169–200; I. Finkelstein and N.A. Silberman, 'Temple and Dynasty: Hezekiah, the Remaking of Judah and the Rise of the Pan-Israelite Ideology', *JSOT* 30 (2006), 259–285.

238 Singer-Avitz, 'Beersheba', 11, 56.

239 Na'aman, 'No Anthropomorphic Graven Image?', 406–408; Herzog, 'The Fortress Mound', 80.

240 Herzog, 'The Fortress Mound', 80.

the trade routes; that the site had contact with its neighbours to the east none-theless is indicated by an ostracon with a *qws* theophoric.[241] In an extensive analysis of the Iron Age pottery at the site, Singer-Avitz suggests that the repertoire indicates that the site's wider economic and political links developed under the *pax Assyriaca* as early as the late eighth century.[242] Two offering dishes have been argued to contain Phoenician letter forms specific to the second half of the seventh century.[243] In Stratum VII, references in the ostraca to 'Kittim' were interpreted by the excavators as references to Phoenician merchants, though the Kittim are more usually thought to be Greeks.[244] Although complicated and unlikely to ever be the focus of agreement, the material at Tel 'Arad conforms to the general picture of the Beersheba and Arad valleys as a forum of intense cultural diversity during the long seventh century.

Nearer the coast, the same cultural *mélange* observed in the Beersheba and Arad valleys may be seen at Tel Haror and Tel Sera'. There, the Edomite pottery—again, locally made—has been found alongside evidence of Assyrian settlements, the latter no doubt strategically established for control of the lucrative trade route approaching its termini at the coast.[245]

Finally, though on the outer fringes of Judahite existence, there are a few sites to note in the southern and eastern Negev. One of these is the fortress at Kadesh Barnea, built in the latter half of the eighth century in conjunction with the rise of Assyrian dominance in the region.[246] The architects and purpose of the site has been the object of some debate: the excavators identified it as a Judahite administrative centre on the trade route from the Red Sea to

---

241   Finkelstein, 'Ḥorvat Qiṭmīt', 158; Singer-Avitz, 'Busayra Painted Ware', 85; Herzog, 'The Fortress Mound', 81–83; Singer-Avitz, 'Arad', 192. A second theophoric has been restored in another ostracon (Herzog, 'The Fortress Mound', 83).

242   L. Singer-Avitz, 'Arad: The Iron Age Pottery Assemblages', *TA* 29 (2002), 184.

243   F.M. Cross, 'Two Offering Dishes with Phoenician Inscriptions from the Sanctuary of Arad', *BASOR* 235 (1979), 75–78. The excavators denied this interpretation, unsurprising given that the bowls were found at the base of the altar, in Stratum X, which Aharoni had attributed to the ninth century (Herzog, Aharoni, Rainey and Moshkovitz, 'The Israelite Fortress', 15). Cross brings that date into question, echoing others who have also cast doubt on the chronology of the strata identified as prior to 701 by Aharoni.

244   Herzog, Aharoni, Rainey and Moshkovitz, 'The Israelite Fortress', 29; compare N. Na'aman, 'Textual and Historical Notes on the Eliashib Archive from Arad', *TA* 38 (2011), 83–93. See 2.2. Egypt on Greeks in the southern Levant in the late seventh century, in connection with Egyptian takeover of the area.

245   Singer-Avitz, 'Busayra Painted Ware', 84; Na'aman, 'Province Systems', 111–112. On the Assyrian remains see Bienkowski and van der Steen, 'Tribes, Trade, and Towns', 39.

246   Finkelstein, 'Kadesh Barnea', 111.

the Mediterranean, while Na'aman has argued that it was the work of and run by Assyrian garrisons from the empire's various vassal kingdoms.[247] On the basis of architectural styles, Finkelstein identified two types of fortresses in the Negev during Iron IIB–C, suggesting that 'En Haseva and Tel el-Kheleifeh, in the Arabah, were built by Assyrians (but probably staffed by locals) and Tel 'Arad and Horvat 'Uza were built by Judahites intending to defend the east-west trade route and the southern frontier.[248] He suggests that Kadesh Barnea has a similar history and pedigree as the latter, with ultimate control in Assyrian hands but indications of Judahite involvement.[249] The site is likely to have served as a locus of interaction between the Assyrians (and whichever military contingents they assigned to the site) and Judahites. Toward the end of the long seventh century, the remains at the site indicate the presence of a number of different groups, including hieratic writing indicative of an Egyptian presence, two Cypro-Phoenician juglets and fragments of Edomite painted ware.[250] The site also exhibits a mix of Edomite, Judahite, Qurayya, Negev and Cypro-Phoenician pottery, in keeping with its probable role as a trade route site.[251]

The preponderance of evidence from the Negev suggests an area of intense (and intensifying) interaction among diverse cultural groups. This reflects especially the central role of this area in regional economic activities and the involvement of a very wide range of groups in these activities.

### The Shephelah

Much of the Shephelah's economic and demographic change in the long seventh century has already been discussed in relation to the economic and political relationships between Judah and Philistia, particularly Ekron. In particular, it is worth recalling the suggestion that Sennacherib's targeting of the Shephelah in 701 was related to an Assyrian attempt to exert more control over

---

247 A. Cohen, 'Variables in Ethnicity', *Ethnic Change* (ed. C.F. Keyes, London, University of Washington Press, 1981), 103; R. Cohen, 'The Iron Age Fortresses in the Central Negev', *BASOR* 236 (1979), 78; Na'aman, 'An Assyrian Residence', 286–287; Na'aman, 'The Kingdom of Judah', 376–377.

248 Finkelstein, 'Kadesh Barnea', 121–122.

249 Finkelstein, 'Kadesh Barnea', 122.

250 R. Cohen, 'The Excavations at Kadesh Barnea (1976–78)', *BA* 44 (1981), 98–100; Beit-Arieh, 'The Edomites', 37; Singer-Avitz, 'Busayra Painted Ware', 84. In light of this Na'aman has suggested that the site came under the control of Egyptians in the wake of the Assyrians' departure from the region (Na'aman, 'The Kingdom of Judah', 376–377). More broadly see Schipper, 'Egypt'.

251 Bienkowski and van der Steen, 'Tribes, Trade, and Towns', 25–28; Beck, 'Ḥorvat Qitmit Revisited', 112; cf. Beit-Arieh, 'The Edomites', 38; Singer-Avitz, 'Busayra Painted Ware', 84.

the region's oil industry and that one of the concrete effects of Sennacherib's invasion was the reorientation of Judah's economy: 'Judah was forced to ship its produce to a new center in the western Shephelah [Ekron], close to the gateway communities of the coast'.[252] After 701 Philistia itself was also closer, as much of the Shephelah came under direct Philistine control.[253]

What remained of a Judahite Shephelah in the seventh century proper was 'only a shadow of the eighth-century peak'.[254] There are accordingly relatively

---

252   Finkelstein and Na'aman, 'The Judahite Shephelah', 75; Finkelstein, 'The Archaeology of the Days of Manasseh', 180; cf. Gitin, 'Tel Miqne-Ekron', 50; Herr, 'Archaeological Sources', 163; Knauf, '"The Glorious Days of Manasseh"', 171; S. Bunimovitz and Z. Lederman, 'Close Yet Apart: Diverse Cultural Dynamics at Iron Age Beth-Shemesh and Lachish', *The Fire Signals of Lachish: Studies in the Archaeology and History of Israel in the Late Bronze Age, Iron Age, and Persian Period in Honor of David Ussishkin* (ed. I. Finkelstein and N. Na'aman, Winona Lake, Ind, Eisenbrauns, 2011), 46–47.

253   The point at which part or all of this region came back under Judahite influence is not clear, primarily because the only two fixed reference points for this period are 701 and 586; while ceramic assemblages aligning closely with the assemblages associated directly with either of these points may be reasonably securely dated, assemblages which do not match either extreme must rely on other factors for more precise dating. For recent discussions see O. Lipschits, O. Sergi and I. Koch, 'Judahite Stamped and Incised Jar Handles: A Tool for Studying the History of Late Monarchic Judah', *TA* 38 (2011), 21–28; Na'aman, 'The Kingdom of Judah', 27, 49, 57–58; N. Na'aman, 'Hezekiah and the Kings of Assyria', *Ancient Israel and Its Neighbors: Interaction and Counteraction* (Winona Lake, Ind., Eisenbrauns, 2005), 98–117; Bunimovitz and Lederman, 'The Final Destruction', 3–4, 20–21; Faust, 'Settlement and Demography', 173; Finkelstein and Na'aman, 'The Judahite Shephelah', 62–65; Fantalkin, 'The Final Destruction of Beth-Shemesh', 252–253; Finkelstein, 'The Archaeology of the Days of Manasseh', 169–187.

254   Faust, 'Settlement and Demography', 173, with survey and references regarding the 'gloomy' seventh-century picture at sites in the region; note also the picture drawn on the basis of the distribution of marked storage jars (Lipschits, Sergi and Koch, 'Royal Judahite Jar Handles', 19–20).

     It has been suggested that some of the shifts in Judah's population which occur during the first part of the seventh century—including settlement in the Beersheba and Arad valleys and the Judean desert region—may be connected to demands for wheat for export, with recent theories of the development of these areas suggest that it was directly linked to the loss of Judah's traditional breadbasket, the Shephelah (Finkelstein, 'The Archaeology of the Days of Manasseh'; Faust and Weiss, 'Judah, Philistia, and the Mediterranean World'). In addition to the discovery of Judahite wheat at Ashkelon, there is an explicit identification of Judah as the source of Phoenicia's grains by the oracle against Tyre in Ezek. 27:17 (Stager, Master and Schloen, *Ashkelon 3*, 737; Faust and Weiss, 'Judah, Philistia, and the Mediterranean World', 71; Weiss and Kislev, 'Plant Remains'); a legal document from Nineveh refers to wheat measured according to the Judahite *se'ah*

few sites to discuss with regard to specific changes in material culture during the long seventh century, given the overwhelming devastation of the majority of the sites in the region combined with the effective reassignment of the area to Philistine control. Judahite consciousness of non-Judahite populations is, as regards the Shephelah, much more basic: an enormous swathe of Judahite territory was no longer under Judahite control but rather under the control of the neighbouring Philistines, whose borders were accordingly far closer to the Judahite heartland, and what population remained in this area found that its previous orientation towards Judah had been pre-empted by an orientation focused on Philistia.

The foremost site of note is Lachish, destroyed during the 701 invasion of Sennacherib. Like most of the Shephelah the site remained essentially uninhabited for several decades, although it appears to have been resettled on a small scale relatively late in the seventh century. As part of recent excavations at the site, one of the excavators undertook the comparative analysis of the ceramic assemblages of Level III, destroyed in 701, and Level II, destroyed in 586.[255] Of particular interest is the significantly larger number of non-Judahite—particularly coastal—vessel forms in the latter assemblage. In the Level III assemblage there was one storage jar of coastal origin (type IIID) and two other vessels (one each of two types in group IIIE) which stood out from

_____

(Faust and Weiss, 'Judah, Philistia, and the Mediterranean World', 82). Note also the suggestion that Tel Beersheba functioned as an administrative centre (in the late eighth century) for the collection and redistribution of grains, perhaps suggesting that there was some precedent for the area's use in this manner (Thareani-Sussely, '"Archaeology of the Days of Manasseh"', 73).That said, Judah is ecologically best suited to wine production, not wheat (Faust and Weiss, 'Judah, Philistia, and the Mediterranean World', 78, cf. 76, 86), suggesting economic motivations other than simple ecological efficiency and pointing toward Judah's integration in the new, international agricultural economic system, whether that system is understood to have been driven by Phoenician and Egyptian influences (Faust and Weiss, Master), by Assyrian influences (Na'aman, Gitin) or by some combination thereof. It is clear that Judah's economy was irrevocably tied to the coastal trading system at this time, either directly, through the supply of oil and other goods to Ekron and beyond, or indirectly, through the constant trespass of trading caravans through the countryside.

255 Zimhoni, 'Two Ceramic Assemblages'; duplicated and supplemented by D. Ussishkin, 'Appendix: Asymmetrical Bowls and Bowls in Assyrian Style', *The Iron Age and Post-Iron Age Pottery and Artefacts* (vol. 4 of *The Renewed Archaeological Excavations at Lachish (1973–1994)*, ed. D. Ussishkin, PIA 22, Tel Aviv, Emery and Claire Yass Publications in Archaeology, 2004), 1900–1906. On the dating of Level III see D. Ussishkin, 'The Destruction of Lachish by Sennacherib and the Dating of the Royal Judean Storage Jars', *TA* 4 (1977), 28–60.

the otherwise Judahite assemblage.[256] In contrast to this relative conformity of ceramic styles in the late eighth century stratum, the seventh-century Level II was significantly more diverse. Two groups of non-Judahite vessels in this assemblage, IID and IIE, appear in much larger quantity than in Level III; these stand out alongside type IIF, a subtype known elsewhere only from Ashdod.[257] The IID and IIE types are also found at Ashdod, in a variant form at Ekron and are also prevalent at Tel Batash. The increase in such coastal types affirms the strong Philistine orientation of the Shephelah during the preceding century and demonstrates its cultural effects at Lachish in particular. Zimhoni traces these changes to the disruption of the economic system occasioned by the invasion of Sennacherib and the political changes attendant on Judah's defeat and geographical dismemberment by the Assyrians. 'The Lachish ceramic assemblage', she writes,

> reflects the environment of *Pax Assyriaca*, an open political and economic system under the aegis of the Assyrian Empire, conditions which continued to prevail later under Egyptian occupation . . . The diverse character of the ceramic assemblage complements the historical picture and can be understood in view of the political changes that took place during that period.[258]

As elsewhere, a major effect of the political and economic changes wrought by the *pax Assyriaca* was a significant alteration in the material culture of the region. Interpreted, the increased diversity in the material culture of Lachish II when compared to Lachish III may be understood to reflect the changes in political and economic control over the area and the attendant diversification of the cultural groups transversing and settling in the Shephelah.

### Jerusalem and Around

Given the various signs of increased cultural interaction between Judah and its neighbours, beginning late in the eighth century and accelerating into the seventh, it will come as no surprise to find that Jerusalem and the surrounding area exhibit signs of similar changes over the period in question.[259] By the sev-

---

256   Zimhoni, 'Two Ceramic Assemblages', 25–27.

257   Zimhoni, 'Two Ceramic Assemblages', 35–36, 41.

258   Zimhoni, 'Two Ceramic Assemblages', 49.

259   Note that the history of Jerusalem as a continuously occupied site and its geo-political significance into the present day have made it a difficult site to excavate on both practical and ideological grounds. The material which is available is often limited in both quantity and context, as only certain parts of the city can be or have been excavated. Exacerbating

enth century, Jerusalem was less than a day's march from the Assyrian border to the north and had Philistia encroaching from the west.[260] Judah's territory had been dramatically reduced, carved away and redistributed to non-Judahites. The territories which were left experienced the long seventh century as a period of increased international and cross-cultural involvement.

A number of sites in the Jerusalem hinterlands begin to sketch the outlines of this picture. Four kilometres south of the city is Ramat Rahel, which may have been a key locus of Assyrian administration.[261] Certainly the later architecture here is generally agreed to be Assyrian or assyrianizing, with Lipschits suggesting that the volute capitals 'were used by the local or Assyrian administration in the vassal kingdoms ... probably as a result of Assyrian encouragement, approval, or sponsorship'.[262] Aharoni's original excavations at the site turned up a painted sherd, variously identified as Assyrian with Syro-Palestinian influences, Assyrian or Greek.[263] A pair of assyrianizing beakers, with a Judahite red burnish, were also found at the site.[264] Among the equine figurines are two two-headed specimens and several additional fragments, of local manufacture, whose nearest parallels seem to be Greek.[265] Elsewhere, a late Iron Age farm structure at Khirbet er-Ras appears to have been built according to Egyptian cubit measurements.[266] At Tel Moza excavators discovered a miniature

---

these issues is that the early archaeological interest in Jerusalem resulted in many of its excavations being conducted using early archaeological techniques.

260  E. Ben Zvi, 'Prelude to a Reconstruction of Historical Manassic Judah', *BN* 81 (1996), 39.

261  Lipschits, Gadot, Arubas and Oeming, 'Palace and Village'; also Na'aman, 'An Assyrian Residence'.

262  O. Lipschits, 'The Origin and Date of the Volute Capitals from the Levant', *The Fire Signals of Lachish: Studies in the Archaeology and History of Israel in the Late Bronze Age, Iron Age, and Persian Period in Honor of David Ussishkin* (ed. I. Finkelstein and N. Na'aman, Winona Lake, Ind., Eisenbrauns, 2011), 219, also 220–222; see also Lipschits, Gadot, Arubas and Oeming, 'Palace and Village', 10–23; Reich, 'On the Assyrian Presence'. On the rationale of an Assyrian presence at the site see already Na'aman, 'An Assyrian Residence'; more recently, Lipschits, Sergi and Koch, 'Royal Judahite Jar Handles', 7 (but contrast Knauf, '"The Glorious Days of Manasseh"').

263  P. Matthiae, 'The Painted Sherd of Ramat Rahel', *Excavations at Ramat Rahel (Seasons 1961 and 1962)* (ed. Y. Aharoni and A. Ciasca, Jerusalem, Hebrew University of Jerusalem, 1964), 85–94; S. Geva, 'The Painted Sherd of Ramat Rahel', *IEJ* 31 (1981), 186–189.

264  E. Stern, 'Stratum V: The Late Judean Period', *En-Gedi Excavations I: Final Report* (ed. E. Stern, Jerusalem, Israel Exploration Society, 2007), 130.

265  A. Ciasca, 'Some Particular Aspects of the Israelitic Miniature Statuary at Ramat Rahel', *Excavations at Ramat Rahel (Seasons 1961 and 1962)* (ed. Y. Aharoni and A. Ciasca, Jerusalem, Hebrew University of Jerusalem, 1964), 95–100.

266  S. Gibson and G. Edelstein, 'Investigating Jerusalem's Rural Landscape', *Levant* 17 (1985), 140.

sceptre-head made of Egyptian blue, which at the time was manufactured only in Egypt; the object itself may also reflect stylistic and conceptual influences from Assyria.[267] At Tel en-Nasbeh, 12 kilometres northwest of Jerusalem, excavations revealed numerous scarabs.[268] Similarly, at Nebi-Samwil, which sits on the main road from the coast to Jerusalem, eight kilometres northwest of the city, excavations turned up a scarab from the Twenty-sixth Dynasty.[269] Five kilometres north of Jerusalem is Tel el-Ful, where the excavators discovered painted bottles thought to be Assyrian in origin and a decorated bowl which may have been imported.[270] A little further afield is the late seventh century site at 'En Gedi, identified by its original excavators as a royal estate.[271] The pottery repertoire included a number of sherds imitating Assyrian palace ware (all locally made); locally-produced sherds of Phoenician jug flasks; a vessel with impressed decorations in Transjordanian style, with Phoenician and Assyrian design influences; several sherds of Cypriot ceramics, of a quality indicating their likely import status; and alabaster bottles and bowls, either Egyptian imports or local imitations of Egyptian products.[272]

---

267    Z. Greenhut, 'The Egyptian-Blue Scepter Head', *Salvage Excavations at Tel Moza: The Bronze and Iron Age Settlements and Later Occupations* (ed. Z. Greenhut and A. De Groot, IAA Reports 39, Jerusalem, Israel Antiquities Authority, 2009), 149–152; I. Segal, 'Analysis of a Blue Sample from the Scepter Head', *Salvage Excavations at Tel Moza: The Bronze and Iron Age Settlements and Later Occupations* (ed. Z. Greenhut and A. De Groot, IAA Reports 39, Jerusalem, Israel Antiquities Authority, 2009), 152–153. On the ceramics, which are mostly Judahite but may contain a few imports see A. Greenhut and A. De Groot, 'The Pottery', *Salvage Excavations at Tel Moza: The Bronze and Iron Age Settlements and Later Occupations* (ed. Z. Greenhut and A. De Groot, IAA Reports 39, Jerusalem, Israel Antiquities Authority, 2009), 79–106; M. Petersson-Solimany and R. Kletter, 'The Iron Age Clay Figurines and a Possible Scale Weight', *Salvage Excavations at Tel Moza: The Bronze and Iron Age Settlements and Later Occupations* (ed. Z. Greenhut and A. De Groot, IAA Reports 39, Jerusalem, Israel Antiquities Authority, 2009), 115–124.

268    J. Zorn, 'Naṣbeh, Tell en-', *New Archaeological Encyclopedia of the Holy Land* (ed. A. Negev and S. Gibson, New York, N.Y., Continuum, 2001), 912–918.

269    I. Magen and M. Dadon, 'Nebi Samwel', *One Land—Many Cultures: Archaeological Studies in Honour of Stanislao Loffreda OFM* (ed. G. Bottini, L. Di Segni and L.D. Chrupcala, Studium Biblicum Franciscanum, Collectio Maior 41, Jerusalem, Franciscan Printing, 2003), 123–124.

270    N.L. Lapp, *The Third Campaign at Tell el-Ful: The Excavations of 1964* (AASOR 45, Cambridge, Mass., ASOR, 1981), 39, 92–94.

271    B. Mazar, T.K. Dothan and I. Dunayevsky, *En-Gedi: The First and Second Seasons of Excavations, 1961–1962* (Atiqot 5, Jerusalem, Hebrew University of Jerusalem, 1966), 21.

272    Stern, 'Stratum V', 130–137, 186–187.

Excavations in Jerusalem itself have yielded a number of significant insights with regard to the city's involvement in international trade during the long seventh century.[273] The city has produced significant quantities of fish bones, strongly suggesting a regular trade route between Jerusalem and the coastal sites where these fish originated; the discovery of various shells, both decorated and undecorated, indicate similar connections.[274]

There are two major groups of these fish remains from Jerusalem. The first comes from the excavations on the Ophel.[275] This is the smaller of the

---

273 One point on which very little agreement exists with regard to the history of Jerusalem is its growth and contraction at various stages over the course of the long seventh century. Given the dominance of the city in seventh century Judah, calculations of the overall population of Judah is similarly contested. With regard to Jerusalem see Broshi, 'The Expansion of Jerusalem'; Na'aman, 'When and How did Jerusalem Become a Great City'; the essays by H. Geva, I. Finkelstein, L. Tatum and R. Reich and E. Shukron in *Jerusalem in Bible and Archaeology: The First Temple Period* (ed. A.G. Vaughn and A.E. Killebrew, SBLSymS, Leiden, Brill, 2003); Finkelstein, 'The Settlement History'; Gibson and Edelstein, 'Investigating Jerusalem's Rural Landscape'; Faust, 'Settlement and Demography'; Z. Zevit, 'Text Traditions, Archaeology, and Anthropology: Uncertainties in Determining the Populations of Judah and Yehud from ca. 734 to ca. 400 BCE', *'Up to the Gates of Ekron': Essays on the Archaeology and History of the Eastern Mediterranean in Honor of Seymour Gitin* (ed. S.W. Crawford, A. Ben-Tor, J.P. Dessel, W.G. Dever, A. Mazar and J. Aviram, Jerusalem, W.F. Albright Institute of Archaeological Research and Israel Exploration Society, 2007), 436–443; Y. Shiloh, 'Judah and Jerusalem in the Eighth-Sixth Centuries B.C.E.', *Recent Excavations in Israel: Studies in Iron Age Archaeology* (ed. S. Gitin and W.G. Dever, AASOR 49, Winona Lake, Ind., Eisenbrauns, 1989), 97–105; G. Barkay, 'Jerusalem of Old Testament Times: New Discoveries and New Approaches', *Strata* 6 (1985–1986), 32–43; and more generally M. Broshi and I. Finkelstein, 'The Population of Palestine in Iron Age II', *BASOR* 287 (1992), 47–60; I. Finkelstein, 'Environmental Archaeology and Social History: Demographic and Economic Aspects of the Monarchic Period', *Biblical Archaeology Today 1990* (ed. A. Biran and J. Aviram, Jerusalem, Israel Exploration Society, 1993), 55–66.

274 Lernau and Lernau, 'Fish Bone Remains'; Lernau and Lernau, 'Fish Remains'; Mienes, 'Molluscs'. Note that the latter constitute possible but not absolute evidence of trade with coastal sites, as the decorated molluscs especially appear to have been traded as luxury items rather than as foodstuffs and therefore are not required to have come to Jerusalem directly from the coast but may have been imported via a third party. More generally, note that the collection of small organic items such as bones has been inconsistent across sites and has not been widespread archaeological practice until recently; accordingly, information on the extent to which the Jerusalem data on the transport of such animal products reflects similar trends outside of the capital will have to wait until further excavations are undertaken.

275 Lernau and Lernau, 'Fish Bone Remains'.

two groups, with the bones all found in one of two locations: the city gate (Building C) or a royal building (Building D). Both are Iron Age loci associated with the eighth and seventh centuries.[276] In this, the earlier published group, the analysts make a point that all the fish found in Jerusalem had to have been imported from elsewhere, as the only local water source is the Gihon which has none. Freshwater fish species are likely to have been obtained from the Yarkon or Jordan rivers (58 kilometres northwest and 36 kilometres east, respectively) while saltwater species would have come from the Mediterranean (64 kilometres west) or the Red Sea (270 kilometres south).[277] Unsurprisingly, all of the saltwater species identified in Jerusalem came from the Mediterranean, not the Red Sea, due no doubt to the logistical difficulties of transporting perishables over a significantly longer distance as well as affirming the stronger trading connections between Judah and the Philistine coastal cities evidenced elsewhere.[278]

The second group of fish bones comes from the city of David excavations and consists of well over 200 bones and bone fragments, most of which are identifiable.[279] The overwhelming majority (85.1%) came from Iron Age II contexts, although unfortunately the published data do not break down the distribution any further.[280] Besides indicating an active trade with coastal areas, the analysts note that the large selection of fish types and the number of exemplars from this period 'may suggest a high standard of living for at least some of the inhabitants of the city', as the preservation and transportation of highly perishable foodstuffs would have resulted in fish being more expensive than locally produced options.[281] These exchanges were part of Judah's involvement in the wider southern Levantine economic system, centred on the coastal ports:

> The fish were part of what Judah got in exchange for its grains (and perhaps also its wine), probably directly from Ashkelon . . . the detailed patterns of exchange that can be demonstrated archaeologically seem to reflect the patter of the more general scenario, and show direct contacts between Judah and Ashkelon.[282]

---

276   Lernau and Lernau, 'Fish Bone Remains', 155.

277   Lernau and Lernau, 'Fish Bone Remains', 155.

278   Lernau and Lernau, 'Fish Bone Remains', 158.

279   Lernau and Lernau, 'Fish Remains', 131. The nine fish families (nine bone and one cartilage) identified in this group include the seven families (all bony) identified in the Ophel (Lernau and Lernau, 'Fish Bone Remains', 158; Lernau and Lernau, 'Fish Remains', 131).

280   There is, however, an enormous increase in the fish remains from Iron Age I to Iron Age II (from six to 160). On the difficulty of Iron Age II stratigraphy in Jerusalem see below.

281   Lernau and Lernau, 'Fish Remains', 135–136.

282   Faust and Weiss, 'Judah, Philistia, and the Mediterranean World', 80.

Similar lines of trade are reflected by the various molluscs collected during the city of David excavations. These break down into those deriving from the Mediterranean, from the Red Sea or from the Nile, with representatives of Mediterranean species somewhat more prominent (this prominence cedes ground to the Red Sea over the course of the period, reaching approximate parity by the end of the period, although the overall numbers are small enough that this may or may not be significant).[283] Like the fish remains, these 'point to an intensive trade between those areas and the inhabitants of the city'.[284] Especially relevant to the present purposes is the significant spike in overall quantities of imported materials in the strata associable with the long seventh century.[285] The publications of the Kenyon excavations also note a number of Mediterranean-sourced shells which were unlikely to have been used for food but perhaps as personal ornaments, as well as a number of worked shells from the Red Sea, which are of additional interest as they have been worked with a variant of a ring and dot motif otherwise only known from Mesopotamia and Syria.[286]

---

283 Once recent and fossil finds are eliminated the data break down as follows: in Stratum 12, two examples from the Red Sea, 13 from the Mediterranean, one from the Nile, one from the Erythraean Sea, one of local origin and one of unknown origin; in Stratum 11, three from the Mediterranean, one from the Red Sea, two from the Nile, one or two of local origin and one of unknown origin; in Stratum 10, two from the Red Sea, three from the Mediterranean, two which could be from either the Red Sea or the Mediterranean, two from the Nile and one from the Erythraean Sea (Mienes, 'Molluscs', 128–129).

284 Mienes, 'Molluscs', 129.

285 Note that, aside from the stratigraphic divisions associated with the destruction of Jerusalem by the Babylonians, the non-destruction of Jerusalem during the eighth and seventh centuries makes delineation of the city's stratigraphy an imprecise art. The relevant strata in the city of David are Strata 10–12: Stratum 12 is identified as pertaining to the eighth century, Stratum 11 is the first half of the seventh century and Stratum 10 is the latter half of the seventh century, culminating in the destruction of 586 (see Shiloh, 'Judah and Jerusalem', 103). There is no differentiation within Stratum 12 and it is accordingly impossible to state definitively that the large numbers of molluscs associated with this stratum are more likely to have originated in the latter part of it, but the near-absence of shells in the stratum associated with the ninth century and the minimal number associated with the tenth indicate a significant change between the ninth and seventh centuries with regard to Jerusalem's trading habits; it seems most plausible to associate this change with the major social and political shift which was the arrival of the Assyrian empire in the southern Levant and the various economic and other changes associated with it.

286 D.S. Reese, 'Marine Invertebrates and Other Shells from Jerusalem (Sites A, C and L)', *The Iron Age Cave Deposits on the South-east Hill and Isolated Burials and Cemeteries Elsewhere*

The Old South Arabian or Greek inscriptions from the City of David have already been mentioned.[287] Strata 12–10 of that area also produced fragments of Cypro-Phoenician juglets as well as Assyrian-inspired jugs, probably of local manufacture; these are most commonly found in the provincial territory to the north.[288] An Assyrian bottle was found in Stratum 10.[289] In the Jewish Quarter excavations the ceramic repertoire includes bowls with Phoenician affinities as well as bowls 'which might be regarded as having Edomite characteristics'.[290] The caves on the south-eastern hill excavated by Kenyon revealed, in Cave II, several juglets imported perhaps from Phoenicia.[291] Cave I produced nearly a dozen carinated bowls whose nearest parallels are to the north; they have been tentatively linked to Assyrian-style wares or neo-Hittite material culture.[292] Other ceramics from Cave II parallel Edomite and especially Phoenician forms, suggesting commercial contacts with the former northern state, Phoenicia, the Transjordan and Philistia.[293] A scaraboid depicting a Horus-falcon; a Hebrew inscription, which the excavators attributed to a north Israelite engraver of the eighth or seventh century; and a jar handle stamped by a scarab of Egyptian origin, with three hieroglyphs, from the seventh or sixth century, were found in secondary contexts in the City of David.[294] A pendant depicting Sekhmet or

---

(vol. 4 of *Excavations in Jerusalem 1961–1967*, ed. I. Eshel and K. Prag, BAMA 6, Oxford, Oxford University Press, 1995), 265–278.

287    Shiloh, 'South Arabian Inscriptions', 9–18; Sass, 'Arabs and Greeks', 59–61.

288    A. De Groot and H. Bernick-Greenberg, 'The Pottery of Strata 12–10 (Iron Age IIB)', *Area E: The Finds* (vol. 7B of *Excavations at the City of David 1978–1985 Directed by Yigal Shiloh*, ed. A. De Groot and H. Bernick Greenberg, Qedem 54, Jerusalem, Hebrew University of Jerusalem, 2012), 74, 77, 81–82.

289    De Groot and Bernick-Greenberg, 'The Pottery of Strata 12–10', 100–101.

290    A. De Groot, H. Geva and I. Yezerski, 'Iron Age II Pottery', *The Finds from Areas A, W and X-2: Final Report* (vol. 2 of *Jewish Quarter Excavations in the Old City of Jerusalem: Conducted by Nahman Avigad, 1969–1982*, ed. H. Geva, Jerusalem, Israel Exploration Society, 2003), 1–49.

291    I. Eshel, 'Two Pottery Groups from Kenyon's Excavations on the Eastern Slope of Ancient Jerusalem', *The Iron Age Cave Deposits on the South-east Hill and Isolated Burials and Cemeteries Elsewhere* (vol. 4 of *Excavations in Jerusalem 1961–1967*, ed. I. Eshel and K. Prag, BAMA 6, Oxford, Oxford University Press, 1995), 34.

292    Eshel, 'Two Pottery Groups', 40.

293    Eshel, 'Two Pottery Groups', 40–62.

294    B. Brandl, 'Scarabs, Scaraboids, Other Stamp Seals, and Seal Impressions', *Area E: The Finds* (vol. 7B of *Excavations at the City of David 1978–1985 Directed by Yigal Shiloh*, ed. A. De Groot and H. Bernick Greenberg, Qedem 54, Jerusalem, Hebrew University of Jerusalem, 2012), 386–387.

Bastet was found in the southern room on the Ophel.[295] Several fragments of *Buxus* wood were found in Stratum 10; these must have been imported, either from northern Iran, Turkey or western Europe to the north or from northern Africa to the south.[296] Cedar wood in the Ophel is likely also to have been imported.[297] Iron Age II lapis lazuli and hematite in the city of David came from the region of modern Afghanistan and from Egypt.[298] Horus eye amulets found in Strata 11 and 10 were probably imported from Egypt or Phoenicia, though they could have been made locally.[299] Though weights calibrated according to foreign standards are known already from the tenth century stratum, there is a substantial increase in the quantity of these essential commercial apparatus in the eighth and seventh centuries.[300]

This period saw an increase in Jerusalem's economic diversity, with the city's inhabitants importing furniture from Syria, ivories from Syria and/ or Mesopotamia, shells from the Red Sea and shells and fish from the Mediterranean and bronze from Cyprus or the Transjordan.[301] Decorative, personal and religious objects appeared in Jerusalem exhibiting influences, if

---

295   E. Mazar and B. Mazar, eds., *Excavations in the South of the Temple Mount: The Ophel of Biblical Jerusalem* (Qedem 29, Jerusalem, Hebrew University of Jerusalem, 1989), 18–19.

296   A. Fahn and E. Werker, 'Macrobotanical Remains', *Stratigraphical, Environmental, and Other Reports* (vol. 3 of *Excavations in the City of David 1978–1985 Directed by Yigal Shiloh*, ed. A. De Groot and D.T. Ariel, Qedem 33, Jerusalem, Hebrew University of Jerusalem, 1992), 106–115.

297   N. Liphshitz, 'Dendroarchaeological Studies 150: The Ophel (Jerusalem) 1986', *Excavations in the South of the Temple Mount: The Ophel of Biblical Jerusalem* (ed. E. Mazar and B. Mazar, Qedem 29, Jerusalem, Hebrew University of Jerusalem, 1989), 143.

298   A. Swersky, 'Gemstones', *Various Reports* (vol. 4 of *Excavations at the City of David 1978– 1985 Directed by Yigal Shiloh*, ed. D.T. Ariel and A. De Groot, Qedem 35, Jerusalem, Hebrew University of Jerusalem, 1996), 268–275; S. Zuckerman, 'Beads and Pendants', *Various Reports* (vol. 4 of *Excavations at the City of David 1978–1985 Directed by Yigal Shiloh*, ed. D.T. Ariel and A. De Groot, Qedem 35, Jerusalem, Hebrew University of Jerusalem, 1996), 276–277.

299   J.M. Cahill, ' "Horus Eye" Amulets', *Various Reports* (vol. 4 of *Excavations at the City of David 1978–1985 Directed by Yigal Shiloh*, ed. D.T. Ariel and A. De Groot, Qedem 35, Jerusalem, Hebrew University of Jerusalem, 1996), 294.

300   A. Eran, 'Weights and Weighing in the City of David: The Early Weights from the Bronze Age to the Persian Period', *Various Reports* (vol. 4 of *Excavations at the City of David 1978– 1985 Directed by Yigal Shiloh*, ed. D.T. Ariel and A. De Groot, Qedem 35, Jerusalem, Hebrew University of Jerusalem, 1996), 221.

301   M.L. Steiner, *The Settlement in the Bronze and Iron Ages* (vol. 3 of *Excavations in Jerusalem 1961–1967*, Copenhagen International Seminar, London, Oxford University Press, 2001), 109–110.

not origins, from Egypt, Phoenicia, Philistia, Mesopotamia and beyond. These manifold material remains from Jerusalem attest to Judah's trading activities in the long seventh century exposing it to outsiders on a significant and meaningful scale, and the remains confirm the city's inclusion in Judah's general trend toward an increased international profile and a greater degree of cross-cultural interaction than attested in previous periods.

## 4      Conclusions

The reality of cultural alterity came home to the population of Judah and Jerusalem in the long seventh century in a way which it had not done before this period: first in a process of gradual internationalisation in the late eighth century, spurred by the appearance of the Assyrian empire in the west and its economic interests in the region, followed by the effects of direct imperial intervention in Judahite geography and politics in 701, with the result that the borders of the Judahite state were drawn dramatically nearer Jerusalem. With the loss of the Shephelah the centre of power lost both the buffer zone between it and the outside world and a significant source of economic self-sufficiency. Deprived of the Shephelah, the outside world was suddenly and forcefully on Jerusalem's doorstep, with the geographic implications of this intrusion reiterated and exacerbated by the necessity of commercial and political engagement to supply its physical needs and protect its remaining state interests. The material evidence from across the region strongly suggests that the Judah of the long seventh century was profoundly affected by the widespread political, social and economic changes wrought by the Assyrian imperial context. Merchants and immigrants from the Transjordanian territories and the Philistine coastal plain were regular features of many Judahite sites from the end of the eighth century onward, while Judah's own inhabitants left witness to their far-flung trading activities at sites across the region. No longer was Judah a sheltered shadow state, its population and its affairs hidden behind the dominant northern kingdom: welcome or not, the outside world had arrived.

# CHAPTER 2

# Identity Formation as an Anthropological Phenomenon

## 1    Introduction

The preceding chapter has laid out archaeological evidence suggesting that the major political, social and economic changes in the southern Levant during the long seventh century led to a recognisable increase in the mobility of people around the region and an associated increase in the diffusion of cultural paraphernalia. The material record illustrates this period as an era of Judah's increased exposure to the diversity of material cultures from other parts of the southern Levant and other parts of the ancient Near East and, by implication, its increased exposure to the people with whom these cultures originated, either directly or indirectly.

The question which now arises concerns the effect of the increased level of cultural interactions which these materials suggest. How might the inhabitants of Judah and Jerusalem have reacted to their interactions with increasing numbers of outsiders, especially in connection with a flourishing regional economic system and occasionally as representatives of other states and powers? In an attempt to formulate a response to this question, this chapter draws on the work of a variety of social anthropologists on the nature and formation of group identity and, in particular, on the nature and formation of ethnic identity.

## 2    Race, Ethnic Identity and Nationalist Identity

Ethnic identity is, as encountered already in the discussion of Edom, a phenomenon which is both difficult to define and difficult to identify with precision. It is closely related to ideas about race and biological descent, on the one hand, and to ideas about the nation or nation-state, on the other. All three of these are attempts to articulate major phenomena of group identity.[1]

---

1    This is not the place for an exhaustive review of the theories pertaining to the origins and functions of group identity formation and the social phenomena they attempt to describe and the appearance of such reviews in recent monographs would render one redundant here.

© KONINKLIJKE BRILL NV, LEIDEN, 2014 | DOI 10.1163/9789004274693_004

## 2.1    *Ethnic Identity*

The prominence of language of ethnic identity in the latter part of the twentieth century has been, in some respects, a result of attempts to focus on cultural
and ideological aspects of group identity without invoking the negative connotations of 'race', a term which has tended to be used to emphasise genetic
components of group identity, sometimes to the near exclusion of group markers such as language, religion and territorial affiliations. Though references to
race are still used in forensic anthropology and related contexts, the heavily
pejorative overtones of this language and its use especially in German National
Socialism have led to the near-abandonment of this terminology in current
discussions about group identity as a social phenomenon.[2]

The status of genetics and biology with regard to the definition of ethnic
phenomena has been and remains varied; one traditional division among
ethnographers has been between those who emphasise a strong genetic component to ethnic phenomena and their cultural expressions (the so-called
primordialists) and those who decentralise genetics in favour of understandings of ethnic identity which prioritise current social context (the so-called
instrumentalists).[3] Although the definition of ethnic groups in terms of strict

---

Instead, this chapter focuses on discussions of identity which promise a degree of explanatory potential for the long seventh century. For much more extensive surveys see M. Banks,
*Ethnicity: Anthropological Constructions* (London, Routledge, 1996); S. Jones, *The Archaeology
of Ethnicity: Constructing Identities in the Past and Present* (London, Routledge, 1997), 56–102;
and the classic essays in J. Hutchinson and A.D. Smith, *Ethnicity* (Oxford, Oxford University
Press, 1996). For recent use of the concept in biblical studies, with extensive introductions
to the relevant literature see D.A. Nestor, *Cognitive Perspectives on Israelite Identity* (LHBOTS
519, London, T&T Clark, 2010), 12–125 and K.E. Southwood, *Ethnicity and the Mixed Marriage
Crisis in Ezra 9–10: An Anthropological Approach* (OTM, Oxford, Oxford University Press,
2012), 19–72. With regard to the philosophy according to which this material is employed,
Banks is worth quoting at some length. 'I do not think', he writes, 'that ethnicity is simply a
quality of groups, and for the most part I tend to treat it as an analytical tool, devised and
used by academics' . . . 'This is not to say that the ethnographic subjects are not responsible
for their "ethnic" actions: they are fully responsible for their actions but it is for the ana-
lyst to decide whether—if at all—ethnicity is a useful tool to make sense of those actions'
(Banks, *Ethnicity*, 6, 186). The use of ethnic identity here is not as an attempt to force either
the archaeological material or the biblical material into anthropological box, but rather the
use of anthropology as a useful tool for making sense of this material.

2    For further discussion see Southwood, *Ethnicity*, 36–41; Nestor, *Cognitive Perspectives*, 12–35.

3    See variously Y. Bromley, 'The Term Ethnos and Its Definition', *Soviet Ethnology and
Anthropology Today* (ed. Y. Bromley, The Hague, Mouton, 1974), 55–72; F. Barth, 'Introduction',
*Ethnic Groups and Boundaries: The Social Organization of Cultural Difference* (ed. F. Barth,
London, George Allen & Unwin, 1969), 9–38; A. Cohen, *Custom and Politics in Urban Africa:*

primordialism has generally been abandoned, due especially to the recognition that most of the cultural phenomena associated with ethnic groups are not immutable and that the supposed genetic relationships within ethnic groups (that is, the idea that all members are biologically related through descent from a common ancestor or ancestors) are often as imagined as they are real, ethnic theorisation has never the less been obliged to recognise and incorporate the fact that the rhetoric of genetic unity is often a significant part of ethnic groups' self-conception, despite its often illusory nature.[4]

As the relative de-emphasis on genetic explanations for ethnic identity suggests, however, one of the major developments in discussions of ethnic phenomena during the twentieth century is a shift towards a widespread emphasis on the contextual social, economic and political function of ethnic identities. Barth's work addressed this in very general terms in his recognition of the role of ethnic identity in boundary formation; the concept has been articulated much more extensively by scholars discussing the often highly practical motives which impel ethnic identity crystallisation.[5] Taking to extreme the observation that an ethnic group's genetic cohesion can be and often is illusory, combined with the fact that the cultural traits associated with a given ethnic identity can change over time, instrumentalist ethnographers have focused on ethnic identity as 'a strategic choice by individuals who, in other circumstances, would chose other group memberships as a mean of gaining some power and privilege'.[6] Ethnic identity, from this perspective, it is 'not so much

A Study of Hausa Migrants in Yoruba Towns (London, Routledge, 1969); N. Glazer and D.P. Moynihan, eds., Ethnicity: Theory and Experience (London, Harvard University Press, 1975); C.F. Keyes, ed., Ethnic Change (London, University of Washington Press, 1981); J.D.Y. Peel, 'The Cultural Work of Yoruba Ethnogenesis', History and Ethnicity (ed. E. Tonkin, M. McDonald and M. Chapman, ASA Monographs 27, London, Routledge, 1989), 198–215. Note that primordialist theories of ethnic identity, especially their emphasis on genetic cohesion, have been highly influential in archaeological as well as biblical conceptions of ethnic identity; witness, for example, K.L. Sparks, Ethnicity and Identity in Ancient Israel: Prolegomena to the Study of Ethnic Sentiments and Their Expression in the Hebrew Bible (Winona Lake, Ind., Eisenbrauns, 1998), in which familial language is taken as the predominant indicator of ethnic sentiment.

4   For discussion see C.F. Keyes, 'The Dialectics of Ethnic Change', Ethnic Change (ed. C.F. Keyes, London, University of Washington Press, 1981), 3–30.

5   For overviews of instrumentalist approaches see Banks, Ethnicity, 24–48; Jones, Archaeology of Ethnicity, 72–84.

6   D. Bell, 'Ethnicity and Social Change', Ethnicity: Theory and Experience (ed. N. Glazer and D.P. Moynihan, London, Harvard University Press, 1975), 171. Note also Wallerstein, known foremost for his articulation of the global economy in terms of core and periphery, who defines ethnic identity as 'the sentiment, shared by a group of people who define their boundaries in cultural terms (a common language, religion, color, history, style of life, and the like, or a

a form of identity as a strategy for corporate action' and a means of manipulating cultural symbols for economic and political gain, 'salient only insofar as it serves to orient people in the pursuit of their interest vis-à-vis other people who are seen as holding contrasting identities'.[7]

This contention—that ethnic identity is all about economic and political efficacy—has not gone unquestioned. The main issue is the extremity to which instrumentalist interpretations may take their conclusions, with a danger especially of implying that the cultural paraphernalia deployed in the ethnic project is as good as plucked out of thin air, with no necessary relationship to any current or previous cultural phenomena known among the individuals now forming the ethnic group. 'While it [ethnic identity] might "function" to justify a special ethnic interest in terms of a higher or wider value', Peel points out, 'it was made plausible by its role in the historic formation of the ethnic groups themselves.'[8] In other words, although ethnic identity may arise in response to specific political, economic and social circumstances and do so because an emphasis on an ethnic form of group identity is useful for its members, it cannot be said that ethnic identity is completely arbitrary. To the contrary, the development of an ethnic identity is based in and draws power from a group's historical and cultural roots.

Attempting to integrate this with the complex realities behind claims to biological unity, Keyes has suggested that the critical point is the concept of 'social descent', that is, the idea that ethnic phenomena rely to a significant degree on the idea of its members' common learned inheritance of the relevant markers of their ethnic heritage.[9] This ethnic 'descent', he suggests, does

---

combination of these), that they must seek to assert or extend their rights in the political arena in order to maintain or improve their material conditions' (I. Wallerstein, *The Capitalist World-Economy* [Cambridge, Cambridge University Press, 1979], 184, cf. 222–230). Such an understanding of ethnic identity was particularly resonant in the United States during the period of the civil rights movement and subsequent political mobilisation of various groups centred on the basis of asserted ethnic affiliation (e.g., Irish-American, black) and elsewhere in the world where power claims were accompanied by assertions of ethnic solidarity.

7   Banks, *Ethnicity*, 34 (less provocatively: 'ethnicity is an artefact, created by individuals or groups to bring together a group of people for some common purpose' [Banks, *Ethnicity*, 39]); Keyes, 'Dialectics', 10.

8   Peel, 'The Cultural Work', 201.

9   Keyes, 'Dialectics', 5–7; compare Emberling's reference to kinship as a social fact, not necessarily a biological fact (G. Emberling, 'Ethnicity in Complex Societies: Archaeological Perspectives', *Journal of Archaeological Research* 5 [1997], 302). Note that Cohen does allow that ethnic groups, by definition, are culture groups; however, he distinguishes the 'cultural factor' from the 'organizational' and 'power (economic-political)' factors, that is, the cultural

not require actual biological descent from parent to child, but rather serves to express the very important idea of cultural continuity between generations of group members. Similarly, in an attempt to articulate a multidimensional concept of ethnic identity which neither accepts claims of biological unity at face value nor dismisses its psychological significance for group cohesion, Jones describes ethnic groups as '*culturally ascribed identity groups, which are based on the expression of a real or assumed shared culture and common descent*'.[10]

As this suggests, prominent in most ethnographic analysis is the phenomena broadly categorised as 'culture' and, in particular, the nature of the cultural similarities which unite members of an ethnic group—especially in light of the simultaneous occurrence of diversity within such groups—and the importance of group members' perceptions of differences between their own cultural practice and the cultural practices of others.[11] Theorising from Bourdieu, Jones has argued that the cultural practices which signify identity affiliations—the practices which are objectified as ethnic symbols—arise from those which resonate with the habitual practices of the group in question.[12] Strengthening identity consciousness is prone to manifest as an exaggeration in the importance of existing features of a given group, to the indifference or detriment of others. As already observed in Chapter One, however, identifying the cultural characteristics which serve this purpose can be extremely difficult; after a brief discussion of nationalist identity, we will be obliged to return to it.

---

form of an ethnic identity from its cultural function of an ethnic identity (A. Cohen, 'Variables in Ethnicity', *Ethnic Change* [ed. C.F. Keyes, London, University of Washington Press, 1981], 328).

10    Jones, *Archaeology of Ethnicity*, 84; italics original.

11    See especially Barth, 'Introduction'; Peel, 'The Cultural Work'; S. Harrison, 'Identity as a Scarce Resource', *Social Anthropology* 7 (1999), 239–251; S. Harrison, 'Cultural Difference as Denied Resemblance: Reconsidering Nationalism and Ethnicity', *CSSH* 45 (2003), 343–361; T.H. Eriksen, *Ethnicity and Nationalism: Anthropological Perspectives* (Anthropology, Culture and Society 1, London, Pluto, 1993); Cohen, 'Variables in Ethnicity'; J. Friedman, 'Notes on Culture and Identity in Imperial Worlds', *Religion and Religious Practice in the Seleucid Kingdom* (ed. P. Bilde, T. Engberg-Pedersen, L. Hannestad and J. Zahle, Studies in Hellenistic Civilization 1, Aarhus, Aarhus University Press, 1990), 14–39; G.C. Bentley, 'Ethnicity and Practice', *CSSH* 29 (1987), 24–55.

12    Jones, *Archaeology of Ethnicity*, 90–91, 120. Identity also tends to crystallise around symbols and similar cues which are usually, though not always, visible, insofar as 'judgments of individual membership are generally made on the basis of symbols that permit discriminations with a significant degree of reliability' (D.L. Horowitz, 'Ethnic Identity', *Ethnicity: Theory and Experience* [ed. N. Glazer and D.P. Moynihan, London, Harvard University Press, 1975], 120).

## 2.2    *Ethnic Identity versus Nationalist Identity*

Given the present study's preference for the terminology of ethnic identity to that of nationalist identity, the distinction between ethnic identity and nationalist identity and why, in particular, the present discussion considers ethnic identity a more useful interpretive tool than nationalist identity merit at least a brief discussion.

It is sometimes argued that ethnic identity and nationalist identity are one and the same phenomenon or that the former does not exist without the latter.[13] However, there is a useful distinction to be made between these two phenomena. Though definitions of nationalist identity vary in much the same way as definitions of ethnic identity, definitions of nationalist identity tend to emphasise the term as describing a community which possesses a political doctrine of the state and 'possesses or claims the right to political identity and autonomy as a people, together with the control of a specific territory'.[14] By contrast, definitions of ethnic identity tend to prioritise its cultural components. Particularly important in distinguishing ethnic identity and nationalist identity, therefore, is that an ethnic group, which focuses on genetic and cultural cohesion, may or may not be linked to the political manifestation of that identity in the form of the nation-state:

> Nationalism, in particular, remains the pre-eminent rhetoric for attempts to demarcate political communities, claim rights of self-determination and legitimate rule by reference to 'the people' of a country. Ethnic solidarities and identities are claimed most often where groups do not seek 'national' autonomy but rather a recognition internal to or cross-cutting national or state boundaries.[15]

---

13    On the relationship between nationalist identity and ethnic identity see variously C. Calhoun, 'Nationalism and Ethnicity', *Annual Review of Sociology* 19 (1993), 211–239; A. Hastings, *The Construction of Nationhood: Ethnicity, Religion and Nationalism* (Cambridge, Cambridge University Press, 1997); A.D. Smith, *The Ethnic Origins of Nations* (Oxford, Blackwell, 1986); J. Hutchinson, 'Ethnicity and Modern Nations', *Ethnic and Racial Studies* 23 (2000), 651–670; E. Gellner, *Nations and Nationalism* (Oxford, Blackwell, 1983); J.A. Armstrong, *Nations Before Nationalism* (Chapel Hill, N.C., University of North Carolina Press, 1982); Eriksen, *Ethnicity and Nationalism*; R.H. Thompson, *Theories of Ethnicity: A Critical Appraisal* (New York, N.Y., Greenwood, 1989).

14    Hastings, *The Construction of Nationhood*, 3; similarly E. Kedourie, *Nationalism* (Oxford, Blackwell, 1993) and also Gellner, *Nations and Nationalism*, who, though he conflates ethnic identity and nationalist identity, considers the latter dependent on the existence of the state.

15    Calhoun, 'Nationalism and Ethnicity', 211, 235.

As Smith puts it: nationalist identity requires territory, ethnic identity does not.[16] Nationalist identity focuses, first and foremost, on territory and the state which is appropriate to govern it. Although nationalist identity often makes use of cultural phenomena in connection with its claims to territorial unity and power, these are less central to the construction of a nationalist identity than they are in the articulation of ethnic identity, where they are indispensable.

This link between nationalist identity and governance means that the extent to which nationalist identity as a phenomenon is associated with nineteenth century intellectual and political developments is also pertinent to the discussion of ancient 'nationalist' identities. According to Kedourie, for example, '[n]ationalism is a doctrine invented in Europe at the beginning of the nineteenth century'.[17] Complicating matters is that many theorists take as their specific example of early nationalist identity the Bible and, specifically, the Jews (though exactly who is meant by the latter, and at what time in

---

16    A.D. Smith, *The Nation in History: Historiographic Debates about Ethnicity and Nationalism* (Menahem Stern Lectures, Hanover, N.H., University Press of New England, 2000), 65; cf. Armstrong, *Nations Before Nationalism*, 7.

17    Kedourie, *Nationalism*, 1; similarly Wallerstein, *The Capitalist World-Economy*; contrast Armstrong, *Nations Before Nationalism*; Hastings, *The Construction of Nationhood*; Smith, *The Nation in History*.

The question of anachronism applies also to the concept of ethnic identity, but as ethnic identity is less tied to specifically modern forms of statehood and government, its attempts to describe a form of group identity connected to kinship and cultural concepts are more readily transferable to an ancient context. On the use of ethnic identity in discussions of the ancient world see A. Leahy, 'Ethnic Diversity in Ancient Egypt', *Civilizations of the Ancient Near East* (ed. J.M. Sasson, New York, N.Y., Charles Scribner, 1995), 225–234; the essays by D. Collon, C. De Bernardi, M. Roaf, G. van Driel and B. Levine in *Ethnicity in Ancient Mesopotamia: Papers Read at the 48th Rencontre Assyriologique Internationale: Leiden, 1–4 July 2005* (ed. W.H. Van Soldt, Leiden, Netherlands Institute for the Near East, 2005); A.E. Killebrew, *Biblical Peoples and Ethnicity: An Archaeological Study of Egyptians, Canaanites, Philistines, and Early Israel, 1300–1100 B.C.E.* (Archaeology and Biblical Studies 9, Leiden, Brill, 2005); Sparks, *Ethnicity and Identity*; E.T. Mullen, Jr, *Narrative History and Ethnic Boundaries: The Deuteronomistic History and the Creation of Israelite National Identity* (SBLSymS, Atlanta, Ga., Scholars, 1993); Nestor, *Cognitive Perspectives*; Southwood, *Ethnicity*; Z. Bahrani, 'Race and Ethnicity in Mesopotamian Antiquity', *World Archaeology* 38 (2006), 48–59; the essays by R.F. Person, Jr. and R.S. Sadler, Jr. in *The Archaeology of Difference: Gender, Ethnicity, Class and the 'Other' in Antiquity: Studies in Honor of Eric M. Meyers* (ed. D.R. Edwards and C.T. McCollough, AASOR 60/61, Boston, Mass., ASOR, 2007); A.C. Hagedorn, 'Looking at Foreigners in Biblical and Greek Prophecy', *VT* 57 (2007), 432–448; R.S. Sadler, Jr., *Can A Cushite Change His Skin? An Examination of Race, Ethnicity, and Othering in the Hebrew Bible* (LHBOTS 425, London, T&T Clark, 2005).

history, is rarely clarified). Hastings, for example, calls the Jews 'the true proto-nation', arguing that the Bible presents 'a developed model of what it means to be a nation—a unity of people, language, religion, territory and government'.[18] Perhaps most prominent in these discussions of biblical nationalist phenomena is Deuteronomy and, given the intention to focus in Chapter Three on the identity concerns of this text in particular, it is worth examining this association in more detail. As the foremost distinctions between ethnic and nationalist identities pertain to their relative emphasis or lack thereof on territorial and political claims, Deuteronomy's attention to these issues are of principal interest.

There is no doubt that Deuteronomy, as a book, is acutely attuned to the question of Israel's possession of the land. Given the numerous passages referring to the land and Israel's possession thereof, combined with laws discussing Israel's leadership and governance, especially in the latter half of the book, it is perhaps not surprising that numerous scholars have been inclined to see Deuteronomy as a 'nationalist' document, a 'national constitution' or similar.[19] Yet the prominence of the land—the single most critical component to the identification of the text in 'nationalist' terms—is characteristic much more of the book's deuteronomistic framework than its deuteronomic core.[20] Though

---

18    Hastings, *The Construction of Nationhood*, 186, 18; note also Hutchinson, 'Ethnicity and Modern Nations', 658–660, who speaks explicitly about the (late) post-exilic period. For discussions see S.D.E. Weeks, 'Biblical Literature and the Emergence of Ancient Jewish Nationalism', *BibInt* 10 (2002), 144–157; E.A. Speiser, '"People" and "Nation" of Israel', *JBL* 79 (1960), 157–163; S. Grosby, *Biblical Ideas of Nationality: Ancient and Modern* (Winona Lake, Ind., Eisenbrauns, 2002); J.L. Wright, 'The Commemoration of Defeat and the Formation of a Nation in the Hebrew Bible', *Prooftexts* 29 (2009), 433–473; M.G. Brett, 'Nationalism and the Hebrew Bible', *The Bible in Ethics: The Second Sheffield Colloquium* (ed. J. Rogerson, M. Davies and M.D. Carroll R., JSOTSup 207, Sheffield, Sheffield Academic, 1995), 136–163; D. Goodblatt, *Elements of Ancient Jewish Nationalism* (Cambridge, Cambridge University Press, 2006).

19    R. Barrett, *Disloyalty and Destruction: Religion and Politics in Deuteronomy and the Modern World* (LHBOTS 511, London, T&T Clark, 2009), 42–47; Grosby, *Biblical Ideas of Nationality*; A.D.H. Mayes, *Deuteronomy* (NCB, London, Marshall, Morgan & Scott, 1981), 55–81; J.G. McConville, *God and Earthly Power: An Old Testament Political Theology, Genesis-Kings* (JSOTSup 454, London, T&T Clark, 2007), 74–98; S.D. McBride, Jr., 'Polity of the Covenant People: The Book of Deuteronomy', *Int* 41 (1987), 229–244; Mullen, Jr, *Narrative History*, 55–85; E. Nielsen, *Deuteronomium* (HAT I/6, Tübingen, Mohr Siebeck, 1995), 7–11; H.D. Preuss, *Deuteronomium* (EdF 164, Darmstadt, Wissenschaftliche Buchgesellschaft, 1982), 182–194; Sparks, *Ethnicity and Identity*, 225–283.

20    Roughly defined, deuteronomic and deuteronomistic are distinguished as the core and the framework of the book, with the core comprising the central legislative

the land is present in the deuteronomic material, it is largely taken for granted. There is no question that the Israelites will live in the land, as part of their Israelite experience, but there is no great emphasis placed on specific territorial possession, nor on the juxtaposition of an Israelite state *vis-à-vis* other southern Levantine or ancient Near Eastern states.[21] In the deuteronomistic material, by contrast, Israelite possession of the land—and the idea of an Israelite land which is recognised on a global stage of other, territorial entities—is a significant issue. This deuteronomistic material is widely understood in terms of exilic attempts to come to grips with the loss of the land in 587; it is hardly surprising to see geography take on a much greater significance. This emphasis manifests in references to the land as having been promised to the ancestors (Deut. 1:6, 35; 6:18, 23; 7:13; 8:1; 10:11; 11:9, 21; 30:20; 31:7, 20) as well as a in a notable theological shift in the conception of Yhwh's relationship with the land: paralleling Israel's exclusive relationship with Yhwh, Yhwh now has an exclusive claim to the land (Deut. 6:14; 7:5, 16, 25; 8:19; 9:16; 11:16). It is in this, deuteronomistic material that the book begins to express a sentiment akin to a nationalist identity, in which control of a fixed geographical territory is an explicit element of group identity.[22] Also worth note is that the deuteronomic material, in addition to its assumption of but relative lack of attention to the land's possession, is not focused on establishing something which might justifiably be construed as a political doctrine of the state. Though the text does address matters of Israelite leadership and the law of the king in particular may be construed as expressing concerns about Israelite autonomy, these concerns are focused on cultural rather than political liberties, in keeping with an overall deuteronomic focus on cultural aspects of Israelite identity. The disinterest in 'Israel's' relationship to the state—Israelite or otherwise—is reflected also in

---

material in Deuteronomy 12–26, a pared-down version of the exhortative introduction in Deuteronomy 6–11 and a conclusion in Deuteronomy 28. More detailed analysis of redactional processes in these chapters may be found in Chapter Three. Even sketched in broad strokes, however, the differences in these two types of text's attitudes to the land are readily recognisable.

21 Note also Hastings' observation that 'political construction is intrinsic not extrinsic to normative ethnicity' (Hastings, *The Construction of Nationhood*, 177); that is, the presence of political/governmental provisions in a deuteronomic text is compatible with its interpretation in terms of ethnic phenomena and does not automate the classification of the text as 'nationalist'.

22 Complicating this, of course, is the land's actual non-possession, and it is no surprise to find divergent opinions as to whether this really constitutes a nationalist phenomenon.

the text's intensely internally-orientated focus.[23] Though motivated by a social, economic and political situation developing on a broadly ancient Near Eastern stage, the deuteronomic concern is with Israelites in the southern Levant and with non-Israelites in the southern Levant who pose a threat to the definition and preservation of Israelite identity.[24] The deuteronomic material is focused on internal issues of cultural praxis rather than political power jockeying with the southern Levantine states or the imperial powers. In the deuteronomistic material, however, this localised debate over Israelite identity shifts towards an international perspective, with an increased level of attention to non-Israelites resident outside the land: it is 'the peoples under all the heavens' who will fear Israel (Deut. 2:25) and a 'distant nation' which Yhwh will employ to exact punishment (Deut. 28:49–50); Israel will be scattered among the nations (Deut. 28:64, cf. Deut. 4:27) and there they will find no rest (Deut. 28:65); it is among the nations that they have been banished (Deut. 30:1) and from which Yhwh will ultimately gather them up (Deut. 30:3). This wider international perspective scarcely exists in the deuteronomic material.

With these relative deuteronomic and deuteronomistic priorities in mind, Calhoun's observation that ethnicities are 'most often claimed where groups do not seek 'national' autonomy but rather a recognition internal to or cross-cutting national or state boundaries' is suggestive.[25] Indeed, as there will be cause to observe on several occasions in Chapter Three, the 'Israelite' identity conceived by the deuteronomic text is not inclusive of all who live on Israelite land. The land alone, in other words, is not the ultimate arbiter of Israelite identity. This and the relative disinterest of the deuteronomic text in state-based, political activities suggests that scholars should not be too quick to assume that the territorial concerns of the book as a whole reflect a nationalist agenda for all its parts.

Ethnic identity and nationalist identity need not, of course, be mutually exclusive; as Hastings argues, 'ethnicities naturally turn into nations', and numerous scholars have devoted studies to understanding the interaction between these two phenomena.[26] Indeed,

---

23    One might also observe the text's persistent failure to make any recognisable reference to an actual political, territorial entity extant in the southern Levant, namely, Judah (or even, to stretch the imagination, Samaria, though the probability of its appearance is low on numerous grounds).

24    C.L. Crouch, 'The Threat to Israel's Identity in Deuteronomy: Mesopotamian or Levantine?', *ZAW* 124 [2012], 541–554; also Chapter Three.

25    Calhoun, 'Nationalism and Ethnicity', 211, 235.

26    Hastings, *The Construction of Nationhood*, 12; see also Smith, *Ethnic Origins of Nations*; Hutchinson, 'Ethnicity and Modern Nations'. Kedourie, *Nationalism*, 71 observes that nationalist identity 'derives the greater part of its strength from the existence of ancient

> The sort of ethnicity which is likely to develop nationalist identity in self-defence is one with control of a clear territorial core . . . [and] . . . the more [a people] have advanced towards a self-conscious separate identity, an identity of language or religion, the more likely they are to respond to intrusion by adopting the option of nationalism.[27]

Though such a development is not automatic, it might be suggested that the more clearly nationalist tenor of the deuteronomistic material represents the development of an ethnic identity into terms more explicitly tied to land and territory, as an ethnic identity previously in control of a territorial core (i.e., Judah) comes under threat. Certainly it is worth emphasising that what scholars frequently describe as nationalist identity—or something like it—in the biblical literature is unlikely to have been an exilic phenomenon *de novo*; while the experience of deportation and exile constituted an extreme threat to group identity, a nationalist response to that threat is unlikely to have materialised from thin air.

For the present discussion, however, ethnic identity and discussions of the formation of ethnic identity are of most use in anticipating responses to the increasingly diverse social, political and economic context of the southern Levant in the long seventh century. Political issues and issues of governance and territory are not wholly absent from the Israelite conception of group identity which arises in response to this context, but concepts of ethnic identity allow for a clearer focus on the cultural and ideological manifestations of Israelite identity formation.

---

communal and religious ties [i.e., ethnic sentiments] which have nothing to do with nationalist theory'. The full passage from Hastings is: 'ethnicities naturally turn into nations or integral within nations at the point when their specific vernacular moves from an oral to written usage to the extent that it is being regularly employed for the production of a literature' (Hastings, *The Construction of Nationhood*, 12; cf. Kedourie, *Nationalism*, 62). Many scholars of the biblical literature would jump directly from here to the assertion that the written nature of the preserved literature itself indicates an underlying nationalist identity. Aside from the aforementioned need to pay close attention to the text's identity priorities, however, what is striking about Deuteronomy is that—for all its writtenness—its self-presentation is as an oral event: a speech (or speeches) directed to a listening audience, addressed as 'you'.

27    Hastings, *The Construction of Nationhood*, 31.

3        The Formation of Ethnic Identity

3.1      *Boundary-Making and Ethnic Identity*

Among the most influential analyses of ethnic identity, as well as the most informative in the specific analysis of the situation in the southern Levant during the long seventh century, are those which relate to the importance of alterity in the process of ethnic identity formation. This trend in ethnic theorisation may be traced most influentially to the work of Barth, who articulated the concept in terms of the experience, articulation and maintenance of boundaries. Barth proposed that the construction of ethnic identity should be understood as a response to a group's discovery of one or more alternative identities and argued that the key feature of a developing ethnic sentiment is the definition and maintenance of boundaries between alternative groups, constructed in opposition to each other.[28] Especially prominent among efforts to articulate the mechanics of this concept has been the work of Bourdieu, who suggests that, over time, a group develops a particular way of living and a particular ways of doing things which is essentially unconscious; the members' 'dispositions' to act in these particular ways arise more or less organically over time in response to the circumstances in which the group finds itself.[29] These dispositions Bourdieu collectively calls the *habitus*; they represent the group's cultural commonality. Intellectually this commonality constitutes the group's *doxic* knowledge—that is, its knowledge and understanding of reality as it corresponds to their own social experience of reality. The critical point for the conscious formation of group identity is when this *doxa* is called into question through contact with another culture, leading to the realisation that the group's own particular *habitus* is not the only one. '[E]xposure to the arbitrariness of cultural practices', Bourdieu observes, 'which had hitherto been mastered in a doxic mode, permits and requires a change "in the level of discourse, so as to rationalize and systematize" the representation of such cultural practices, and, more generally, the representation of the cultural tradition

---

28     Barth, 'Introduction'. Similarly A.P. Cohen, *The Symbolic Construction of Community* (London, Tavistock, 1985), who describes ethnic identity as a means of making and articulating 'us versus them' sentiments.

29     P. Bourdieu, *Outline of a Theory of Practice* (Cambridge Studies in Social Anthropology 16, transl. R. Nice, Cambridge, Cambridge University Press, 1977). Subsequent usage of Bourdieu includes, among various others, Bentley, 'Ethnicity and Practice'; M. Dietler and I. Herbich, 'Habitus, Techniques, Style: An Integrated Approach to the Social Understanding of Material Culture and Boundaries', *The Archaeology of Social Boundaries* (ed. M.T. Stark, London, Smithsonian Institute, 1998), 232–263; Nestor, *Cognitive Perspectives*; Jones, *Archaeology of Ethnicity*.

itself'.[30] Similarly emphasising the importance of interaction in the formation of ethnic identity, Emberling and Yoffee suggest that

> ethnic identity depends on perception of similarity and difference. It is not any specific feature of a group of people, but the recognition of significant difference between its members and outsiders that distinguishes it as a group separate from others ... it is an aspect of social relations.[31]

In other words, ethnic identity is provoked by interaction with others and, more specifically, by the recognition that a group's existing traditions and practices are not the only possible traditions and practices.[32]

Not all experiences of alterity, however, produce the same response; ethnic formation phenomena are most likely to occur in situations in which the groups on either side of the boundary are, in a significant number of respects, very similar.[33] Underlying this observation are two points. First, it is comprehensible in terms of rationalisation and systematisation of the *doxa* that an alternative *habitus* which is radically different actually requires less comprehensive explanation than an alternative *habitus* which is only slightly different from the native *habitus*. In the latter case, the confrontation of minor differences in the context of overall similarity poses a greater challenge to explanation than the broad strokes of total difference. Second, and similarly, the latter situation is practically more likely, insofar as a certain degree of what Barth calls 'congruence of codes and values' is required for interaction to occur in

---

30    Bourdieu, *Outline of a Theory of Practice*, 233; for discussion see Jones, *Archaeology of Ethnicity*, 95. Jones especially wants to see a fusion of the primordialist and instrumentalist theories here, arguing that the differences which become objectified as significant ethnic symbols are derived not from thin air but rather are cultural practices which resonate with the habitual practices of the people in question (their *habitus*, in Bourdieu's language) (Jones, *Archaeology of Ethnicity*, 90–91).

31    G. Emberling and N. Yoffee, 'Thinking about Ethnicity in Mesopotamian Archaeology and History', *Fluchtpunkt Uruk: Archaeologische Einheit aus Methodologischer Vielfalt: Schriften für Hans J. Nissen* (ed. H. Kuehne, R. Bernbeck and K. Bartl, Rahden, Marie Leidorf Verlag, 1999), 273.

32    Compare Eriksen: 'If a setting is wholly mono-ethnic, there is effectively no ethnicity, since there is nobody there to communicate cultural difference to' (Eriksen, *Ethnicity and Nationalism*, 34). Barthian/instrumentalist theories of ethnic identity have played a significant role in the 'new' archaeology; see Jones, *Archaeology of Ethnicity*, 26–29.

33    In Harrison's words, 'it is only when people identify with one another that a felt need can arise to differentiate themselves' (Harrison, 'Cultural Difference', 345; cf. Harrison, 'Identity as a Scarce Resource').

the first place.[34] That is, there must be a certain level of similarity between two groups in order for individuals from those groups to be able to interact; representatives of two wholly dissimilar *habitus* may fail to challenge each other's ways of doing things simply on the basis of mutual incomprehensibility. In order for an alternative *habitus* to properly present a challenge to another, its representative(s) must be accessible to the other. At a most fundamental level, for example, they must be able to communicate, such as by speaking the same or a similar language; beyond basic conversance, an encounter such as a commercial endeavour requires similar ideas about the procedures through which a sale or exchange is effected, while participation in religious rituals requires overlap in the deities recognised as deserving of worship as well as similar expectations of proper procedure. As a result of this requisite degree of similarity, interaction between congruent groups is both more likely and more potent because the alternative presented is not so alien as to be inconceivable: it occurs in a framework which is fundamentally familiar. If the groups are not to become indistinguishable, each unique practice—whether those already extant or those formulated for the purpose—must bear a proportionally greater burden in the definition of the group's common cultural property, being not merely one among many but rather one among few. Exposure to an alternative culture is not alone enough to prompt concerns about identity; the alternative must be sufficiently similar to the known as to be threatening in its ambiguity.

In practice, then, it is not surprising to see the most stringent efforts at delineation occurring in circumstances of overall similarity.[35] Harrison observes that 'the most elaborate and extreme forms of ethnic 'othering' are more likely to occur in relationships that are in some sense close, rather than in distant ones'; indeed, 'ethnic groups may sometimes conceive themselves as in conflict not so much because they have irreconcilably different identities, but rather because they have irreconcilable claims or aspirations to the *same* identities'.[36] Ethnic identity may often be a matter of relatively small differences highlighted against a background of relative similarity; 'the symbolization of ethnic identification is primarily focused on style of life distinctiveness within the larger framework of much more nearly uniform . . . social structure'.[37] In

---

34    Barth, 'Introduction', 16.

35    Barth, 'Introduction', 16.

36    Harrison, 'Cultural Difference', 345; Harrison, 'Identity as a Scarce Resource', 239.

37    T. Parsons, 'Some Theoretical Considerations on the Nature and Trends of Change in Ethnicity', *Ethnicity: Theory and Experience* (ed. N. Glazer and D.P. Moynihan, London, Harvard University Press, 1975), 65.

the southern Levantine context, this suggests that the primary *foci* of ethnic identity phenomena are likely to be others who are largely similar in language and culture.

### 3.2    *Social Change and Ethnic Identity*

As already implied, one of the major triggers for the formation or crystallisation of group identity is social, political or economic change, especially insofar as this change results in the exposure of a group to outsiders in a more extensive or sustained way. 'Ethnic change', Keyes explains, 'is a dialectical process that begins when a people experience a radical shift in their social circumstances (when they migrate to a new society or are incorporated into a new political order)'.[38] More specifically, the cause of ethnic change is the challenge posed by the new situation to a community's established way of doing things (its cultural practice) and its established way of thinking about existence (its ideology). In Bourdieu's terms, the presentation of an alternative practice poses a challenge to a community's *doxic* understanding of its *habitus*, requiring a change 'in the level of discourse, so as to rationalize and systematize' the *habitus*.[39]

There are perhaps as many specific kinds of social change which might impel the explicit articulation of identity discourse as there are ethnic groups. One type of change which is of particular interest in discussion of the long seventh century, however, is the change(s) associated with major shifts of political power.

> A new ethnic identity often develops when a state conquers or otherwise encompasses previously independent groups. These may be relatively bounded, well-defined groups such as other states, or they may be less-bounded, relatively undifferentiated agricultural communities or hunter-gatherers. The newly formed ethnic groups in these situations thus arise on the margins of expanding states.[40]

The situation in the southern Levant might reasonably be described in these terms. Noting especially the allowance for a sliding scale of control—that nascent ethnic groups may be conquered outright by the state in question, or may

---

38    Keyes, 'Dialectics', 3.

39    Bourdieu, *Outline*, 233.

40    G. Emberling, 'Ethnicity in Complex Societies: Archaeological Perspectives', *Journal of Archaeological Research* 5 (1997), 308; cf. Emberling and Yoffee, 'Thinking about Ethnicity', 274.

come less directly under its sway—it would be unsurprising to observe the advent of Assyrian influence provoking ethnic identity formation processes in parts of the southern Levant.[41] The economic and social changes prompted in the region as a result of Assyrian dominance and influence translated Assyrian expansionism into real terms in the form of the myriad individuals and groups now passing through—and occasionally resident—in Judah and Jerusalem, even though these would likely have manifested themselves less frequently as the direct faces of Assyrian power than as the more immediate alterities of the cultural variety of the rest of the southern Levant. In either case or in combination, however, the circumstances of the long seventh century prevailed to present Judah with unavoidable evidence of alternatives to its particular *habitus*.

Useful to bear in mind in the consideration of such circumstances is that, by forcing the systematisation of group practice in response to alternatives, the experience of alterity can effect changes in the *habitus* itself, as well as in the community's doxic understanding of the *habitus*. Recognition of this is informative for understanding the rapid changes associated with the long seventh century and, in particular, the erratic correspondence between the cultural practices recorded materially and the practices claimed by biblical texts. Keyes explains that,

> As people evolve new patterns of social adaptation to their changed circumstances, they begin to reassess the saliency of the cultural basis of their ethnic identities. And, as new cultural meanings are given to their identities, they also develop social patterns in accordance with the premises of their identities.[42]

As noted already, the Israelite identity which the deuteronomic material develops seems often only tangentially connected to the cultural practices of Judah as witnessed by the archaeological record. Understanding the deuteronomic project as an instance of ethnic identity formation, developing in response to changing circumstances, helps to explain why the deuteronomic material appears to be altering the social patterns of Israelite identity: it is a witness to a process of re-evaluation of existing cultural praxis and the evolution of new patterns of identity expression in accordance with the development of

---

41    Broadly, see L.G. Herr, 'Archaeological Sources for the History of Palestine: The Iron Age II
       Period: Emerging Nations', *BA* 60 (1997), 114–183.
42    Keyes, 'Dialectics', p. 3.

the identity itself. Related to this uncomfortable, transitioning juxtaposition between past and future identities is the recognition that,

> Under conditions of rapid social change and certain tendencies to anomic social disorganization and alienation, intensification of 'groupism' and the highly emotional loading of the status of group membership and identity is one major type of reaction. Like many other such phenomena it may involve a complex combination of potential and, to a certain degree, actual disruptive consequences for social solidarity and, at the same time, a kind of a constructive mode of reintegration of population elements into structures which are less anomic and alienative than their members might otherwise be exposed to.[43]

In other words, the development of new or changing identities in response to change may involve not only the contiguous development of a single identity but the fragmentation of an existing identity into multiple new identities. In terms of lived realities in Judah, an intensified emphasis on group identity in the face of rapid social change suggests a complex impact on the community, anticipating the community's initial fragmentation in search of stronger cohesive principles. It is evident within the deuteronomic text, for example, that the 'Israel' constructed by the deuteronomic identity project is meant to comprise only a portion of the population which inhabits the land. In pursuit of a secure identity, the deuteronomic identity project fragments this wider community, comprising the entire population of the land, by rejecting a regional solidarity in favour of a closely-defined, limited 'Israel'. Articulated anthropologically, a general degree of social solidarity among the inhabitants of the land, in which a wide variety of cultural practices were shared by most of the population and in which there is a relatively high tolerance for cultural diversities, is disrupted by the aggressive intensification of Israelite identity undertaken in the deuteronomic identity project.

### 3.3   *Manifestations of Ethnic Identity Formation*

The primordialist framework, while not adopted by the majority of ethnographers, has profoundly affected archaeological interpretation of material culture and, in the form of its emphasis on genetic or biological connections among group members, is probably the form of ethnic identity which has most frequently found its way into discussions of biblical texts, including Deuteronomy, and in the latter especially prominent in discussions of its its

---

43    Parsons, 'Some Theoretical Considerations', 68–69.

use of familial language (primarily אח, brother). As observed already, while claims of genetic unity—real or imagined—are a very common part of ethnic self-conceptions, they are far from the only expression of ethnic identity.

Cohen, mentioned already as an especially ardent defender of the idea of ethnic identity as primarily a functional phenomenon, proves especially useful in this arena due to his emphasis on the practical aspects of identity formation; because he is so adamant that ethnic identity is not an ever-present aspect of human existence but is fully grounded in social and political realities, his analysis pays particular attention to the ways in which ethnic sentiments manifest themselves. His analysis may be split into two broad categories. First, he outlines a number of specific methods by which a group can articulate and achieve its particular distinctiveness. Second, he pays particular attention to the role of religious practice in the formation of identity, discussing especially its effectiveness as an upper-level cognitive framework in which ethnic identity may be articulated, akin in this respect to the kinship concepts more commonly observed in this regard.

In discussing both of these types of ideological framework, Cohen suggests that kinship-based ideologies tend to occur in relatively segmentary political systems, while ritual ideologies tend to predominate in more centralised societies. He emphasises, however, that they are not mutually exclusive. Kinship ideologies function by '[e]xploit[ing] the strong sentiments and emotions that are associated with primary relationships between members and the elementary family'.[44] Ritual ideologies tap into the broader social nature of humanity and 'exploit the emotional anxieties of men in facing the perennial problems of existence, of life and death, health and illness, happiness and misery.'[45] Both are means by which a group may mobilise existing social relations into a (self-perpetuating) phenomenon of group identity.[46]As will be discussed in

---

44    Cohen, *Custom and Politics*, 209.

45    Cohen, *Custom and Politics*, 209.

46    Cohen speaks of the 'ritual and moral mechanisms' which serve to condition members' moods, attitudes and beliefs, 'impos[ing] a heavy burden on the "conscience" and will of men and require[ing] continuous sharpening of their normative sensibilities' (Cohen, *Custom and Politics*, 210–211). In time this develops into a self-reinforcing feedback loop, in which the norms of the group are so solidly entrenched in the ideology of the group's members that the ideology itself 'becomes an autonomous factor which can motivate people to action' (Cohen, *Custom and Politics*, 208). The development of this kind of description of ethnic phenomena into the language used by Bourdieu is not difficult to conceive.

greater detail in Chapter Three, elements of both of these ideological types appear in the deuteronomic text.[47]

Cohen's study of the Hausa offers a practical example of the role of religion in ethnic identity articulations. The Tijaniyya form of Islam was adopted by the Hausa just at the moment that the majority of the city's non-Hausa were converting to Islam; by adopting the more specific Tijaniyya form, the Hausa established a narrative of group origins distinct from this increasing general population of Yoruba Muslims in the city. Separate religious observances also facilitated the development of a Hausa endo-culture (a type of cultural feed-back loop) by promoting members' interaction with other members and dis-couraging social interaction outside the group. Religious observance thus acts as a mechanism for the isolation of community members as well as justifying this isolation. In this way the Hausa's distinctive religious identity

> brought about processes which halted the disintegration of the bases of the exclusiveness and identity of Sabo. The reorganization of the Quarter's religion was at the same time a reorganization of the Quarter's political organization. A new myth of distinctiveness for the Quarter was found. The Quarter was now a superior, puritanical, ritual community, a reli-gious brotherhood, distinct from the masses of Yoruba Moslems in the city, complete with its separate Friday Mosque, Friday congregation, and with a separate cemetery.
>
> The localization of ritual in the Quarter inhibited the development of much social interaction with the Yoruba. On the other hand, the intensi-fication and collectivisation of ritual increased the informal social inter-actions within the Quarter, under Hausa traditional values, norms, and customs.[48]

---

47  It is perhaps due to the dual nature of 'Israelite' society in the long seventh century that both kinship and ritual ideologies appear in the deuteronomic texts: on the one hand, the book is tending toward, indeed advocating, a centralising system, in which a ritual ideology is the more natural; on the other, it is working from an essentially small-scale, largely rurally based social structure, to which kinship ideology compellingly speaks. Interestingly, Cohen also suggests that groups which are 'informally' organised make more use of their moral, ritual and economic powers to effect these distinctions than groups which are formally organised and backed by physical power (Cohen, *Custom and Politics*, 207). Judah's physical power in most of the long seventh century was meagre, making it perhaps unsurprising that deuteronomic efforts toward identity formation are heavily dependent on 'soft' forms of power.

48  Cohen, *Custom and Politics*, 185. Note that Cohen uses 'political' in a broad sense inclusive of marriage ties, friendship, etc.; see Cohen, *Custom and Politics*, 193.

The new religious and ritual phenomenon, in other words, acted to insulate and solidify the community's cultural and collective identity. A more recent study of Muslims in New York City has made similar observations regarding the effectiveness of religion in the articulation of both individual and group identities.[49] In explaining why religion is especially effective in facilitating and reinforcing group identity, Cohen concludes that

> Religion provides an ideal 'blueprint' for the development of an informal political organization. It mobilizes many of the most powerful emotions which are associated with the basic problems of human existence and gives legitimacy and stability to political arrangements by representing these as parts of the system of the universe. It makes it possible to mobilize the power of symbols and the power inherent in the ritual relationships between various ritual positions within the organization of the cult. It makes it possible to use the arrangements for financing and administering places of worship and associated places for welfare, education, and social activities of various sorts, to use these in developing the organization and administration of political functions. Religion also provides frequent and regular meetings in congregations, where in the course of ritual activities, a great deal of informal interaction takes place, information is communicated, and general problems are formulated and discussed. The system of myths and symbols which religion provides is capable of being continuously interpreted and re-interpreted in order to accommodate it to change economic, political and other social circumstances.[50]

The intimate relationship between Israelite religion and Israelite identity will be a familiar refrain throughout the next chapter; emphasising here the function of religion in the formation of identity acts as a counter to the extent to which scholars tend to be absorbed with the religious ideas of biblical books in and for themselves. Bearing in mind the social function of religious phenomena in creating and facilitating identity, recognising that they may not be mere expressions of abstract intellectual theologising, will help to integrate the

---

49    L. Peek, 'Becoming Muslim: The Development of a Religious Identity', *Sociology of Religion* 66 (2005), 215–242. Peek also observed that, as of 2005, there were still very few studies of identity which address the role of religion in this respect.

50    Cohen, *Custom and Politics*, 210; cf. C. Geertz, *The Interpretation of Cultures: Selected Essays* (London, Fontana, 1973); P.L. Berger, *The Sacred Canopy: Elements of a Sociological Theory of Religion* (Garden City, N.Y., Doubleday, 1969).

biblical text's observable interests into the social, economic and political context of the long seventh century.

Finally, given that ethnic identity may be understood as substantially to do with the identification, articulation and defence of group boundaries, it is productive to consider specific ways in which a given group might go about identifying, articulating and defending its distinctiveness *vis-à-vis* outsiders. The actual differentiation of ethnic groups may take various forms; aside from assertions of genetic relations among members, perhaps the foremost of these tend to relate to aspects of culture: ethnic identity may be understood as 'refer[ring] to aspects of relationships between groups which consider themselves, and are regarded by others, as being culturally distinctive'.[51] Culture in this sense may include, though is not limited to, language, diction and script; dress and personal ornamentation; foodways, accommodation and other elements of daily life; and religious belief and practice. As noted in the discussion of Edom, scholars have identified as potential ethnic markers such varied phenomena as household structure, 'because of its close, meaningful relationship with daily life', aspects of ritual practice, including mortuary rituals, and cuisine; material objects 'used in and that structures every day domestic life'; complex technologies and decorations which cross-cut a number of media; behaviours concerned with symbolising ethnic identity, the goal of which are communicative and for which differences and distinctions should be pronounced; behaviours which are learnt as part of the socialisation process of the group, such as manufacturing techniques and stylistic preferences, although these may become less important in situations of market exchange or large territorial diffusion; and behaviours reflecting economic or political strategy.[52] As the length and generality of this list suggests, the cultural features which delimit boundaries may be extremely varied; there is certainly 'no invariable pattern as to which cultural differences will be seized upon by groups as emblematic of their ethnic differences'.[53] Cultural markers can also be extremely fluid, changing over time as the role of gatekeeper shifts among different specific points of practice and as practices themselves change.[54]

---

51    Eriksen, *Ethnicity and Nationalism*, 4.

52    Emberling, 'Ethnicity in Complex Societies', 325, 318; M. Hegmon, 'Technology, Style, and Social Practices: Archaeological Approaches', *The Archaeology of Social Boundaries* (ed. M.T. Stark, London, Smithsonian Institute, 1998), 277; Kamp and Yoffee, 'Ethnicity in Ancient Western Asia', 96; Hodder, *Symbols in Action*, 187.

53    Keyes, 'Dialectics', 7.

54    Note Barth, 'Introduction', 14: 'The cultural features that signal the boundary may change, and the cultural characteristics of the members may likewise be transformed, indeed,

Functionally, however, the development of group cohesion requires 'the creation and strengthening and utilization of different kinds of myths, beliefs, norms, values, and motives'.[55] Though by no means producing an exhaustive list of possibilities, Cohen provides a useful preliminary list of means by which such 'myths, beliefs, norms, values, and motives' may be articulated, providing a starting point for the discussions to follow. First, a group may articulate and legitimate its separation from other groups by reference to unique myths of origins, which are often accompanied by claims to superiority. Second, groups will often emphasise the genetic cohesiveness of the group's membership, especially in terms of the current generation's claims to lineal descent from previous generations of group members and a theoretical, if not always practical, emphasis on endogamy, particularly in cases where the descent principle is not particularly strong. Third, a group will frequently discourage all or most social interaction outside the group, for obvious reasons. Fourth, there can be a development of an 'endo-culture', that is, the mutual reinforcement of existing values, norms and beliefs through informal interaction primarily or wholly with other group members who share these; religious phenomena are especially conducive to facilitating such informal interactions, in the context of more formal worship practices. Fifth, there is a tendency to establish spatial proximity among group members. Sixth and finally, groups will tend to homogenise themselves through the elimination of sub-cultures.[56] Each of these is at work in the efforts of the deuteronomic material to delineate a distinctive Israelite identity.

---

even the organizational form of the group may change—yet the fact of continuing dichotomizations between members and outsiders allows us to specify the nature of continuity, and investigate the changing cultural form and content.' See also the discussion of the difficulty of identifying relevant cultural difference in the archaeological record in Chapter One.

55    Cohen, *Custom and Politics*, 208.
56    Cohen, *Custom and Politics*, 202–204.

# Deuteronomy as Identity Formation Project

## 1 Introduction

The preceding has established the social, political and economic atmosphere of the long seventh century as likely to have provoked acute identity issues among the population of the southern Levant, including Judah. In this third chapter the objective is to conduct an experiment in the implications of those conclusions for the reading of a specific text. Because of the tendency to classify the book's identity concerns as indicators of part or all of its origins in the exilic period or later, the text chosen for this experiment is Deuteronomy and, more specifically, its deuteronomic core, as it is the pre- or post-exilic date of this material which is primarily at stake in such discussions.

As is well known by even the novice student of Deuteronomy, the book's origins in the seventh century have been variously argued and asserted for much of the last two centuries, especially since de Wette associated the book with the law book purportedly discovered in the temple during renovations ordered by Josiah.[1] Much of the scholarship in the interim has assumed that Deuteronomy, in one form or another, may be traced to the seventh century. Most recently, however, the reliability and motives of the material in 2 Kings which gave rise to this historical-critical lynchpin have been called into question, with the consequence that its relevance to discussions of Deuteronomy's origins and purpose must be heavily discounted.[2] With this in mind the present investigation has endeavoured to proceed, insofar as possible, without

---

1  W.M.L. de Wette, *Beiträge zur Einleitung in das Alte Testament* (2 vols., Hildesheim, Olms, 1806–1807).

2  F. Stavrakopoulou, *King Manasseh and Child Sacrifice: Biblical Distortions of Historical Realities* (BZAW 338, Berlin, de Gruyter, 2004); E. Ben Zvi, 'Prelude to a Reconstruction of Historical Manassic Judah', *BN* 81 (1996), 31–44; E.A. Knauf, 'The Glorious Days of Manasseh', *Good Kings and Bad Kings: The Kingdom of Judah in the Seventh Century B.C.E.* (ed. L.L. Grabbe, LHBOTS 393, London, T&T Clark, 2005), 164–188; R.H. Lowery, *The Reforming Kings: Cults and Society in First Temple Judah* (JSOTSup 210, Sheffield, JSOT, 1991); L.A.S. Monroe, *Josiah's Reform and the Dynamics of Defilement: Israelite Rites of Violence and the Making of a Biblical Text* (Oxford, Oxford University Press, 2011); P.R. Davies, 'Josiah and the Law Book', *Good Kings and Bad Kings: The Kingdom of Judah in the Seventh Century B.C.E.* (ed. L.L. Grabbe, LHBOTS 393, London, T&T Clark, 2005), 65–77.

regard to the 2 Kings account, though this must bear in mind that the assumptions of other secondary literature are not always explicit.

Untethered from 2 Kings, the origins and purpose of a deuteronomic text must seek out other reference points for chronological anchor.[3] The intention in what follows is to attempt a reading of a number of passages in the book against the long seventh century's social, economic and political background, as described in Chapter One, and according to the anthropological possibilities raised by Chapter Two. If such a reading is successful, it will challenge the dating arguments which insist that the book's interest in Israelite identity is a reason to locate either the deuteronomic text as a whole or the parts of the book which deal with identity to the exilic period or later.[4]

---

3   One such reference, widely touted, is the Succession Treaty of Esarhaddon (also known as the Vassal Treaty of Esarhaddon, or VTE). This tradition begins with R. Frankena, 'The Vassal-Treaties of Esarhaddon and the Dating of Deuteronomy', *OTS* 14 (1965), 122–154 and M. Weinfeld, 'Traces of Assyrian Treaty Formulae in Deuteronomy', *Bib* 46 (1965), 417–427 and continues through H.U. Steymans, 'Eine assyrische Vorlage für Deuteronomium 28:20–44', *Bundesdokument und Gesetz: Studien zum Deuteronomium* (ed. G. Braulik, HBS 4, Freiburg, Herder, 1995), 119–141; H.U. Steymans, *Deuteronomium 28 und die Adê zur Thronfolgeregelung Asarhaddons: Segen und Fluch im Alten Orient und in Israel* (OBO 145, Göttingen, Vandenhoeck & Ruprecht, 1995); E. Otto, 'Treueid und Gesetz: Die Ursprünge des Deuteronomiums im Horizont neuassyrischen Vertragsrechts', *ZABR* 2 (1996), 1–52; E. Otto, *Das Deuteronomium: Politische Theologie und Rechtsreform in Juda und Assyrien* (BZAW 284, Berlin, de Gruyter, 1999); B.M. Levinson, 'Textual Criticism, Assyriology, and the History of Interpretation: Deuteronomy 13:7a as a Test Case in Method', *JBL* 120 (2001), 211–243; and B.M. Levinson, 'Esarhaddon's Succession Treaty as the Source for the Canon Formula in Deuteronomy 13:1', *JAOS* 130 (2010), 337–348; its influence is felt also in innumerable commentaries, articles and monographs. I have undertaken an analysis of the relationship between Deuteronomy, VTE and the Assyrian treaty and loyalty oath tradition elsewhere and will not repeat those arguments here; suffice it to observe that the affinities are too inadequate to justify the chronological weight they have been asked to bear. A relationship between VTE and Deuteronomy is too tenuous to use in dating a deuteronomic text to the seventh century.

4   It goes nearly without saying that the book was adopted and adapted by a number of subsequent generations; redactional and editorial fault lines are evident on even a superficial reading of the text, with its repetitive introductions and multiple appendices. Raising the possibility of deuteronomic identity issues as deriving from the long seventh century's social and economic context should not be interpreted as implying either that the entirety of the book or that every instance of its identity concerns must be pre-exilic. Following on from the historical and anthropological argument in Chapters One and Two, the objective is rather to emphasise that the text's interest in Israelite identity cannot, without further analysis and without additional support, be taken as a diagnostic indicator of its origins in the exile or thereafter. The possibility of Israelite identity issues in the pre-exilic period must be recognised and taken into account in the analysis of individual texts.

As noted already, attention to identity concerns in Hebrew Bible texts has usually focussed on the effects of the Babylonian exile and the Persian milieu of the post-exilic period. This orientation has frequently coloured interpretations of Deuteronomy, both with regard to specific texts as well as interpretations of the book's origins more generally. With rare exception, mention of the book's interests in identity occurs in reference to passages considered later additions and reflecting later interests.[5] With a few prominent exceptions, such discussions have also been dominated by the language of nationalism and nationalist identity—especially with discussions of Jewish nationalist identity in the exilic and post-exilic periods—a preference for the language of nationalism which reflects a scholarly conceptualisation of identity issues in terms focused on territory and the political activities of the state.[6] The most

5   Thus H.-J. Fabry, 'Deuteronomium 15: Gedanken zur Geschwister-Ethik im Alten Testament', *ZABR* 3 (1997), 92–111 on Deuteronomy 15; O. Kaiser, 'Von Ortsfremden, Ausländern und Proselyten—Vom Umgang mit den Fremden im Alten Testament', *Gott, Mensch und Geschichte: Studien zum Verständnis des Menschen und seiner Geschichte in der klassischen, biblischen und nachbiblischen Literatur* (BZAW 413, Berlin, de Gruyter, 2010), 41–62 on Deuteronomy 7; N. Levtow, *Images of Others: Iconic Politics in Ancient Israel* (Biblical and Judaic Studies 11, Winona Lake, Ind., Eisenbrauns, 2008), 143–153 on Deuteronomy 4 and 12; A.D.H. Mayes, 'Deuteronomy 14 and the Deuteronomic World View', *Studies in Deuteronomy in Honour of C.J. Labuschagne on the Occasion of his 65th Birthday* (ed. F. García Martínez, A. Hilhorst, J.T.A.G.M. van Ruiten and A.S. van der Woude, VTSup 53, Leiden, Brill, 1994), 165–181 on Deuteronomy 14; note also attribution of the book's 'brother' language to an exilic or late author by, among others, Fabry, 'Deuteronomium 15'; E. Nicholson, *Deuteronomy and the Judaean Diaspora* (Oxford, Oxford University Press, 2014), 52, 134; T. Veijola, *Das 5. Buch Mose: Deuteronomium: Kapitel 1,1–16,17* (ATD 8,1, Göttingen, Vandenhoeck & Ruprecht, 2004). Among commentators see especially Veijola, *Das 5. Buch Mose*, and G. Braulik, *Deuteronomium 1–16,17* (NEchtB 15, Würzburg, Echter, 1986); G. Braulik, *Deuteronomium II: 16,18–34,12* (NEchtB 28, Würzburg, Echter, 1992). E.T. Mullen, Jr, *Narrative History and Ethnic Boundaries: The Deuteronomistic History and the Creation of Israelite National Identity* (SBLSymS, Atlanta, Ga., Scholars, 1993) similarly presupposes that the identity concerns in Deuteronomy derive from an exilic deuteronomistic revision involving the entire Deuteronomistic History as a nationalist project.

6   Discussions of Israelite, Judahite and/or Jewish nationalist identity (the distinctions among which are not always made as clear as they ought to be) include D. Goodblatt, *Elements of Ancient Jewish Nationalism* (Cambridge, Cambridge University Press, 2006); Mullen, Jr, *Narrative History*; S.D.E. Weeks, 'Biblical Literature and the Emergence of Ancient Jewish Nationalism', *BibInt* 10 (2002), 144–157; J.L. Wright, 'The Commemoration of Defeat and the Formation of a Nation in the Hebrew Bible', *Prooftexts* 29 (2009), 433–473; R. Barrett, *Disloyalty and Destruction: Religion and Politics in Deuteronomy and the Modern World* (LHBOTS 511, London, T&T Clark, 2009); S. Grosby, *Biblical Ideas of Nationality: Ancient and Modern* (Winona Lake, Ind., Eisenbrauns, 2002). This situation is complicated by the

recent example of this is Nicholson's *Deuteronomy and the Judean Diaspora*, a revision and development of several earlier articles and essays which, collectively, represent a major departure from the author's *oeuvre* of the preceding half century.[7] Nicholson argues for Deuteronomy's location in the exilic period on the grounds of its acute concern 'to defend and reinforce national identity and community survival against ethnic, cultural, and religious assimilation' and, more specifically, Deuteronomy's articulation of these concerns in terms of the internal threats to Israelite identity—'indigenous outsiders' and 'bad insiders', drawing on Stulman's terminology—and its 'depoliticizing' of the Israelite community, most especially in its circumscription of the role of the king.[8]

Aside from the initial presupposition that Israelite identity issues are to be associated with the exilic period, the first difficulty with Nicholson's line of argument is its conflation of Israelite ethnic identity with Judahite political identity:

> in Deuteronomy Israel is a 'depoliticzsed' [sic] society whose collective identity is expressed socially in terms of 'brotherhood' and defined culturally as 'the people of Yahweh' ... The Israel that had been constituted as a state or two states with appropriate political institutions has been eclipsed, and here replaced by a collective identity and self-awareness that is distinctively different.[9]

---

propensity of discussions of the nature and history of nationalist phenomena to turn to the biblical material as an ancient example; see, for example, A. Hastings, *The Construction of Nationhood: Ethnicity, Religion and Nationalism* (Cambridge, Cambridge University Press, 1997); J. Hutchinson, 'Ethnicity and Modern Nations', *Ethnic and Racial Studies* 23 (2000), 651–670. Grosby, *Biblical Ideas of Nationality* and Goodblatt, *Elements* also form part of this debate.

7   Nicholson, *Deuteronomy and the Judaean Diaspora*; contrast E. Nicholson, *Deuteronomy and Tradition* (Oxford, Basil Blackwell, 1967).

8   Nicholson, *Deuteronomy and the Judaean Diaspora*, 50.

9   Nicholson does spend some time arguing specifically against a pre-exilic context for Deuteronomy's identity issues, primarily in response to Stulman, as well as against a post-exilic context, against Assmann (interspersed throughout Nicholson, *Deuteronomy and the Judaean Diaspora* 41–73). His objections with regard to the former, however, are focused entirely on the association of such concerns with the purported surge in nationalist sentiments under Josiah which—aside from the questionable reliability of such accounts—he finds incompatible with Deuteronomy's ominous tone (Nicholson, *Deuteronomy and the Judaean Diaspora*, 50–53). The only other potential spark for Israelite identity concerns in the pre-exilic period which is entertained in the discussion is Assyrian imperial (political) power, specifically in connection with the law of the king (Nicholson, *Deuteronomy and the*

Nicholson explicitly ties pre-exilic Israelite identity to the political state: as a result, he is compelled to conclude that the non-political identity presented by Deuteronomy must be exilic.

Chapter Two discussed the usefulness of maintaining a distinction between ethnic identity and nationalist identity and, in particular, noted the prominence of the political and state components of the latter. The consequences of failing to differentiate between these phenomena are evident in Nicholson's argumentation, which rests heavily on what Nicholson calls the 'depoliticizing' of Israelite identity and which he relates to the destruction of the Judahite state in the wake of Jerusalem's defeat by the Babylonians. As Nicholson himself observes, however, the 'Israel' with which Deuteronomy is concerned is not a collection of ardent Israelites, battling for political autonomy, but a community which is in contention with itself, over itself.[10] The focus, in other words, is not the protection of an Israelite state against one or more foreign states, but the preservation of an Israelite cultural identity threatened by exposure to and the temptation to adopt practices considered non-Israelite. This is ethnic identity, not nationalist identity: the kind of identity 'most often claimed where groups do not seek 'national' autonomy but rather a recognition internal to or cross-cutting national or state boundaries'.[11] In this context it is essential to emphasise that the deuteronomic entity called 'Israel' is not co-terminous with Judah or its population. To conclude that a lack of focus on political or state phenomena is indicative of the non-existence of a Judahite state is to create a false co-dependence between pre-exilic Israelite identity and Judahite political identity.[12] The so-called 'depoliticizing' of the Israelite community in Deuteronomy is not, in fact, a depoliticization at all: merely a reflection of the ethnic, rather than nationalistic, orientation of its conception of Israelite identity.

---

*Judaean Diaspora*, 107–109, 117–134; to the purpose and referents of this law we will return below). The possibility that the atmosphere of the long seventh century might be perceived more comprehensively as a threat to Israelite identity is not considered.

10    Nicholson, *Deuteronomy and the Judaean Diaspora*, 50–53, 67–73; Nicholson draws especially on the language and concepts of 'encroachment' articulated in L. Stulman, 'Encroachment in Deuteronomy: An Analysis of the Social World of the D Code', *JBL* 109 (1990), 613–632.

11    Calhoun, 'Nationalism and Ethnicity', 211, 235.

12    On whether 'nationalist identity' would be appropriate terminology for an identity focused on the Judahite state see Chapter Two.

As Nicholson's easy conflation suggests, discussions of Israelite identity in the pre-exilic period, when they do occur, almost always do so in connection with supposed nationalist sentiments under Josiah.[13] This paradigm is typified by two of the rare discussions of pre-exilic identity concerns, both of which address Deuteronomy in particular. The first of these is a brief venture by Lohfink, which suggests that the book reflects Judah's 'culture shock' in response to the advent of Assyrian power.[14] Though Lohfink draws on elements of the anthropological material discussed in Chapter Two—he speaks of the challenge to a group's world view posed by the presentation of an alternative— he is bound by the assumption that the alternative involved was Assyrian and therefore a fundamentally political, territorial and state-orientated phenomenon.[15] As became clear from the archaeological record discussed in Chapter One, however, the effects of Assyrian domination sometimes appeared in the form of actual Assyrians but, more often, the diversity of cultural contact during the long seventh century was manifest in the form of Judah's fellow inhabitants of the southern Levant. Similarly, although Stulman is one of the few to draw attention to the possibility of identity phenomena in the pre-exilic period, he operates within a paradigm which assumes that such phenomena occur in direct response to Assyria.[16] Aware of the text's internal focus, his assumption of a distant, Assyrian menace and articulation of the book's identity issues in terms of a state-based nationalist identity project oblige him to conclude that the book 'appears to lack internal coherence and clarity'.[17]

There has been some use of ethnic identity language in discussions of Deuteronomy, with Sparks' *Ethnicity and Identity in Ancient Israel* probably the most well-known.[18] Subtitled *Prolegomena*, Sparks' object is to provide a broad survey of 'ethnic sentiment' across the eighth, seventh and sixth century literature of Judah and Israel. In so doing he naturally spends substantial time with Deuteronomy. However, despite the apparent focus on expressions of 'ethnic' identity, Sparks' propensity to refer to Yhwh as a 'national deity' and

---

13    Note that Nicholson's argument against a pre-exilic date is focused exclusively on this context (Nicholson, *Deuteronomy and the Judaean Diaspora*, 50–53).

14    N. Lohfink, 'Culture Shock and Theology', *BTB* 7 (1977), 12–22.

15    Lohfink, 'Culture Shock', 18: 'Would not the crisis which Deuteronomy encounters be really that culture shock in which Judah of necessity must have fallen when it came under an Assyrian sovereignty?'

16    Stulman, 'Encroachment in Deuteronomy', 613–632.

17    Stulman, 'Encroachment', 615.

18    K.L. Sparks, *Ethnicity and Identity in Ancient Israel: Prolegomena to the Study of Ethnic Sentiments and Their Expression in the Hebrew Bible* (Winona Lake, Ind., Eisenbrauns, 1998).

to the book as the agenda of 'national reformers' and a programme of 'national renewal' belies a persistently nationalist orientation.[19] In addition, Sparks restricts his definition of ethnic identity to perception of common ancestry ('ethnic kinship'); other aspects of ethnic identity are relegated to the category of 'other modes of identity'.[20] In keeping with this definition, Sparks' discussion of Deuteronomy begins with and is dominated by concepts of genealogical relationship, particularly its references to the ancestors and the use of brother language.[21] He concludes that there is 'nothing exceptionally "powerful" about the [other modes of identity] outlined by Deuteronomy, especially in regard to the "ethnic" aspect of Israelite identity'.[22] From the more complex anthropological perspective on ethnic identity discussed in Chapter Two, such a statement is startling. Although common to most expressions of ethnic identity, the perception of shared genetic history constitutes only one manifestation of ethnic identity among many: ethnic identity is difficult to pin down, precisely because of the range of practices which may function as ethnic identity markers. As the following will demonstrate, there are many elements to Israelite ethnic identity beyond the perception of simple genealogical descent.

Perhaps inevitably, this lack of attention to the wider possibilities of ethnic phenomena leads Sparks to the conclusion that 'the primary purpose of these ethnic expressions in Deuteronomy was to exploit the natural sentiment of kinship as a motivation factor in the effort to promote the Deuteronomic idea of mono-Yahwistic fidelity' ... 'Even in its most ethnic guise—"kill the Canaanites"—Deuteronomic identity was concerned primarily with religious identity rather than ethnic purity'.[23] This assertion is repeated frequently and in various forms, always contending that Deuteronomy's real interest is in

---

19    Sparks, *Ethnicity and Identity*, 260–261, 264, 267 and elsewhere; compare, among many others, Stulman, 'Encroachment'; Lowery, *The Reforming Kings*; Barrett, *Disloyalty and Destruction*. Like Stulman and Lohfink, he also operates within an Assyrian paradigm.

20    Sparks, *Ethnicity and Identity*, 4, 13. In the latter category he mentions language, culinary legislation, a centralised cult and Sabbath worship as possible positive markers for identity and abstention from the worship of foreign deities, divination and death cult rituals as negative markers (Sparks, *Ethnicity and Identity*, 265–267).

21    Sparks, *Ethnicity and Identity*, 226–228, 230–231, 236–238, 245–249, 263–267.

22    He is right, however, to pick up on the fact that, prior to the deuteronomic project, 'there is probably little about these prohibited practices that was essentially "non-Israelite"' (Sparks, *Ethnicity and Identity*, 267). As has already been suggested in the Introduction and will be discussed in more detail in what follows, the deuteronomic project is significantly constructive in its intent, homogenising Israelite practice in the creation of an idealised Israel.

23    Sparks, *Ethnicity and Identity*, 227, 234.

religious purity rather than in ethnic identity.[24] Unfortunately, by limiting Israelite ethnic identity to expressions of genealogical cohesion and then prioritising Deuteronomy's attention to overtly religious practices, Sparks fails to recognise the function of religion itself as an expression of ethnic identity.

The focus of attention in the following is the deuteronomic core—roughly defined as the legal material in Deuteronomy 12–26, its hortatory introduction in Deuteronomy 6–11 and its warning conclusion in Deuteronomy 28—as these are the chapters whose pre- or post-exilic origins are most at stake in discussions of the book's identity issues; most of the rest of the book is either recognised as deuteronomistic or later or as earlier material which has been appended to a deuteronomic core.[25] In these chapters the text addresses itself to matters of Israelite ethnic identity, working both to define what it is to be Israelite as well as to defend that identity once established. As discussed in Chapter Two, the exact mechanisms by which a group will seek to construct and then to perpetuate its identity are myriad and will vary from group to group (hence the notorious difficulty of producing a universally applicable definition of such groups). It is therefore unsurprising to see the deuteronomic interest in Israelite identity take a variety of forms, ranging from the legislation of specifically Israelite practices and the prohibition of non-Israelite practices to efforts to isolate Israelites from the potentially corrupting influence of non-Israelites. Religion as a key element in the formation of ethnic identity is evident in the predominance of ritual in many of the individual expressions of Israelite identity, and the first part of this chapter is especially devoted to these phenomena. Ritual identity is especially associated with centralised or centralising society and in this regard it is notable the degree to which the deuteronomic identity formation project is intertwined with a centralising ritual and cultural agenda—scholarly focus on which has tended to dominate the discussion of deuteronomic interests to the exclusion of all else.[26] As Cohen

---

24    Sparks, *Ethnicity and Identity*, 260, 263, 264, 267.

25    For the sake of space and efficacy, redactional issues relating to deuteronomistic and post-deuteronomistic editorial activity in the midst of this deuteronomic core will be dealt with as they arise and only as necessary.

26    Given the nature of the book and its preservation among the sacred texts of a religious community it is unsurprising that most commentators have focused on the theological implications of the deuteronomic presentation of Yhwh as Israel's sole deity and the imperative to worship Yhwh at a single cult site. Though the identification of Yhwh as the sole acceptable object of Israelite worship is a vital aspect of the book's theology and purpose, it should not be mistaken for an abstract theological project: it constitutes a significant part of the identity-formation project in progress in the deuteronomic material. Cultic practice is a major component of Israel's cultural identity, with worship and ritual forms providing a prominent venue in which practices peculiar to Israelites may be regu-

emphasised, however, ritual and kinship identity phenomena are far from mutually exclusive and—especially given the centralising, rather than centralised, nature of the Israelite society depicted in this material—it is not surprising to also observe a significant kinship component to the deuteronomic identity project, this being perhaps the most commonly recognised identity component of the book.[27] It is to this type of phenomenon to which the latter part of the chapter turns.

Subsumed within both of these categories of identity ideologies occur a wide range of more specific identity-formation mechanisms. In many of these instances the identity formation and identity protection mechanisms described by Cohen are recognisable: references to unique myths of origins and claims to superiority; emphasis on genetic cohesiveness as well as spatial proximity among members; discouragement of interactions with outsiders, including placing a high value on endogamy; the development of an endoculture and the use of worship practices to facilitate this; and the elimination of sub-cultures. These include efforts to homogenise Israelite culture, recognisable especially in light of recent archaeological discoveries regarding the actual diversity of practice in Judah, including the widespread worship of multiple, non-Yahwistic deities; the discouragement of social interaction with non-Israelites and the concomitant development and reinforcement of an Israelite mono-culture, such as in the emphasis on endogamous marriage and the isolation of the king from his non-Israelite analogues; an emphasis on genetic cohesiveness, manifest concretely in the aforementioned prioritisation of endogamy as well as abstractly in the use of familial language; references to a uniquely Israelite myth of the community's origins in Egypt, shot through with a sense of superiority predicated on Yhwh's preference for Israel; and, last but not least, efforts to establish spatial proximity among members of the group—manifest, interestingly, in the deuteronomic material less in its emphasis on the importance of the land as a whole to Israelite identity (an emphasis which comes to the fore in the deuteronomistic material) and more in its efforts to force the Israelites themselves to converge towards a single space: the single, centralised cult site.

---

larly displayed. The worship of Yhwh as a specifically Israelite deity and the rejection of all other deities as non-Israelite is the centrepiece of a group of imperatives designed to distinguish the cultic features of Israelite cultural practice.

27    Thus, for example, Sparks, *Ethnicity and Identity*, 225–267, L. Perlitt, '"Ein einzig Volk von Brüdern": Zur deuteronomischen Herkunft der biblischen Bezeichnung "Bruder"', *Deuteronomium-Studien* (FAT 8, Tübingen, Mohr, 1994), 50–73; Braulik, *Deuteronomium 1–16,17*; Braulik, *Deuteronomium II*.

The following observations are likely only a portion of the deuteronomic laws and exhortations concerned with Israelite ethnic identity. As already observed, the recognition of the relevant ethnic identity markers of any given culture can be difficult even in contemporary anthropological research; this is only exacerbated by a distance of two and a half millennia. Many of the practices highlighted here are those which the text is more or less explicit in marking as matters of Israelite identity, or regarding which the discoveries of archaeologists and ancient Near Eastern scholars happen to be available to inform the interpretation of the deuteronomic text. Inevitably this can be only a partial image; there is no way of knowing what other practices may eventually come to illuminate the deuteronomic concerns, nor those which will continue to evade our awareness in consequence of our own ignorance. It may even be the case that future discoveries demand that one or more of the following interpretations be abandoned. The plurality of the evidence for deuteronomic identity issues and the representation of these concerns through nearly every chapter of the core, however, suggests that, future nuancing and individual disagreements regarding specific texts aside, the significance of these concerns for understanding the overall purpose and the origins of this core should not be underestimated.

Finally, before embarking on this reading of the deuteronomic material in the long seventh century, it should be clarified that this is not a grandiose claim to have identified the single governing and exclusive interest of the deuteronomic text. Israelite identity is by no means the only matter to which the deuteronomic text attends; indeed, on one or two occasions there will be reason to observe that identity concerns have been subordinated to other deuteronomic interests. It is, however, a deeply determining element of the deuteronomic outlook and one which has been both underestimated and undertheorised. In what follows the intent is to make a case that various of the major (centralisation, monolatry) and minor (cult offerings, slavery) elements of the deuteronomic text—some of which have proved otherwise baffling—may be read as reflecting a concern for the definition and protection of Israelite identity, arising out of the social, economic and political circumstances of the long seventh century.


## 2      Defining Israel: Praxis, Proximity and Origins

Analysis begins with the passages in which the deuteronomic legislation is designed to define a distinctively Israelite cultural practice, differentiating it from that of non-Israelites. As already noted, many of the features of Israelite identity formation are ritually-oriented, focused on the peculiarities of Israelite cultic praxis in particular. As discussed in Chapter Two, religion often plays a significant role in the articulation and reinforcement of a group's identity. In 'the creation and strengthening and utilization of different kinds of myths, beliefs, norms, values, and motives', religion can serve as an umbrella system for mythology and belief, most obviously, but—as is especially evident in the legal formulation of much of the deuteronomic material—it can also be employed to articulate and reinforce group norms, values and motives.[28] Israelites behave in certain defined ways because these are the norms of Israelite behaviour laid down by the Israelite god, Yhwh; they are inherently valued as deriving from the divine will and adherence to these norms is motivated by a belief in their divine origins. In the case of Israel's exclusive relationship with Yhwh, religion has a further identity function insofar as this exclusive Yahwism acts to isolate Israelites from non-Israelites, both practically—Israelite identity revolving heavily around Yahwistic practices in which Israelites come into contact with other Israelites while avoiding the non-Yahwistic practices of non-Yahwists and, concomitantly, non-Israelites—as well as ideologically, providing an unequivocal point of difference between Israelites and non-Israelites.

Other practices are more broadly cultural in nature, although, as will become evident in what follows, the separation between these categories is far from absolute, reflecting the general permeation of religion and cult into all aspects of life and practice and acting as a reminder that such a division should not be pursued with too much stringency. Many of the imperatives and exhortations which follow are focused on the homogenisation of Israelite practice; others are designed to establish spatial proximity among Israelites or emphasise the Israelites' shared history.

### 2.1    *Homogenising Israelite Ritual: Exclusive Yahwism*
'Israel' is a Yahwistic community. This fact is perhaps the single most distinctive feature of Israelite culture and Israelite identity as defined by the deuteronomic project. Israel is distinguished from all other identity groups by virtue of its identification with Yhwh. Israel is further distinguished by its exclusive worship of Yhwh: unlike non-Israelites, who may have a chief deity but nonetheless worship multiple deities, Israel worships only one deity, Yhwh. Israel is thus distinguished not only by the identity of and its association with its

---

28    A. Cohen, *Custom and Politics in Urban Africa: A Study of Hausa Migrants in Yoruba Towns* (London, Routledge, 1969), 208.

particular deity but also by the way in which it acts in relation to that deity, forsaking all others and becoming characterised by its highly unusual, mono-latrous worship practice.

Israel's peculiar worship of Yhwh is the focus of the opening exhortative Shema as well as multiple legislative passages. The Shema's function is horta-tory, a rhetorical call to Israelites to acknowledge the fundamentally Yahwistic character of their existence as Israelites; Deut. 13:2–19; 16:21–22; and 17:2–7 reinforce this from a legal perspective, alongside the numerous references in other laws to Yhwh as 'your god' (אלהיך). These passages converge to effect a homogenisation of Israelite religious culture.[29] As is now generally recognised, actual religious practice and belief in pre-exilic Judah was diverse and far from exclusively Yahwistic.[30] The recurring emphasis in the deuteronomic text on the Israelites' sole worship of Yhwh represents a rejection of this diversity in favour of the worship of a single deity at a single cult site.

### Exhortation

Israel's Yahwistic peculiarity is a point of emphasis already from opening of the deuteronomic text, the Shema ('Hear, O Israel...') in Deut. 6:4.

> The first four chapters of Deuteronomy are all but universally agreed to be secondary (or tertiary, or beyond) (re-)introductions to the book's deuteronomic material. The status of Deuteronomy 5 is disputed; the view taken here is that it is a (re-)introduction added on analogy to a sim-ilar use of the Decalogue prior to the Covenant Code. Between Deut. 6:1 and 12:1 matters become more complex and there is little agreement. The text here identified as deuteronomic includes Deut. 6:4–13 (excluding the expansion of אבתיך in 6:10 with לאברהם ליצחק וליעקב); Deut. 7:1–4a? (per-haps excluding the list of seven nations but not certainly); Deut. 8:6–11a, 12–14, 17–18a; 10:12, 20. The excision of non-deuteronomic material is on the following grounds. Deuteronomy 6:1–3 is a new introduction after the addition of the Decalogue in Deuteronomy 5. Deuteronomy 6:14–19 contains erratic shifts between plural and singular address, raising suspicions compounded by the pre-emptive declaration against other gods, evidently a reflection of the exilic experience of destruction (and

---

29    See Cohen, *Custom and Politics*, 204.

30    See, recently, the essays in F. Stavrakopoulou and J. Barton, eds., *Religious Diversity in Ancient Israel and Judah* (London, T&T Clark, 2010).

probably contextually prompted by the emphatic Deut. 6:13). This and a number of other passages use deuteronomistic phrases and ideas: 'signs and portents' (Deut. 6:22; 7:19) and 'a mighty hand (and outstretched arm)' (Deut. 6:21; 7:8, 19; 11:2) about events in Egypt and 'what is right (and what is good) in the eyes of YHWH', as well as depicting the possession of the land as conditional on obedience to the law, an exilic and deuteronomistic perspective (Deut. 6:20–25; 7:12–16; 8:1–5; 8:11b; 10:13; 10:22–11:15; 11:16–32). Deuteronomy 7:6 uses language familiar from Deut. 14:2 and there deemed at least secondary to the original deuteronomic material.[31] Deuteronomy 7:4b–16, like several of these passages, is erratic in its choice of address and Deut. 7:4b–5 reflects the wisdom of exilic hindsight, like Deut. 6:14–17 and 8:19. Deuteronomy 7:9–10 and 10:14–17 use late, universalistic language in their descriptions of YHWH. Deuteronomy 7:17–24 and 9:1–3 are both tangents reassuring the audience of their success in conquest, the former appealing to the Egypt tradition and characterised by deuteronomistic language; Deut. 7:22 is an even later explanation of the failure to completely eliminate all non-Israelites from the land. The language of תועבה and חרם in Deut. 7:25–26 seem deuteronomic until the application of these terms to objects of worship instead of worship practices is noted. Similarly unusual use of deuteronomic material occurs in Deut. 10:18–19, which picks up on the deuteronomic interest in the גר to declare that YHWH loves the גר and therefore the Israelites ought to love the גר also (note that here and Deut. 23:8 are the only places in Deuteronomy where the Israelites' status as גרים in Egypt are used to motivate a commandment). Deuteronomy 8:1–5 reflects the deuteronomistic, conditional interpretation of the promise of the land; the passage is also another instance of recycled deuteronomic material, namely the positive use of the phrase 'which you did not know and your ancestors did not know' (אשר לא ידעת ולא ידעון אבתיך), which contrasts with the use of similar phrases in a negative sense elsewhere (Deut. 13:3, 7, 14; also 11:28). Deuteronomy 8:15–16 depends on 8:1–5; Deut. 8:18b–20 is peppered with language typical of late additions; and Deut. 9:7–10:11 is a long deuteronomistic riff on the subject of 'you are a people stiff of neck' (כי עם קשה ערף; Deut. 9:6) which already presupposes the covenant-making in Deuteronomy 5, while Deut. 10:22–11:15 is an elaboration of

---

31 E. Nielsen, *Deuteronomium* (HAT I/6, Tübingen, Mohr Siebeck, 1995), 97, who retains it, nonetheless admits that it is not really typical deuteronomic, or even deuteronomistic, language.

'these great and fearful things which your eyes saw' (את נגדלת ואת הנוראת
האלה אשר ראו עיניך; Deut. 10:21) and reflects a particular interest in the
present generation (Deut. 11:2, 8); note the related disinterest in identifying the patriarchal triumvirate as the audience's ancestors in Deut. 9:27.
Deuteronomy 11:18–20 is a poor citation of Deut. 6:4–9, culminating a
deuteronomistic conditional on the promise of the land to the ancestors
(Deut. 11:21, 22–25).[32]

This credo 'serves to create an identity for this people ... a confession is made
by them that will serve to shape their identity and their way in the world'.[33]
Israelites are fundamentally and ultimately Yahwistic: an Israelite who is not
Yahwistic is not an Israelite. Not only this, however, but Israelites are exclusively Yahwistic: an Israelite who worships another god alongside or in addition to YHWH is also not an Israelite. These two essential elements of Israelite
Yahwism are articulated in the two halves of Deut. 6:4. The first half, 'Hear,
O Israel, YHWH is our god' (שמע ישראל יהוה אלהינו), establishes that Israel
is defined as a people which recognises YHWH as its deity. The second half,
'YHWH alone' (יהוה אחד), establishes that it is only YHWH whom the Israelites
recognise in this way.

Because of the centrality of this text in both Deuteronomy and in later
Judaism, its location at the opening of the deuteronomic material and the
level of interest its syntax and meaning has elicited, it is worth taking a brief
moment to examine it more closely. The Hebrew is terse; while no individual
word is unclear, the absence of verbs makes several renderings grammatically
possible. Translated word for word, it reads: 'Hear Israel YHWH our god YHWH
one' (שמע ישראל יהוה אלהינו יהוה אחד). Depending on the placement of the
understood verb(s) and the division of words into clauses, this has been variably understood to mean any or all of the following: 'YHWH is our god; YHWH

---

32    For more detailed discussions of redactional matters see variously M. Weinfeld,
      *Deuteronomy 1–11: A New Translation with Introduction and Commentary* (AB 5, London,
      Doubleday, 1991); Braulik, *Deuteronomium 1–16,17*; Nielsen, *Deuteronomium*; A.D.H. Mayes,
      *Deuteronomy* (NCB, London, Marshall, Morgan & Scott, 1981); Veijola, *Das 5. Buch Mose*;
      R.D. Nelson, *Deuteronomy* (OTL, London, Westminster John Knox, 2004); M. Weinfeld,
      *Deuteronomy and the Deuteronomic School* (Oxford, Clarendon, 1972); G. von Rad,
      *Deuteronomy* (transl. D. Barton, OTL, London, SCM, 1966).

33    P.D. Miller, *Deuteronomy* (IBC, Louisville, Ky., John Knox, 1990), 98.

is one';[34] 'Yhwh is our god, Yhwh alone';[35] 'Yhwh our god is one Yhwh';[36] and 'Yhwh our god, Yhwh is one'.[37]

The first uncertainty concerns the first half of the statement, יהוה אלהינו. Is this a statement in and of itself ('Yhwh is our god') or are these in apposition, anticipating the rest of the sentence ('Yhwh our god ...')? Elsewhere in the book יהוה and אלהים with a suffix do not appear as subject and predicate but in apposition, a tendency which might support a rendering beginning with 'Yhwh our god ...'.[38] However, the location of this statement at the beginning of the text weakens the strength of a strictly grammatical comparison, as every subsequent reference to יהוה אלהינו\אלהיך\אלהיכם effectively constitutes a short-hand recollection of the entire statement here. The point emphasised by both this original statement and its subsequent iterations, however, is clear: Yhwh is Israel's god. This forms the foundation for all subsequent exhortation (You will do this because Yhwh commands it and Yhwh is your god).

That only Yhwh is Israel's god (and the corollary, that the audience does this thing which Yhwh commands and not that thing which some other deity might command because only Yhwh is Israel's god and no other gods may claim this status) is rendered explicit by the second part of the verse: יהוה אחד. אחד is multivalent and in English may be rendered as 'one', emphasising the singularity of the deity, or as 'alone', emphasising the exclusivity of Israel's relationship with the deity.[39] It is likely that most, if not all, of the various nuances picked up by different renderings of the verse are intended by the statement: that Yhwh is Israel's god, that Yhwh alone is Israel's god, and that Yhwh is a single divine entity. All of these express and contribute to the deuteronomic

---

34    J.G. Janzen, 'On the Most Important Word in the Shema (Deuteronomy VI 4–5)', VT 37 (1987), 280–300; Veijola, *Das 5. Buch Mose*, 174.

35    J.H. Tigay, *Deuteronomy* (JPS Torah Commentary, Philadelphia, Pa., JPS, 1996), 76; D.L. Christensen, *Deuteronomy 1:1–21:9, revised* (2nd edn., WBC 6A, Nashville, Tenn., Thomas Nelson, 2001), 141; Mayes, *Deuteronomy*, 176; Nelson, *Deuteronomy*, 86.

36    Weinfeld, *Deuteronomy 1–11*, 337; von Rad, *Deuteronomy*, 62; S.R. Driver, *Deuteronomy* (ICC, Edinburgh, Charles Scribner, 1895), 89.

37    Braulik, *Deuteronomium 1–16,17*, 55; Nielsen, *Deuteronomium*, 84; R.W.L. Moberly, '"Yahweh is One": The Translation of the Shema', *Studies in the Pentateuch* (ed. J.A. Emerton, VTSup 41, Leiden, Brill, 1990), 209–215; L.-J. Bord and D. Hamidović, 'Écoute Israël (Deut. vi 4)', VT 52 (2002), 13–29. Of those translating with 'one', the sense is usually related to number; Bord and Hamidović, however, understand it as meaning unique.

38    Nelson, *Deuteronomy*, 90; Nielsen, *Deuteronomium*, 86; Weinfeld, *Deuteronomy 1–11*, 337; Moberly, '"Yahweh is One"', 213–214; Bord and Hamidović, 'Écoute Israël', 19.

39    HALOT 1, *s.v.* אחד.

agenda, emphasising that Yʜwʜ and only Yʜwʜ has claim to be Israel's deity, that only Yʜwʜ ought therefore to be worshipped and that Yʜwʜ's unified nature implies a unified system of worship.[40] It might also be suggested that the singularity of Yʜwʜ parallels and anticipates the singularity of Israel itself.

Ultimately and despite its grammatical and interpretational multivalency, the meaning of this verse for the identity of Israel is straightforward: it articulates a vision of Israel characterised by an exclusive relationship between Israel and Yʜwʜ and identifies that exclusivity as the most fundamental feature of Israel's existence. This, above all else, defines Israel: 'You will love Yʜwʜ your god with all your heart and with all your soul and with all your might' (ואהבת את יהוה אלהיך בכל לבבך ובכל נפשך ובכל מאדך, Deut. 6:5).[41]

### Legislation

The enactment of this characterisation of Israel as specifically Yahwistic is the focus of Deut. 13:2–19; the point is developed elsewhere especially in Deut. 17:2–7 and 16:21–22 as well as reiterated in the numerous references to Yʜwʜ as 'your god' (אלהיך).

Deuteronomy 13:2–19 highlights the importance of exclusive Yahwism to Israel's identity by presenting three exemplary challenges to Israel's distinctively and exclusively Yahwistic character and their extreme consequences: exhortations to worship other gods pronounced, in turn, by the diviner (Deut. 13:2–6), the family member (Deut. 13:7–12) and the inhabitants of a particular city (Deut. 13:13–19). In each case an individual or group pursues the worship of deities other than Yʜwʜ and encourages members of the Israelite community to do the same. The incompatibility of the worship of other deities with

---

40    Compare the argument of W. Herrmann, 'Jahwe und des Menschen Liebe zu Ihm: Zu Dtn. vi 5', *VT* 50 (2000), 47–54, that the singularity and undivided nature of Yʜwʜ demands the singular and undivided loyalty of the Israelites; similarly, for the suggestion that the statement יהוה אחד is meant to convey the fidelity of Yʜwʜ, on which the fidelity of the Israelites to Yʜwʜ is predicated see Janzen, 'On the Most Important Word', though he curiously downplays the polyvalency of meaning implied by his argument.

41    Note the use in Deut. 6:5 of love language, which emphasises this exclusivity and reiterates the notion of Israel's absolute loyalty to Yʜwʜ alone (see discussions in W.L. Moran, 'The Ancient Near Eastern Background of the Love of God in Deuteronomy', *CBQ* 25 [1963], 77–87; D.J. McCarthy, 'Notes on the Love of God in Deuteronomy and the Father-Son Relationship between Yahweh and Israel', *CBQ* 27 [1965], 144–147; S. Ackerman, 'The Personal is Political: Covenantal and Affectionate Love (*'āhēb, 'ahăbâ*) in the Hebrew Bible', *VT* 52 [2002], 437–458; B.T. Arnold, 'The Love-Fear Antinomy in Deuteronomy 5–11', *VT* 61 [2011], 551–569), as does the threefold repetition of כל לבבך—כל נפשך—כל מאדך :בכל. On the unity of Deut. 6:4 and 6:5 see Herrmann, 'Jahwe und des Menschen Liebe zu Ihm', 50–54, with further references.

membership in an Israelite community defined as fundamentally and exclusively Yahwistic, however, means that these individuals or groups are no longer Israelite and, in connection with the challenge which their non-Israelite practices pose to a Yahwistic Israel, must be removed from the community (cf. Deut. 20:10–16).[42]

In light of the discussions in Chapter Two it is especially worth emphasising that each of these cases deals with persons problematic to Israelite identity precisely because they are otherwise extremely similar to Israelites. These persons are 'in your midst' (בקרבך): persons who, according to other criteria, are part of the Israelite community. The conflict arises not because they are wholly alien to the Israelites addressed by the deuteronomic text but because their similarity to those addressees makes them the most acute challenge to the deuteronomic conception of Israel: the challenge is 'not so much because they have irreconcilably different identities, but rather because they have irreconcilable claims or aspirations to the *same* identities'.[43] These worshippers of other gods probably consider themselves Israelite. The non-Yahwistic Israelite identity which they enact, however, is incompatible with the exclusively Yahwistic Israelite identity articulated by the deuteronomic identity project.

In connection with this point, it is worth highlighting that Israelite identity is not solely ascribed—that is, accorded by virtue of birth or other event beyond the individual's control—but rather contains a strong element of achieved identity—that is, identity which is gained by virtue of deliberate action or inaction on the part of the individual.[44] The focus on the book's

---

42    Observing the connection of violence to identity formation, Reeder describes this as 'constructive violence', that is, 'violence that intends good' (C.A. Reeder, *The Enemy in the Household: Family Violence in Deuteronomy and Beyond* [Grand Rapids, Mich., Baker, 2012], 8).

43    S. Harrison, 'Identity as a Scarce Resource', *Social Anthropology* 7 (1999), 239; note also F. Barth, 'Introduction', *Ethnic Groups and Boundaries: The Social Organization of Cultural Difference* (ed. F. Barth, London, George Allen & Unwin, 1969), 16.

44    For a discussion of ascribed and achieved identity in the modern American Muslim context see L. Peek, 'Becoming Muslim: The Development of a Religious Identity', *Sociology of Religion* 66 (2005), 215–242; more briefly and more generally, M. Banks, *Ethnicity: Anthropological Constructions* (London, Routledge, 1996), 117. On religious identity as achieved identity see P.E. Hammond, 'Religion and the Persistence of Identity', *Journal for the Scientific Study of Religion* 27 (1988), 1–11; R.S. Warner, 'Work in Progress Toward a New Paradigm for the Sociological Study of Religion in the United States', *American Journal of Sociology* 98 (1993), 1044–1093. Ascribed and achieved identities are rarely absolute, nor are they mutually incompatible: 'Ethnic identities are neither ascribed nor achieved: they are both' (T.H. Eriksen, *Ethnicity and Nationalism: Anthropological Perspectives* [Anthropology, Culture and Society 1, London, Pluto, 1993], 57).

use of kinship language has focused most attention on ascriptive elements of Israelite identity, but there are several passages in the deuteronomic material, including this one, which indicate that deuteronomic Israelite identity is not entirely of that type. To the contrary, a person whose ascriptive qualities, namely birth into the Israelite community, pre-dispose him (or her) to identification as Israelite is able to effectively renounce that identity by acting in such a way as to achieve non-Israelite status, especially by failing to enact the primary feature of Israelite identity, namely, exclusive Yahwistic worship.[45] An Israelite, in other words, can cease to be an Israelite if he or she fails to act like an Israelite.[46]

The first exemplar of an Israelite whose ascriptive status has been lost and who now threatens to lead (other) Israelites into achieving non-Israelite status is the diviner: 'a prophet or a dreamer of a dream' (נביא או חלם חלום), who invites the addressee to 'go after other gods' (נלכה אחרי אלהים אחרים).[47]

---

45  Cf. Reeder, *The Enemy*, 23: 'The foundation of Israelite identity is devotion to Yahweh alone... within this construction of identity, idolaters, be they Canaanites or errant descendants of Abraham, are automatically identified as outsiders simply because they do not fear Israel's God.' This dual characterisation of Israelite identity as both achieved and ascribed has also been noted by D.A. Nestor, *Cognitive Perspectives on Israelite Identity* [LHBOTS 519, London, T&T Clark, 2010], 200–201.

46  Conversely, the deuteronomic material also conceives of the possibility of an ascribed non-Israelite achieving Israelite status; see 3.2.4. Exceptions on the war captive and the Edomite.

47  On dreams as a form of divination see A. Jeffers, *Magic and Divination in Ancient Palestine and Syria* (SHANE 8, Leiden, Brill, 1996), 125–139. The prophet is the divinatory specialist identified by Deut. 18:9–22 as the acceptable Yahwistic method of communication with the divine (see 2.4.1. Divination); the dreamer is not mentioned as either forbidden or favoured. It is unclear whether the mention of the latter is meant to indicate that both the ostensibly Yahwistic diviner (the prophet) as well as an unsanctioned and non-Yahwistic diviner (the dreamer) are potential sources of non-Yahwistic, non-Israelite activities, or if it is meant to refer to two types of permissible divination whose Yahwistic authenticity nonetheless cannot be taken for granted. On the dreamer of Deut. 13:4 as a diviner deriving from an extra-biblical source, perhaps implying that an overtly non-Israelite diviner is intended; see J. Pakkala, 'Der literar- und religionsgeschichtliche Ort von Deuteronomium 13', *Die deuteronomistischen Geschichtswerke: redaktions- und religionsgeschichtliche Perspektiven zur 'Deuteronomismus'-Diskussion in Tora und Vorderen Propheten* (ed. M. Witte, K. Schmid, D. Prechel and J.C. Gertz, BZAW 365, Berlin, de Gruyter, 2006), 125–137, with further references. On the statement—apparently quoted—that these are gods whom the addressee does not know see variously A. Bartor, *Reading Law as Narrative: A Study in the Casuistic Laws of the Pentateuch* (Ancient Israel and Its Literature 5, Atlanta, Ga., Society of Biblical Literature, 2010), 129–131; J. Stackert, 'The Syntax of Deuteronomy 13:2–3 and the Conventions of Ancient Near Eastern Prophecy', *JANER* 10 (2010), 159–175;

The offence to which the diviners tempt the addressee is the worship of deities other than Yʜᴡʜ: a practice which will serve to sever the characteristically (deuteronomic) Israelite connection with Yʜᴡʜ alone.[48] 'Die Apostasie in "deiner Mitte" (6.12.15 17⁷) zerstört das, was Israel zu Israel macht.'[49] The deuteronomic Israelite community is defined by the worship of Yʜᴡʜ: the pursuit of worship of gods other than Yʜᴡʜ renders a person effectively non-Israelite. If left unchecked, this threatens to eradicate the Israelite character of the entire Israelite community. The presence of non-Yahwistic worship activities in the midst of the community is thus a challenge and a threat to its existence and must be eliminated absolutely and without delay. The emphasis throughout these cases is that the threat is 'in your midst' and must be eradicated 'from your midst' (Deut. 13:2, 6, 12, 14, 15): note again that the threat to Israel's identity as a Yahwistic community is from inside the community.[50]

---

J. Stackert, 'Mosaic Prophecy and the Deuteronomic Source of the Torah', *Deuteronomy in the Pentateuch, Hexateuch, and the Deuteronomistic History* (ed. R.F. Person, Jr. and K. Schmid, ꜰᴀᴛ II 56, Tübingen, Mohr Siebeck, 2012), 47–63, 56–57. The latter also discusses the apparently odd syntactical structure of Deut. 13:2–3.

48   Stackert, 'Mosaic Prophecy', 54: 'Verse 4 reveals the imagined scenario as a test, and it is one that leads the literary and practical aspects to its desired end, an end restated with emphatic syntax in v. 5: "After *YHWH YOUR God* shall you walk, and *him* you shall fear; *his commands* shall you keep, and *him* shall you obey; *him* shall you serve, and *to him* shall you cling."' This point is, in light of the considered similarities between Deuteronomy 13 and ᴠᴛᴇ, often articulated in terms of loyalty to Yʜᴡʜ (M. Nissinen, 'The Dubious Image of Prophecy', *Prophets, Prophecy and Prophetic Texts in Second Temple Judaism* [ed. M.H. Floyd and R.D. Haak, ʟʜʙᴏᴛs 427, London, T&T Clark, 2006], 30; Otto, *Das Deuteronomium*; T.C. Römer, *The So-Called Deuteronomistic History: A Sociological, Historical and Literary Introduction* [London, T&T Clark, 2007], 76; Barrett, *Disloyalty and Destruction*; B.M. Levinson, '"But You Shall Surely Kill Him!": The Text-Critical and Neo-Assyrian Evidence for MT Deuteronomy 13:10', *Bundesdokument und Gesetz: Studien zum Deuteronomium* [ed. G. Braulik, ʜʙs 4, Freiburg, Herder, 1995] 37–63).

49   Braulik, *Deuteronomium 1–16,17*, 103.

50   See C.L. Crouch, 'The Threat to Israel's Identity in Deuteronomy: Mesopotamian or Levantine?', *ᴢᴀᴡ* 124 (2012), 541–554. Using the language of 'encroachment', Stulman also draws attention to the internal orientation of the deuteronomic text: 'the most profound threat to Israel's survival', he observes, 'is posed not by enemies who live far away but by "indigenous outsiders" (i.e., bad insiders) who coinhabit the land' (Stulman, 'Encroachment', 615, cf. 626). 'You will burn the evil from your midst' appears several other times in Deuteronomy (Deut. 17:7, 12; 19:19; 21:21; 22:21, 22, 24; 24:7). In all cases except Deut. 19:19, it follows punishment by death, indicating its use as a signalling phrase for severe threats to the community.

The second apostasy example deals with the case of a close family member or friend.[51] This is one of the clearest cases in which the deuteronomic focus on the dangers to Israelite identity which derive from those nearest and most similar to the Israelites is evident: the abandonment of Israel's Yahwistic character is not a matter of an outside entity appearing and threatening to overrun the cultural capital of the Yahwistic community but an internal phenomenon in which competing claimants to the same Israelite identity are eroding the distinctive features of the deuteronomic version of this community, through the pursuit of practices identifiable with deities other than Yhwh.[52] As Reeder observes,

> The enemy within is a member of the household, someone who should be an Israelite, who instead rejects what Deuteronomy posits as the ideal for Israelite identity. This enemy endangers the family and the community as a whole by worshiping idols and attempting to spread idolatry in Israel, by refusing to learn to be an Israelite . . . For the good of the family and the covenant community, this enemy must be destroyed.[53]

---

51  For a more detailed discussion of this list and its origins see Levinson, 'Textual Criticism'.

52  Which deities the author had in mind is not entirely clear, other than that they were ones 'which you and your ancestors did not know' (אשר לא ידעת אתה ואבתיך)—probably an allusion to Israel's 'knowing' Yhwh in the exodus from Egypt. The expansion of Deut. 13:8—'from the gods of the peoples which surround you, those who are near to you or those who are far from you, from the end of the land to the end of the land' (מאלהי העמים אשר סביבתיכם הקרבים אליך או הרחקים ממך מקצה הארץ ועד קצה הארץ)—aside from its awkward syntax and erratic choice of person, also casts a much broader net than that with which the typical deuteronomic material concerns itself: it 'expands the perspective beyond indigenous gods to those of neighboring peoples' (Nelson, *Deuteronomy*, 172). The similar terminology in the war laws in Deut. 20:10–16 is particularly striking when the contrast in concern between the two texts is noted: whereas Deut. 20:10–16 is concerned about the local threat and not especially troubled by the possibility of cultural contamination from distant peoples, Deut. 13:8 is indiscriminate in its warnings. The verse makes most sense understood as a later addition to the Levant-orientated deuteronomic material, aimed at widening the scope of concern to include the Mesopotamian deities encountered especially in exile. On the probability that this is a redactional addition to the text see Mayes, *Deuteronomy*, 234; Nielsen, *Deuteronomium*, 143–145; Veijola, *Das 5. Buch Mose*, 280.

53  Reeder, *The Enemy*, 58.

The emphatic, repetitive instructions in Deut. 13:9 reflect the particular difficulty which might be envisioned in response to a commandment to execute
a member of one's own family (even more so than a member of one's own
community), but reiterate that not even the family bond may override the
demands of exclusive allegiance to YHWH.[54] Again, mere virtue of birth is not
enough to ensure an Israelite of his or her status as such; an Israelite must
also act like an Israelite in order to maintain Israelite status and identity. That
this case represents a threat not merely to a point of theological doctrine but
more fundamentally to the community's existence as a recognisable entity is
reiterated by the final explanation, in Deut. 13:11, regarding the rationale for the
person's death: 'he sought to push you away from YHWH your god, who brought
you out from the land of Egypt, from the house of servitude' (בקש להדיחך מעל
יהוה אלהיך המוציאך מארץ מצרים מבית עבדים). Israel's identity and existence are
tied to its departure from Egypt, the departure from Egypt is equated with
worship of YHWH, who effected that departure, and worship of YHWH is therefore inseparable from Israel's own identity. To abandon YHWH is to cease to be
Israelite.

The final case concerns an entire (Israelite) city ('one of your cities', אחת
עריך) and highlights similar issues and objectives to the two cases preceding.
Here, however, there is a clear stage in which the rumour of apostasy must be
verified, because in this instance the statement is reported second hand rather
than heard by the addressee (cf. Deut. 17:2–7). It also lacks a clear statement of
the purpose of the destruction of the perpetrator(s), akin to 'so you may burn
the evil from your midst' of the first case (Deut. 13:6) and 'so all Israel will hear
and fear and will not act again according to this wicked thing in your midst' in
the second (Deut. 13:12).[55]

The proposed action is the pursuit of other gods; that it is YHWH from
whom the inhabitants of the city are lured and that this is connected to the
identity of the Israelites as Yahwistic is understood in the statement that it is
'other' (אחרים) gods that are sought and that these are gods 'whom you do not
know' (אשר לא ידעתם, Deut. 13:14). The similarity to the legislation in Deut.
20:15–16 regarding the destruction of non-Israelite cities suggests a shared concept in both passages, namely, that populations which present an alternative

---

54    Tigay, *Deuteronomy*, 132; Veijola, *Das 5. Buch Moses*, 289.

55    Given the generally supposed revision of the last verses of the case to render the burning
      of the city as a sacrifice to YHWH, it is possible that the original explanation for the situa-
      tion was obliterated in the process (so Mayes, *Deuteronomy*, 236–237; Veijola, *Das 5. Buch
      Mose*, 5, 281; see also Driver, *Deuteronomy*, 155; Tigay, *Deuteronomy*, 135).

to deuteronomic Israel are to be destroyed on account of the challenge they pose to this deuteronomic conception (cf. also Deut. 7:1–4a). The apostate city is destroyed because, by worshipping deities other than Yhwh, it renders itself non-Israelite according to the deuteronomic definition of Israel as Yahwistic.[56] Lest this non-Israelite city confuse its non-Yahwistic, non-Israelite practices with the Yahwistic Israelite community, it must be eliminated.[57]

A more generalised form of this principle appears in Deut. 17:2–7.[58] The separation of this general form of the law from the particular examples in Deut. 13:2–19 has often been noted in connection with redactional arguments. Whether these originally formed a sequence of four apostasy laws and whether the text should be reorganised in order to reunite them is, however, no longer agreed.

---

56    Cf. the observation of R. Barrett, *Disloyalty and Destruction: Religion and Politics in Deuteronomy and the Modern World* (LHBOTS 511, London, T&T Clark, 2009), 143: 'an Israelite who unites with other gods effectively becomes a Canaanite, a lure to idolatry for the rest of Israel, whose destruction is required for the safety of the nation'.

57    Again, the emphasis on this being an internal issue is reiterated by the reappearance of the phrase 'from/in your midst' (מקרבך, בקרבך, Deut. 13:14, 15). The on-going importance of eradicating the proximate threat is clear from the recourse to capital punishment.

58    The presence of deuteronomistic language in Deut. 17:2–7, though typically noted, is not usually deemed sufficient to source the entirety of the passage from a deuteronomistic hand. The final phrase of Deut. 17:2 (לעבר בריתו) and the reference to Yhwh (not) commanding in Deut. 17:3b (אשר לא צויתי) are typically suspect, along with the worship of astral deities in the same verse (שמש או לירח או לכל צבא השמים). Nielsen, for example, identifies all three of these as deuteronomistic but recognises Deut. 17:2abα, 3a, 4–7 as deuteronomic (Nielsen, *Deuteronomium*, 173). Mayes similarly locates the deuteronomistic material in the early part of the section but includes all of Deut. 17:3 as secondary (leaving Deut. 17:2abα, 4–7), making an argument that the secondary level is thus a deuteronomistic attempt to transform a generic law into a specific law about apostasy (Deut. 17:3a being vital to this revised emphasis) (Mayes, *Deuteronomy*, 262–263, 266). However, he concedes that the connection of Deut. 17:3b to 17:3a is grammatically awkward, implicitly suggesting that the two parts of the verse are most likely the result of two different hands. Given that the latter half is associated much more clearly with deuteronomistic material elsewhere (Kings, Jeremiah), the former's claims to ante-date it would seem to be strengthened accordingly. The immediately preceding material in Deut. 16:21–22, not to mention the material elsewhere on the subject, gives no reason to doubt the viability of a deuteronomic interest in whether the audience is worshipping Yhwh exclusively.

The conventional view since Dillmann is that the laws belong together.[59] However, Deut. 17:2–7 may be interpreted as an exemplar case for establishing legal precedent for multiple witnesses in a capital case; this is Levinson's view.[60] Levinson's ultimate conclusion, however—that Deut. 17:2–7 is a later revision of the case in Deut. 13:7–12—is based on the contention that these two laws' focus on the individual renders them fundamentally similar and that, accordingly, the differences in the actions which they instruct—that Deut. 13:10 directs 'you' to put the offender to death immediately while Deut. 17:4b–7 requires a trial—renders them incompatible, with one necessarily later than the other.[61] However, this overlooks a critical difference between the two cases: in Deut. 13:7–12 the addressee is the direct recipient of the proposal to worship deities other than YHWH, whereas in Deut. 17:2–7 the addressee has only heard about this activity second hand. Having not himself been a witness to the offence, the addressee cannot immediately act; the report requires substantiation. In this respect the law in Deut. 17:2–7 more closely resembles Deut. 13:13–19, in which the non-Yahwistic activities are also discovered by a third party. As in Deut. 17:2–7, Deut. 13:13–19 requires that the matter be properly investigated before the death penalty is applied. In Deut. 13:13–19 the point about multiple witnesses is not pursued; this suggests that the judicial question about appropriate witnesses is more the point of Deut. 17:2–7, while non-Yahwistic worship is the focus of the laws in Deut. 13:2–19. Note also that the second hand nature of the discovery in Deut. 13:13–19 highlights the fact that these laws are ultimately not laws about 'incitement' as much as they are laws about non-Yahwistic worship: by the time the addressee hears about the original incitement, the

---

59   Thus S. Dempster, 'The Deuteronomic Formula *kî yimmāṣēʾ* in the Light of Biblical and Ancient Near Eastern Law', *RB* 91 (1984), 188–211 and P.E. Dion, 'Deuteronomy 13: The Suppression of Alien Religious Propaganda in Israel during the Late Monarchical Era', *Law and Ideology in Monarchic Israel* (ed. B. Halpern and D.W. Hobson, JSOTSup 124, Sheffield, JSOT, 1991), 159–160, but see B.M. Levinson, *Deuteronomy and the Hermeneutics of Legal Innovation* (Oxford, Oxford University Press, 1997), 104–109 for a review and a critique. For recent discussion see also M. Aspinen, 'Getting Sharper and Sharper: Comparing Deuteronomy 12–13 and 16:18–17:13', *Houses Full of All Good Things: Essays in Memory of Timo Veijola* (ed. J. Pakkala and M. Nissinen, Publications of the Finnish Exegetical Society 95, Göttingen, Vandenhoeck & Ruprecht, 2008), 42–61; Barrett, *Disloyalty and Destruction*, 132.

60   Levinson, *Deuteronomy and the Hermeneutics of Legal Innovation*, 107–127.

61   Cf. W.S. Morrow, *Scribing the Center: Organization and Redaction in Deuteronomy 14:1–17:13* (SBLMS 49, Atlanta, Ga., Scholars, 1995), 22.

rest of the city's inhabitants have already succumbed, requiring them to be put to death as well. The capacity of the deuteronomic material to juggle multiple issues simultaneously should also not be discounted; the pervasiveness of deuteronomic identity concerns renders highly likely the possibility that a deuteronomic author deliberately chose a case of non-Yahwistic incitement in order to reiterate Israel's Yahwistic character while making a juridical point.[62] Also possible is that that Deut. 17:2–7 represents a general principle regarding non-Yahwistic worship, declared exhortatively in Deut. 6:4 and used paranetically in Deut. 13:2–19 to emphasise the importance of this point at all levels and in all parts of the community.

The offence is identified in Deut. 17:3 as the worship of non-Yahwistic deities and in Deut. 17:4 as instigation to pursuit of non-Yahwistic practices, the former representing a specific example of the latter.[63] Here as in Deut. 13:2–19, the temptation to worship deities other than YHWH is manifest in the shape of individuals

---

62    Dion, 'Deuteronomy 13', 159–162 suggests that it reflects the 'author's obsession'.

63    The mention of the deities as particularly the astral ones—sun, moon, stars—is not typically deuteronomic but is more typically deuteronomistic (e.g., Deut. 4:19; 2 Kgs. 23:4; Nielsen, *Deuteronomium*, 173; Nelson, *Deuteronomy*, 216; von Rad, *Deuteronomy*, 117). It is most convincing to view their identification as part of an exilic deuteronomistic revision aimed at reapplying the deuteronomic religious-cultural delineations to a situation in which the most significant threat came from Mesopotamian culture rather than West Semitic culture.

Note that the instigating statement in Deut. 17:4, 'Let us do this alien thing in Israel' (נעשתה התועבה הזאת בישראל), is not a statement which would actually occur on the lips of an instigator. Bartor suggests that this type of 'quotation' of direct speech occurs in laws related to idolatry (Deut. 13:2–6, 7–12, 13–19) as a means by which the author can undermine the desire to pursue non-Yahwistic cultic practice, by rendering the practices in negative terms: 'By exposing the negative values of the Canaanite cult, which make it inappropriate for the worship of YHWH, he seeks not only to prevent an action but also to undermine the desire to perform such acts' (Bartor, *Reading Law*, 124–125). In this case, however, Bartor argues that Deut. 17:4 is actually *not* a citation of direct speech (despite appearances to the contrary), principally on the grounds that in the other cases the supposed speaker is attempting to instigate non-Yahwistic practices rather than actually being caught in the act of performing them (Bartor, *Reading Law*, 125). The text, however, is rendering a sequence of events from the perspective of the law enforcer, who only discovers the instigating declaration after the discovery of the illicit practices. Like Deut. 13:13–19, the second hand character of the case means that punishment is not simply to do with incitement.

whose ascriptive identity would render them part of the Israelite community.[64] Again, the most problematic threat to identity is from those who are nearest and in other respects most similar. Provided that the rumours of non-Israelite behaviours can be substantiated, such persons are to be expurgated, reiterating that the definition of the Israelite community first and foremost as a community of YHWH-worshippers precludes the possibility of members who pursue the worship of other deities.[65] Individuals who do not worship YHWH exclusively lose their status as members of the Israelite community; any individual pretending to such membership while engaging in non-Yahwistic worship must be unequivocally ejected as a non-Israelite.

Deuteronomy 16:21 and 16:22 are direct prohibitions of cultural acts associated with deities other than YHWH.[66] In the first of these, 'you will not plant an אשרה for yourself, any wooden thing' (לא תטע לך אשרה כל עץ), this is evident already from the vocabulary: אשרה is a well-known deity as well as the most likely candidate for Yahweh's consort. Although references to אשרה in the Hebrew Bible are primarily in similarly polemical material, there is ample evidence to indicate an active cult involving אשרה alongside YHWH in Judah and Israel.[67] The most famous comes from inscriptions referring 'YHWH and

---

64    Again, the law's underlying interest in eliminating pretenders to Israeliteness from the Israelite community is made especially clear by the phrase 'in/from your midst' (מקרבך, בקרבך) in Deut. 17:2, 7. The issue, the language implies, is less that there are individuals in the world who worship deities other than YHWH, or even the suggestion that other deities might exist, so much as the revelation of such a person within a community defined by its exclusive devotion to YHWH.

65    Again, however, certain standards of justice override this point: here as in Deut. 13:13–19, failure to uphold the basic character of Israelite identity requires confirmation. See similarly under 3.3.3. The גר.

66    So already Driver, *Deuteronomy*, 203–204; Mayes, *Deuteronomy*, 263–265; Christensen, *Deuteronomy 1:1–21:9*, 363–364; Tigay, *Deuteronomy*, 161–162; Nielsen, *Deuteronomium*, 180. The latter, interestingly, ties the deuteronomic concern here to the objectives of centralisation, rather than non-Yahwistic practices; this seems to ignore the extent to which centralisation itself is designed toward the latter end—a point which Nielsen is, in fact, inclined to acknowledge: 'Die dt Polemik gegen die Mazzeben mag vielleicht eher aus der Forderung der Kultzentralisation als aus dem Bestreben, den kana'anäischen Einfluß zu beseitigen, enstanden sein' (Nielsen, *Deuteronomium*, 184; see also 2.2. Establishing Spatial Proximity).

67    There are many, many articles and monographs on אשרה in the Hebrew Bible, in archaeology and in the ancient Near East; among others see G. Braulik, 'The Rejection of the Goddess Asherah in Israel: Was the Rejection as Late as Deuteronomistic and Did it Further the Oppression of Women in Israel?', *The Theology of Deuteronomy: Collected Essays of Georg Braulik, O.S.B.* (BIBAL Collected Essays 2, North Richland Hills, Tex.,

his *'šrh'* found at Kuntillet 'Ajrud and at Khirbet el-Qom; the pictorial depictions from Kuntillet 'Ajrud have provoked discussion and speculation as well.[68] Although the debate over the exact nature of אשרה in these texts continues to rage, it is clear that either a deity called Asherah or a cult object identified using the same name was an integral part of Yahwistic practice until quite a late stage. Again, the deuteronomic identity project is engaged in a battle over the very nature of what it is to be an Israelite, with the deuteronomic claim that this entails the exclusive worship of YHWH central to this point. Expressed in a different way, the deuteronomic project is, in its emphasis on an exclusively Yahwistic Israel, engaged in the homogenisation of Israelite practice, suppressing alternative sub-cultures and their alternative conceptions of Israelite identity.[69]

A particularly notable element of the prohibition in Deut. 16:21 is that it is not categorical; it is specifically 'near to the altar of Yahweh your god' (אצל מזבח יהוה אלהיך) that the אשרה is banned. In an expression of sentiments

BIBAL, 1994), 165–182; J. Day, *Yahweh and the Gods and Goddesses of Canaan* (JSOTSup 265, Sheffield, Sheffield Academic, 2002); M.S. Smith, *The Early History of God: Yahweh and the Other Deities in Ancient Israel* (2nd edn., Grand Rapids, Mich., Eerdmans, 2002), xxx–xxxvi, 108–147; S.M. Olyan, *Asherah and the Cult of Yahweh in Israel* (SBLMS 34, Atlanta, Ga., Scholars, 1988); J.M. Hadley, *The Cult of Asherah in Ancient Israel and Judah: Evidence for a Hebrew Goddess* (University of Cambridge Oriental Publications 57, Cambridge, University of Cambridge, 2000); W.G. Dever, *Did God Have a Wife? Archaeology and Folk Religion in Ancient Israel* (Grand Rapids, Mich., Eerdmans, 2005); U. Winter, *Frau und Göttin: Exegetische und Ikonographische Studien zum Weiblichen Gottesbild im Alten Israel und in dessen Umwelt* (OBO 53, Göttingen, Vandenhoeck & Ruprecht, 1983), 479–629; all include numerous further references.

68   Note also the Jerusalem pictorial inscription recently published by G. Gilmour, 'An Iron Age II Pictorial Representation from Jerusalem Illustrating Yahweh and Asherah', *PEQ* 141 (2009), 87–103; Gilmour argues that the image depicts YHWH and Asherah. On the inscriptions see O. Keel and C. Uehlinger, *Gods, Goddesses, and Images of God in Ancient Israel* (transl. T.H. Trapp, Minneapolis, Minn., Fortress, 1998), 225–232 (Kuntillet 'Ajrud) and 237–240 (Khirbet el-Qom), with further references; J. Emerton, 'New Light on Israelite Religion: The Implications of the Inscriptions from Kuntillet 'Ajrud', *ZAW* 94 (1982), 2–20; also Hadley, *The Cult of Asherah*; on the associated imagery, likewise Keel and Uehlinger, *Gods, Goddesses, and Images of God*, 210–225. Keel and Uehlinger conclude that the אשרה in question is most convincingly understood as a cult object rather than the goddess, but the extent to which these were clearly distinct gives rise to significant question (Keel and Uehlinger, *Gods, Goddesses, and Images of God*, 232–237; similarly J. Emerton, '"Yahweh and His Asherah": The Goddess or Her Symbol', *VT* 49 [1999], 315–337). For the suggestion that אשרה itself was a noun meaning 'consort', subsequently elevated to the status of a proper name see B. Margalit, 'The Meaning and Significance of Asherah', *VT* 40 (1990), 268–297.

69   Cohen, *Custom and Politics*, 204.

similar to those which will be noted below, the deuteronomic issue with the אשרה is less its existence than its potential to contaminate or confuse distinctively Israelite cultural practice, deuteronomically defined as fundamentally and exclusively Yahwistic, when it occurs in proximity to this Israelite Yahwism. The objection to the practice is its failure to be exclusively Yahwistic; as, in order to be an Israelite practice, it must be exclusively Yahwistic, its ambiguity in this regard renders it rejected as not properly Israelite. As with other prohibited practices in the deuteronomic material, the problem relates to the possibility of confusion—both theological and cultural—on the part of worshippers with regard to the identity of the deity(ies) they worship. Even if the deity for whom the אשרה was erected was YHWH, the similarity between an אשרה cult directed toward or associated with YHWH and an אשרה cult associated with a goddess Asherah is deeply ambiguous. Very similar to an outright cult of אשרה, at least superficially, an אשרה in the Yahwistic cult blurs the distinction between the exclusively Yahwistic cult the deuteronomic material is trying to establish and cults involving non-Yahwistic deities; it is hardly surprising that the deuteronomic author outlaws it.

Deuteronomy 16:22 bans a practice with similarly problematic divine associations; מצבות are common cultic paraphernalia across much of the southern Levant.[70] Indeed, the widespread use of מצבות in a range of religious traditions is acknowledged elsewhere in the Hebrew Bible: it appears as a traditional Yahwistic cult object elsewhere (Gen. 28:18; Josh. 24:26; Hos. 3:4; 10:1–2) despite an association with Baal (2 Kgs. 3:2; 10:26–27) and with monuments to the dead (Gen. 35:19–21; 2 Sam. 18:18).[71] The less ubiquitous annihilation of מצבה

---

70    T.N.D. Mettinger, *No Graven Image? Israelite Aniconism in Its Ancient Near Eastern Context* (ConBOT 42, Stockholm, Almqvist & Wiksell, 1995). On the identification of מצבות see E. Bloch-Smith, '*Maṣṣēbôt* in the Israelite Cult: Argument for Rendering Implicit Cultic Criteria Explicit', *Temple and Worship in Biblical Israel* (ed. J. Day, LHBOTS 422, London, T&T Clark, 2005), 28–39. Graesser suggests that that the uninscribed מצבות in Judah were part of a specifically Levantine practice, as uninscribed מצבות are common in the Levant but rarely found in Egypt or Mesopotamia, where inscriptions and reliefs predominate (C.F. Graesser, 'Standing Stones in Ancient Palestine', *BA* 35 [1972], 34–35; see also J.V. Canby, 'The Stelenreihen at Aššur, Tell Halaf, and *Maṣṣēbôt*', *Iraq* 38 [1976], 113–128).

71    Nelson, *Deuteronomy*, 219; Tigay, *Deuteronomy*, 161–162. J. Day, 'Asherah in the Hebrew Bible and Northwest Semitic Literature', *JBL* 105 (1986), 406 suggests that they were associated with the male deity, in counterpart to the female אשרה. The monuments' generalised associations may explain why there is nothing in Deut. 16:22 regarding the location where מצבות are prohibited; such monuments could have been erected anywhere. Note that they seem to be opposed also in Hos. 10:1–2; this may indicate that the deuteronomic legislation is here reiterating an existing injunction rather than innovating, as in the case of the אשרה.

practices from the Hebrew Bible may perhaps be attributed to its lack of explicit connection to a specific non-Yahwistic deity: there is no god called מצבה nor, conversely, are the objects in question called בעלים or something similarly obvious. Nevertheless, the scattered references to מצבות in the Hebrew Bible, which seem especially to associate them with Baal and/or ancestral cults, suggest that either these associations or, more generally, the widespread use of such cultic paraphernalia in the southern Levant rendered them antithetical to the deuteronomic programme in their non-Yahwistic ambiguity, provoking this ban.[72] As Graesser has observed, 'without any specific indication by an inscription, different individuals could easily attach diverse meanings to the same stone', hinting at the same type of ambiguity to which deuteronomic material elsewhere objects.[73]

## 2.2    Establishing Spatial Proximity: Centralisation

The rationale for the centralisation of the Yahwistic cult at a single cult site in Deuteronomy 12 has been the objective of immense scholarly speculation.[74]

---

72    On their rejection as 'Canaanite', already Driver, *Deuteronomy*, 204; Christensen, *Deuteronomy 1:1–21:9*, 364; Nielsen, *Deuteronomium*, 184. On ancestral or funerary cults see T.J. Lewis, *Cults of the Dead in Ancient Israel and Ugarit* (HSM 39, Atlanta, Ga., Scholars, 1989); J.C. de Moor, 'Standing Stones and Ancestor Worship', UF 27 (1995), 1–20 and F. Stavrakopoulou, *Land of Our Fathers: The Roles of Ancestor Veneration in Biblical Land Claims* (LHBOTS 473, London, T&T Clark, 2010). The latter associates them especially with boundaries (both physical and metaphysical). On types and uses of מצבות see Graesser, 'Standing Stones'.

73    Graesser, 'Standing Stones', 35. Tigay, *Deuteronomy*, 161–162, who tends to be more conscious of the significance of non-Yahwistic practices for Deuteronomy than most, similarly suggests that they are categorically rejected because 'the distinction between legitimate and idolatrous pillars was apparently too difficult to maintain'.

74    Recent attempts include Ben Zvi, 'Prelude'; S. Chavel, 'The Literary Development of Deuteronomy 12: Between Religious Ideal and Social Reality', *The Pentateuch: International Perspectives on Current Research* (ed. T.B. Dozeman, K. Schmid and B.J. Schwartz, FAT 78, Tübingen, Mohr Siebeck, 2011), 303–326; R.E. Clements, 'The Deuteronomic Law of Centralization and the Catastrophe of 587 B.C.E.', *After the Exile: Essays in Honour of Rex Mason* (ed. J. Barton and D.J. Reimer, Macon, Ga, Mercer University Press, 1996), 5–25; B. Halpern, 'The Centralization Formula in Deuteronomy', VT 31 (1981), 10–38; B. Halpern, 'Jerusalem and the Lineages in the Seventh Century BCE: Kinship and the Rise of Individual Moral Liability', *Law and Ideology in Monarchic Israel* (ed. B. Halpern and D.W. Hobson, (JSOTSup 124, Sheffield, JSOT, 1991), 11–107; Knauf, 'The Glorious Days of Manasseh'; A. Rofé, 'The Strata of the Law about the Centralization of Worship in Deuteronomy and the History of the Deuteronomic Movement', *Deuteronomy: Issues and Interpretation* (OTS, London, T&T Clark, 2002), 97–102; N. Steinberg, 'The Deuteronomic Law Code

No doubt there are a number of factors involved in this legislation. From the perspective of the deuteronomic interest in identity formation, however, several features of this law are particularly noteworthy. The chapter manifests a number of identity mechanisms: its instruction of a single worship site for Israel's deity is itself distinctive, representing a rejection of the existing diversity of cultic sites and an exception in the broader ancient Near Eastern context; it underscores the exclusively Yahwistic nature of the Israelite cult by associating that worship with an exclusively Yahwistic cult site, away from non-Yahwistic sites elsewhere; and the drive to centralise Israel's Yahwistic worship serves simultaneously to gather the Israelites into a restricted, proximate space relative to each other and, by doing so, to promote the mutual reinforcement of Israelite culture by promoting interaction with fellow Israelites.

To begin with perhaps the most distinctive aspect of this chapter's contribution to Israelite identity: the effect of the law on the spatial distribution of the Israelites is remarkable. As already noted, one of the mechanisms by which a group may facilitate and reinforce its members' shared identity is to establish a degree of spatial proximity among those members.[75] The most familiar of such efforts is probably the tendency of groups to associate their collective identity with a particular piece of geographic territory. A territorial form of this mechanism is indeed evident in Deuteronomy's interest in the Israelites' claims to the land, mostly in the deuteronomistic material, though present also to a lesser degree in the deuteronomic material.[76] Centralisation, however,

---

and the Politics of State Centralization', *The Bible and Liberation: Political and Social Hermeneutics* (ed. N.K. Gottwald and R.A. Horsley, Maryknoll, N.Y., Orbis, 1993), 365–375; E. Reuter, *Kultzentralisation: Entstehung und Theologie von Dtn 12* (BBB 87, Frankfurt, Anton Hain, 1993). The veracity and/or success of any such programme is also contested; see, among others, L.S. Fried, 'The High Places (*Bāmôt*) and the Reforms of Hezekiah and Josiah: An Archaeological Investigation', *JAOS* 122 (2002), 437–465; B. Gieselmann, 'Die sogenannten josianische Reform in der gegenwärtigen Forschung', *ZAW* 106 (1994), 223–242; Herzog, 'Perspectives'; Knauf, 'The Glorious Days of Manasseh'; Lowery, *The Reforming Kings*; N. Na'aman, 'The Debated Historicity of Hezekiah's Reform in the Light of Historical and Archaeological Research', *ZAW* 107 (1995), 179–195; Monroe, *Josiah's Reform*; and the essays by Z. Herzog, R.G. Kratz, J. Pakkala and H. Schaudig in R.G. Kratz and H. Spieckermann, eds., *One God—One Cult—One Nation: Archaeological and Biblical Perspectives* (in collaboration with B. Corzilius and T. Pilger, BZAW 405, Berlin, de Gruyter, 2010).

75    Cohen, *Custom and Politics*, 204.

76    The deuteronomic material presupposes an audience (already) in possession of the land, for whom this possession is not under ultimate question (its extent, perhaps, but not its existence); this assumption of the land's possession is evident already from Deut. 6:10–11. The deuteronomic mythology of Israel's origins in Egypt, outside this land, however,

goes beyond the broad spatial proximity among Israelites implied by claims to the land and legislates a much more immediately intensified proximity among members by compelling their presence at a single cult site.[77] By instructing the Israelites to focus their ritual practice at a single cult site and requiring their presence there for the performance of essential rites, the centralisation legislation focuses Israelite identity on highly localised space and effects the congregation of the Israelites themselves at that site on a regular basis (cf. Deut. 16:1–17). This assembly has the additional effect of promoting regular interaction among Israelites, creating a forum for the formation and reinforcement of an Israelite monoculture in which challenges to Israelite identity are minimal.[78]

---

provides an unusual twist on the otherwise common association of a group's identity with a particular territory. Israel's association with its land is a double-edged sword: offering the geographical cohesiveness which facilitates group identity but containing a fundamental threat to the unity and distinctiveness of Israel, namely, the non-Israelite inhabitants present in the land prior to Israel's claim and their various deities and practices which the Israelites might be tempted to imitate, to the denigration of Israelite distinctiveness.

77   This is the case whether the original form of the text is located in Deut. 12:13–19, as is most commonly concluded, or in Deut. 12:20–28, as has been argued by Chavel, 'The Literary Development'; alternatively see, for example Halpern, 'The Centralization Formula'; Römer, *The So-Called Deuteronomistic History*.

78   Cohen, *Custom and Politics*, 203. Contrast Hagedorn, who contends that '[c]entralization in Deuteronomy does not mean a centralization of the people in close vicinity to the sanctuary' (A.C. Hagedorn, 'Placing [A] God: Central Place Theory in Deuteronomy 12 and at Delphi', *Temple and Worship in Biblical Israel* [ed. J. Day, LHBOTS 422, London, T&T Clark, 2005], 202). Certainly the text does not envision the continual presence of the Israelites at the sanctuary, but this should not diminish the ideological significance of centralisation. Elsewhere, Altmann has argued that cultic food consumption (of which the centralised cult in Deuteronomy 12 is one instance) in Deuteronomy is an identity-formation activity; in these meals 'they both become and create their group identity and grow in their sense of belonging to the group through the textually prescribed experience (P. Altmann, *Festive Meals in Ancient Israel: Deuteronomy's Identity Politics in Their Ancient Near Eastern Context* [BZAW 424, Berlin, de Gruyter, 2011], 62). Altmann's contention that this is formulated specifically as anti-Assyrian polemic is not adequately substantiated, but he is nonetheless right to highlight the importance of collective activities in establishing and reinforcing group identity (cf. R.G. Kratz, 'The Idea of Cultic Centralization and Its Supposed Ancient Near Eastern Analogies', *One God—One Cult—One Nation: Archaeological and Biblical Perspectives* [ed. R.G. Kratz and H. Spieckermann in collaboration with B. Corzilius and T. Pilger, BZAW 405, Berlin, de Gruyter, 2010], 129: 'the idea of cultic centralization neither fits the rationality of neo-Assyrian politics nor any Judean anti-Assyrian political movement'.)

The centralisation legislation also contributes to Israelite identity formation in other ways. Most fundamentally, for the deuteronomic text to demand
a centralised cult is for it to differentiate the worship of Yhwh from other
ancient Near Eastern worship practices in a visible and demonstrable fashion,
making the explicit restriction of Yahwistic worship to a single cult site itself
a means of distinguishing the Yahwistic cult from that of any other god. The
restriction of a deity's worship to a single cult site is an exceptional move in
the ancient Near Eastern context. Other gods may have had principal shrines
or temples, but no other deity in the ancient Levant of which evidence sur-
vives could be worshipped only at a single cult site. Both Kratz and Schaudig
note that Mesopotamian gods tend to be associated with only a single temple
site (though this at times seems to have been more theory than practice); yet,
though these deities may have only had one 'temple', they could clearly be worshipped elsewhere, in various locations.[79] These localised divine phenomena
raise doubts especially about proposals contending that Yahwistic centralisation ought somehow to be considered a challenge to a 'centralised' Assyrian
cult.[80] Nearer to home, the southern Levant is scattered with cult sites to a
wide variety of deities, with no apparent limitation. Notably, all the analogies
which have been put forth for deuteronomic centralisation are Mesopotamian;
no one has yet proposed any similar phenomenon in the southern Levant. In
the southern Levantine context, therefore, the singularity of this imperative
appears to have been all the more remarkable.[81] Though other ancient Near

---

79    H. Schaudig, 'Cult Centralization in the Ancient Near East? Conceptions of the Ideal
      Capital in the Ancient Near East', *One God—One Cult—One Nation: Archaeological
      and Biblical Perspectives* (ed. R.G. Kratz and H. Spieckermann in collaboration with
      B. Corzilius and T. Pilger, BZAW 405, Berlin, de Gruyter, 2010), 147–152; Kratz, 'The Idea
      of Cultic Centralization', 125–126. The worship of Assyrian deities in provincial and vas-
      sal territorials has been the subject of long-standing debate; see variously J.W. McKay,
      *Religion in Judah under the Assyrians, 732–609 B.C.* (SBT 26, London, SCM, 1973); M.D.
      Cogan, *Imperialism and Religion: Assyria, Judah and Israel in the Eighth and Seventh
      Centuries B.C.E.* (SBLMS 19, Missoula, Mont., Scholars, 1974); H. Spieckermann, *Juda unter
      Assur in der Sargonidenzeit* (FRLANT 129, Göttingen, Vandenhoeck & Ruprecht, 1982); S.W.
      Holloway, *Aššur is King! Aššur is King!: Religion in the Exercise of Power in the Neo-Assyrian
      Empire* (CHANE 10, Leiden, Brill, 2001).
80    Note also that the apparent dearth of local Mesopotamian shrines may be as much a func-
      tion of archaeological interest in the region's capitals as of historical reality.
81    In other attempts to explain the deuteronomic centralisation in a wider ancient Near
      Eastern context, the preparations undertaken for war or siege have sometimes been seen
      to provide an explanation for a sudden impetus toward a centralised cult in the long sev-
      enth century. Although the evidence is not extensive, there is material to suggest that
      cultic paraphernalia could be 'centralised' in advance of an anticipated military attack.

Eastern gods had primary sites of worship or locations with which they were especially associated, the deuteronomic Yhwh is the only one for whom an attempt to restrict the cult to one site and one site only is known.[82] Inherent to the centralisation law itself, then, is its distinctiveness as a cultural practice, over and against the cultural practices of any other god. The act of centralisation is a distinctively Yahwistic practice; by its very peculiarity, it sets up Yahwistic worship in opposition to the worship of other, non-Yahwistic deities. In defining Israelite Yahwism as enacted at a single cult site, centralisation differentiates Israelite practice from the religious practice of non-Israelites.

Finally, the concentration of Yahwistic worship at a single cult site serves to help defend Israelite worship practices against confusion with and contamination by non-Israelite practices by isolating them from these practices.[83] Such an arrangement would have facilitated further efforts to differentiate the Yahwistic cult from non-Yahwistic cults, allowing the close oversight of cultic practice.[84] This is rendered a particularly prominent motivation of the chapter by the later introduction in Deut. 12:2–7, but it is also explicit in its conclusion, which may be deuteronomic; Nielsen has argued that Deut. 12:29–31 is not a late editorial addition but represents the chapter's original introduction.[85] It is certainly notable that these verses have tended to be dismissed by commentators searching for the deuteronomic intent of the centralisation legislation, ostensibly on the grounds of their similarity to Deut. 12:2–7 but also on the

---

Ben Zvi, for example, has noted the potential relevance of such a 'centralising' process of cultic paraphernalia to the reports of cultic centralisation undertaken by Hezekiah, suggesting that this arose in anticipation of 701 as an attempt to protect the region's sancta; particularly when viewed in hindsight, this could be seen as the first steps toward a cult increasingly centred on Jerusalem (Ben Zvi, 'Prelude', 36; similarly Halpern, 'Jerusalem and the Lineages'; M. Weinfeld, 'Cult Centralization in Israel in the Light of a Neo-Babylonian Analogy', *JNES* 23 [1964], 202–212; Lowery, *The Reforming Kings*; cf. Clements, 'The Deuteronomic Law of Centralization', who also points to (potential) conquest to explain centralisation, but to 587 rather than 701; for discussion see also Kratz, 'The Idea of Cultic Centralization', 130–136; Schaudig, 'Cult Centralization', 146–147). If preparations for 701 did result in such a process, the deuteronomic material might represent an attempt at it subsequent institutionalisation in service of identity formation, seized upon as a facilitator of Israelite identity.

82    See Kratz, 'The Idea of Cultic Centralization', 125–126 for discussion.

83    Cohen, *Custom and Politics*, 203.

84    For example J.B. Miller, *The Ethics of Deuteronomy: An Exegetical and Theological Study of the Book of Deuteronomy* (D.Phil. diss., University of Oxford, 1995), 152–153, who argues that the object of centralisation was to prevent 'inadvertent' idolatry.

85    Nielsen, *Deuteronomium*, 135, 141–142.

assumption that the identity concerns they identify cannot have been part of a pre-exilic deuteronomic text. The supposition that Israelite particularity is only of concern from the exilic period has already been rejected. The suggestion that these verses must stand or fall alongside the deuteronomistic introduction is also problematic: the supposed connection to Deut. 12:2–7 lies in the similarity of these sections' general sentiment, especially a shared interest in non-Israelites, but the latter is hardly diagnostic and closer attention to the two passages reveals their inconsistency. Thus Deut. 12:2–7 speaks in the second masculine plural while Deut. 12:29–31 speaks in the second masculine singular; this chapter is one of the few sections in which such shifts between plural and singular address appear to be consistently significant from a redaction-critical point of view. That part of the concern of the centralisation project is to reduce the risk to Israelite practice presented by the reality of non-Israelites is consistent both with the various instructions which endeavour to isolate the Israelites from non-Israelites as well as with the multicultural realities witnessed by the material remains of seventh century Judah. Even if these verses are not deuteronomic they probably reflect an additional function of the centralisation imperative.

In various ways, centralisation serves the interests of deuteronomic identity formation. The restriction of a deity's worship to a single cult site is itself a peculiarly Israelite practice. Its emphasis on exclusivity in the location of Yahwistic worship parallels the emphasis on the exclusivity of Israelite Yahwism while facilitating the (re)enforcement of this exclusivity through focusing Yahwistic practice away from the non-Yahwistic cults enacted elsewhere by non-Israelites. Most significantly, it brings together the Israelites into a single, communal Israelite space in which Israelite practice and Israelite identity may be reinforced.[86]

---

86  It is, very briefly, worth mentioning the contribution of the foregoing two sections to the debate regarding the unity of Deuteronomy 12 and Deuteronomy 13 (on which see Dion, 'Deuteronomy 13'; C. Koch, *Vertrag, Treueid und Bund: Studien zur Rezeption des altorientalischen Vertragsrechts im Deuteronomium und zur Ausbildung der Bundestheologie im alten Testament* [BZAW 383, Berlin, de Gruyter, 2008]; Morrow, *Scribing the Center*; Otto, 'Treueid und Gesetz'; Otto, *Das Deuteronomium*; Pakkala, 'Der literar- und religionsgeschichtliche Ort'). The extraction of one of these chapters—usually of Deuteronomy 13 and often in connection to its supposed connection to VTE or another Assyrian treaty or loyalty oath—fails to recognise that both are manifestations of deuteronomic identity concerns. *Kultuseinheit* and *Kultusreinheit* are not randomly juxtaposed concerns but related components of a deuteronomic interest in defining, reiterating and enforcing a distinctively Yahwistic Israelite identity: Deuteronomy 12 brings the Israelites together,

2.3    *A Common Mythology of Origins: Exodus from Egypt*

Another one of the mechanisms by which Israel's identity as a cohesive people is established is the deuteronomic text's regular appeal to a common Israelite myth of origins, namely, to the origins of Israel in the experience of exodus from Egypt.[87] This mythology of origins is one of the more recognisable feature of ethnic groups and is certainly one of the most fundamental:

> In spite of the difficulty of being specific about criteria features and com-
> ponents, what social scientists have called ethnic groups do belong to
> a relatively distinct sociological type. This is a group the members of
> which have, both with respect to their own sentiments and those of non-
> members, a distinctive identity which is rooted in some kind of distinc-
> tive sense of its history.[88]

For Israel this sense of history is its memory of its departure from Egypt. This arises first in Deut. 6:12–13 and is reiterated throughout the deuteronomic text, which regularly refers to 'Yhwh who brought you out of the land of Egypt' (יהוה אלהיך הוציאך מארץ מצרים; יהוה אשר הוציאך מארץ מצרים and similar) or reminds the Israelites of their origins in Egypt (עבד היית בארץ מצרים and simi-lar), often using it as a motivator to encourage a particular course of action.[89]

---

forming and reinforcing Israelite identity while the Israelites are assembled as a com-munity in close spatial proximity and Deuteronomy 13 addresses the enforcement of that identity when the Israelites are away from the central site. 'Deut 12 prepares an environ-ment conducive to loyalty [to Yhwh], Deut 13 . . . deals with those who would undermine that loyalty' (Barrett, *Disloyalty and Destruction*, 131).

87    Cohen, *Custom and Politics*, 202. For contrasting perspectives on the place of Egypt in Israel's self-understanding see F.V. Greifenhagen, *Egypt on the Pentateuch's Ideological Map: Constructing Biblical Israel's Identity* (JSOTSup 361, Sheffield, Sheffield Academic Press, 2002) and P.A.H de Boer, 'Egypt in the Old Testament: Some Aspects of an Ambivalent Assessment', *Selected Studies in Old Testament Exegesis* (ed. C. van Duin, OTS 27, Leiden, Brill, 1991), 152–167; also K. Schmid, *Genesis and the Moses Story: Israel's Dual Origins in the Hebrew Bible* (transl. J. Nogalski, Siphrut 3, Winona Lake, Ind., Eisenbrauns, 2010).

88    T. Parsons, 'Some Theoretical Considerations on the Nature and Trends of Change in Ethnicity', *Ethnicity: Theory and Experience* (ed. N. Glazer and D.P. Moynihan, London, Harvard University Press, 1975), 56. Like shared ancestry, whether these shared historical origins are real or imagined is largely beside the point. On the degree of historical reality required of such traditions see the discussion in Chapter Two and the references there.

89    On the variety of the formulations of references to Egypt see B.S. Childs, 'Deuteronomic Formulae of the Exodus Traditions', *Hebraïsche Wortforschung, Festschrift zum 80.*

Referring to similar language in Leviticus and Numbers, Greifenhagen under-scores that these reiterative statements function to differentiate Israel, explic-itly from Egypt but implicitly from all others.[90] The evocation of Egypt in many of the deuteronomic text's motive clauses reflects the event's cultural implica-tions for Israelite identity: as a community which traces its history to its extrac-tion and differentiation from Egypt, Israel has a responsibility to maintain this differentiation.

Though the multiple ways of referring to the exodus from Egypt may reflect particular nuances in emphasis, the unifying theme of all of these statements is the centrality of the event for the community's definition of itself: 'Israel was Israel in the strictest sense only from Egypt onward.'[91] An Israelite is someone who shares in this history, who lays claim to the exodus tradition and the nar-rative of Israelite origins which it articulates. The interrelation of Israel's iden-tity as the worshippers of Yʜᴡʜ and Israel's identity as a people with a shared

---

*Geburtstag von Walter Baumgartner* (ed. B. Hartmann, E. Jenni, E.Y. Kutscher, V. Maag, I.L. Seeligmann and R. Smend, VTSup 16, Leiden, Brill, 1967), 30–39; S. Kreuzer, 'Die Exodustradition im Deuteronomium', *Das Deuteronomium und seine Querbeziehungen* (ed. T. Veijola, Schriften der Finnischen Exegetischen Gesellschaft 62, Göttingen, Vandenhoeck & Ruprecht, 1996), 81–106; I. Schulmeister, *Israels Befreiung aus Ägypten: Eine Formeluntersuchung zur Theologie des Deuteronomiums* (Österreichische Biblische Studien 36, Frankfurt, Peter Lang, 2010).

90    Greifenhagen, *Egypt on the Pentateuch's Ideological Map*, 162. 'Egypt . . . is not only or pri-marily a pointer to a determinate location or people, but functions more as a multivalent metaphor or symbol in which the geographic or ethnographic referent is overdetermined by the values or ideology of the producers' (Greifenhagen, *Egypt on the Pentateuch's Ideological Map*, 6). The identity formation function of Israel's exodus from Egypt at the hand of Yʜᴡʜ is of course not unique to the deuteronomic material; nevertheless it is notable the degree to which it is emphasised by it: 'That Deuteronomy has been saturated by the exodus tradition is shown by the approximate 50 places in the book that refer to Exodus' (Schmid, *Genesis and the Moses Story*, 69 n. 127). Kreuzer, 'Die Exodustradition im Deuteronomium', 87–88 attempts to differentiate between deuteronomic references to Yʜᴡʜ having brought Israel out of Egypt and deuteronomistic references to Israel's slavery in Egypt as an ethical motivator, but the experience of slavery is too intimately associated with Yʜᴡʜ's deliverance to be rendered secondary so neatly. He also contends that the deuteronomic exodus tradition is confined to the Passover-Unleavened Bread legislation and has nothing to do with either centralisation or exclusive Yahwism, but his rejection of the exodus in Deut. 13:11 is predicated on this assumption and is therefore circular, while the peculiarly deuteronomic conflation of Passover and Unleavened Bread can hardly be said to be anything but fundamentally affected by centralisation.

91    Schmid, *Genesis and the Moses Story*, 125, cf. 145–146.

history in Egypt reinforces the significance of this history for Israel's identity, insofar as the former is predicated on the latter having been effected by YHWH; Israel and YHWH are inextricably linked because YHWH founded Israel by bringing the people who would become Israel out of Egypt.[92]

Nevertheless, this particular communal history also presents an in-built danger for Israelite identity: the external origins of the Israelites implies a land previously inhabited by non-Israelites. This issue arises almost immediately in the introduction, with the emphasis that these inhabitants must be avoided or eradicated in order to protect Israelite distinctiveness. The constant reminders that Israel came out of Egypt—in the introduction and throughout the text— function to counteract this danger by reiterating Israel's special status, as the specific people which YHWH extracted from another people to be particularly associated with YHWH himself and by reiterating that the Israelites who are now in the land are irrevocably distinct from the land's non-Israelite inhabitants. For the deuteronomic author and his audience to confess that Israel constitutes those whom YHWH brought out from Egypt is to define Israel as different from the inhabitants of the land who do not share in this history.

### 2.4    *Further Differentiation of Israelite Practice*

As central as the worship of YHWH is to Israel's self-definition, the deuteronomic identity project is not limited to the characterisation of Israel as a Yahweh-worshipping community. The definition of an unambiguously Israelite cultural identity via the differentiation of Israelites from non-Israelites and the subsequent protection of that identity is, rather, a recurring theme of deuteronomic texts. This section is devoted to recognising this issue in a wide range of deuteronomic passages. Some of these have previously been noted as pertaining to issues of Israelite identity, but often this has occurred in connection to claims that they are exilic and/or secondary passages, with an implicit corollary that these issues are not primary to the deuteronomic agenda. The preceding chapters have established that the historical social, political and commercial circumstances of the long seventh century provided ample impetus for concern with ethnic identity formation. This concern is evident not only in the differentiation of Israelite cultural practice as exclusively Yahwistic but also in a large number of other passages in which the Israelite cultural identity is first distinguished, then protected.

---

92    Schulmeister, *Israels Befreiung aus Ägypten*, 309: the exodus is 'grundlegend für die Beziehung zwischen Jahwe und seinem Volk Israel'.

2.4.1        Divination

The long section between Deut. 16:18 and Deut. 18:22 on the leadership roles allotted for the Israelite community culminates with the role of the prophet, presented as the antithesis of the preceding divinatory practitioners (Deut. 18:9–22). The passage breaks down into two main parts: Deut. 18:9–14, which prohibits certain divinatory practices, mostly clearly technical, and Deut. 18:15–22, which promises and regulates the intuitive divinatory role of prophet.[93]

This first section sets itself up as commanding a differentiation between the types of actions in which the addressed audience is to engage and those in which non-Israelites engage: 'When you come to the land which YHWH your god is giving to you, you will not learn to act according to the alien practices of these nations' (לעשות תלמד לא לך נתן אלהיך יהוה אשר הארץ אל בא אתה כי כתועבת הגוים ההם, Deut. 18:9). 'These behaviors', as Nelson puts it, 'are treated as markers of the ethnic boundary between the doomed "nations" and "you."'[94]

The attestations elsewhere to Israelite pursuit of some of these practices suggest that this is not a rote rehearsal of alien practices for rhetorical effect, but an attempt to deliberately differentiate Israelite practice by classifying certain divinatory practices as culturally ambiguous and consequently unacceptable among Israelites. What follows is programmatic, not descriptive; both biblical and extra-biblical materials indicate the existence of non-prophetic means of communicating with the divine, not least in their persistent prohibition (Lev. 19:31; 20:6, 7; Isa. 8:19; 19:3; 1 Samuel 28). As with exclusive Yahwism, the deuteronomic project is engaged in a process of homogenisation, rejecting an existing diversity of divinatory practices in favour of a single method of communication with the divine. Compounding the significance of this process for Israelite identity is its effect on Israelite distinctiveness; the prioritisation of intuitive prophecy to the exclusion of all technical forms of divination sets Israelite praxis apart from other ancient Near Eastern divinatory hierarchies.

The practices rejected in Deut. 18:10–11 comprise a wide range of technical divinatory methods, by their number probably intended to represent all such techniques.[95] The first named is 'one who crosses his son and his daughter over

---

93    On the terminology of intuitive and technical divination see J. Stökl, *Prophecy in the Ancient Near East: A Philological and Sociological Comparison* (CHANE 56, Leiden, Brill, 2012), 7–11.

94    Nelson, *Deuteronomy*, 232. On תועבה as connoting the alienness of the practices to which it refers see 2.4.5. תועבה.

95    For discussion of the divinatory activities listed here and their wider biblical and ancient Near Eastern contexts see Jeffers, *Magic and Divination*, 25–143 and F.H. Cryer, *Divination*

in the fire' (מעביר בנו ובתו באש).[96] While the original context and purpose of the practice is inevitably difficult to ascertain given the ideological baggage it now carries in the biblical text, it hardly seems impossible to imagine that it may have been classed among divinatory practices: reading the organs of sacrificial animals is a classic form of technical divination. Perhaps something along such lines was carried out on the bodies of sons and daughters passed through the fire. Though later texts, other passages seem to support an association between crossing a child over fire and divination (2 Kgs. 17:17; 21:6). Nielsen in particular suggests that '[m]it diesem Ritual dürfte es sich um eine mantische, in den Jahwekultus des 8. und 7. Jahrhunderts aufgenommene Unternehmung handeln, die in der späteren Überlieferung als Kinderopfer, und danach als ausgesprochen Heidnisches, dem Ba'al oder den anderen Göttern gewidmet, aufgefaßt worden ist.'[97] Whether the phrase refers to a nonlethal ritual involving children or full-on child sacrifice remains debated but, whatever the precise nature of the practice, it also appears to have been associated with non-Israelites.[98] Its rejection here represents a rejection of a practice with ambiguous cultural associations, inadequately unique to Israel, and the rejection of a form of communication with the divine which fails to differentiate Israelite divinatory priorities and Israel's relationship with YHWH from non-Israelites' relationships with their deities.

Though their remits are not as clear as might be desired, the remaining practitioners are readily recognisable as technical diviners. The קסם קסמים is usually rendered by 'diviner', 'one who makes predictions' or some other generalising term. The remit of the מעונן is probably more specific, but the

---

        *in Israel and Its Ancient Near Eastern Environment: A Socio-Historical Investigation* (JSOTSup 142, Sheffield, JSOT, 1994), 229–305. Deuteronomy 18:9–14 may be developing Exod. 22:17, which condemns the female diviner to death, but the extent to which the deuteronomic text expands and extends the rudimentary prohibition of Exodus makes the relationship of little more than the most basic redactional interest.

96     For discussion see Stavrakopoulou, *King Manasseh*, with further references; also J.A. Hackett, 'Religious Traditions in Israelite Transjordan', *Ancient Israelite Religion: Essays in Honor of Frank Moore Cross* (ed. P.D. Miller Jr., P.D. Hanson and S.D. McBride, Philadelphia, Pa., Fortress, 1987), 125–136; O. Boehm, 'Child Sacrifice, Ethical Responsibility and the Existence of the People of Israel', *VT* 54 (2004), 145–156; M. Weinfeld, 'Burning Babies in Ancient Israel: A Rejoinder to Morton Smith's Article in JAOS 95 (1975), 477–479', *UF* 10 (1978), 411–413; M. Smith, 'A Note on Burning Babies', *JAOS* 95 (1975), 477–479.

97     Nielsen, *Deuteronomium*, 186.

98     2 Kgs. 16:3; 17:17; 21:6; 23:10; Jer. 7:31; 19:5; 32:35; Ezek. 20:31; Deut. 12:31. Note that the condemnations of child sacrifice in the biblical texts persistently condemn it on the grounds of its association with non-Israelites and deities other than YHWH.

precise nature of his expertise is unclear. Suggestions include divination by clouds or other meteorological phenomena, divination by noises or a specialism in incantations. The מנחש is similarly a matter of guesswork; translations usually offer something general like 'one who seeks omens'. The speciality of the 'sorcerer' (מכשף) is opaque. Deuteronomy 18:11 names the חבר חבר, the charmer, alongside two or possibly three persons whose enquiries related to the deceased: 'one who enquires of the shades' (שאל אוב), 'one who seeks after the dead' (דרש אל המתים) and the 'soothsayer' (ידעני). The second and third of these appear together frequently; the fourth is perhaps meant to indicate that both casual and professional attempts to gain insight through enquiry of the dead are prohibited.[99] Although the particularities of these many forms of divination are beyond certainty, the length and permutations of the list suggest that it is meant to represent a wide range of technical divinatory practices.

These practices are identified as non-Israelite in Deut. 18:9: 'you will not learn to act according to the alien practices of these nations' (לא תלמד לעשות כתועבת הגוים ההם).[100] Because these divinatory practices are associable with non-Israelites, they must be avoided by YHWH's Israelite followers as part of

---

99    J. Blenkinsopp, 'Deuteronomy and the Politics of Post-Mortem Existence', *VT* 45 (1995), 1–16 notes that a number of the divinatory professions listed in this section (though not all) involve mediation with deceased ancestors, suggesting that this is part of an overall interest of the deuteronomic material in breaking down its audience's affinities with the ancestors and building up those to the state instead. Certainly there is a notable difference between the nearly complete disinterest in the ancestors which is evidenced by the core deuteronomic material and the much more substantiative focus on an ancestral connection with the past in the deuteronomistic material.

100   Mayes, *Deuteronomy*, 279 suggests that Deut. 18:10–12a is a pre-deuteronomic list incorporated and revised in a deuteronomic vein by Deut. 18:9, 12b; similarly Nielsen, *Deuteronomium*, 179, who sees Deut. 18:10–12a as polemic against Ahaz. Note that it is unlikely that the various descriptions of certain practices as תועבה originated together as some type of תועבה law collection (contra J. L'Hour, 'Les interdits *to'eba* dans le Deutéronome', *RB* 71 [1964], 481–503); it is much more likely that its prevalence in the deuteronomic material reflects the deuteronomic interests in this quarter and its attendant regular application of the term. Whether or not this list has pre-deuteronomic origins, it is likely that the descriptions of these practices as תועבה derive from the deuteronomic hand, in keeping with similar terminology in Deut. 12:31; 13:15; 14:3; 17:1, 4; 20:18; 22:5; 23:7, 19; 24:4; 25:16. For further discussion of this phrase see 2.4.5. תועבה; note especially that this language may function not only as a description of non-Israelite associations but as a means of articulating the alienating effect of certain actions on the intimacy of the relationship between YHWH and an individual.

their programme of distinctiveness.[101] An Israelite who engages in such practices risks both his exclusive relationship with YHWH and his identification
as an Israelite. Those who follow YHWH are expected to be distinct from the
nations and to apply that distinctiveness to their behaviours and practices;
those who fail to do so alienate themselves from YHWH.

The prohibition of practices deemed non-Israelite is not, however, the only
object of this section; Deut. 18:9–14 forms the negative complement for a presentation of prophecy as the sole acceptable means of Israelite communication with YHWH in Deut. 18:15–22.[102] The declaration in Deut. 18:9 that Israel
will not pursue the practices of non-Israelites anticipates the positive imperative of what the Israelites will do *vis-à-vis* the נביא in Deut. 18:15 ('to him you
will listen', אליו תשמעון), effectively rendering it a statement of Israel's atten-
tiveness to the prophet in contrast to non-Israelites' lack of attention to such
persons.[103] As almost all commentators recognise, the Yahwistic prophet is presented as the means by which communication between Israelites and YHWH is
to occur. The lengthy first half of the section, in which other various mediation
techniques are prohibited while being emphatically identified as practices of
other peoples, is designed as a foil to the presentation of the Israelite prophet.[104]

---

101    This point is reiterated in the late, perhaps priestly, explanation in Deut. 18:13: 'You will
       be wholly with YHWH your god' (תמים תהיה עם יהוה אלהיך). On the date see Nielsen,
       *Deuteronomium*, 186; Mayes, *Deuteronomy*, 281–282.

102    While it is usually agreed that significant parts of the prophecy section in Deut. 18:15–22
       derive from a later deuteronomistic hand, it is at the same time generally supposed that
       at least some basic identification of prophecy as the means by which Israel is to commu-
       nicate with YHWH was included in the original deuteronomic material, in contrast to the
       preceding prohibited forms (see Mayes, *Deuteronomy*, 262, 282; Nielsen, *Deuteronomium*,
       174–175). Given the expansionism in the section, perhaps only Deut. 18:15 provided the
       original counterpoint to the preceding (and in light of the rather late identification of
       Moses as a נביא, probably without the specification that this will be a prophet 'like me',
       כמני; see Stökl, *Prophecy in the Ancient Near East*, 171–186). For interpretations of the
       entire prophecy section as exilic or later see Nissinen, 'The Dubious Image'; H.L. Bosman,
       'Redefined Prophecy as Deuteronomic Alternative to Divination in Deut. 18:9–22', *Acta
       Theologica* 16 (1996), 1–23; E.W. Nicholson, 'Deuteronomy 18.9–22: The Prophets and
       Scripture', *Prophecy and Prophets in Ancient Israel: Proceedings of the Oxford Old Testament
       Seminar* (ed. J. Day, LHBOTS 531, London, T&T Clark, 2010), 151–171.

103    This is effectively the point of Deut. 18:14, whatever its redactional status: 'for these
       nations whom you are dispossessing will listen to sign-interpreters and predictors, but
       you—thus does YHWH your god not give for you' (כי הגוים האלה אשר אתה יורש אותם אל
       מעננים ואל קסמים ישמעו ואתה לא כן נתן לך יהוה אלהיך; see Mayes, *Deuteronomy*, 282).

104    Nelson, *Deuteronomy*, 232; Blenkinsopp, 'Deuteronomy', 11; Bosman, 'Redefined Prophecy', 11.

The involvement of this legislation in matters of Israelite identity is reiterated by the twofold specification that the prophet will be 'from among you, from your brothers' (מקרבך מאחיך). The brother language represents a circling of the wagons, protecting Israelite identity by creating a self-reinforcing system, stripped of interactions with non-Israelites.[105]

As already noted, however, many of the practices enumerated in the first half of this section as characterising other cultures' communication practices with the divine are attested as practices pursued also by the inhabitants of Judah, with varying degrees of tolerance and opposition. At the same time, many other cultures in the ancient Near East employed prophets to communicate with their gods. The deuteronomic author could hardly thus suppose that reliance on prophetic mediation was truly a distinctively Israelite method of communication with the divine. What is unique about the deuteronomic emphasis on intuitive divination, however, is the hierarchy of divinatory authority which it represents. Though the evidence for and about prophetic activity in other ancient Near Eastern cultures is limited by the vagaries of preservation, it is notable that in both the cultures in which prophetic activities are best attested—at Mari and among the Assyrians—prophetic messages from the gods were considered a less dependable form of communication, one which at Mari was at times obliged to undergo a verification process and which in Assyria is far less prominent in the archival material than other forms of divination.[106] In other words, the technical forms of divination were considered a superior, more reliable means of communicating with the deity than the intuitive forms, including prophecy.

---

105  Cohen, *Custom and Politics*, 203; cf. C. Geertz, *The Interpretation of Cultures: Selected Essays* (London, Fontana, 1973).

106  Compare the standard editions of the Assyrian material: four prophecy collections and just over half a dozen oracle reports (SAA 9), compared to dozens and dozens of astrological reports and enquiries (SAA 4; SAA 8) and letters from scholars (SAA 10). For discussion see the introductions in the SAA volumes as well as M. de Jong Ellis, 'Observations on Mesopotamian Oracles and Prophetic Texts: Literary and Historiographic Considerations', *JCS* 41 (1989), 136–137, with further references; Stökl, *Prophecy in the Ancient Near East*, 81–86; Stackert, 'The Syntax of Deuteronomy', 162–164; also E.J. Hamori, 'Echoes of Gilgamesh in the Jacob Story', *JBL* 130 (2011), 625–642, who observes that the gender of the prophet at Mari was part of (but not the only) motivation for verification. On gender differences between Assyrian and Yahwistic prophetic personnel see J. Stökl, 'Ištar's Women, YHWH's Men? A Curious Gender-Bias in Neo-Assyrian and Biblical Prophecy', *ZAW* 121 (2009), 87–100. For the suggestion that even prophecy is severely circumscribed see Stackert, 'Mosaic Prophecy'.

The deuteronomic model reverses this hierarchy. Through a progressive process of eliminating all other means of contact with the deity as unacceptably associated with the practices of non-Israelites, the text leads the audience to the conclusion that prophecy, though poorly regarded and seen as unreliable by non-Israelites, will be Israel's characteristic means of communicating with its god. Instead of residing at the bottom of the divinatory pile the prophet stands at the top, while the technical practitioners whose skills were prized by their neighbours are devalued to the point of complete rejection.[107] Such an order of preference constitutes a clear deviation from the norms of divinatory practice in the rest of the ancient Near East.

Though perhaps also motivated by a perception that the more 'direct' means of communication with the deity which prophecy represented was in keeping with a deuteronomic emphasis on exclusive reliance on YHWH—not on the knowledge of the technical diviner—in the elimination of all divinatory practices other than prophecy and its attendant reordering of the divinatory hierarchy the deuteronomic legislation defines prophecy as the sole acceptable form of Israelite divinatory activity while simultaneous distinguishing Israelite divinatory activities from non-Israelite divinatory activities. Although this section undoubtedly contains later accruals in light of the particularities of biblical literature and imagery, the basic reversal in priorities which it contains constitutes a fundamental fissure between Israelite and non-Israelite divination practices.

### 2.4.2      Cult Officials

It is perhaps not surprising that the extent of the deuteronomic interest in Israelite distinctiveness has been generally overlooked: the imperatives which define particular aspects of Israelite cultural practice collectively constitute several of the most obscure passages in Deuteronomy. Two of these injunctions—which may or may not be related to each other—appear in Deut. 23:18 and Deut. 23:19. Deuteronomy 23:18 prohibits a son or daughter of Israel from becoming either קדש or קדשה; Deut. 23:19 concerns the types of offerings permissible for presentation to YHWH. Given the appearance of the term זונה in Deut. 23:19 and the long-standing scholarly assumption that the ancient Near East was rife with cult-related sexual practices (variously referred to as sacred marriage, sacred prostitution and cult[ic] prostitution), these verses are often understood to be referring to some type of sexual practices,

---

107     Braulik is one of the few commentators to note this juxtaposition between these technical forms of communication with the divine and the non-technical form, prophecy, advocated in Deut. 18:15–22 (Braulik, *Deuteronomium II*, 135).

associated with the cult, which the deuteronomic author wished to eradicate. These two declarations have also been taken to refer, in parallelism, to the same phenomenon in the sacred (Deut. 23:18) and profane (Deut. 23:19) spheres, first with reference to women (Deut. 23:18a, 19) and then with reference to men (Deut. 23:18b, 19).[108] Most commonly, the קדש and the קדשה are interpreted as individuals whose sexual services were linked to and occurred at a cult site, while the זונה and the euphemistically-identified כלב are understood as the secular equivalents.

The role of the קדש and the קדשה remains one of the highly contested but largely unknown elements of Israelite cultural practice. The name alone, employing the same root whence derives the terms for 'holy', 'holiness' and 'sanctuary', strongly suggests a link to the cult, with texts both in and out of the Hebrew Bible indicating that this is a justifiable association: biblical narrative texts refer to קדש(ה) in connection with the cult several times (1 Kgs. 14:24; 15:12; 22:47; 2 Kgs. 23:7), while the *qdš(t)* at Ugarit was a ritual specialist associated with temples, as was the Mesopotamian *qadištu*.[109]

The first issue at stake is whether the masculine and feminine forms of the noun are to be understood as referring to masculine and feminine practitioners of a single common act, or if they ought to be taken as referring to two entirely different categories. The latter is instinctively dubious yet commonly pursued: thus, in Deut. 23:18 the female in question, the קדשה, is engaged in sexual activities, while the male, the קדש, is not.[110] As Westenholz notes, however, 'it is contrary to reason to separate the male and female counterparts of the same office in order to deduce that the male was a Canaanite cultic functionary and the female was a irreligious prostitute on the basis that it is a synonym of *zōnā*.'[111] The improbability of such a distinction is observable, among other places, in the use of the masculine plural term in 2 Kgs. 23:7 in a context

---

108   Whether this is a justifiable case of parallelism may be disputed: Deut. 23:18 comprises two separate sentences and is in the third person, while 23:19 is an apodictic second masculine singular with a single verb and double object.

109   J.G. Westenholz, 'Tamar, *Qĕdēša, Qadištu*, and Sacred Prostitution in Mesopotamia', HTR 82 (1989), 249–265; cf. K. Nyberg, 'Sacred Prostitution in the Biblical World?', *Sacred Marriages: The Divine-Human Sexual Metaphor from Sumer to Early Christianity* (ed. M. Nissinen and R. Uro, Winona Lake, Ind., Eisenbrauns, 2008), 310; Nelson, *Deuteronomy*, 280–281; Tigay, *Deuteronomy*, 215–216.

110   See, for example, E.A. Goodfriend, 'Prostitution (Old Testament)', ABD 5:507–510; note also P. Bird, 'The End of the Male Cult Prostitute: A Literary-Historical and Sociological Analysis of Hebrew *qādēš-qĕdēšîm*', *Congress Volume: Cambridge 1995* (ed. J.A. Emerton, VTSup 66, Leiden, Brill, 1997), 37–80.

111   Westenholz, 'Tamar, *Qĕdēša, Qadištu*', 248.

which clearly includes women.[112] As Westenholz indicates, evidence in favour of a distinction is usually traced to the supposed parallelism of Deut. 23:18 and Deut. 23:19: according to Nyberg, for example, the parallelism in these verses of קדשה with זונה and קדש with כלב suggests that the feminine terms ought to be associated with the provision of sexual acts while the masculine are to be associated with cultic activities of some (other) kind.[113] The significance and referents of זונה and כלב in Deut. 23:19 will be addressed in greater detail momentarily; anticipating those conclusions somewhat, neither of the terms should be understood as relating to sexual practices or their practitioners, rendering the basis of a sexual interpretation for קדשה moot. One might also wish to note that the syntax of Deut. 23:18 differs from that of Deut. 23:19; Deut. 23:18a and 23:18b contain full and independent statements pertaining to the קדשה and קדש respectively, while Deut. 23:19 names אתנן זונה and מחיר כלב in a short list.

In any event it is highly unlikely that the services to the cult of either the קדשה or the קדש were sexual in nature; though they are obliquely associated with sexual activity in a few places (Hos. 4:14 in particular, possibly also Gen. 38:21–22), most of the texts adduced to support the existence of sexual activity in the context of the cult derives from the language used in prophetic texts to describe the unfaithfulness of the people to Yhwh, rather than from references to actual persons (e.g., Hos. 2:7; Jer. 2:20–23; 3:6–9).[114] Furthermore, the idea that sexual activities were frequently associated with sacred sites and cultic activities in the ancient Near East has been called into question, with its prevalence in modern biblical scholarship being traced to the historically dubious accounts of Herodotus and Lucian and, in particular, the influence of the former via Frazer's *The Golden Bough*.[115] The presumed sexual content of these

---

112    Nyberg, 'Sacred Prostitution', 309; Westenholz, 'Tamar, *Qĕdēša, Qadištu*', 248.

113    Nyberg, 'Sacred Prostitution', 310.

114    Nyberg, 'Sacred Prostitution', 312 suggests that Hos. 4:14 should be understood in this way and M.-T. Wacker, '"Kultprostitution" im Alten Israel? Forschungsmythen, Spuren, Thesen', *Tempelprostitution im Altertum: Fakten und Fiktionen* (ed. T.S. Scheer, OikSAW 6, Berlin, Verlag Antike, 2009), 81 similarly suggests that the link between זונות and קדשות in Deuteronomy and Hosea is rhetoric intended to render קדשות objectionable by simple association. I.E. Riegner, *The Vanishing Hebrew Harlot: The Adventures of the Hebrew Stem ZNH* (Studies in Biblical Literature 73, Oxford, Peter Lang, 2009), 112, 117 understands them as cultic functionaries involved in sacrifice.

115    See especially J. Assante, 'Bad Girls and Kinky Boys? The Modern Prostituting of Ishtar, Her Clergy and Her Cults', *Tempelprostitution im Altertum: Fakten und Fiktionen* (ed. T.S. Scheer, OikSAW 6, Berlin, Verlag Antike, 2009), 23–54; contrast H.-J. Stipp, 'Die *Qedešen* im

prohibitions must therefore be abandoned. It is more likely that the קדשים are cult functionaries or ritual specialists of some kind, not sexual hirelings.

Regardless of the precise function of the קדשה and the קדש, it is clear that the deuteronomic text objects to these persons. More significantly, the text does not object in general terms—nor, notably, with reference to sexual mores—but on the grounds that it is specifically for Israelites that this cultic profession is unacceptable: 'A קדשה will not be *from the daughters of Israel*, nor will a קדש be *from the sons of Israel*' (לא תהיה קדשה מבנות ישראל ולא יהיה קדש מבני ישראל; italics supplied). Apparently the deuteronomic author has no objection to קדשים as such; implicitly, at least, the text permits non-Israelite קדשים. This prohibition is not a prohibition on general principle. Rather, the point of the law is to identify this cultic vocation as unequivocally non-Israelite and therefore incompatible with claims to Israelite identity. While the precise nature of the vocation may be unclear to us, the prohibition's intention to identify it as a non-Israelite practice is not.

In this respect, a few further remarks *vis-à-vis* קדשים in the Hebrew Bible are valuable. First, it perhaps affirms an understanding of the קדש as in some way (deuteronomically) non-Israelite that the three masculine singular references to the קדש in Kings (1 Kgs. 14:24; 15:12; 22:47), though of variable historical reliability, speak of him as 'in the land'—an allusion to the non-Israelite inhabitants—and in association with acts performed ככל התועבת הגוים ([sic] 1 Kings 14:24). The קדשים may very well, therefore, have been comprised primarily of non-Israelites, at least according to a deuteronomic definition. Second, Riegner's recent examination of the root זנה deals in passing with the aforementioned passage in Hos. 4:14, in which קדשות are paralleled to זונות and which Riegner understands as a term referring to non-Yahwistic practice. The parallelism, which has thus usually been taken to identify the קדשות as prostitutes, may thus be better understood an attempt to associate these persons with non-Israelite practices.[116] Finally, although the temporal and geographical distance makes it impossible to state with any confidence, it may not be coincidental that one of the extra-biblical attestations of the *qdš* is at Ugarit, where the *klb* is also attested. Both, therefore, may be used here with

---

Alten Testament', *Die Erzväter in der biblischen Tradition: Festschrift für Matthias Köckert* (ed. A. Hagedorn and H. Pfeiffer, BZAW 400, Berlin, de Gruyter, 2009), 209–240.

116  Riegner, *The Vanishing Hebrew Harlot*, 112. Compare Bird, 'The End of the Male Cult Prostitute', 46, who associates the קדשות with 'the persisting forms of Israelite cultic life that were rooted in indigenous tradition', also on the basis of Hosea.

reference to cultic personnel whom the deuteronomic author wished to identify as (problematically) non-Israelite.[117]

Ironically, the erroneous assumption of rampant cultic sexuality in the
ancient Near East may have produced an element of truth in the traditional
scholarly interpretations of this verse. The deuteronomic author was, indeed,
deeply concerned by the prospect of Israelites engaging in cultic practices
associable with (deuteronomically defined) non-Israelites; the practices in
question are simply not sexual in nature. Deuteronomy 23:18 may be most
clearly interpreted—even in the absence of particularities regarding the cultic
role in question—as dealing with the cultic vocations permissible to members
of the Israelite community: an attempt to eliminate cultic offices which might
confuse the procedures of the Yahwistic cult with those of non-Yahwistic cults.
This differentiation of Israelite practice is part of the wider context of deuteronomic identity concerns.

### 2.4.3    Voluntary Offerings

Though the relationship of Deut. 23:18 and Deut. 23:19 as parallel references to
sacred and profane sexual practices by women and men respectively must be
abandoned, revised interpretations of these verses indicate a common concern
with cultic aspects of distinctive Israelite cultural practice. In Deut. 23:19 two
types of voluntary offerings are specified as impermissible: מחיר כלב, usually
translated as 'the purchase price of a dog', and אתנן זונה, usually rendered 'the
hire price of a prostitute'. As already noted, the אתנן זונה has universally been
understood to refer to sexual acts performed for a price and it is this which has
so strongly influenced scholarly interpretations of Deut. 23:18–19: as Deut. 23:19
refers to sexual practices, so too must the prohibitions on the קדשה, the קדש
and the כלב.[118] That such an association with regard to קדשה and קדש is erroneous has already been established.

That both the אתנן זונה and the מחיר כלב, despite their obscurity, pertain
to details of cultic praxis is indicated by the specification that the funds in
question are not to cross the bounds of 'the house of Yʜᴡʜ your god for

---

117    M.I. Gruber, 'Hebrew qĕdēšāh and Her Canaanite and Akkadian Cognates', UF 18 (1986),
        133 n. 1.

118    Driver, Deuteronomy, 264; Braulik, Deuteronomium II, 173; Nielsen, Deuteronomium, 220,
        222. For a recent attempt see M. Simon-Shoshan, 'Ain't Nothing but a Hound Dog? The
        Meaning of the Noun klb in Northwest Semitic Languages in Light of Bt Rosh Hashanah
        4a', A Common Cultural Heritage: Studies on Mesopotamia and the Biblical World in Honor
        of Barry L. Eichler (ed. G. Frame, E. Leichty, K. Sonik, J.H. Tigay and S. Tinney, Bethesda,
        Md., CDL, 2011), 177–194.

any voluntary offering' (בית יהוה אלהיך לכל נדר).[119] That these offerings are addressed as a matter of cultural definition—akin to that seen in Deut. 23:18—is indicated by the statement that 'both of them are an abomination of YHWH your god' (כי תועבת יהוה אלהיך גם שניהם), with the תועבה terminology and the evocative reminder that the Israelite audience is fundamentally and exclusively Yahwistic indicating that the objection to these practices is concerned with (non-)Yahwistic, (non-)Israelite cultural practices.

The initial appearance of אתנן זונה in the verse has usually infected the interpretation of מחיר כלב, prompting interpretations attempting to identify כלב as a euphemism for a man who performs sexual acts for hire.[120] However, no evidence of כלב used in this way appears in the Hebrew Bible and nothing similar has surfaced from anywhere else in the ancient Near East.[121] While this hardly makes the suggestion impossible, it does make it difficult. Given also that the search for a sexual interpretation of כלב has been driven by the sexual interpretation for all of Deut. 23:18–19, which must now be abandoned, the particular need to locate a sexual meaning for מחיר כלב is no longer required. It might also be noted that the verse's emphatic final word, '*both* of them' (שניהם), tends to suggest that the ban on bringing מחיר כלב to the house of YHWH and the ban on bringing אתנן זונה should be understood as two independent elements of the injunction, related by virtue of their potential as voluntary offerings and allowed accordingly to share a verb, but not parallel repetitions of the same thing.

---

119   The phrase is particularly noteworthy given that this is the only explicit mention of the temple in the entire book (Nelson, *Deuteronomy*, 281; Nielsen, *Deuteronomium*, 223).

120   Thus, for example, Driver, *Deuteronomy*, 265.

121   The sole possible exception to this blanket statement is involves the *assinnu*, a Mesopotamian cult functionary devoted to Ishtar, whose title is associated in some lexical lists with a sign which may be read as 'dog', and who has frequently been associated with sexual cultic profligacy. The sign in question, however, is variably interpreted and no further evidence of such terminology has yet been found; the association between Ishtar's cultic functionaries and rampant sexual activity is also highly problematic (see Assante, 'Bad Girls and Kinky Boys?', 23–29, 37–49; I. Zsolnay, 'The Misconstrued Role of the *Assinnu* in Ancient Near Eastern Prophecy', *Prophets Male and Female: Gender and Prophecy in the Hebrew Bible, the Eastern Mediterranean and the Ancient Near East* (ed. C. Carvalho and J. Stökl, Ancient Israel and its Literature 15, Atlanta, Ga., Society for Biblical Literature, 2013), 81–99; S.M. Maul, '*kurgarrû* und *assinnu* und ihr Stand in der babylonischen Gesellschaft', *Außenseiter und Randgruppen: Beiträge zu einer Sozialgeschichte des Alten Orients* [ed. V. Haas, Xenia 32, Konstanz, Universitätsverlag Konstanz, 1992], 159–171).

Barring the interpretation of כלב as a euphemistic term for a male sex worker, however, an obvious alternative interpretation has remained lacking. Nelson suggests that it could be a term for a devoted follower of a particular god and, by extension, the devoted follower of a particular non-Yahwistic god, or that it might have something to do with real dogs: dogs were considered unclean, so might be thought to be contaminating the funds by association, though in what context remains obscure.[122] More tantalizing has been the discovery of hundreds of dog burials in Persian-period Ashkelon and the attendant suggestion that the reference here could be to a cultic practice involving actual dogs, but a cultic context of the Ashkelon burials is not clear and the animals were certainly not sacrificial.[123] Closer to home, sacrifice involving canines also appears in Isa. 66:3, albeit also later than the period to which Deut. 23:19 speaks. A background to the deuteronomic text which involved non-Yahwistic cultic practices with dogs might go some way toward explaining both what is opposed—bringing funds to the temple to purchase dogs for sacrifice—and why it is opposed in the language of תועבה, if such a practice was known and associated with cultic traditions not exclusively Yahwistic. The lack of chronologically proximate material or textual witness, however, means that this can be no more than speculation.

There is, however, another possibility. In the texts from Ugarit—where the *qdš(t)* has already been met—there appears a cult official identified as *klb*.[124] Elsewhere in ancient Near Eastern texts the term is used to describe a devoted servant.[125] It is possible, therefore, that this prohibition of bringing the fees of a *klb* to the house of YHWH לכל נדר—'for any offering' or 'for (i.e., to fulfil) any

---

122 D.L. Christensen, *Deuteronomy 21:10–34:12* (WBC 6B, Nashville, Tenn., Thomas Nelson, 2002), 549–550; Nelson, *Deuteronomy*, 281.

123 Tigay, *Deuteronomy*, 216, followed by Christensen, *Deuteronomy 21:10–34:12*, 547. For discussions of the Ashkelon material see L.E. Stager, 'Why Were Hundreds of Dogs Buried at Ashkelon?', *BAR* 17 (1991), 27–42; P. Wapnish and B. Hesse, 'Pampered Pooches or Plain Pariahs? The Ashkelon Dog Burials', *BA* 56 (1993), 55–80; B. Halpern, 'The Canine Conundrum of Ashkelon: A Classical Connection?', *The Archaeology of Jordan and Beyond: Essays in Honor of James A. Sauer* (ed. M.D. Coogan, J.A. Greene and L.E. Stager, SAHL 1, Winona Lake, Ind., Eisenbrauns, 2000), 133–144. Note also that one of the more likely factors playing into the Ashkelon burials is the Zoroastrian reverence for canids, with attendant chronological implications.

124 Gruber, 'Hebrew *qĕdēšāh*', 133 n. 1; note also a fourth century inscription from Kition (Goodfriend, 'Prostitution [Old Testament]', 5:507).

125 CAD 8, *s.v. kalbu*; Goodfriend, 'Prostitution (Old Testament)', 5:507. The Akkadian usage, however, appears to be a deliberate form of self-abasement in correspondence with superiors, rather than a specific title.

vow'—is an attempt to eliminate a specific cultic practitioner from the context of Yahwistic worship. As with the previous suggestion, chronological and geographical distance make straightforward conclusions impossible (although the possibility of an antecedent phenomenon in this case is somewhat more promising than subsequent attestations only), but it is possible that the deuteronomic choice of terminology here is deliberately targeted at a ritual specialist whose (deuteronomically) Yahwistic credentials were suspect. The deuteronomic legislation would, in that case, again be weeding out practices with the potential to blur the lines between Israelite and non-Israelite praxis, as in Deut. 23:18.

This leaves, finally, the prohibition of the אתנן זונה. The understanding of this phrase as referring to the fees of a sex worker holds the privileges of both tradition and consensus. Nevertheless, the context of this prohibition is very clearly cultic and, as has been quite thoroughly established already, the evidence for sexual activity associated with cultic praxis in the ancient Near East is slim, approaching non-existent. Indeed, when such activity is supposed to be the background for Deut. 23:18–19, it has not been Deut. 23:19 that has been thought to be the verse addressing cultic sexual activities, despite the verse's explicit cultic context; that (misplaced) honour has gone to Deut. 23:18. Deuteronomy 23:19 has been thought to refer to the commercial sale of sex.

Ironically, it is now the reference to the אתנן זונה in Deut. 23:19, employing language associated with prostitution in a clearly cultic context, which provides one of the few possible witnesses to cult-related sexual activities, by suggesting that the זונה might have played some such role in connection with the cult. The prohibitions preceding (Deut. 23:18) address the permissibility of specific cultic practitioners, the מחיר כלב probably relates to a similar issue and the cultic context is affirmed by the qualification of both the אתנן זונה and the מחיר כלב as inappropriate as voluntary offerings specifically. The cultic context, in other words, is irrefutable. The question thus becomes whether to fly in the face of all evidence regarding the non-existence of cult-related prostitution and take this single phrase as evidence for the presence of sex workers in connection with sacred sites. The possibility persists, however remotely, that there was a system of gifts and offerings at the temple which included a type of offering connected to sexual activity with a member of the temple's cultic personnel: an enacted element of prayers for fertility would seem the obvious context. It is also possible that it was this practice which led to the preponderance of prophetic characterisations of worship practices to which they were opposed in terms of prostitution—Hosea's rhetoric is a common example, and Micah might be similarly classed.

Rather than ignore all evidence to the contrary, however, it is also possible to turn the sequence on its head: to envision that the concept of an exclusive relationship between YHWH and YHWH's worshippers was expressed metaphorically in terms of marital fidelity—as well-attested in numerous texts, including Hosea and Ezekiel—and to suggest that this terminology led to the derisive designation of offerings which were thought to betray this exclusive relationship as 'prostitute donations', meaning something akin to 'the donations of those who are religiously promiscuous in the manner of prostitutes'. Understood thus, אתנן זונה is a derogative term for cult offerings whose Yahwistic pedigree is in doubt and the ban in Deut. 23:19 is a prohibition of offerings which do not meet the exacting requirements for exclusive Yahwistic worship.[126] Such an interpretation would make sense of these prohibitions in their immediate context as well as in the wider context of deuteronomic concern to establish an exclusively Yahwistic cultural practice which distinguishes Israelite practice from that of non-Israelites, with the added advantage of better cohering with what is known of cultic practice elsewhere in the ancient Near East.

From a slightly different angle, other evidence in favour of the interpretation of אתנן זונה as a phrase for offensively non-Yahwistic offerings occurs in a recent study into the root זנה, which argues that the root's core meaning is 'to participate in non-Yahwistic religious practice' and that it is in this sense that the majority of uses of the root are properly interpreted, with only in a handful of texts that it means 'to prostitute' or 'to be promiscuous'.[127] If this thesis is correct, Deut. 23:19 would make even better sense in its immediate context, with אתנן זונה referring to non-Yahwistic voluntary donations and Deut. 23:18–19 thus consistently focused on the eradication of a series of specific non-Yahwistic cultic functionaries and practices, cohering with the wider interests of the deuteronomic text.

---

126   The otherwise redundant 'for *any* voluntary offering' (לכל נדר) might support such a reading, if it is an attempt to indicate that in no circumstances were any offerings not exclusively Yahwistic to be brought to the temple.

127   Riegner, *The Vanishing Hebrew Harlot.* Riegner suggests that it is the confusion of these variant meanings, combined especially with the prophets' metaphorical presentations of the YHWH-Israel relationship as a marital relationship which has been betrayed by Israel's pursuit of non-Yahwistic practices, which has turned the prophetic language accusing Israel of non-fidelity to YHWH into language accusing Israel of 'prostitution'. Riegner focuses especially on Hosea, where the marriage metaphor is especially prominent, but emphasises that the clear issue for Hosea is Israel's pursuit of non-Yahwistic cult practices, not Israel's sexual practices.

2.4.4       Transvestitism

Deuteronomy 22:5 has attracted attention from scholars primarily as a result of its use of a motivation clause with תועבה, hinting that the issue involved in this prohibition is more than a mere passing preference. The verse comprises three parts, including the תועבה clause; the first prohibits the כלי גבר from being (היה) upon a woman and the second prohibits said גבר from donning (לבש) the שמלת אשה. The motivation of this imperative has been suggested to lie in an attempt to prevent men from avoiding military duty and women from accompanying the army;[128] to relate to the use of male and female attire in sympathetic magic rituals designed to affect the sexual potency of an individual or his enemy;[129] to reflect a wider concern for avoiding the improper mixture of categories, perhaps stemming from the reproductive requirements of agrarian society;[130] to stem from the purported associations of transvestite behaviour with foreign deities or foreign cult practices;[131] to relate to concerns about the use of clothing as disguise;[132] or to derive from some combination of one or more of these.[133]

Given that the few images available show civilian men and women wearing largely similar attire, it is surely right to suppose that the issue here is something more particular than merely the swapping of clothing. This is also strongly suggested by the particularity of the vocabulary the verse employs. The attire denied to women is כלי גבר: although the precise nuance of כלי is disputable, it is most likely to be referring either to weaponry or to some specific

---

128    C.M. Carmichael, *The Laws of Deuteronomy* (London, Cornell University Press, 1974), 147–148.

129    H.A. Hoffner, 'Symbols for Masculinity and Femininity: Their Use in Ancient Near Eastern Sympathetic Magic Rituals', *JBL* 85 (1966), 332–334.

130    P.J. Harland, 'Menswear and Womenswear: A Study of Deuteronomy 22:5', *ExpTim* 110 (1998), 75–76; N.S. Fox, 'Gender Transformation and Transgression: Contextualizing the Prohibition of Cross-Dressing in Deuteronomy 22:5', *Mishneh Todah: Studies in Deuteronomy and Its Cultural Environment in Honor of Jeffrey H. Tigay* (ed. N.S. Fox, D.A. Glatt-Gilad and M.J. Williams, Winona Lake, Ind., Eisenbrauns, 2009), 70–71.

131    W.W. Hallo, 'Biblical Abominations and Sumerian Taboos', *JQR* 76 (1985), 37; W.H.P. Römer, 'Randbemerkungen zur Travestie von Deut. 22,5', *Travels in the World of the Old Testament: Studies Presented to Professor M.A. Beek on the Occasion of His 65th Birthday* (ed. M.S.H.G. Heerma van Voss, Ph. H.J. Houwink ten Cate and N.A. van Uchelen, SSN 16, Assen, Van Gorcum, 1974), 217–222.

132    S. Schroer, 'Die Problematik der Verkleidung im Alten Israel', *Diasynchron: Beiträge zur Exegese, Theologie und Rezeption der hebräischen Bibel: Walter Dietrich zum 65. Geburtstag* (ed. T. Naumann and R. Hunziker-Rodewald, Stuttgart, Kohlhammer, 2009), 338–339.

133    H.T. Vedeler, 'Reconstructing Meaning in Deuteronomy 22:5: Gender, Society, and Transvestitism in Israel and the Ancient Near East', *JBL* 127 (2008), 459–476.

'implement' of the גבר, who in turn is not identified with the generic term for 'man' (איש) but the more specific גבר, the term used of men as warriors.[134] Vedeler has recently argued that גבר is used here as a deliberate means of focusing on the most hyper-masculine manifestation of Israelite manhood; men identified by this term are those distinguished by their strength and virility in particular.[135] It thus seems reasonable to suggest that the law is concerned with the extremes of gender roles: not all men's attire, in generic terms, is prohibited for the woman to wear, but specifically the attire characteristic of a man in his military persona. This leads to the question of why the author does not want women wearing the attire characteristic of hyper-masculine men and why hyper-masculine, military men are to avoid womenswear. Suggestions have included a concern with the blurring of sex or gender divisions, homosexual role-playing or other sexual activity and, most frequently, non-Israelite religious practices, the spectre of which is raised especially by the appearance of תועבה.[136]

That other ancient Near Eastern cultures conceived both of the possibility of a 'third sex' which was neither male nor female (either androgynous or, more usually, hermaphrodite) and the possibility of gender identification at odds with biologically-defined sex, reflected especially in references to transvestitism, is witnessed by an abundance of extra-biblical material.[137] These are most extensively witnessed by the Mesopotamian repertoire, but there is also evidence for such concepts in the southern Levant, in the Transjordan,

134 The common translation of כלי as 'clothing' is based on the plural form having this meaning in rabbinic Hebrew; in biblical Hebrew, however, it normally means 'weapon', 'implement' or 'vessel' (HALOT 2, *s.v.* כלי).

135 Vedeler, 'Reconstructing Meaning', 469–472; thus HALOT 1, *s.v.* גבר; contra H. Kosmala, 'The Term *geber* in the Old Testament and in the Scrolls', *Congress Volume: Rome 1968* (VTSup 17, Leiden, Brill, 1969), 159–169.

136 References as above; among the commentaries note especially Tigay, *Deuteronomy*, 200 and Mayes, *Deuteronomy*, 307, citing Römer, 'Randbemerkungen zur Travestie von Deut. 22,5' on the Mesopotamian Ishtar cult. Nielsen, *Deuteronomium*, 211, 214 points chronologically further afield to Lucian's *De Dea Syria* (15, 26, 51) and a description there of a fertility cult involving the exchange of clothing in the course of worshipping the fertility deity; Braulik, *Deuteronomium II*, 161–162, prefers a Canaanite target but notes also the Mesopotamian Ishtar cult.

137 See Fox, 'Gender Transformation', 52–53; Vedeler, 'Reconstructing Meaning', 464–469; W. Roscoe, 'Priests of the Goddess: Gender Transgression in Ancient Religion', *HR* 35 (1996), 213–217.

in Philistia and in the Beersheba-Arad valley.[138] Although Nelson rightly cautions that cultural anthropology has recorded forms of gender transformations in many different contexts, including but not limited to the ritual sphere, transvestitism in the ancient Near East is known only in the cultic realm.[139] That the text is prohibiting some practice considered typical of or with associations to non-Israelite cultural or religious practice is a plausible interpretation of this otherwise isolated imperative, especially in light of the evidence for various forms of gender ambiguity, both human and divine, in both the southern Levant and Mesopotamia.[140] In this respect it is relevant to note that the particular nuances of גבר include not only implications of strength and virility on the part of the man in question but also that the man is in a close, obedient relationship with Yhwh.[141] While Vedeler focuses on the importance of the former in Israelite gender ideology, suggesting that the concern in Deut. 22:5 is the threat which (cultic) transvestitism poses to the virility of the

---

138  R. Kletter, 'Pots and Polities: Material Remains of Late Iron Age Judah in Relation to Its Political Borders', *BASOR* 314 (1999), 19–54, 381–385; P. Beck, 'Human Figurine with Tambourine', *Tel 'Ira: A Stronghold in the Biblical Negev* (ed. I. Beit-Arieh, MSIA 15, Tel Aviv, Tel Aviv University, 1999), 386–394; and Fox, 'Gender Transformation', 57–58 for references to the southern Levantine material; also Fox, 'Gender Transformation', 61–62 for an Egyptian depiction of transvestite performers from the southern Levant. Fox rejects the possibility of a cultic interpretation of Deut. 22:5 on the grounds that there is no evidence for Israelite borrowing of Mesopotamian cult rituals (Fox, 'Gender Transformation', 66). While that point has been under dispute for decades, the southern Levantine material renders the point academic: there are various witnesses to similar ideas in the southern Levant with which the Israelite Yahwists were likely familiar. Whether the hermaphrodite figurines in question are best understood as deities or humans is not yet clear.

139  Nelson, *Deuteronomy*, 268; Vedeler, 'Reconstructing Meaning', 464–469. For an entertaining account of a number of more recent transvestites see C.J.S. Thompson, *Mysteries of Sex: Women Who Posed as Men and Men Who Impersonated Women* (London, Hutchinson, 1974).

140  Vedeler, 'Reconstructing Meaning', 464–469 focuses especially on the Mesopotamian material surrounding Ishtar/Inanna, but note also Fox, 'Gender Transformation', 57–58, 61–62. As with Deut. 23:2, it should be remembered that the dominance of Mesopotamian comparisons reflects the relative abundance and paucity of Mesopotamian and Levantine witnesses, respectively; the evidence which does exist indicates that similar ideas and practices occurred also in the southern Levant. While locating the target of deuteronomic ire is in these instances inevitably imprecise, the more numerous witnesses to Mesopotamian practice should not lead to a default assumption that it is the Mesopotamian cultural sphere which the deuteronomic material has in its sights.

141  Kosmala, 'The Term *geber*', 162–164, cf. 164–167 on Job; Vedeler, 'Reconstructing Meaning', 172.

hyper-masculine גבר, Kosmala's work suggests that any threat to a man's status as גבר would also constitute a threat to his relationship with YHWH. Combined with the concentration of the evidence for ancient Near Eastern transvestitism in connection with deities and their cults, this reinforces the idea that Deut. 22:5 has to do with the risks which the behaviours it describes pose to the Israelite male's unique and exclusive relationship with YHWH. The verse is thus a case in which the deuteronomic legislation aims to protect the relationship between the Israelite and YHWH and to do so by differentiating Israelite practice from non-Israelite.

### 2.4.5    תועבה: Sacrificial Offerings, Weights and Diet

There are a large number of passages in Deuteronomy, some of which have already been discussed, which describe individual acts or practices with the term תועבה, traditionally rendered into English as 'abomination, abhorrent thing' or similar. Though the English thus emphasises the hatefulness of the person, object or practice thus described, without indicating the cause for hatred, the Hebrew usage suggests a more specific function of indicating the alien or alienating character of these entities: people, practices and objects described as תועבה are somehow strange or distant—'alien'—from the perspective of the text.[142] This nuance has been often acknowledged in the context of Deuteronomy's concerns about non-Israelites, in no small part because in the cases where the objection to the practice in question is made explicit the consistent point of reference is the association of the practice(s) with non-Israelites, especially the previous inhabitants of the land. This is obvious in the prohibitions regarding the use of images of non-Israelite gods (Deut. 7:25–26); certain divinatory practices involving children (Deut. 12:31, cf. Deut. 18:10) and a wide range of technical divinatory practices, opposed to the intuitive (prophetic) divinatory methods which are used by Israelites (Deut. 18:9–12); as

---

142    E. Gerstenberger, 'תעב t'b pi. to abhor', TLOT 3:1431; cf. L'Hour, 'Les interdits to'eba', 503. The identification of a person, object or practice as 'alien' usually occurs from an Israelite perspective, though not always (e.g., Gen. 46:34); in practice תועבה is therefore often used to indicate something which is 'non-Israelite', but its use is not limited to this meaning. I hope to address this in greater detail in a forthcoming study. Previous discussions include L'Hour, 'Les interdits'; R.E. Clements, 'The Concept of Abomination in the Book of Proverbs', Texts, Temples and Traditions: A Tribute to Menahem Haran (ed. M.V. Fox, V.A. Hurowitz, A. Hurvitz, M.L. Klein, B.J. Schwartz and N. Shupak, Winona Lake, Ind., Eisenbrauns, 1996), 211–225; P. Humbert, 'Le substantif to'ēbā et le verbe t'b dans l'Ancien Testament', ZAW 72 (1960), 217–237; H.D. Preuss, 'תּוֹעֵבָה tô'ēḇâ; תעב t'b', TDOT 15:591–604; see also W. McKane, Proverbs: A New Approach (OTL, London, SCM, 1970), 301–302; Weinfeld, Deuteronomy and the Deuteronomic School, 265–267, 268, 296, 323, cf. 226.

well as the worship of deities other than Yʜᴡʜ, Israel's particular god (Deut. 13:15; 17:4; cf. 27:15; 32:16).[143] In addition to these texts, in which the association between a specific practice and non-Israelites is explicitly stated, there are also a number of passages in which a given practice is simply described as תועבה, without further elaboration. The wider interpretation of this terminology as denoting a person's, practice's or object's alienness suggests that such concerns ought to be borne in mind in these more obscure passages as well.

In some cases, including a number of those discussed in this section, the association of the practice with non-Israelites is still (just about) recognisable to the modern reader, as with the legislation regarding voluntary offerings (Deut. 23:19) and transvestitism (Deut. 22:5). In others the matter remains obscure, with the role of the prohibitions in differentiating Israelite practice now signalled only by the use of תועבה. Included in this category are the sacrificial offerings of Deut. 17:1, the (dis)honest weights of Deut. 25:13–16 and the dietary prescriptions of Deut. 14:3, 21. This section, on the definition of Israelite practice, will conclude by briefly examining each of these.

The sacrifice of imperfect animals is identified as תועבה, non-Israelite, in Deut. 17:1. A number of commentators note that the verse reiterates a principle apparent already from Deut. 15:21–23.[144] The law is repeated in its general sense also in Lev. 22:20–21, where it lacks the distinguishing תועבה language, ignoring

---

143    It should be noted that, while some of the things described with this terminology, both in the deuteronomic material and elsewhere in the Hebrew Bible, can be persuasively argued to reflect practices known to have been engaged in by non-Israelites (according to any definition), the indications that many of the practices thus stigmatised were also engaged in by 'Israelites' at one time or another suggests that the use of תועבה language is constructive as well as descriptive in intent: it is used to actively create an 'Israelite' identity by advocating the abandonment of certain practices on the grounds that they are 'non-Israelite'. Compare, for example, the constructive capacity of ethnic identity formation as described by Cohen, *Custom and Politics*; Barth, 'Introduction'; see also J.D.Y. Peel, 'The Cultural Work of Yoruba Ethnogenesis', *History and Ethnicity* (ed. E. Tonkin, M. McDonald and M. Chapman, ᴀsᴀ Monographs 27, London, Routledge, 1989), 198–215; C.F. Keyes, 'The Dialectics of Ethnic Change', *Ethnic Change* (ed. C.F. Keyes, London, University of Washington Press, 1981), 3–30. Note also Southwood's discussion of the language of 'foreignness' in Ezra 9–10 (K.E. Southwood, *Ethnicity and the Mixed Marriage Crisis in Ezra 9–10: An Anthropological Approach* [ᴏᴛᴍ, Oxford, Oxford University Press, 2012], 191–211). Elsewhere, Varšo suggests that the recurrence of תועבה in the so-called law of office is meant to emphasise the role of these persons in eliminating non-Israelite practices (M. Varšo, 'Abomination in the Legal Code of Deuteronomy: Can an Abomination Motivate?', *ZABR* 13 [2007], 254–255).

144    Halpern, 'The Centralization Formula', 29; Nelson, *Deuteronomy*, 218; Driver, *Deuteronomy*, 205.

the deuteronomic concerns about distinctiveness in lieu of characteristically priestly concerns about purity and perfection.[145] Though hardly determinative on its own, the deuteronomic law's appearance in the midst of other laws directed at differentiating Israelite praxis contributes to the interpretation of Deut. 17:1 as interested in limiting the audience's religious-cultural practices to those which are distinctively Israelite (Deut. 16:21–22; 17:2–7).

The law about just weights and measures is occasionally identified as arising from the Israelites' relationship with their neighbours (Deut. 25:13–16).[146] Interpreting the law in this light is not necessary, but given the persistent association of the תועבה language with this issue it may be proposed as at least one possible, even probable, interpretation. It should also be noted that interpreting the תועבה language as an indicator of concerns about alien or alienating associations helps smooth the apparent disjuncture between the wisdom context in which this law is usually perceived as having its roots and the present deuteronomic context: in the usual interpretation of תועבה renders its appearances in Proverbs as an expression of social ethics and its appearances elsewhere, including Deuteronomy, as relating to the cult. In such a dichotomised understanding of תועבה, this law sits awkwardly: its nearest affinities appear to be to the wisdom texts, but nevertheless its current location is squarely in the deuteronomic text and its usage of תועבה.[147] The peculiarity is pre-empted when תועבה is understood in both Proverbs and Deuteronomy (and elsewhere) as denoting the alien or alienating quality of the person, practice or object so described. Understanding the term as indicating non-Israelite associations (real or rhetorical) explains the addition of a motivation clause to a law whose imperative would have been self-evident as a matter of social ethics but bears no apparent relationship to the cult by suggesting that its appearance here is intended to indicate a concern regarding specifically Israelite cultural practice.

---

145   Though note, curiously, the additional specification that such animals are not to be accepted from a foreigner, perhaps hinting at the differentiation discerned (or desired) by Deut. 17:1.

146   Mayes, *Deuteronomy*, 314, who however identifies it as deuteronomistic; Nelson, *Deuteronomy*, 301–302 limits the deuteronomistic addition to Deut. 25:15, which prevents the תועבה statement from coming directly after the positive injunction in that verse and instead has it follow directly from the negative command in Deut. 25:13–14 as is more usual; Nielsen, *Deuteronomium*, 230 maintains almost the entirety of the section as deuteronomic (Deut. 25:13a, 14a, 15–16a).

147   Braulik, *Deuteronomium II*, 190.

Last but not least, the dietary laws in Deut. 14:3, 21a, 21b probably also fall into the category of deuteronomic ethnic identity legislation.[148] The intervening list of clean and unclean animals is closely related to a similar list in Lev. 11:2–23 and that a substantial portion of this section has either been taken over from the Leviticus text or derives from some shared source is generally assumed.[149] Most interesting in this regard is the significant difference between the Deuteronomy and Leviticus versions of the list, namely, the statement in Deut. 14:3 which now acts as a heading for the whole: 'You will not eat any alien thing' (לא תאכל כל תועבה). Missing in the Leviticus version, this categorical statement instructs the Israelites to distinguish themselves in their culinary praxis just as they distinguish themselves in other cultural praxis.[150]

---

148  The preceding injunction regarding mourning practices (Deut. 14:1) is probably also related to the definition of Israelite cultural praxis. Its plural verbs and the extensive biblical records of the practice until quite a late period—including the prohibition of the same or similar practices in Leviticus—suggest, however, that it is part of the continual revision of the deuteronomic identity concerns for new circumstances. The holiness language which has crept into this chapter—not to mention the duplications in the lists of clean and unclean animals—likewise seems to indicate redactional activity undertaken with the priestly material in mind; given the interests of this latter in Israelite identity definition and protection, an interest in the deuteronomic material is hardly surprising. On the practice itself see Lewis, *Cults of the Dead*, 99–104; J. Gray, 'The Book of Job in the Context of Near Eastern Literature', *ZAW* 82 (1972), 262–263. On the significance of foodways to identity see Altmann, *Festive Meals*, 42–66 and references there.

149  Nelson, *Deuteronomy*, 177–178; Weinfeld, *Deuteronomy 1–11*, 30; following W.L. Moran, 'The Literary Connection between Lv. 11:13–19 and Dt. 14:12–18', *CBQ* 28 (1966), 271–277; previously Driver, *Deuteronomy*, xi. See also R. Achenbach, 'Zur Systematik der Speisegebote in Leviticus 11 und in Deuteronomium 14', *ZABR* 17 (2011), 161–209, regarding the relation of these to the rest of the Pentateuch. Mayes, *Deuteronomy*, 238 retains only Deut. 14:2–3, 21ff. as deuteronomic, while Veijola, *Das 5. Buch Mose*, 294 reverses this to identify Deut. 14:1–2, 21b as secondary additions; Braulik, *Deuteronomium 1–16,17*, 108 identifies the entirety of Deut. 13:2–14:21 as a 'digression', although whether this means it is also secondary is not immediately evident.

150  The insertion of this list at this point in the text has the simultaneous effect of explicating the identification of the clean and unclean as deriving from their alien associations and elaborating an originally blanket statement into meticulous, if theoretical, detail: though it has been suggested that one of the factors governing the cleanness or uncleanness of a given animal was that animal's use in the cultic practices of non-Israelites—with references sometimes to texts such as Isa. 65:3–4 (cf. Deut. 14:8); Isa. 66:3, 17 (cf. Deut. 14:8, 19, but note that שור and שה are permitted in Deut. 14:4) and Ezek. 8:9–10 (cf. Deut. 14:19)—it is usually now admitted that this cannot be consistently applied as an explanation for all of the animals disallowed by this text. For the classic presentation of this argument see

This is a general statement about the development and pursuit of a distinctively Israelite culinary practice; what follows addresses more specifically what may be eaten (Deut. 14:4–20) and the way in which it may be prepared (Deut. 14:21–29). 'You may eat this but not that; you may prepare it like this but not like that: you are not like non-Israelites.' Nelson rightly observes that the law here constitutes an attempt 'to construct and reconstruct endangered boundaries around Israel's peoplehood ... The idea held in common [with Deuteronomy 12–13] is that Israel is different from other peoples ... [b]y forbidding these customs and foods, Deuteronomy seeks to distinguish Israel from other peoples, defining chosen peoplehood in terms of cultural behavior.'[151] The idea that certain cultural practices define the Israelites is already a clear deuteronomic theme by Deut. 14:3; the author resumes the issue of animal slaughter—to explain that the centralisation of sacrificial slaughter need not preclude meat consumption by those at some distance from the single sacrificial site (Deut. 14:22–29)—by emphasising that the changes in sacrificial rules must not be accompanied by dietary behaviour not in keeping with a distinctively Israelite praxis.

Elaborating the general statement of Deut. 14:3 in two specific ways are Deut. 14:21a and 14:21b. The former, which prohibits the consumption of carrion by any Israelite but permits its gift to the גר and its sale to the foreigner, explicitly legislates different behaviour for the Israelite and the non-Israelite.[152] Non-Israelites—of any kind—may eat carrion; Israelites do not. Throughout

---

M.T. Douglas, *Purity and Danger: An Analysis of Concepts of Pollution and Taboo* (London, Routledge, 1969).

151   Nelson, *Deuteronomy*, 175–176. Similarly Mayes, 'Deuteronomy 14', 165: these laws 'are the means by which the people of Yahweh are to demonstrate their separateness from the peoples and cultures of their environment.' Interestingly, however, he concludes that the chapter cannot have been an original part of the lawcode on the grounds that its world view presupposes a community which is separate from and intolerant of outsiders and in which status is ascribed by birth, whereas the rest of the book reflects the eventual acceptance of some outsiders, such as the גר, and a status which is not acquired at birth but dependent on behaviour. Once the emphasis on innate community status is recognised as deriving from the close connections to the priestly holiness material, however, the same emphasis on behaviour as is witnessed elsewhere is readily evident.

152   The primarily singular form of the injunctions in Deut. 14:21 seem to imply that they follow on from the singular Deut. 14:3, with the plural of Deut. 14:4–20 an interjection; the initial plural in Deut. 14:21 attempts to smooth over the break. While in keeping with the underlying idea of a differentiated Israel, the reiteration of the holiness idea (cf. Deut. 14:1–2) is perhaps likely to be part of a holiness-orientated editorial hand in this chapter (and elsewhere, cf. Deut. 7:6; 23:14; 28:9); alternatively, it may have been the impetus for such intervention, given that the idea of YHWH's holiness and the potential for this to

these chapters the objective is to differentiate between the way that Israelites do things and the way non-Israelites do things: Israelites sacrifice at a single site, while non-Israelites sacrifice at many; Israelites worship a single god, YHWH, while non-Israelites worship many gods and gods other than YHWH; Israelites and non-Israelites eat and prepare their food differently.

The half verse at Deut. 14:21b has provoked all manner of explanations regarding who might have been boiling young goats in the milk (or fat, depending on the pointing of חלב) of their mothers and why the author felt the need to object to the practice.[153] Particularly popular has been the suggestion that a Ugaritic ritual text describes just such a practice in a cultic context and that the practice was therefore a common 'Canaanite' one.[154] If correct, the deuteronomic injunction becomes comprehensible as one of the many aimed at eradicating culturally ambiguous practices. As convenient as such a background would be for the current thesis, re-examination of the Ugaritic text has undermined the reading and evidence for this practice outside the Hebrew Bible remains lacking.[155] Accordingly any suggestion that the practice was rejected because of its cultural or cultural-cultic ambiguity remains conjectural—although certainly possible, if not highly likely, if Deut. 14:21b is viewed as still under the תועבה rubric announced in Deut. 14:3—and suggestions that the issue is violation of maternal relations (cf. Exod. 22:29;

---

have implications for human behaviour is hardly innovative and is already present in the Exodus parallel (Exod. 22:29–30).

153  For a history of scholarship see S. Schorch, '"A Young Goat in Its Mother's Milk"? Understanding an Ancient Prohibition', *VT* 60 (2010), 116–130; on the pointing see J.M. Sasson, 'Ritual Wisdom? On "Seething a Kid in Its Mother's Milk"', *Kein Land für sich allein: Studien zum Kulturkontakt in Kanaan, Israel/Palaestina und Ebirnâri für Manfred Weippert zum 65. Geburtstag* (ed. U. Hübner and E.A. Knauf, OBO 186, Göttingen, Vandenhoeck & Ruprecht, 2002), 294–308.

154  Already Maimonides, but gaining momentum in the twentieth century in connection with KTU 1.23; for more recent variants see O. Keel, *Das Böcklein in der Milch seiner Mutter und Verwandtes: Im Lichte eines altorientalischen Bildmotivs* (OBO 33, Freiburg, Universitätsverlag, 1980), who bases his argument on iconographic grounds, and E.A. Knauf, 'Zur Herkunft und Sozialgeschichte Israels: "Das Böckchen in der Milch seiner Mutter"', *Bib* 69 (1988), 153–169; contrast especially M. Haran, 'Das Böcklein in der Milch seiner Mutter und das Säugende Muttertier', *TZ* 41 (1985), 135–159.

155  R. Ratner and B. Zuckerman, 'A Kid in Milk? New Photographs of KTU 1.23, Line 14', *HUCA* 57 (1986), 51 concluded, categorically, that 'no introductory biblical textbook, biblical commentary, biblical history, Bible dictionary entry or encyclopedia article should cite this comparison as a clear example of religious or cultural interplay between ancient Israel and its neighbors' (although they do not completely exclude the possibility, either).

Lev. 22:27–28; Deut. 22:6–7), some kind of abuse connected to festival celebrations, on the basis of the law's context in Exod. 23:19; 34:26, or a prohibition of
eating the animal while still suckling, remain possible.[156]

### 2.5    Summary

The homogenisation of Israelite culture through the elimination of diverse sub-
cultures and the differentiation of Israelites from non-Israelites forms a major
component of the deuteronomic identity project. Exclusive Yahwism acts to
differentiate Israelites by virtue of the identity of their particular deity as well
as through the peculiar practice of worshipping a single deity. This Yahwistic
peculiarity is supported through the physical congregation of Israelites at a single cult site, with spatial proximity promoting regular interaction among group
members and reinforcing common beliefs and values. A common mythology
of Israel's origins in an exodus from Egypt unites the group around a shared
past. Ritual practices, including the particularities of cultic officials, divinatory experts and permissible offerings, contribute to Israelite differentiation.
Collectively, these features of Israelite identity go some way towards achieving
the deuteronomic identity project.

---

156    Schorch, '"A Young Goat"', argues for the last of these; in the process of rejecting the
       suggestion of Knauf, 'Zur Herkunft' (that the prohibition should be connected to wor-
       ship of Anat and Astarte) he contends that there is no proof for the idea 'that the idea
       was a means of self-delimitation'. Against Schorch see P. Guillaume, 'Binding "Sucks": A
       Response to Stefan Schorch', *VT* 61 (2011), 335–337 (referring to his earlier P. Guillaume,
       'Thou Shalt Not Curdle Milk with Rennet', *UF* 34 [2002], 213–215, which connects the
       law to cheese production). Possible humanitarian explanations are cited by M. Haran,
       'Seething a Kid in Its Mother's Milk', *JJS* 30 (1979), 23–35; J. Milgrom, *Leviticus 1–16: A New
       Translation with Introduction and Commentary* (AB 3, New York, N.Y., Yale University
       Press, 1991), 739; C.J. Labuschagne, 'Divine Speech in Deuteronomy', *Das Deuteronomium:
       Entstehung, Gestalt und Botschaft* (ed. N. Lohfink, BETL 68, Leuven, Leuven University
       Press, 1985), 111–126. Christensen, *Deuteronomy 1:1–21:9*, 288 follows Labuschagne in sug-
       gesting that it has something to do with the apparent presence of blood in milk imme-
       diately after birth, which would provide an additional link between this verse and the
       subsequent one; Veijola, *Das 5. Buch Mose*, 301 concludes that entire prohibition is an
       addition deriving from the general context of food and animals, but the reversed citation
       style of Deut. 14:21b–22 when compared to Exod. 23:19; 34: 26 suggests that the elimina-
       tion of Deut. 14:21b demands the elimination also of Deut. 14:22; the latter exhibits no
       justification for its removal and Veijola, *Das 5. Buch Mose*, 2 does not attempt it.

3        Defending Israel: Kinship, Segregation and the Formation of an
         Endo-culture

The formation of Israelite identity is a complex undertaking, operating on
ideological as well as practical levels and across a wide range of social contexts, both ritual and otherwise. The simple differentiation of Israelites from
non-Israelites, while important, is not in itself enough to support and perpetuate Israelite identity. Having gone some way towards defining Israelite identity, the deuteronomic project works to protect Israelite identity from outside
encroachments by isolating Israelites, insofar as possible, from non-Israelites.
Indeed, the importance of the protection of the peculiarities of Israelite norms
and practice has been already anticipated, with Deut. 13:2–19 achieving the
simultaneous reiteration of the importance of exclusive Yahwism to Israelite
identity as well as the deliberate elimination of threats to that exclusivism.
Further efforts to this end revolve mainly around the elimination of potential
avenues of interaction between Israelites and non-Israelites, in order to deny
Israelites the opportunity of engaging with and absorbing cultural practices
of non-Israelites. Such opportunities divide between those occurring on the
personal level—marriage and family—and those with their primary locus on
the community level—the king, the conduct of warfare and the official stance
*vis-à-vis* foreigners. Like the concentration of the Israelite population at the
single cult site, this type of identity formation activity acts both to discourage social interaction outside the group and to encourage social interaction
inside it, thereby creating a self-perpetuating endo-culture, in which 'primary
relations ... are governed by [the group's] specific values, norms, and beliefs'.[157]
This prioritisation of in-group interaction is often and unsurprisingly articulated in terms of kinship, '[e]xploit[ing] the strong sentiments and emotions
that are associated with primary relationship between members and the elementary family'.[158] As will be seen, kinship language is especially prominent in
the legislation which protects Israelite identity by legislating preferential treatment for Israelites, subtly but deliberately differentiating between Israelites
and non-Israelites.

3.1      *Segregation of the Israelite Family from Non-Israelites*
A number of the preceding discussions have highlighted the importance for
identity formation of the encouragement and facilitation of group socialisation, especially for the reinforcement of group values, norms and beliefs.

---

157    Cohen, *Custom and Politics*, 203.
158    Cohen, *Custom and Politics*, 208–109.

Conversely, a critical mechanism for protecting this newly-forming identity is the discouragement of social interactions outside the group.[159] Although the protection of Israelite identity through the discouragement of interactions with non-Israelites occurs perhaps most blatantly in the deuteronomic rejections of non-Israelites at the community-wide level, the deuteronomic efforts to dissociate Israelites from non-Israelites occurs also at the family level, with the protection of Israelite identity through the discouragement of intermarriage in particular.

### 3.1.1      Intermarriage

Given the propensity of ethnic identity to be articulated in terms of genetic cohesion (real or rhetorical), perhaps the single foremost threat to a distinctively Israelite identity is the possibility of the dissolution of that identity through intermarriage with non-Israelites.[160] The practice of endogamy contributes in a fundamental way to a group's mythology of common genetic origins, lending it the appearance of reality as well as acting as a mechanism for enforcing a group's cultural commonality by dictating that the most primary of primary relationships will be governed by the common values shared by members of the group.[161] It comes as no surprise to see Southwood opine that 'intermarriage is in many ways the "bottom line" of ethnicity' ... '[e]ndogamy is a particularly effective device for maintaining the durability of group boundaries and of the transmission of group identity through time, since a mixed union may mean not only the defection of a member of the group, but also a loss of

---

159    Cohen, *Custom and Politics*, 203.

160    Though the imagined nature of genetic cohesion may be readily recognisable as myth, it remains necessary: 'There is nothing strange or modern in overlooking a gap between the real and the mythical. The latter establishes the necessary moral unity of a group.... The recognition of ancestry pretends, "imagines" if you like, a genetic origin which may not be biologically correct. It remains socially correct, however, and even morally necessary to define the social mythically in terms of the genetic' (Hastings, *The Construction of Nationhood*, 170). Intermarriage has been discussed in the context of Ezra-Nehemiah and the identity concerns of the post-exilic period extensively, but the commonality, if not universality, of the phenomenon gives little reason to limit its occurrence among identity-conscious Israelites to the post-exilic period alone. On that period see Southwood, *Ethnicity*; C. Hayes, *Gentile Impurities and Jewish Identities: Intermarriage and Conversion from the Bible to the Talmud* (Oxford, Oxford University Press, 2002); both with further references.

161    Cohen, *Custom and Politics*, 203.

the children'.[162] Warning similarly regarding the problematic consequences of exogamy for identity, Lehmann observes its assimilatory effects: 'Nothing ties such settlements as closely as intermarriage. Long term observations of intermarriage show that previously distinct groups assimilated to the point of sharing a common culture...[It] tie[s] individuals, families, settlements and more comprehensive groups together.'[163] In the case of Israelite and non-Israelite, the clear danger of intermarriage is that the regular integration of non-Israelites into the group through intermarriage runs the risk of the Israelites' assumption and assimilation of the non-Israelites' norms and practices.

As already observed, the mythology of an Israel with origins outside the land, in Egypt, presents a particular conundrum in this respect: Israel's origins outside the land imply the presence of non-Israelites in the land (Deut. 20:15–16 notwithstanding). Already Deut. 6:12–13 warns against the confusion which may arise as a result of exposure to these non-Yahwistic inhabitants, namely the temptations posed by their gods and associated cultural practices, reminding the Israelites that their identity is rooted in its peculiar relationship to YHWH and its collective experience of YHWH in a departure from Egypt. Though other deities are not named, the reiteration that it is 'YHWH your god you will fear and him you will serve and by his name you will swear' (את יהוה אלהיך תירא ואתו תעבד ובשמו תשבע, Deut. 6:13; note the emphatic syntax) alludes to the possibility that the newly-settled Israelites might be tempted to worship the local deities, who might be given credit for these 'great and good cities which you did not build and houses full of everything good which you did not fill, hewn cisterns which you did not hew, gardens and olive trees which you did not plant, so you may eat and be sated' (ערים גדלת וטבת אשר לא בנית

---

162    Southwood, *Ethnicity*, 62, 67. Similarly: 'Ethnicity defines the group within which one is normally expected to marry' (Hastings, *The Construction of Nationhood*, 168).

163    G. Lehmann, 'Reconstructing the Social Landscape of Early Israel: Rural Marriage Alliances in the Central Hill Country', *TA* 31 (2004), 155–156. Hastings observes that 'ethnic' and 'nationalist' identities have different interests *vis-à-vis* intermarriage: 'intermarriage across ethnic borders strengthens territorial nationhood but threatens ethnic nationhood and is anathema to ethnic nationalists' (Hastings, *The Construction of Nationhood*, 206). The deuteronomic emphasis on endogamy perhaps therefore reflects the degree to which the deuteronomic argument is internal to the inhabitants of Judah, rather than a 'nationalist' project concerned primarily with the territorial unity and integrity of Judah. The focus, in other words, is not on building up the connections among all the inhabitants of Judah, in the name of buttressing a nationalist Judahite unity; the 'Israelite' cultural identity, the Israelite 'ethnic identity', is primary.

ובתים מלאים כל טוב אשר לא מלאת וברת חצובים אשר לא חצבת כרמים וזיתים אשר לא נטעת ואכלת ושבעת, Deut. 6:10b–11).[164]

More explicit references to the vehicle of this temptation comes shortly thereafter, as the text turns to the land's inhabitants (Deut. 7:1–4a).[165] In light of the foregoing the risk is obvious: intermarriage with the land's existing inhabitants means intimate social interactions with persons outside the Yahwistic Israelite community: persons who enact a wide range of non-Yahwistic, non-Israelite practices. If the silent land and its inert blessings posed a danger to the Israelites' Yahwistic exclusivity and its attendant distinction, how much greater might be the danger from a persuasive inhabitant of one's own bed? The speaker accordingly adjures the audience to shun contact with these inhabitants (Deut. 7:2–3), explicitly warning of the danger they pose (Deut. 7:4a).

It is pertinent at this point to mention Nielsen, whose analysis of these chapters whittles the many expansions down to Deut. 6:4–13; 7:1a, 3, 6; 8:7–11a, 12–13, 17–18a; 10:12, 20–21a. The principal distinction between his analysis and the one

---

164 Veijola, *Das 5. Buch Mose*, 211 summarises the chapter's topic as 'das Leben in der materiellen Fülle des verheißenen Landes als Bedrohung für die Identität Israels'. However, he declares that this concern cannot relate to the pre-exilic period and must be a post-exilic addition (Veijola, *Das 5. Buch Mose*, 212). As Nelson, *Deuteronomy*, 139 states in relation to one of the more explicit reiterations of this theme (Deut. 11:10–21), 'satiation (v.15) usually brings with it the danger of apostasy (6:11–12; 8:10–11, 12–17; 31:20). Moreover, the subject of rain and fertility seems to lead naturally to the topic of "other gods," to whose power these good things might be credited (v.16).' As the subsequent warning about straying from YHWH indicates, the issue at hand is indeed the exclusive and particular relationship between YHWH and Israel. On these types of signals indicating a genuinely West Semitic context for the deuteronomic material see Crouch, 'The Threat to Israel's Identity', 543–553.

165 The stereotyped catalogue of nations in Deut. 7:1b may or may not be original and is frequently excised. The list is not identical to the list in Deut. 20:17 (and there it is accompanied by a suspicious plural), tending against the rote insertion of a list in both locations by a later editor; perhaps Deut. 7:1b is the precedent for Deut. 20:17. On these lists see Weinfeld, *Deuteronomy 1–11*, 362–363; Braulik, *Deuteronomium 1–16,17*, 62; B.J. Collins, 'The Bible, The Hittites, and the Construction of the "Other"', *Tabularia Hethaeorum: Hethitologische Beiträge Silvin Košak zum 65. Geburtstag* (ed. D. Groddek and M. Zorman, Dresdner Beiträge zur Hethitologie 25, Wiesbaden, Harrassowitz, 2007), 153–161; J. Van Seters, 'The Terms "Amorite" and "Hittite" in the Old Testament', *VT* 22 (1972), 64–81; C. Houtman, 'Die ursprünglichen Bewohner des Landes Kanaan im Deuteronomium: Sinn und Absicht der Beschreibung ihrer Identität und ihres Charakters', *VT* 52 (2002), 51–65; H.M. Niemann, 'Das Ende des Volkes der Perizziter: Über soziale Wandlungen Israels im Spiegel einer Begriffsgruppe', *ZAW* 105 (1993), 233–257.

offered here is in the originality of the apostasy theme: Nielsen eliminates any mention of other deities associated with the inhabitants of the land, considering it a deuteronomistic elaboration, and emphasises the ban on intermarriage which his redactional analysis leaves at the centre of the original text: 'im Zentrum steht das Verbot des connubium mit den Kanaʻanäern, das durch das Auserwähltsein des Volkes begründet ist; dieses Verbot wird von Warnungen, Jahwe im schönen Lande nicht zu vergessen, umrahmt, und der Inhalt des ersten und des letzten Gebots ist: Jahwe zu lieben und ihn zu fürchten. Die dtr Redaktion hat diese Warnungen mit dem Verbot des Fremdgötterdienstes verdeutlicht'.[166] While Nielsen's analysis rightly accentuates the importance laid by the text on the distinctiveness of YHWH's people, over and against the people of the land—a distinctiveness threatened by intermarriage—he underestimates the extent to which the distinctiveness of the Israelites is fully caught up in their association with YHWH (and only YHWH). He accordingly does not acknowledge the extent to which the actual threat posed by the inhabitants of the land is related to their status as worshippers of other deities.

The power of a non-Israelite to sway the thoughts and behaviours of a Yahwistic Israelite with whom he or she is in intimate, familiar contact has already been noted in conjunction with the legislation in Deut. 13:2–19, where the particular danger of the close family member or friend forms an entire point of exhortation and legislation on its own. In the deuteronomic text, however, Deut. 13:2–19 is revisiting a point already made in Deut. 7:1–4a. Here the explicit threat is from persons who are non-Israelite but with whom an Israelite might conceivably join in marriage.[167] Similarly, the reason that 'you will not intermarry with them: you will not give your daughter to his son and his daughter you will not take for your son' (לא תתחתן בם בתך לא תתן לבנו ובתו לא תקח לבנך, Deut. 7:3) is anticipated in the Shema: 'YHWH is our god, YHWH alone'. The marriage of Yahwists to the inhabitants of the land is problematic precisely because these non-Israelite inhabitants of the land do not worship YHWH: 'for it will turn your son aside from me, and they will serve other gods'

---

166  Nielsen, *Deuteronomium*, 89; Mayes, *Deuteronomy*, 181 makes a similar claim when he contends that the destruction of previous inhabitants and the warning about worshipping those inhabitants' gods 'are in fact treated quite separately' and are 'abruptly' joined in Deut. 7:16; contrast Nelson, *Deuteronomy*, 98.

167  That this exists as a viable possibility raises interesting questions with regard to the actual identity of the 'Israelites' and 'non-Israelites' which, unfortunately, are too complex to address here. This focus on dangers immediately proximate to the Israelites in the land, however, suggests a battle over Israelite identity which is at its most intense with respect to those with 'irreconcilable claims or aspirations to the *same* identities' (Harrison, 'Identity as a Scarce Resource', 239).

(בי יסיר את בנך מאחרי חעבדו אלהים אחרים, Deut. 7:4). Because these people do not worship Yhwh, they do not know or adhere to the distinctively Yahwistic identity which is the foremost characteristic of Israelites. Kinship and ritual identities are inseparable: the rejection of the non-Israelite inhabitants of the land as potential marriage partners derives from the Israelites' identity as exclusive Yahwists and the incompatible association of these non-Israelites with other gods.

Before moving on, it is worth drawing out the implications of the deuteronomic logic of Israelite identity at this point. In the discussion of Deut. 13:2–19 there was cause to observe that the deuteronomic concept of Israelite identity is, ultimately, as achieved rather than ascribed. Here too, this logic is visible. As Hayes observes,

> Although this absolute ban applies to the seven Canaanite nations only, the moral-religious rationale motivating it has an important consequence: It can both broaden and limit the ban. The rationale can *broaden* the scope of the prohibition because it can be argued that intermarriage with any Gentile (not just one from the seven Canaanite nations, but any Gentile) who turns an Israelite to idolatry should be prohibited. At the same time it does not render the law of *universal* application. On the contrary, the clear implication of this rationale is that only those exogamous unions that result in the moral or religious alienation of the Israelite partner are prohibited.[168]

Regardless of whether the list of nations in Deut. 7:1b is original, Hayes' underlying point is valid: the ultimate issue in this injunction is the threat to Israelite identity represented by the prospect of an Israelite's marriage to a non-Israelite. As already seen and as will be seen elsewhere, the prioritisation of praxis reflects a primary deuteronomic focus on cultural identity which belies the ostensible genetic emphasis of even the endogamy principle itself. Although the deuteronomic text advocates endogamy as a means of protecting Israelite identity, it is—quite astutely—aware that it is not genetic purity which is at ultimately stake but cultural differentiation. This prioritising of cultural identity renders it capable already in principle of overriding genetic bonds in the delineation of who is or is not an Israelite: thus Deut. 13:2–19, in which rejection of the Israelite cultural characteristic of exclusive Yahwistic worship overrides even the nearest genetic bonds, and Deut. 21:10–14, in which occurs the reverse. In Deut. 7:1–4a the explicit danger is that these non-Israelites persons

---

168    Hayes, *Gentile Impurities*, 25 (italics original).

adhere to a distinct and non-Israelite set of cultural practices. Intermarriage with such persons means intimate contact with persons outside the Yahwistic Israelite community and the exposure of Israelites to non-Israelite practices, risking an assimilative process.

### 3.1.2    Levirate Marriage

That Israel is not merely a matter of the present generation but concerns also the future has been highlighted by the discussion of its promotion of endogamous marriage. Similar issues are at stake in the levirate marriage tradition (Deut. 25:5–8), which is explicitly concerned with the genealogical perpetuation of the Israelite community: ensuring that a family will persist in the instance of a deceased man who had no children is part of a basic concern for the continuity of the community.[169] Beyond the general importance of reproduction for the perpetuation of a community and its identity, however, the passage's interest in the preservation of Israelite identity is also evident from several more specific points of phrasing and terminology. Perhaps the most obvious of these is the opening phrase: 'If brothers live together' (כי ישבו אחים יחדו). This has been the subject of significant scrutiny in attempts to determine whether the law is meant to be limited to only those cases in which property is yet to be divided; it is rarely, however, recognised as forming part of the language of brotherhood which is common to the deuteronomic material.[170] As numerous scholars have observed, there are a variety of reasons that a man might not wish to perform the duties of a levir. Although the deuteronomic law

---

169    Note that the identification of the children of such unions as the descendants of their natural fathers in the cases of Judah (Gen. 46:21) and Boaz (Ruth 4:21) suggest that the literal perpetuation of the 'name' of the deceased man is not the only expression of this intention; on the significance of property inheritance see E.W. Davies, 'Inheritance Rights and the Hebrew Levirate Marriage: Part 1', *VT* 31 (1981), 141–142; R. Westbrook, *Property and the Family in Biblical Law* (JSOTSup 113, Sheffield, JSOT, 1991), 74–77; see also E. Otto, 'False Weights in the Scales of Biblical Justice? Different Views of Women from Patriarchal Hierarchy to Religious Equality in the Book of Deuteronomy', *Gender and Law in the Hebrew Bible and the Ancient Near East* (ed. V.H. Matthews, B.M. Levinson and T. Frymer-Kensky, London, T&T Clark, 1998), 138–140. There have been numerous studies of the phenomenon of levirate marriage in biblical texts; see Westbrook, *Property and the Family*, 69–89 and D.E. Weisberg, 'The Widow of Our Discontent: Levirate Marriage in the Bible and Ancient Israel', *JSOT* 28 (2004), 403–429, with further references.

170    E.W. Davies, 'Inheritance Rights and the Hebrew Levirate Marriage: Part 2', *VT* 31 (1981), 264–266; Westbrook, *Property and the Family*, 77–80. It is noted for its use of brother language by L. Perlitt, *Deuteronomium* (BKAT 5, Neukirchen-Vluyn, Neukirchener Verlag, 1990–), 58.

acknowledges such deterrents—to the point of providing an escape clause for one truly determined against the undertaking—the familial language which introduces the imperative is designed to motivate through the evocation of a sense of community and familial obligation, like the references to brotherhood which motivate difficult legislation elsewhere (cf. Deut. 15:1–18).[171] Similarly, it is not merely a name for an individual man which is achieved by the institution of levirate marriage, but a name 'in Israel' (Deut. 25:7, 10, בישראל; cf. 25:6, מישראל): this suggests that at stake, as far as the practice's deuteronomic rendering is concerned, is not only the perpetuation of an individual but the perpetuation of Israel itself. Language which evokes this wider community is used deliberately to motivate compliance with an ultimately unenforceable instruction.[172]

In addition to expressions which appeal to feelings of community and brotherhood to motivate behaviour in the community's interest, the law also uses negative language to describe the woman's fate, if the levir fails to act, referring explicitly to the possibility that the woman might end up estranged from the community: the woman will end up 'outside, belonging to a strange man' (החוצה לאיש זר, cf. Judg. 12:9). Though commentators usually understand this to mean marriage to another man and therefore marriage outside the family, with translations following suit (thus 'the wife of the deceased shall not be married

---

171    See 3.3.1. Preferential Treatment of the Israelite 'Brother'. Contrast Weisberg, who contends that 'nothing about the relationship of brothers in the Hebrew Bible would suggest that a man could expect altruism or affection from his brother' (Weisberg, 'The Widow of Our Discontent', 412–413); the obvious exception to this rule, however, is the deuteronomic text, which deliberately speaks of the Israelite community as a community of 'brothers'. On the appeal to familial relations as well as common history in Egypt to evoke empathy in motivation of particular ethical behaviours in Deuteronomy see T. Kazen, *Emotions in Biblical Law: A Cognitive Science Approach to Some Moral and Ritual Issues in Pentateuchal Legal Collections* (Sheffield, Sheffield Phoenix, 2011), 102–109.

172    Note also the use of public humiliation which, despite commentators' tendency to focus on the ritual as an escape clause for the unwilling levir, would have presented a substantiative deterrent in a society with a significant social emphasis on honour and shame. Weisberg raises an interesting question regarding the widow's role in this ritual: 'the language of the ritual suggests that the widow represents her deceased husband, the acknowledged victim of the levir's refusal. Does the widow also represent the community, whose expectations the levir has scorned?' (Weisberg, 'The Widow of Our Discontent', 409). The preponderance of brother language and references to the wider Israelite community suggest that the answer to this is likely yes. The anthropological literature on shame and shaming as motivators of action is extensive; see S.M. Olyan, 'Honor, Shame, and Covenant Relations in Ancient Israel and Its Environment', *JBL* 115 (1996), 202–204 and T.M. Lemos, 'Shame and Mutilation of Enemies in the Hebrew Bible', *JBL* 125 (2006), 227–229, with further references.

outside the family to a stranger' [NRSV], 'the wife of the deceased shall not be married to a stranger, outside the family' [JPS]), this is not quite what the text actually says (and for which one might expect איש אחר or the like). Rather, it is the risk that the woman's connection to the community will be severed by her subsequent attachment to an 'outsider', a 'strange man', which is presented as motivation for the levir to act. The double emphasis of זר and החוצה articulates the nature of the envisioned threat, namely, that it is not simply the possibility of the woman being with another man (maritally or otherwise) which is the problem, nor that she might remain unmarried altogether, but the possibility that she—along with her children and, perhaps, the property involved—might end up with a non-Israelite.[173] Davies' pursuit of the implications of the formal disavowal of the duties of the levir notes that, assuming the brothers' father to be already deceased, the widow's dead husband's share in the property would go to the recalcitrant levir (and, if the father is not dead already, his subsequent death would have the same effect).[174] Noting the problematic moral implications of this, Davies nonetheless concludes that 'the only alternative, surely, would have been to allow the widow herself to inherit the property, and since she would probably have remarried outside her husband's family (cf. Ruth i 9), the ancestral estate would inevitably have passed completely out of the hands of the original owner'.[175] Precisely this danger, writ on not merely the familial level—in which case the woman's marriage to *any* other man would be problematic—but against the background of the entire Israelite community—hence the emphasis on the danger of the איש זר specifically— may be the reason that the deuteronomic law is so intent on encouraging the levir: 'such a mixed union may mean not only the defection of a member of the group, but also a loss of the children.'[176] Indeed, it is notable that it is only in the deuteronomic law, with its particular concern for Israelite identity, that the law of the levirate appears; though it or something like it appears to lie

---

173 One may presume that one component of the situation described is the economic precariousness of the widow; without husband or (grown) child, her options for providing for herself would have been limited (witness the repeating injunctions elsewhere to have care for the widow [Deut. 14:29; 16:11, 14; 24:17, 19, 20, 21]). Barring her successful reincorporation into a male-headed household her fate would have been uncertain; though it is difficult to guess at the options available to a woman in such a position, prostitution or travel in search of better prospects (cf. Ruth) spring most quickly to mind; both of these pose significant problems for the preservation of the woman's (and any subsequent children's) Israelite identity.

174 Davies, 'Inheritance Rights', 262–263.

175 Davies, 'Inheritance Rights', 263.

176 Southwood, *Ethnicity*, 67.

behind Genesis 38 and possibly Ruth, neither the Covenant Code nor the priestly legislation mention it.

### 3.1.3    Remarriage

Deuteronomy 24:1–4 deals with a man who marries and divorces a woman, then wishes to remarry the same woman after she has been married to another man. 'Esoteric' hardly seems adequate: it is difficult to imagine that such a situation occurred on a sufficiently regular basis such that the deuteronomic writer felt obliged to legislate against it. The explanations concocted by commentators to explain the law's meaning and rationale are so diverse as to indicate no small puzzlement and very little agreement over the passage. The disagreements revolve primarily around the interpretation of the phrase ערות דבר in Deut. 24:1 and the trifold motive clause in Deut. 24:4. Philo's interpretation, seeing the ערות דבר as a reference to adultery, has been generally rejected on the grounds that Deut. 22:22 addresses the case of the adulterous wife by prescribing the death penalty, whereupon the woman would hardly be in the position to remarry, although the presumption of total consistency between these laws has also been questioned and the possibility that the husband may have retained a certain degree of discretion in such matters proposed.[177] However, if ערות דבר is not understood to be a reference to adultery, there is little consensus on its referent: some type of sexual 'perversion' on the part of the wife, discovered only after marriage;[178] 'some sort of abnormal or displeasing physical or physiological abnormality on the part of the woman';[179] the woman's indecent exposure of her genitalia;[180] or, indeed, any aspect of the wife or her behaviour other than adultery, either immoral or merely unbecoming.[181] Similarly disputed is the law's rationale: the protection of the first husband;[182] conversely, the protection of the woman's right to remarry and the limitation of the rights

---

177    E. Otto, 'Das Verbot der Wiederherstellung einer geschiedenen Ehe: Deuteronomium 24,1–4 im Kontext des israelitischen und judäischen Eherechts', *UF* 24 (1992), 301–310; B.S. Jackson, 'The "Institutions" of Marriage and Divorce in the Hebrew Bible', *JSS* 56 (2011), 221–251.

178    A.J.M. Garrett, 'A New Understanding of the Divorce and Remarriage Legislation in Deuteronomy 24:104', *JBQ* 39 (2011), 245–250.

179    T. Scacewater, 'Divorce and Remarriage in Deuteronomy 24:1–4', *JESOT* 1 (2012), 69.

180    R.M. Davidson, 'Divorce and Remarriage in the Old Testament: A Fresh Look at Deuteronomy 24:1–4', *Journal of the Adventist Theological Society* 10 (1999), 5–7.

181    A. Phillips, 'Some Aspects of Family Law in Pre-exilic Israel', *JSOT* 23 (1973), 355.

182    Garrett, 'A New Understanding', 245–250.

of the first husband;[183] the prevention of the woman's economic exploitation by the first husband;[184] and the prevention of sexual impurity akin to adultery have all been proposed as possibilities.[185]

Part of the peculiarity of the law is its declaration that the woman (or the act) is objectionable specifically on the grounds that it is (or makes her) תועבה הוא לפני יהוה (Deut. 24:4), apparently suggesting that it is dealing with an issue of cultural differentiation of some kind. Although the nature of the issue remains opaque, one interesting suggestion is noted by Tigay, who refers to Maimonides' suggestion that the law is designed to prevent wife-swapping and suggests that the practice behind Deut. 24:1–4 might mirror a practice known as *mut'a*, in which a marriage is contracted temporarily and then dissolved shortly thereafter.[186] While such an interpretation is conjectural, it is one way of accounting reasonably well for the law's oddities, including one of the law's most notable peculiarities: bearing in mind the shorter ancient life span in which the marriages described by Deut. 24:1–4 must be supposed to have occurred, three genuine marriages in succession presses the bounds of plausibility (especially, perhaps, given that it is the probability of a woman's death in childbirth which would have been the most likely cause of marriage dissolution). While technically possible, this seems surely so rare in practice as to make its particular prohibition superfluous. The fact that the first man might anticipate resuming his relationship with the woman at some point in the future also strongly suggests that a short-term arrangement is presupposed for both the first and second marriages (it also implies a community in which the number of women available for such 'marriages' is limited, as a larger number of available women would obviate the need to return to the same woman).

---

183  Otto, 'Das Verbot', 309; Otto, 'False Weights', 137–138; R. Westbrook, 'The Prohibition on Restoration of Marriage in Deuteronomy 24:1–4', *Studies in Bible, 1986* (ed. S. Japhet, ScrHier 31, Jerusalem, Magnes, 1986), 387–406.

184  Braulik, *Deuteronomium II*, 176–177.

185  C. Pressler, *The View of Women Found in the Deuteronomic Family Laws* (BZAW 216, Berlin, de Gruyter, 1993), 46–61; Davidson, 'Divorce and Remarriage', 2–22. See also the literature reviews in Scacewater, 'Divorce and Remarriage', 73–76; J.C. Laney, 'Deuteronomy 24,1–4 and the Issue of Divorce', *Bibliotheca Sacra* 149 (1992), 9–13.

186  Tigay, *Deuteronomy*, 220, though Tigay rejects the theory on the grounds that the woman is divorced due to the man disliking her (having found the elusive ערות דבר in her). However, mistresses and sex workers fill a role which is by definition temporary; the man discarding the woman on the grounds of disliking her, or once the relationship had grown tiresome to him (once he had 'uncovered her secrets', perhaps), would be in keeping with the nature of such a relationship. See 2 Samuel 13 for a witness that ancient authors could be as aware of the fraught emotional waters of sexual relations as their modern analogues.

The passage at Deut. 24:1–4 about remarrying a former wife may, therefore, be plausibly understood as an attempt to prohibit prostitution thinly veiled by the guise of temporary marriage; Pressler's contention that much of the rhetoric in this law is linked to purity issues suggests, perhaps, that the author chose to deploy concepts of purity—rendering the remarriage akin to adultery and thereby acquiring the connotations of impurity associated therewith—in order to reinforce his rejection of this practice.[187]

That the practice is described in terms of תועבה suggests that there are also underlying issues of Israelite identity and cultural praxis involved in the legislation banning its implementation. Unfortunately, the precise threat to Israelite identity which is imagined here remains opaque. Perhaps the women who resorted to the profession were those without family or other ties to the community who were accordingly perceived as outsiders; perhaps those frequenting them were supposed to be mostly the itinerant population of merchants and other international visitors, or inclusive of the locals considered deuteronomically non-Israelite. In any case the mixing—both social and genetic—of populations and cultures arising from such interaction could be perceived as a threat to community integrity. The issue might equally have been the anomaly which such women and any children produced would have presented to a community whose traditions were safeguarded by the family; without a clear place in the community structure they might have been perceived as weak links in the protection and preservation of community tradition and identity.[188] It is impossible to be confident in the details, but that these verses reflect a degree of concern about the integrity of the community seems likely.

### 3.2    Segregation of the Israelite Community from Non-Israelites
In addition to the discouragement of social interactions with non-Israelites in the immediate family context, the deuteronomic material also moves to discourage interactions with non-Israelites at the wider community level. This discouragement takes several forms, including the isolation of the Israelite royal figurehead, the legislation of total destruction for proximate non-Israelites (echoing in reverse the efforts of centralisation to facilitate proximity among Israelites) and the outright exclusion of outsiders from the community.

---

187    Pressler, *The View of Women*, 46–61. Note also the possibility of editorial complicating of the motivations of this verse; see, e.g., Mayes, *Deuteronomy*, 323.

188    On family and identity in Deuteronomy see Reeder, *The Enemy*, 17–58.

3.2.1    The King

The law of the king has long posed an interpretive and historical crux. As most commentators readily admit, the description of the royal role as it now stands is a far cry from any historical institution in Judah: one need only compare the descriptions in the royal psalms to realise that kingship in Judah was a much more significant and powerful role that the deuteronomic law would have its reader believe, even before comparing the narratives about kings in the books named after them and the various prophetic complaints directed at their behaviour.[189] Even if these latter were meant to be unflattering, the sheer frequency of references to royal behaviour exceeding deuteronomic limitations and the variety of texts in which such references appear makes it likely that the kings of Judah, whatever the limitations they faced as a result of the small size and consequence of their territory and whatever opposition they faced from among their subject population—which, if difficult to trace, is nonetheless sufficiently prevalent as to suppose that it reflects some real tradition of opposition to kingship—were possessed of power and possessions which outstripped those described by Deut. 17:14–20.[190]

Unsurprisingly, the tenuous relationship between reality and the kind of kingship described by this law has led to the suggestion that it must have been added, or at least modified, after the kingdoms of Israel and Judah had fallen and their kings were coming to be blamed for this fact: the poor stature of Deuteronomy's king reflects an exilic demotion of the nation's leader as a result of deuteronomistic apportioning of blame for the exile onto Judah's and Israel's kings.[191] Yet, though the author limits the king's power, he presumes

---

189   For a discussion of ancient Near Eastern kingship and kingship in the Deuteronomistic History see B.M. Levinson, 'The Reconceptualization of Kingship in Deuteronomy and the Deuteronomistic History's Transformation of Torah', *VT* 51 (2001), 511–519.

190   Various parts of Deut. 17:14–20 are thought, according to different analyses, to be of later origin than the principal legislation. Of these the most frequently questioned is the section in Deut. 17:18–20 on the reading and learning of the law, due especially to its anachronistic reference to 'this law' (התורה הזה) and to Deuteronomy as a book (ספר); the conditionality of the land which is implied by Deut. 17:20b is also suspect. Deuteronomy 17:16b shifts suddenly and without motivation into a plural, raising doubts about its originality as well.

191   E. Nicholson, '*Traditum* and *traditio*: The Case of Deuteronomy 17:14–20', *Scriptural Exegesis: The Shapes of Culture and the Religious Imagination: Essays in Honour of Michael Fishbane* (ed. D.A. Green and L.S. Lieber, Oxford, Oxford University Press, 2009), 46–61; cf. Nicholson, *Deuteronomy and the Judaean Diaspora*, 101–134, in which the poor stature of the king is the highlight of Deuteronomy's 'depoliticizing' of Israel; Davies, 'Josiah and the Law Book'; J. Pakkala, 'The Date of the Oldest Edition of Deuteronomy', *ZAW* 121

his existence. The text also uses מֶלֶךְ, the normal title, rather than alternative reflecting a reduced status, as Ezekiel uses נָשִׂיא. Against protests that the king as described in this law is not realistic during the period of the monarchy, one might equally observe that the deuteronomic presentation of an Israel which exclusively worships Yhwh is also idealised: yet this is not taken as a reason to deny the existence of the idea. The relationship between the ideal Israel and the real Judah is not direct. To recognise the unreality, even implausibility, of the law of the king is not to reject it as unimaginable. There are a number of reasons why an author working in a time of kingship might, as an expression of ideological priorities, choose to legislate an extremely limited form of kingship.[192] Indeed, the limitations placed on the Israelite king by this law are comprehensible as expressions of the deuteronomic ethnic identity concerns arising from the social, political and economic context of the long seventh century.

How do each of these limitations serve deuteronomic identity concerns? Though a number of the motivation clauses are opaque, the focus in Deut. 17:14–17 is on the king's high-risk position as a prominent nexus of Israelite interaction with non-Israelites, a position which, as the foregoing anticipates, goes against the deuteronomic instinct to protect Israelite identity by

---

(2009), 388–401; M. Nevader, *Yahweh versus David: The Monarchic Debate of Deuteronomy and Ezekiel* (OTM; Oxford: Oxford University Press, 2014); N. Lohfink, 'Distribution of the Functions of Power: The Laws Concerning Public Offices in Deuteronomy 16:18–18:22', *A Song of Power and the Power of Song: Essays on the Book of Deuteronomy* (ed. D.L. Christensen, transl. R. Walls, Sources for Biblical and Theological Study 3, Winona Lake, Ind., Eisenbrauns, 1993), 345–349; R. Achenbach, 'Das sogenannte Königsgesetz in Deuteronomium 17,14–20', *ZABR* 15 (2009), 216–233; note also A.C. Hagedorn, *Between Moses and Plato: Individual and Society in Deuteronomy and Ancient Greek Law* (FRLANT 204, Göttingen, Vandenhoeck & Ruprecht, 2004), 140–146, 154–156, who reads these verses against a fifth century background.

192   One particularly interesting possibility concerns the relative significance of ethnic cultural priorities over national political ones. As Calhoun has observed, ethnicities are 'most often claimed where groups do not seek "national" autonomy but rather a recognition internal to or cross-cutting national or state boundaries' (C. Calhoun, 'Nationalism and Ethnicity', *Annual Review of Sociology* 19 [1993], 211). The much stronger deuteronomic emphasis on the cultural praxis of Israel, rather than the political power of Judah *vis-à-vis* other southern Levantine states or the Assyrian empire has already been suggested as indicating that the focus of the deuteronomic project is not a state-based nationalist identity but a broadly-based programme of cultural praxis operable within an overarching imperial framework; the relative minimisation of the national figurehead, the king, would be in keeping with this focus. Contrast especially Nicholson, *Deuteronomy and the Judaean Diaspora*.

discouraging interaction outside the group. His very existence is confusable with the practices pursued by the Israelites' neighbours: rhetorically, at least, the Israelite king exists precisely because the population has said 'Let me set over myself a king, *like all the nations which surround me*' (אשימה עלי מלך ככל הגוים אשר סביבתי; Deut. 17:14, emphasis added). Even before the king's function is addressed, the text recognises that the Israelites' desire for a king like all the surrounding non-Israelites contradicts everything for which the deuteronomic material stands.[193] Given that such a person is apparently nevertheless unavoidable, the deuteronomic author legislates the royal role in such a way as, first, to minimise the major avenues of risk presented by the king's position, thereby securing Israel's insularity, and by doing so to, second, effectively render the Israelite king unlike his non-Israelite analogues.

With regard to the latter, the text's first movement in this direction is that the Israelite king will be distinctive from non-Israelite kings insofar as he must be chosen by Yhwh, Israel's particular deity (שום תשים עליך מלך אשר יבחר יהוה אלהיך בו, Deut. 17:15a).[194] If Israel's king cannot be distinguished from non-Israelite kings in his royal capacity as such, he should be distinguished by virtue of the Israelite deity who renders him royal. The phrasing aligns Yhwh's choice of king with Yhwh's choice of a single cult site, meant both to be distinctive and to ensure the distinctiveness of Israel's practice.

Next, the law insists that the king be from among the Israelites' 'brothers' (מקרב אחיך), not a 'foreigner' (איש נכרי אשר לא אחיך הוא, Deut. 17:15b). This specification has several functions. First, it incorporates the law of the king into the identity-orientated brother language used elsewhere (also, notably, in connection with especially difficult laws). In so doing it locates the king squarely in the deuteronomic identity project. At the same time, it reiterates the particularly Israelite character of Israelite kingship, much like the specification that the king will be appointed by Yhwh.

In addition to these ideological functions, this injunction also has a practical purpose. It was standard imperial practice to first appoint a puppet ruler and, ultimately, an imperial governor, in cases of persistent rebellious

---

193 Highlighting, perhaps, the extent to which the existence of such a figurehead is considered unavoidable: 'ein Zugeständnis an die geschichtliche Wirklichkeit', in von Rad's terms (G. von Rad, *Das fünfte Buch Mose: Deuteronomium* [ATD 8, Göttingen, Vandenhoeck & Ruprecht, 1964], 85).

194 Although, as Mayes, *Deuteronomy*, 271 notes, this element of Deut. 17:15aβ (אשר יבחר יהוה אלהיך בו) is frequently seen as deuteronomistic due to its apparent tension with Deut. 17:14, Bartor's argument that this is part of the text's careful sublimation of the royal house to Yahwistic oversight is persuasive (Bartor, *Reading Law*, 46–47).

activity by a vassal state; these persons might be natives but could equally be outsiders.[195] Though the insistence that Israel have an Israelite king has often struck commentators as odd, this concern to appoint a native ruler is explicable as an issue arising from imperial policies during the long seventh century.[196] The warning against foreign rulers is, in effect, an adjuration of rebellious political activities because of their dangerous consequences.[197]

---

195   See N. Na'aman, 'Ekron under the Assyrian and Egyptian Empires', *BASOR* 332 (2003), 81–91, 83 on the installation of new dynasties in Ekron and Gaza and the certain knowledge of the former, at least, in Judah. A similar process likely also occurred in eighth-century Israel (M. Van De Mieroop, *A History of the Ancient Near East: ca. 3000–323 BC* [2nd edn., Oxford, Blackwell, 2007], 248–252). Hamilton raises this practice in connection with this prohibition, concluding that it constitutes 'a refusal to submit to incorporation into the Assyrian provincial system' (M.W. Hamilton, 'The Past as Destiny: Historical Visions in Sam'al and Judah under Assyrian Hegemony', *HTR* 91 [1998], 241). He fails, however, to distinguish between provincial status, to which Judah was never converted under the Assyrians, and vassal status and, with regard to the latter, the multiple stages through which a vassal state might progress, depending on its degree of cooperation with Assyria. It cannot be a rejection of submission to Assyria but must be understood as a warning against (further) resistance.

196   Commentators have offered a wide variety of explanations for this seemingly inexplicable injunction (in Daube's words, 'no sane person would have contemplated enthroning a foreigner'; D. Daube, 'One from among Your Brethren Shall You Set King over You', *JBL* 90 [1971], 480). Nelson, *Deuteronomy*, 223 points toward the threat of the forcible enthronement of Tabeel (Isa. 7:6) and to Abimelech (Judges 8–9; also Daube, 'One from among Your Brethren'). Mayes, *Deuteronomy*, 272 notes attempts to link the clause to Omri or Ahab and Jezebel; Tigay, *Deuteronomy*, 167 favours the possibility of a coup by foreign mercenaries; Nielsen, *Deuteronomium*, 185 suggests that the possibility is mentioned because of the innate temptation posed by the foreignness of the institution itself; Braulik, *Deuteronomium II*, 128 suggests that the son of a foreign wife is excluded here. Nicholson argues for a recollection of Ahaz's submission as a vassal to a foreign, Assyrian king (E. Nicholson, ' "Do Not Dare to Set a Foreigner over You": The King in Deuteronomy and "The Great King," ' *ZAW* 118 [2006], 46–61; cf. Nicholson, '*Traditum* and *traditio*', 51–54 and Nicholson, *Deuteronomy and the Judaean Diaspora*, 101–134); also referring to the appearance of the Assyrians, though in the context of discussion of the related 1 Samuel 8, is M. Leuchter, 'A King Like All The Nations: The Composition of I Sam 8,11–18', *ZAW* 118 (2005), 555. Hagedorn, *Between Moses and Plato*, 141 deems it a post-exilic antithesis to Deutero-Isaiah's presentation of Cyrus.

197   Though P. Dutcher-Walls, 'The Circumscription of the King: Deuteronomy 17:16–17 in Its Ancient Social Context', *JBL* 121 (2002), 604–605, 609–615 focuses primarily on the internal political machinations which might prompt the stipulations of the law, she also suggests that this occurs within the larger imperial framework as 'a strategy of acquiescence to the domination of Assyria' (Dutcher-Walls, 'The Circumscription of the King', 615); contrast Hamilton, 'The Past as Destiny', 230–248, who argues that Deut. 17:14–17 and its depiction

The insistence that the king over Israel be himself an Israelite is an attempt to ensure that the leader of the Israelite, Yahwistic community is a community insider, aware of and in support of the various practices which constitute the Israelite community's particular identity. To risk the acquisition of a non-Israelite king is to risk a ruler who is neither an Israelite himself nor aware or concerned about the preservation of a Yahwistic Israelite identity. Here and throughout this law the text aims at 'insulating parts of the culture[] from confrontation and modification'.[198]

The importance of minimising the danger posed by the king's role as nexus of interaction with non-Israelites is also in mind in the subsequent elements of the legislation, beginning with the acquisition of horses (לא ירבה לו סוסים, Deut. 17:16a). Though nearly every phrase in the verse has had the verdict of 'meaning uncertain' bestowed upon it by one commentator or another, the sense remains reasonably coherent. The horses which the king is not permitted to multiply are associated with Egypt, as the verse itself makes explicit. Nelson wonders whether this might refer to an exchange in which a king sent mercenaries to Egypt in exchange for the horses he needed to supply his own cavalry; alternately, it might have a commercial referent, acting as a means of prohibiting trade with Egypt, or be intended to evoke an image of the exodus, reversed, with the identity-formation effect of the exodus undone and the people effectively dissolved.[199] Mayes suggests that it is a metaphor for political alliances, while Dutcher-Walls suggests that it constitutes a rejection of the

---

of a relatively weakened king constitutes anti-Assyrian subversiveness. Given the afore-mentioned difficulties with his initial premise, combined with the specific texts to which he appeals, one wonders whether he might have a better case for arguing that the parts of Deuteronomy with which his argument is concerned derive from an anti-Babylonian revision.

198   Barth, 'Introduction', 16.

199   Nelson, *Deuteronomy*, 224. Tigay, *Deuteronomy*, 167 prefers one of the first two options; Nielsen, *Deuteronomium*, 185 favours the military option. Driver, *Deuteronomy*, 212 straddled both, seeing a reference to either ambassadors or merchants sent to Egypt for cavalry. Also common is the suggestion that the mention of Egypt and of foreign wives (Deut. 17:17) indicates that the entire law of the king is intended to be anti-Solomonic rhetoric (thus M.A. Sweeney, 'The Critique of Solomon in the Josianic Edition of the Deuteronomistic History', *JBL* 114 [1995], 615–616, referring to 1 Kgs. 10:1–25, 26–29; see also G.N. Knoppers, 'The Deuteronomist and the Deuteronomic Law of the King: A Reexamination of a Relationship', *ZAW* 108 [1996], 329–346, for a comparison of deuteronomic and deuteronomistic views of kingship). Though not restricting the issue to Solomon exclusively, Nicholson, '*Traditum* and *traditio*', views Deut. 17:14–20 as an *ex eventu* critique of kingship.

foreign 'entanglements' required to procure the beasts, perhaps also aimed at limiting the existence of the king's standing army.[200] This military-political angle is probably the most likely, especially given that the combination of horses and Egypt together is used elsewhere in biblical texts as a cipher for Judah's military and political machinations with that nation (cf. Isa. 30:1–7; 31:1–3). However, the impulse toward the link between Egypt and identity should not be overlooked; it reflects an important part of the problem posed by potential military involvement with Egypt. The most certain means of provoking Assyrian military interference in local affairs was for a vassal state to attempt to form a rebellious alliance with another nation. Egypt in particular was a favourite to which restive Levantine vassals, Judah included, were known to turn—almost inevitably with disastrous consequences. These consequences typically included the removal of the rebellious king and his replacement with an individual of Assyrian choosing, sometimes but not always from the old king's own dynastic house. Against the long seventh century's background of Assyrian domination in the Levant, therefore, this connects to and reiterates the declaration that the king must be an Israelite and not a foreigner. Involvement with Egypt, symbolised by the exchange of horses, poses a concrete threat to Israelite isolationism and is accordingly prohibited.[201] Rendering the warning especially effective is that departure from Egypt is the event which crystallised the nation's identity; thus return to Egypt represents the loss of identity which rebellious alliances threaten to bring about—indeed, brought full circle through reliance on Egyptian military might.[202]

The rest of the law continues this focus on protecting of the Israelites' distinctive identity through isolationism. Deuteronomy 17:17 extends the language of Deut. 17:16 to prohibit the king's acquisition of numerous wives: 'and

---

200    Mayes, *Deuteronomy*, 272; also Christensen, *Deuteronomy 21:10–34:12*, 385–386, with some
         uncertainty; Dutcher-Walls, 'The Circumscription of the King', 603, 608. Note especially
         Dutcher-Wall's contextualisation of this isolationism in the realities of the Assyrian
         empire; she suggests that Deut. 17:16 adapts local royal ideology to the reality of Assyria's
         domination rather than rejecting it (Dutcher-Walls, 'The Circumscription of the King',
         615). One should note that the possibility of Egypt as an ally in rebellion is chronologically
         limited by Egypt's subordination to Assyria for at least part of the middle of the seventh
         century.

201    Even if the specific identification of Egypt is deemed secondary (as D.J. Reimer, 'Con-
         cerning Return to Egypt: Deuteronomy XVII 16 and XXVIII 68 Reconsidered', *Studies in the
         Pentateuch* [ed. J.A. Emerton, VTSup 41, Leiden, Brill, 1990], 217–229), the underlying con-
         cern to deter potentially explosive military alliances may be maintained.

202    See Greifenhagen, *Egypt on the Pentateuch's Ideological Map*, 184–186 for a broader discus-
         sion of this trope.

he will not multiply women for himself' (ולא ירבה לו נשים). The king's wives were the concrete manifestation of and living seal on international treaties and alliances; the prohibition's repetition of language from Deut. 17:16 reiterates that the objection to both horses and women lies in this quarter. Their existence is additionally opposed in cultural terms, insofar as the incorporation of non-Israelites into the royal household endangered the king's fidelity to his own cultural traditions: 'and he will not multiply women for himself *so he will not turn his heart away*' (ולא ירבה לו נשים ולא יסור לבבו, Deut. 17:17aβ). The verb סור, though not exclusively used of 'turning away from' the worship of Yʜᴡʜ, suggests that the concern here is the threat which such women could pose to Israelite peculiarity, representing the intimate primary relationships which should involve only shared Israelite norms and values.[203] Finally, the acquisition of much gold and silver is a warning about the risks associated with the region's flourishing commercial activities. Though lucrative, probably especially so for the king and his fellow elites, economic development was the very source of the Israelite identity crisis reflected in the deuteronomic text. It concomitantly forms a third variant on the imperatives against rocking the imperial boat: in conjunction with military and political forms of rebellion, among the first expressions of a vassal state's rejection of imperial control was the withholding of tribute. The warning to the Israelite king not to gather silver and gold to himself constitutes a veiled admonishment to pay his tribute on time and thereby avoid provoking punitive measures. This Israelite king is to secure his throne and Israel's insularity by behaving as a loyal vassal, avoiding alliances secured by the exchange of goods or by the exchange of women, and by paying his tribute on time. In keeping with the rest of the deuteronomic material, the law of the king is intensely concerned with the threat of the Israelites' exposure to non-Israelite cultural practices through interactions with non-Israelites and with the risk of incursions into the community by outsiders, whether directly, in the form of a non-Israelite sovereign, or indirectly, in the form of the creeping influences of on-going, regular interaction.

In its efforts to protect Israelite identity, the deuteronomic royal legislation creates a king who is not 'a king like all the nations', effectively differentiating

---

203   Nicholson, '*Traditum* and *traditio*', 52–53. See also Cohen, *Custom and Politics*, 209. As it is all wives which are prohibited in large number and not only explicitly foreign ones it is not unreasonable to suppose that the author's concerns extended to the excessive acquisition of royal wives in and for itself. Nonetheless, it is the cultural threat which is identified explicitly. Given the evidence that the cultural threats to the developing Israelite identity were as likely to be from within Judah as from without, it seems likely that native wives could also be perceived as a threat if they were not deuteronomically Israelite.

the Israelite king from his non-Israelite counterparts by virtue of the limitations placed upon him. The Israelite king does not engage in international political alliances, does not amass a powerful army or an extensive harem and does not enrich the royal coffers or himself. As so many commentators have noted, the king presented in these verses is unlike any king known in the ancient Near East. In Mullen's terms, '[t]hough a king might make Israel "like all the nations" (*kĕkol-haggōyīm*; v. 14), the nature of the kingship would distinguish Israel, in ideal terms, from those other groups.'[204] Despite the people's having desired to be like the nations by having a king, the deuteronomic law effectively subverts these intentions by delineating a royal role which sets Israel's ruler apart, just as the laws before and after do the same for the population as a whole.

### 3.2.2    Warfare

The war laws in Deut. 20:10–18 dictate the ruthless elimination of non-Israelites from the territory claimed for Israelite habitation. Of this, Deut. 20:10–14 constitutes normal ancient Near Eastern practice.[205] It is not, however, in keeping with the deuteronomic interest in segregating Yahwistic Israelite practice from that of non-Israelites, and it is unsurprising to see a secondary development in Deut. 20:15–16, designed to ensure that co-mingling does not occur.

> It is not uncommon to identify all of Deut. 20:15–18 as a deuteronomistic, late editorial layer. Following the scholarly trend toward seeing identity issues as arising primarily in the exile, my own earlier analysis took this stance. However, recognising the similarity of sentiment between these verses and many of the deuteronomic texts suggests that there is no necessary reason to assume that the ordinary rules in Deut. 20:10–14 are deuteronomic and that the more stringent legislation must be deuteronomistic. If anything, the lack of concern about a proximate non-Israelite population in Deut. 20:10–14—'whether or not these besieged towns submit to conquest on the part of the Israelites, the majority of the people are destined to become part of the population of Israel'—suggests that it is not deuteronomic but pre-deuteronomic, revised in a deuteronomic vein by Deut. 20:15–16 and subsequently rendered in more explicit terms

---

204    Mullen, Jr., *Narrative History*, 74; see also the discussion in Barrett, *Disloyalty and Destruction*, 210–217.

205    C.L. Crouch, *War and Ethics in the Ancient Near East: Military Violence in Light of Cosmology and History* (BZAW 407, Berlin, de Gruyter, 2009), 184–188.

by Deut. 20:17–18.[206] Note especially the differentiation between the singular Deut. 20:15–16, which specifies a change in the legislation in order to facilitate the elimination of the immediate proximate threat of non-Israelites inhabiting cities (to be) also inhabited by Israelites, and the plural Deut. 20:17–18, which elaborate on this instruction in order to specify both who is condemned and why (the latter picking up the deuteronomic language of differentiation in its use of תועבות); the use of singular versus plural is by no means an infallible redaction-critical tool, but it is striking that it is only Deut. 20:17–18 which shift, inexplicably, into plural before the text reverts back to singular in Deut. 20:19.

The motivation of this revision is precisely the same as that which underlies numerous other laws in the deuteronomic material, namely, protecting Israel from the threat to the distinctiveness of Israelite identity posed by proximity to and interaction with non-Israelites. Most commentators echo Miller's statement that 'the Deuteronomist seeks to show, either implicitly or explicitly, that the purpose of the ban was to remove all aspects of the Canaanite religion and culture so that the worship of the Lord, the God of Israel, might not be corrupted'.[207] While the identification of the danger in terms of the named list of Israel's predecessors in the land in Deut. 20:17 and the articulation of the issue in the language of תועבות in Deut. 20:18 make this explicit, the

---

206   Christensen, *Deuteronomy 1:1–21:9*, 444; cf. A. Rofé, 'The Laws of Warfare in the Book of Deuteronomy: Their Origins, Intent and Positivity', *JSOT* 32 (1985), 28–30; also C. Hayes, 'Intermarriage and Impurity in Ancient Jewish Sources', *HTR* 92 (1999), 8–9. There is an abundance of literature on the *ḥrm* language and its ideology; note especially Monroe's study of the *ḥrm* traditions in Moab, Sabā and the Hebrew Bible, in which she highlights their particular focus on the nexus between land, deity and peoplehood (L.A.S. Monroe, 'Israelite, Moabite and Sabaean War-herem Traditions and the Forging of National Identity: Reconsidering the Sabaean Text RES 3945 in Light of Biblical and Moabite Evidence', *VT* 57 [2007], 318–34). She classifies the 'interest in protection against contamination' in Deut. 7:2–5; 20:18 as not strictly part of the *ḥrm* tradition itself, but identity defined in terms of deity and land and identity defined in terms of praxis are both essential to the type of group identity under discussion.

207   Miller, *Deuteronomy*, 41. In keeping with the idea that issues about Israelite identity arose first and foremost in the exile, the majority of commentators see the desire to eliminate non-Israelites as supporting a deuteronomistic assignment for all of Deut. 20:15–18. In counterpoint, arguing that the (deuteronomistic) *ḥrm* materials constitute 'a polemic against supporters of a nationalistic, anti-foreigners policy', namely, Ezra and his ilk, see Y. Hoffman, 'The Deuteronomistic Concept of the Herem', *ZAW* 111 (1999), 196–209.

differentiation between 'the cities which are very distant from you' (לכל הערים
הרחקת ממך מאד) and those which are 'here among the cities of these nations'
(מערי הגוים האלה הנה) which occurs in Deut. 20:15 already indicate that the
concern is with non-Israelites who are present in the land and which, by virtue of their presence, present a potential locus for the dissolution of Israelite
identity. Again, those closest to the community pose the greatest threat to its
preservation.[208]

### 3.2.3 Exclusion from Israel

The most blatant efforts at the defence of Israel's cultural borders are the outright exclusions of non-Israelites from the Israelite community. These may
be explicit and specifically ethnically-based exclusions, as in the case of the
Ammonite and Moabite and probably in the case of persons of mixed Israelite
and non-Israelite heritage, or may take more general form, as in the case of
the eunuch. Though sometimes opaque, the intention in each of these cases
appears to be the minimisation or elimination of Israelites' social interactions
with non-Israelites.

Given the preceding observations regarding the deuteronomic conception
of Israelite identity as ultimately achieved rather than simply ascribed, it will
come as little surprise to find that there are also exceptions to what might be
expected to be an absolute deuteronomic rejection of all non-Israelites' interactions with Israelites.

*Ammon and Moab*

The most explicitly ethnically based rejection of Israelite association with non-
Israelites occurs in Deut. 23:4, in which the Ammonite and the Moabite are
declared to never be permitted to join the Israelite community.

The exclusions in Deut. 23:2–9 are each articulated with reference to
entry into the קהל יהוה (not the בית יהוה, reference to which in Deut. 23:19

---

208    Barth, 'Introduction', 16; 'Cultural Difference', 345. The text effectively dismisses non-
       Levantine affairs from the deuteronomic remit, as Deut. 20:15–16 limits the militarily sen-
       sible but—relatively speaking—mild set of instructions recounted in Deut. 20:10–14 to
       only those populations which are beyond Israel's immediate proximity. As with the refer-
       ences to the threat which is 'in your midst', the danger to Israel is the immediate danger
       posed by non-Israelites living alongside Israelites. Note in this regard also the recent case
       by Wright that the following verses, Deut. 20:19–20, should not be understood as anti-
       Assyrian polemic but as part of an internal Israelite discussion (J.L. Wright, 'Warfare and
       Wanton Destruction: A Reexamination of Deuteronomy 20: 19–20 in Relation to Ancient
       Siegecraft', *JBL* 127 [2008], 423–458).

is highly unusual); in each of these cases the focus is on the exclusion of non-Israelites from the Yahwistic community.[209] This is contrary to the interpretation of Olyan, who contends that the issue under consideration is cultic participation specifically, referring to Lam. 1:10; Isa. 56:3–7; and Ezek. 44:7, 9 in interpreting 'to enter the assembly' as parallel in meaning to 'enter the house' or 'enter the sanctuary'.[210] However, Lam. 1:10 does not preclude a primary understanding of קהל as referring to the community rather than a sacred building and neither Isa. 56:3–7 nor Ezek. 44:7, 9 refer to the קהל at all. While exclusion from the Israelite community would imply exclusion from the sanctuary frequented by that community, temple-access does not appear to be the primary issue here. The broader understanding of the קהל יהוה as the Israelite community, rather than sanctuary specifically, also makes sense as a reflection of the deuteronomic interest in the general discouragement of Israelites' interactions with non-Israelites; it is not only at the sanctuary that such interactions are dangerous but whenever and wherever they might occur.

The basis of the rejection in Deut. 23:4 on ethnic grounds is reflected in the use of generational, genetic language.[211] Neither the Ammonite nor the Moabite are ever permitted to join the community, even after ten generations; the language suggests that ethnic concepts of ancestry and familial descent are key in the logic of this imperative.[212] Although, as already observed, much of the

---

209    Thus M. Zehnder, 'Anstösse aus Dtn 23,2–9 zur Frage nach dem Umgang mit Fremden', *FZPhTh* 52 (2005), 304.

210    S.M. Olyan, *Disability in the Hebrew Bible: Interpreting Mental and Physical Differences* (Cambridge, Cambridge University Press, 2008), 27–28; also S.M. Olyan, 'Equality and Inequality in the Socio-Political Visions of the Pentateuchal Sources', *JHS* 10 (2010), 38–39; S.M. Olyan, '"Anyone Blind or Lame Shall Not Enter the House": On the Interpretation of Second Samuel 5:8b', *CBQ* 60 (1998), 221–223; F.-L. Hossfeld, 'Volk Gottes als "Versammlung"', *Unterwegs zu Kirche: Alttestamentliche Konzeptionen* (ed. J. Schreiner, QD 110, Freiburg, Herder, 1987), 123–142.

211    The extant justification for the exclusion is expansionary, based on a tradition of the Ammonites' and the Moabites' lack of hospitality in Israel's approach to the land. Other explanations of the prohibition include, on the basis of the preceding laws and the narratives about Lot's daughters in Genesis 19, appeal to sexual behaviours associated with these peoples (thus Hossfeld, 'Volk Gottes als "Versammlung"', 129; A.R. Hulst, 'Der Name "Israel" im Deuteronomium', *OTS* 9 [1951], 97).

212    'The tenth generation' should be taken as symbolic of completeness, synonymous with the final 'forever' (עד עולם) (Christensen, *Deuteronomy 21:10–34:12*, 536; Nelson, *Deuteronomy*, 278; the exclusion is likely meant as a categorical statement, even if one or the other is an addition per Nielsen, *Deuteronomium*, 216; Mayes, *Deuteronomy*, 316).

deuteronomic material is concerned with Israelites who threaten to become non-Israelites by virtue of the pursuit of non-Israelite practices, emphasising the achieved elements of Israelite identity, these verses focus on ascribed identity, rejecting on apparently genetic grounds the possibility that these non-Israelites might be able to become Israelites. It is perhaps the strongest statement in the deuteronomic text of the significance of ascriptive identity in the deuteronomic identity logic; although the repeated emphasis on Israelites' common origins in Egypt and the use of brother language imply similar thinking, it is the rejection here of those who lack this genetic linkage to the Israelite community which makes this explicit.

The verse's expression of the problematic nature of non-Israelites in relation to the community of Israelites raises, of course, the question of why the text does not simply announce a blanket ban of all non-Israelites. As von Rad put it, it is 'verwunderlich, daß die Reihe nicht aus einer pauschalen Anweisung besteht'.[213] Partial exceptions to the rule are addressed below; here it seems worthwhile to consider why Ammonites and Moabites are singled out for exclusion. The answer, perhaps, lies in the text's fiction: the three most probably original nations addressed in Deut. 23:4–9 were Ammon, Moab and Edom. Between these three, all of the non-Israelites in the Transjordan are represented. While it is difficult to be certain how much of the Mosaic speech form was contained in the deuteronomic original, the emphasis on Egypt presupposes a tradition of entry into the land from elsewhere; if that entry was understood as via the Transjordan, these would be the non-Israelites which Israel has, in narrative terms, already encountered.[214] One might also note that, among southern Levantine populations, the material culture of Judah (and the northern kingdom) most closely resembled that of the Transjordan

---

213     von Rad, *Das fünfte Buch Mose*, 104; the full quotation is 'So ist es bei der schroffen Exklusivität der Jahwereligion anderen Kulten gegenüber verwunderlich, daß die Reihe nicht aus einer pauschalen Anweisung besteht'. Similarly Tigay, *Deuteronomy*, 211: 'There is no blanket exclusion of foreigners as such, nor any racial objection to them'.

214     Another possibility is that the trio was originally a quartet formed of the four classic foreign nations of Ammon, Moab, Edom and Philistia (cf. Amos 1–2; Ezekiel 25), with Philistia displaced by Egypt. In this case it is the omission of Philistia which is unexpected; with this in mind Zehnder, 'Anstösse aus Dtn 23,2–9' explains the absence of the Philistines in terms of the Mosaic pretense of approach from the east, while Nielsen, *Deuteronomium*, 220 suggests that Philistia may be the unnamed target of Deut. 23:2. Kaiser, 'Von Ortsfremden', 54 suggests that both Philistia and Phoenicia were tacitly overlooked as a consequence of them being only on the horizon of the author's consciousness (which he locates in the Persian period).

until quite late.[215] The particular attention to Ammon and Moab may therefore reflect another instance of greater intensity in identity concerns *vis-à-vis* those of greater cultural similarity.[216] While Edom is excepted from the universalising exclusion on the grounds of its peculiar familial relationship to Israel, Ammon and Moab represent the norm: non-Israelites are excluded from the Israelite community.[217]

### Offspring of Mixed Heritage

Though now opaque due to its unusual vocabulary, Deut. 23:3 is likely a variant on the concept of exclusion of those who are not of Israelite ancestry. In this verse, the ממזר is denied inclusion into the community. The difficulty is to what or to whom the term refers; traditional translations simply reflect the guess that the term has something to do with a person resulting from illicit sexual intercourse of some kind ('Those born of an illicit union shall not be admitted to the assembly of the LORD' [NRSV], 'No one misbegotten shall be admitted into the congregation of the LORD' [JPS]). Rabbinical interpretation understood a ממזר to be the product of an incestuous or otherwise too closely related marriage, based on Deut. 23:1 and the interpretation of Moab and Ammon's exclusion in Deut. 23:4 as a consequence of their incestual origins (cf. Gen. 19:30–38).[218] Mayes extends the possibilities to include other forms of prohibited marriage, while Braulik follows Craigie in deriving the term from נזר, to dedicate, and concluding that the forbidden union involved was that with a cult prostitute.[219]

---

215    L.G. Herr, 'Archaeological Sources for the History of Palestine: The Iron Age II Period: Emerging Nations', *BA* 60 (1997), 114–183; Keel and Uehlinger, *Gods, Goddesses and Images of God*.

216    Barth, 'Introduction'; Harrison, 'Cultural Difference'; Harrison, 'Identity as a Scarce Resource'.

217    It is also interesting to note Olyan's suggestion that 'the original law in Deut 23:4–9 concerned only the exclusion of circumcised peoples (Ammonites, Moabites, Edomites, and Egyptians) from the assembly (see Jer 9:24–25); uncircumcised peoples are not even mentioned in that context' (Olyan, '"Anyone Blind or Lame"', 222 n. 18). Though there is cause to question the inclusion of Egyptians in this list (see 3.2.4. Exceptions) this observation does raise the possibility that the focus on these particular peoples may be a consequence of the particular 'congruence of codes and values' to which Barth, 'Introduction', 16 refers.

218    Driver, *Deuteronomy*, 260; Tigay, *Deuteronomy*, 211; Nelson, *Deuteronomy*, 275; Mayes, *Deuteronomy*, 316. Reversing this, Christensen, *Deuteronomy 21:10–34:12*, 534 argues that the idea that Ammon and Moab were the product of incest was derived from Deut. 23:3–4.

219    Mayes, *Deuteronomy*, 316 (cf. Hayes, *Gentile Impurities*, 26); Braulik, *Deuteronomium II*, 170; on the (un)likelihood of the latter see 2.4.2. Cult Officials.

The term itself only appears otherwise at Zech. 9:6, and on that basis
Nielsen concludes that it refers to a person whose parents are of different races (a 'Mischling', in his terms): that is, a person with a non-Israelite
parent.[220] Although the Zechariah text does not define the term, it is interesting to note that its usage is in the context of a threat to the Philistines existence
*qua* Philistines, suggesting that, whatever its precise referent, the term probably does reflect sensitivities about ethnic identities. Although the definition
of the ממזר is problematic, there is therefore some justification for seeing him
as a person with a parent of non-Israelite origin. If this is the case, this verse is
designed to exclude those whose parentage was a source of potential identity
confusion, due either to the ambiguous genetic heritage (note again the use of
generational language) or, more to the point, the ambiguous cultural heritage
attendant upon such parental diversity. This interpretation, as Nielsen notes,
would also give the entire passage some semblance of logical sequence: a law
rejecting anyone who commits an act which causes him to resemble a non-
Israelite in Deut. 23:2; a law rejecting anyone confused—explicitly genetically
but also implicitly culturally—by possession of a non-Israelite parent in Deut.
23:3; and a law rejecting non-Israelites outright in Deut. 23:4.[221] The law would
thus fall into the category of attempts to exclude non-Israelites from the community, on the grounds of genetic confusion and, implicitly, that interaction
with the ambiguous or mixed cultural practices of such persons threaten to
blur the clarity of Israelite cultural practice.

Ultimately, Deut. 23:3 is stated too obscurely to allow a confident assertion
regarding what it meant to prohibit or why its author intended do so. The

---

220   Nielsen, *Deuteronomium*, 221.

221   Nielsen, *Deuteronomium*, 221: 'Sollte diese Wiedergabe das Richtige treffen, würde das
        Gemeindegesetz eine gewisse Steigerung enthalten: Weder Entfremdete (V. 2), noch
        Halbfremde (V. 3), noch Ganzefremde (V. 4) könnten zur Gemeinde Jahwes Zutritt
        erhalten.' It is worth noting that, if correct, this prohibition is also closely aligned with
        the imperative contained in Deut. 7:1–4a regarding marriage to non-Israelites. Indeed,
        strictly speaking, this law would seem redundant; if Israelites follow Deut. 7:1–4a and
        do not marry non-Israelites, the question of the eligibility of the product of such a mar-
        riage to enter the community should never arise. However, as emphasised throughout,
        the identity project on which the deuteronomic material is embarked is a work in prog-
        ress. Though the idea of endogamous marriage is expressed in Deut. 7:1–4a, the reality is
        addressed by Deut. 23:3: children whose parents are not both committed Israelites are
        not admissible to the Israelite community. Note again that it is the cultural, especially
        Yahwistic, identity of the non-Israelite which is the core issue in Deut. 7:1–4a and that
        this same concern is here reflected in the reference to the Israelite community as the קהל
        יהוה, with the Yahwistic identity of Israel serving as *pars pro toto* for all Israelite practice.

evidence which is available, however, suggests that the concern of the imperative reflects identity issues similar to those found in other deuteronomic material, with Deut. 23:3 preventing the Israelite community from interacting with individuals whose heritage was a source of potential alterity. Although the details of the prohibition remain obscure, approaching it with identity issues in mind offers a compelling articulation of its presence and purpose.

### Eunuchs

Among the cases in which the deuteronomic material appears to be addressing matters of cultural definition are a few whose precise categorisation is somewhat ambiguous, insofar as it is not immediately evident whether they are attempting to differentiate a distinctive Israelite cultural practice *vis-à-vis* a practice of non-Israelites or whether they are attempting to achieve this same end by the means of the exclusion of actual non-Israelites from the community. One of these is Deut. 23:2, which prohibits the entry into קהל יהוה of any male whose genitalia have been crushed (דכא) or severed (כרות). Two aspects of this prohibition are particularly noteworthy.

First, the usual interpretation of this description is that it is meant to refer to men who have been castrated to some degree or another, either deliberately or by accident. On this basis many interpretive efforts have turned to the person of the סריס, an individual who appears intermittently in the narratives about the kings of Israel and Judah.[222] In these texts the סריס is associated with the court; he appears to have been a royal official close to the king. With regard to the deuteronomic text it may be observed that in some of these passages the סריס is either explicitly declared to be incapable of reproducing (Isaiah 56) or, due to the nature of his work among the royal wives and concubines, likely to have been so (Esther). In the former case, the stereotyped aspect of the statement indicates that sterility is a characteristic more or less associated with the class, rather than an exceptional case.[223]

---

222    1 Sam. 8:15; 1 Kg. 22:9; 2 Kg. 8:6; 9:32; 23:11; 24:12, 15; 25:19; Jer. 29:2; 34:19; 38:7; 41:16.

223    The positive inclusion of the סריס in Isa. 56:3–5 as something remarkable has been interpreted as supporting a pre-exilic date for Deut. 23:2, although this has also been questioned (see Nelson, *Deuteronomy*, 278 and Nielsen, *Deuteronomium*, 219 in favour; but J.L. Wright and M.J. Chan, 'King and Eunuch: Isaiah 56:1–8 in Light of Honorific Royal Burial Practices', *JBL* 131 [2012], 99–119, for an argument against Isaiah 56 having much to do with Deut. 23:2 at all; note also Christensen, *Deuteronomy 21:10–34:12*, 536, who renders the two texts compatible by understanding Deut. 23:2 to be referring only to deliberate castration and Isaiah 56 therefore to refer only to those for whom the emasculation was accidental or due to illness).

The biblical association between the סריס, the royal servant and castration is paralleled in the various sources regarding Assyrian, Babylonian and
Persian practices, with the potential for a connection to these highlighted by
the Akkadian term for such persons, *ša rēši*, whence the Hebrew term derives.[224]
Best known are the numerous depictions on the Assyrian palace reliefs of
beardless males engaged in administrative activities and serving as attendants
to the king, but various texts similarly suggest an above-average correlation
between the title *ša rēši* and castration.[225]

This correlation, however, does not appear to be absolute, and it is in this
regard that the failure of Deut. 23:2 to use the term סריס is noteworthy. The
absence of what might seem to be a generic term for the most common category of such persons may suggest that, as in Mesopotamia, the Hebrew סריס
might—but might not—be a eunuch, and that the author of this prohibition wished to specify that it was not the royal official, as such, to whom he
objected, but to genital mutilation. This, in turn, seems to suggest two things.
First, although it would be in keeping with the limitations placed on the king in
Deut. 17:14–17, this particular law does not appear to be targeting royal aggran-
disement of power or a peculiarly royal risk of exposure to non-Israelites.[226]
Conversely, it indicates that there is some deuteronomic issue with castration,
most likely of the deliberate variety.[227]

---

224   For a review of the ancient Near Eastern materials see S. Cornelius, '"Eunuchs"? The
      Ancient Background of *Eunouchos* in the Septuagint', *Septuagint and Reception: Essays
      Prepared for the Association for the Study of the Septuagint in South Africa* (ed. J. Cook,
      VTSup 127, Leiden, Brill, 2009), 323–329 and Wright and Chan, 'King and Eunuch', 104–111,
      with further references. On the connection between סריס and the Akkadian *ša rēši* see
      H. Tadmor, 'Rab-saris and Rab-shakeh in 2 Kings 18', *The Word of the Lord Shall Go Forth:
      Essays in Honor of David Noel Freedman in Celebration of His Sixtieth Birthday* (ed. C.L.
      Meyers and M. O'Connor, Special Volume Series (American Schools of Oriental Research)
      1, Winona Lake, Ind., Eisenbrauns, 1983), 279–285 and H. Tadmor, 'Was the Biblical *saris*
      a Eunuch?', *Solving Riddles and Untying Knots: Biblical, Epigraphic, and Semitic Studies
      in Honor of Jonas C. Greenfield* (ed. Z. Zevit, S. Gitin and M. Sokoloff, Winona Lake, Ind.,
      Eisenbrauns, 1995), 317–325.
225   On the biblical סריס as eunuchs see especially Tadmor, 'Rab-saris and Rab-shakeh' and
      Tadmor, 'Was the Biblical *saris* a Eunuch?', the latter suggesting that word and institution
      entered Hebrew via Phoenician, before the Assyrians arrived in the eighth century.
226   See Wright and Chan, 'King and Eunuch', 104–108, with further references, on the rationale
      of employing eunuchs in the royal entourage.
227   Scholars are rightly hasty to point out the possibility of accidental injury of the sort Deut.
      23:2 appears to describe, but short of statistical data on the frequency of such injuries
      (and, more pertinently, the number of these which would not result in fatal infection) it
      is impossible to definitively determine whether Deut. 23:2 has such accidental injuries in

This brings us back to the law itself and, in particular, to its second note-worthy feature: that it is 'in the assembly of Yнwн' (בקהל יהוה) that such per-sons may not enter. In contrast to Deut. 23:19, which prohibits the entry of certain voluntary offerings into 'the house of Yнwн' (בית יהוה), the ban here is concerned with the קהל יהוה, the community of Yahwistic practitioners. This suggests that the issue in this prohibition is unlikely to be perceived cultic imperfection or cultic impurity, of the sort which prevents the sacrifice of a physically imperfect animal in Deut. 17:1 or the performance of altar service by an imperfect priest in Lev. 21:17–23; the issue is not, apparently, at this specific level of proximity to sacred space but rather at the broader level of inclusion in the Yahwistic community.[228] Again, then, arises the question: what is the deuteronomic problem with deliberately castrated males? Two options arise; both seem equally plausible and both, perhaps, represent part of the concern of this text.

First, there is the suggestion that the deliberately-castrated man, possibly a סריס, is a non-Israelite.[229] This proposal has traditionally been based primarily on the fact that סריס is clearly a loan word from *ša rēši* and is, as such, the only known transliteration of a foreign title in Hebrew.[230] There is also the possibil-ity that close attendants to the king would have been more likely to be imported mercenaries than locals with potentially conflicting loyalties; one is actually specified as 'the Cushite' (הכושי, Jer. 38:7).[231] This is supported in Deut. 23:2 by the text's own statement that the person in question 'may not enter … the assembly of Yнwн' (לא יבא … בקהל יהוה). Aside from implying that the person in question is an outsider whose admissibility into the Yahwistic community is

---

mind. Given, however, the probably rarity of such injuries and the generally assumed rule of legislation which presumes that most laws target a known and reasonably prevalent practice, it seems more likely that Deut. 23:2 is dealing with deliberate mutilations.

228 As, e.g., Tigay, *Deuteronomy*, 210–211; compare Olyan, 'Equality and Inquality', 38–39, who assumes that the individual in question is (already) an Israelite (see also above regarding the קהל יהוה).

229 See Nielsen, *Deuteronomium*, 200; Tigay, *Deuteronomy*, 210; Driver, *Deuteronomy*, 259.

230 N.S. Fox, *In the Service of the King: Officialdom in Ancient Israel and Judah* (HUCM 23, Cincinnati, Ohio, Hebrew Union College Press, 2000), 277.

231 Cf. 2 Samuel 18; 20; 1 Kings 1; 2 Kings 11. N. Na'aman, 'Textual and Historical Notes on the Eliashib Archive from Arad', *TA* 38 (2011), 83–93, 89 notes that mercenaries are always sta-tioned with the king; Fox considers it 'quite feasible' for eunuchs to have been imported from Syria or Mesopotamia to serve in this capacity. Fox also suggests that the non-Israelite origin of the סריסים is supported by the legal aversion to castration ('in light of Israelite law, it seems highly unlikely that the society produced eunuchs from its own people'), but this has the danger of becoming circular (Fox, *In the Service of the King*, 202–203).

under contention (rather than an Israelite whose pursuit of such practices will result in expulsion), the focus of the next several verses (arguably all of them) is on the refusal of entry into the Yahwistic community to non-Israelites and each of the subsequent commands uses this exact phraseology.

If the eunuchs in question are indeed non-Israelites, there naturally arise questions of both their origin and their reason for a presence in Judah sufficiently regular as to warrant the present prohibition. Two options appear viable. First, as already suggested, it is possible that they are among the סריסים, imported to serve as the king's closest attendants. Such individuals might have been from almost any ancient Near Eastern region. Equally possible is that this law has in view some of the Assyrian administrative staff present in Judah as part of its inclusion in the empire. It is admittedly difficult to imagine that any meaningful number were inclined to join the Israelite community—again, the issue is not just participation in worship but inclusion in the community—but the possibility is there. Of course, the use of eunuchs was probably widespread in the ancient Near East (certainly it seems absurd to assume that it was restricted to only Israel, Judah and Assyria) and, given this, it is also possible that ambassadors or other officials visiting from the southern Levant may also be in mind here.[232] In either case—whether the eunuchs in question are servants of the Judahite king or in the employ of other regional powers—this law's purpose is isolationist, attempting to maintain the clarity of Israel's boundaries by disallowing the presence among Israelites of persons whose origins are elsewhere.

Given, however, that there is no real reason to assume that eunuchs in the service of the Judahite king could only be imported from elsewhere, it is also possible that at least part of the motive of Deut. 23:2 is akin to what we have seen in other deuteronomic texts, with its object to prohibit among Israelites the pursuit of practices which may be interpreted as characteristic of non-Israelites. Indeed the verse may have a double function: both prohibiting the entry of non-Israelite eunuchs into the Israelite community as well as rejecting, by implication, any Israelites who pursue a practice primarily associated with non-Israelites.

Finally, it has also been suggested that the deuteronomic objection to the man whose genitalia are injured (פצוע) is that such a man will be unable to bear children.[233] Such inability has been a significant factor in the use of eunuchs

---

232   See Tadmor, 'Was the Biblical *saris* a Eunuch?'; Fox, *In the Service of the King*, 202–203; also
       Cornelius, '"Eunuchs"?', 328 for the practice also in Babylonia at this time.

233   Christensen, *Deuteronomy 21:10–34:12*, 534; see also Nelson, *Deuteronomy*, 278; Mayes,
       *Deuteronomy*, 315.

in various royal households for millennia, but the association with royal power does not seem to be in mind here. The inability to procreate, however, may make sense in the context of the deuteronomic concern for community continuity. Indeed, the combination of these two concerns may aptly address the core of the deuteronomic objection, with the law prohibiting those who are doubly incapable of ensuring the survival of the Israelite Yahwistic community: first, by virtue of being or associating themselves with non-Israelites and, second, by virtue of an inability to produce a new generation of Israelites.[234]

### 3.2.4    Exceptions

Despite the multiplicity of means by which the deuteronomic text undertakes to distinguish Israelite cultural practice from non-Israelite and to protect that distinctiveness by discouraging interaction with non-Israelites, there nonetheless exist two exceptions to the deuteronomic determination to avoid mixing with non-Israelites. In the case of the Edomite this reflects the paradoxical potential of genetic relationship with Israel and in the case of the war captive the ultimate conception of Israelite identity as a status achieved rather than ascribed.

### The Edomite

The first exception follows on from the explicit exclusion of the Ammonites and Moabites: Deut. 23:8–9 specifically permits the admission to the community of the Edomite and the Egyptian. Aside from the anthropological questions raised by these verses, to which we will return momentarily, there are several difficult grammatical elements which obscure their intent. First, in Deut. 23:8 the addressee is instructed not to תעב *pi.* either the Edomite or the Egyptian, the former on the grounds of familial-ethnic ties ('for he is your

---

234    A number of scholars have also noted the possibility that the ban reflects the rejection of a non-Israelite cultic practice, which would fit neatly with the tendency toward such legislation in the deuteronomic material (e.g., Tigay, *Deuteronomy*, 210–211). Nielsen, *Deuteronomium*, 219–220 suggests an association with 'Canaanite' cultic practices and points out that if the ban was directed at Phoenician and/or Philistine practices this would round off the catalogue of neighbouring nations which are addressed in the subsequent verses; Braulik, *Deuteronomium II*, 170 suggests that the ban relates to some form of 'Canaanite' religiosity and contends that the persons are not eunuchs but the *pater familias* engaged in some kind of ritual castration, though whence he derives this notion is unclear. Evidence for such a cultic practice, however, is lacking; there is no mention of such a practice elsewhere in the Hebrew Bible and the only extra-biblical evidence is a reference in Lucian to a religious ceremony in Syria during the Hellenistic period; the possibility remains but cannot be proven.

brother', כי אחיך הוא) and the latter on the basis of Israel's residence in Egypt ('for you were a גר in his land', כי גר היית בארצו). Traditionally the verb has been understood to mean something like 'to hate, detest, despise', but the usage of both noun and verb across a wide range of texts suggests that the תעב stem is associated with a sense of the alienness of the person, practice or object in under discussion. In this passage, this makes notably better sense of the text: rather than a vague statement not to 'hate' the Edomite or the Egyptian, Deut. 23:8 is instructing that the Israelite should not treat him like a non-Israelite.

The implications of this are unpacked in Deut. 23:9: 'Sons who are borne to them, the third generation: he may come to them in the assembly of Yhwh' (בנים אשר יולדו להם דור שלישי יבא להם בקהל יהוה). In what at first seems a contradiction of the preceding rejection of those with non-Israelite heritage in Deut. 23:2–4, the text presents a mechanism by which a non-Israelite may be admitted to the Israelite community. It will come as no surprise that these verses are often thought to be a later addition, inconsistent with deuteronomic cultural logic.[235] There is some cause, however, to think that part of this law might have some deuteronomic antiquity, not least the very specific usage of the 'brother' language in the explanation for the admission of the Edomite— paradoxically, drawing on precisely that genetic, ascribed element within deuteronomic identity logic which was prominent in Deut. 23:3–4—as well as the verse's positive attitude regarding Edom, in contrast to the vehement polemicizing against Edom which appears in the wake of the fall of Judah (e.g., Obadiah).[236]

If the entire passage is not to be rejected wholesale, the technical peculiarities are worthy of scrutiny. There are difficulties with the text of Deut. 23:8–9 which indicate that it has been subject to elaboration and suggest that only

---

235   Mayes, *Deuteronomy*, 316; Perlitt, *Deuteronomium*, 152; Hulst, 'Der Name "Israel"', 87–88, 100–101.

236   For an interpretation of this last in explicitly ethnic terms see A.C. Hagedorn, 'Edom in the Book of Amos and Beyond', *Aspects of Amos: Exegesis and Interpretation* (ed. A.C. Hagedorn and A. Mein, LHBOTS 536, London, T&T Clark, 2011), 41–57. On the relationship between Israel and Edom see, among others, J.R. Bartlett, *Edom and the Edomites* (JSOTSup 77, Sheffield, JSOT, 1989); B. Dicou, *Edom, Israel's Brother and Antagonist: The Role of Edom in Biblical Prophecy and Story* (JSOTSup 169, Sheffield, JSOT, 1994); also J.M. Tebes, '"You Shall Not Abhor an Edomite, for He is Your Brother": The Tradition of Esau and the Edomite Genealogies from an Anthropological Perspective', *JHS* 6 (2006), n.p. and the essays in D.V. Edelman, ed., *You Shall Not Abhor an Edomite for He Is Your Brother: Edom and Seir in History and Tradition* (Archaeological and Biblical Studies 3, Atlanta, Ga., Scholars, 1995).

one of the two peoples now named is original to the deuteronomic intent. First, the masoretic punctuation reflects a significant break between Deut. 23:8a and Deut. 23:8b, presenting them as independent imperatives. This is also signalled by the duplicated syntactical structure and separate motive clauses: 'You will not treat an Edomite like an alien, because he is your brother' (Deut. 23:8a) and 'You will not treat an Egyptian like an alien, because you were a גר in his land' (Deut. 23:8b). The strict separation of these imperatives is muddled by Deut. 23:9: 'the sons which are borne to them' in Deut. 23:9aα are referenced in the plural, apparently referring to the offspring of both Edomite and Egyptian collectively, before the standard singular phrasing for entering the assembly appears in Deut. 23:9b (cf. Deut. 23:3, 4).The reference to the sons is stilted, collectivising the preceding so that both the Edomite and the Egyptian, until now handled separately, may be dealt with together by the solitary permissive phrase in Deut. 23:9b.

Other factors also suggest that only one of these foreigners was originally permitted entry into the community and, to be precise, that this was the Edomite and not the Egyptian. First, there is the extreme wariness of Egypt in the law of the king; by comparison, the welcome here sits uncomfortably, at best, with the multivalent avoidance tactics advocated there. Contributing to this incongruity is the differentiating effect of the numerous references to Israel as an entity which was brought out of Egypt by YHWH.[237] As Greifenhagen puts it, 'if the Egyptian can enter the assembly of YHWH, then the whole process of Israel's separation from Egypt is brought full circle back to its beginnings.'[238] Additionally, although the mention of the גר in the explanation of why the Egyptian may be permitted to join the assembly is a very clever way of linking the imperative to deuteronomic interests in that quarter, it is inconsistent with those interests. This is one of only two instances in which an imperative is justified on the grounds of Israel's having been גרים in Egypt; the only other such motivation is Deut. 10:19, which is certainly not deuteronomic.[239] Other justifications based on Egypt are rooted in it having been a place of slavery, where

---

237    See Greifenhagen, *Egypt on the Pentateuch's Ideological Map*, 160–167, especially 162, and
         2.3. A Common Mythology of Origins. Tigay, *Deuteronomy*, 213 derives the unusually posi-
         tive attitude toward Egypt here from the tradition of Egypt having been a haven in time
         of famine; cf. M.D. Cogan, 'The Other Egypt: A Welcome Asylum', *Texts, Temples, and
         Traditions: A Tribute to Menahem Haran* (ed. M.V. Fox, V.A. Hurowitz, A. Hurvitz, M.L.
         Klein, B.J. Schwartz and N. Shupak, Winona Lake, Ind., Eisenbrauns, 1996), 65–70.

238    Greifenhagen, *Egypt on the Pentateuch's Ideological Map*, 195.

239    On this see J.E. Ramírez Kidd, *Alterity and Identity in Israel: The גר in the Old Testament*
         (BZAW 283, Berlin, de Gruyter, 1999), 86–95.

the Israelites were עֲבָדִים (Deut. 15:15; 16:12; 24:22, cf. 6:12; 8:14; 13:5). The current text's openness toward the Egyptian, especially on the grounds of having been גֵּרִים, sits oddly with the rest of the deuteronomic text.

In addition to these indications against Egypt are factors in favour of Edom. The language of brotherhood used to justify the treatment of Edom as not an alien, although exceptional in a pre-exilic context in relation to Edom, is in keeping with deuteronomic rationale used when justifying laws which distinguish between Israelites and non-Israelites. As elsewhere, this brother language appears in what might be perceived as a particularly difficult law to implement. The use of familial language to justify the Edomite's potential inclusion among the Israelites also draws on the rhetoric of common ancestry which is especially common to articulations of ethnic unity.[240]

Relevant to this exceptional potential for the Edomite is Tebes' recent analysis of the tradition of Edom as Judah's 'brother', which draws on archaeological material to suggest that this tradition originated in the late Iron Age 'as a conflation of different, yet contemporary, oral traditions within the circle of local Negev population groups to mentally accommodate to this new sociopolitical and demographic situation'.[241] Specifically, Tebes sees the Edom-Judah 'brotherhood' as a means by which the inhabitants of the Negev attempted to incorporate their lived, side-by-side experience into their intellectual and

---

240    On this see Cohen, *Custom and Politics*, 202; S. Jones, *The Archaeology of Ethnicity: Constructing Identities in the Past and Present* (London, Routledge, 1997), 84; Keyes, 'Dialectics of Ethnic Change', 5–7. The generational language is also appropriate as a means of specifying that the Edomite may be classed as an Israelite only after an appropriate transitional period; by specifying that full admission into the community may be gained only by a future generation, the verse implicitly acknowledges that these offspring will have been resident alongside the Israelite cultural community rather than their own cultural community for some time. The third generation (or fourth, depending on how the verse is read) indicates that the individual in question is part of a family which has done so for some decades. Though it is not explicitly stated, the text implies that the individuals to be allowed into the community have been resident long enough to assimilate to Israelite norms. On the relevance of generational identity to ethnic identity see J. Ahn, *Exile as Forced Migrations: A Sociological, Literary, and Theological Approach on the Displacement and Resettlement of the Southern Kingdom of Judah* (BZAW 417, Berlin, de Gruyter, 2011), with further references. Note, also, Horowitz's classification of types of assimilation: assimilation may entail amalgamation (A+B=C) or incorporation (A+B=A). The exceptions to Israel's isolationism are clearly of the latter kind; the incorporation of the Edomite after this transitional period is not anticipated to alter Israelite identity but disappear into it (D.L. Horowitz, 'Ethnic Identity', *Ethnicity: Theory and Experience* [ed. N. Glazer and D.P. Moynihan, London, Harvard University Press, 1975], 115).

241    Tebes, '"You Shall Not Abhor an Edomite"', 3.

ideological frameworks. The 'sociopolitical and demographic situation' which Tebes describes is part and parcel of the wider phenomenon occurring in the southern Levant at this time: the phenomenon which is the major driving factor in the deuteronomic effort to differentiate Israelites from non-Israelites.

At first glance, the deuteronomic admission of an Edomite non-Israelite into the community seems to present evidence against the argument that the deuteronomic text is dedicated to differentiating and minimising the interaction between Israelites and non-Israelites. There is never, however, a single, predictable reaction provoked by a given set of social, political and economic circumstances. While the separatist response observable in the majority of the deuteronomic material is indeed the dominant response to situations of this type, it is not the only possible response. Other factors can come into play and affect the way in which heightened interaction with outsiders is perceived, managed and incorporated into a group's identity narrative. Indeed, as Tebes and others have noted, a number of indicators suggest an extraordinary relationship between Edom and Israel, namely, a tradition of proximity in the religious histories of Edom and Israel and, in particular, a tradition which locates YHWH's origins in territory with Edomite affinities.[242] The use of familial language in Deut. 23:8 to articulate the Edomite's unusual potential as a future Israelite makes sense in an identity framework in which significant weight can be given to traditions of common descent, provoked by notions of just such a familial relationship with Edom.[243]

### The War Captive

The second of the exceptions to the exclusion of non-Israelites from proximity to Israelites is Deut. 21:10–14, which allows an Israelite man to marry a female

---

242    Tebes, '"You Shall Not Abhor an Edomite"', 11–12; M. Rose, 'Yahweh in Israel, Qaus in Edom?', *JSOT* 4 (1977), 28–34; Bartlett, *Edom and the Edomites*; L. Zalcman, 'Shield of Abraham, Fear of Isaac, Dread of Esau', *ZAW* 117 (2005), 405–410; Hagedorn, 'Edom in the Book of Amos'; Dicou, *Edom, Israel's Brother*, 170–181; J.M. Hutton, 'Southern, Northern and Transjordanian Perspectives', *Religious Diversity in Ancient Israel and Judah* (ed. F. Stavrakopoulou and J. Barton, London, T&T Clark, 2010), 149–174, especially 161–167, as well as numerous biblical and extra-biblical texts linking YHWH to Edom, Seir, Teman, etc.

243    If Tebes is correct in locating the origins of this process already in the eighth century, chronology may also help to explain the decision to allow Edomites a possible entry into the community: by the time the wider phenomenon reached a sufficient crisis point to provoke the deuteronomic identity project, an earlier, localised response to the beginning stages of this phenomenon was already embedded.

prisoner of war.[244] At first glance, it appears to be in tension with Deut. 7:1–4a and Deut. 20:15–16, insofar as the latter implies that no women from a defeated population are allowed to live (and should therefore not be available for anything, marriage or otherwise) and the former explicitly prohibits intermarriage with the indigenous population. This has, unsurprisingly, led some to conclude that both Deut. 7:1–4a and Deut. 20:15–18 constitute later redactions of an original deuteronomic text for which interaction with non-Israelites was not an issue. However, there is a difference between Deut. 21:10–14 and the two previous instructions. Both Deut. 7:1–4a and Deut. 20:15–16 apply specifically to Israel's fellow-inhabitants in the land. The opening phrase of Deut. 21:10, however—'If you go out to battle' (כי תצא למלחמה)   implies that the enemy from whom the woman is captured is outside the land; if so, she is removed from the remit of either Deut. 20:15–16 or Deut. 7:1–4a and placed in the category of persons described in Deut. 20:10–14.[245] This would render Deut. 21:10–14 consistent with the general deuteronomic disinterest in those outside the land.[246] As the corollary to the propensity of identity phenomena

---

244   On the integrity of the chapter see G.J. Wenham and J.G. McConville, 'Drafting Techniques in Some Deuteronomic Laws', *VT* 30 (1980), 248–252, (though note the on-going scholarly uncertainty regarding this law's textual relationship to Deut. 20:10–18 especially). On the integrity of the law itself commentators are generally agreed, with a tendency to raise the possibility that it reflects an early or perhaps even pre-deuteronomic tradition (Nielsen, *Deuteronomium*, 202–207; Mayes, *Deuteronomy*, 201–203; contra Otto, *Das Deuteronomium*, 229–233, who attributes it to the Persian period in counter to the exclusivism of Ezra and Nehemiah. As already emphasised, however, identity concerns need not be limited to the exilic and post-exilic periods; the very limited extent of this law also speaks against such a broad remit).

245   Cf. Mayes, *Deuteronomy*, 303; Nelson, *Deuteronomy*, 260; Driver, *Deuteronomy*, 244–245; Christensen, *Deuteronomy 1:1–21:9*, 474; contra Rofé, 'Laws of Warfare', 30. Braulik, *Deuteronomium II*, 154 suggests that the casuistic formulation of the law itself presupposes that the audience is already in the land at the point at which the law is employed and that the enemy in question must therefore be foreign rather than local. Tigay writes that the law 'apparently does not regard them [foreign women] as posing the same threat to Israel's religious integrity as would Canaanites. Perhaps it assumes that since they are separated from their own culture, they will quickly assimilate to Israel's ways and will not attract their husbands to their own native religion' (Tigay, *Deuteronomy*, 193–194).

246   Combined with the text's overall disinterest in both foreigners in general and with Mesopotamians in particular, this presents the intriguing possibility that the deuteronomic text tacitly allows the marriage of Israelites to non-Israelites as long as the non-Israelites in question are true foreigners. If this is the case, it would confirm the relatively neutral—if not positive—attitude toward Assyrian power indicated by the deuteronomic text.

to be most intense *vis-à-vis* proximate and largely similar alternatives, this makes sense.[247]

Such permissiveness with regard to a woman truly foreign, rather than local but not Israelite, relies on the practical elements of such a situation to assist in the protection of Israelite distinctiveness. A certain degree of existing similarity is usually required for an outsider to represent a significant threat; heritage which is almost wholly unfamiliar is a simpler matter to reject. To this end the extent to which the woman is deliberately and methodologically estranged from her former life and everything associated with it is particularly obvious. While she is permitted to mourn for them, her parents are gone; with them goes the most decisive link with her past (any husband being already presumed dead).[248] It is not specified whether the parents are mourned for because actually dead or because they are absent; while the father might be dead in battle, there is no particular reason to assume likewise for the mother. The mourning for the parents is also mentioned after she puts aside 'the mantle of her captivity', suggesting that the loss of her parents is directly related to her extraction from the general sea of captives and the cultural milieu they represent: a loss occasioned by her symbolic separation from the group from which she originated rather than by her parents' physical death. Pressler suggests that the law is designed to provide a means for a man to marry a woman who has no family member to conclude a marriage contract on her behalf; even if this were not actually the case (that is, the woman's parents were still alive), the law effectively makes it so, rendering the woman a blank slate, without ancestry, history or identity.[249] Nelson observes that the assimilative threat posed by intermarriage would be eliminated by their effective death: 'there would be no family to entangle Israel into pagan practices'.[250]

---

247    Barth, 'Introduction'; Harrison, 'Identity'; S. Harrison, 'Cultural Difference as Denied Resemblance: Reconsidering Nationalism and Ethnicity', *CSSH* 45 (2003), 343–361.

248    H.C. Washington, '"Lest He Die in the Battle and Another Man Take Her": Violence and the Construction of Gender in the Laws of Deuteronomy 20–22', *Gender and Law in the Hebrew Bible and the Ancient Near East* (ed. V.H. Matthews, B.M. Levinson and T. Frymer-Kensky, London, T&T Clark, 1998), 204 especially notes the possibility of a previous husband, even the possibility of previous children; also H.C. Washington, 'Violence and the Construction of Gender in the Hebrew Bible: A New Historicist Approach', *BibInt* 5 (1997), 324–363. The text does not specify their non-existence, yet it effectively renders them as though they did not exist: like the setting aside of the parents yet going beyond it, the ties of the woman to her past represented by the spouse and the child are written out entirely.

249    Pressler, *The View of Women*, 102–103 n. 2.

250    Nelson, *Deuteronomy*, 260.

The specification of a mourning period of a full month perhaps affirms this; while it is a logical amount of time to delay the subsequently-permitted intercourse as a means of ensuring the paternity of any offspring, it is longer than what appears elsewhere to be the norm for mourning rites. It seems best interpreted as a symbolically significant liminal period, in which the woman transitions from non-Israelite to Israelite.[251] Also representing the woman's change of loyalties is the shaving of the head; although a number of both rabbinic and modern commentators suppose this to be a means of making the woman unattractive in order to test the man's commitment and affection—his decision to wed having been described in Deut. 21:11 as due to her beauty—shaving the head is more convincingly understood as a symbolic divestiture of her native affiliations, as is the changing of her clothes: 'Wenn die Frau das "Kleid der Gefangenschaft" ablegt, dann verliert sie alles, was sie mit der Vergangenheit und dem für Israel Fremde und Feindliche verbindet'.[252] As Nelson puts it, 'the wife-to-be is shedding bits of her former self-hood'.[253] Supporting this transitional effect is the stipulation that, if divorced in future, the woman must not be sold; rather, she must be treated as the Israelite woman she has become (Deut. 21:14). Linking the text to the 'brother' ethics already discussed, Nielsen concludes that 'Das Dtn schützt sie ausdrücklich wie jeden israelitischen Bruder—vgl. 24[7]—vor einem Sklavenschicksal'.[254] As Bechmann observes, this law aims 'nicht auf kriegsgefangene Frauen generell, sondern nur auf die Übernahme einer schönen fremden Gefangenen in das Haus und Bett eines israelitischen Mannes'.[255] The law is not a general *carte blanche* for the incorporation of non-Israelite women into the community but a law addressing the potential for a person whose identity is so unfamiliar as to pose almost

---

251   See V.W. Turner, *The Ritual Process: Structure and Anti-Structure* (New York, N.Y., Aldine, 1969); A. Van Gennep, *Les rites de passage* (Paris, Picard, 1981); cf. Pressler, *The View of Women*, 12–13.

252   U. Bechmann, 'Die Kriegsgefangene Frau (Dtn 21,10–14)', *BK* 4 (2005), 201; though note that Bechmann's suggestion that she then remains unclothed seems unlikely.

253   Nelson, *Deuteronomy*, 259; similarly Mayes, *Deuteronomy*, 303; Braulik, *Deuteronomium II*, 155. Mayes, *Deuteronomy*, 301–302 contends however that the point of the law is the captive's rights, not the 'subsidiary, and in the present context quite superfluous, provisions dealing with the actions to be performed by the captive when taken into her master's house'; he deems Deut. 21:12b–13 to be an older, pre-deuteronomic element. However, in such a case one must wonder why the deuteronomic author left such 'superfluous' elements in if they were not germane to his point.

254   Nielsen, *Deuteronomium*, 207; cf. Braulik, *Deuteronomium II*, 155; Nelson, *Deuteronomy*, 259.

255   Bechmann, 'Die Kriegsgefangene Frau', 200.

no threat to be rendered an Israelite, in a manner consistent with the deuteronomic identity framework. The text appears to presuppose that such wives exist; under what circumstances and how they might be incorporated into the Israelite community in such a manner as to eliminate their non-Israelite character and thereby protect the distinctiveness of the community from the threat which that non-Israelite past represents, limited though it may be, is the matter at stake. Isolation, both geographical and cultural, is the solution proffered by the text.

Ultimately this passage raises interesting questions about the nature of 'Israeliteness'; it reiterates that, though theoretically ascribed through birth into the Israelite community, Israelite identity may sometimes be achieved by individuals to whom the status was not automatically accorded at birth. This idea of Israelite identity has already been noted in the logic of other passages, Deut. 13:2–19 most prominent among them, which understand Israeliteness as something which may be lost as a result of failure to act like an Israelite. Conversely, here Israeliteness is something which may be gained as a result of positive action.[256] In Eriksen's terms, '[i]dentities are ambiguous, and . . . this ambiguity is connected with a negotiable history and a negotiable cultural content'.[257]

### 3.3  *Differential Treatment of Israelites and Non-Israelites*

The deuteronomic effort to avoid social interaction and cultural assimilation to non-Israelite practices by simply avoiding non-Israelites as far as possible could not cover all eventualities. The *realia* of life in the long seventh century was such that non-Israelites would inevitably be encountered eventually. The non-Israelites in question could be true foreigners, from distant places, or might be non-Israelites resident alongside Israelites in Judah. The stringent deuteronomic efforts to curtail Israelite interaction with the latter especially have already been observed; what follows will consider the deuteronomic response to the foreigners the Israelites might be expected to encounter as

---

256   Whether this was voluntary or forced is another matter; on the realities behind this law see Washington, 'Violence', 342–352; Washington, ' "Lest He Die" ', 202–207; S.B. Thistlethwaite, ' "You May Enjoy the Spoils of Your Enemies": Rape as Biblical Metaphor for War', *Semeia* 61 (1993), 64–65.

257   Eriksen, *Ethnicity*, 73. Similarly: 'Ethnic identities are neither ascribed nor achieved: they are both' (Eriksen, *Ethnicity*, 57). Hastings, *The Construction of Nationhood*, 170, speaking more generally, notes that: 'In adopting the ancestors and gods of one's hosts, one's conquerors or even those one has conquered, one is adopting their *mores* and a shared moral community which leaps beyond any genetic bond, without, however, disallowing the latter's symbolic meaning.'

well as examining the peculiar case of the גר, apparently resident alongside the Israelites but allowed an exceptional degree of toleration, motivated by other deuteronomic interests. First, however, it turns to the use of explicitly ethnic language of brotherhood in certain deuteronomic laws and the preferential treatment of Israelites with which this language is associated.

### 3.3.1     Preferential Treatment of the Israelite 'Brother'

One of the characteristics of the deuteronomic legislation most often cited as evidence for its in-group mentality is its use of the language of brotherhood. This language is widespread in the deuteronomic material, appearing in almost every chapter of the deuteronomic core and rarely escaping commentators' notice.[258] The relevance of this type of language to discussions of deuteronomic Israel as an ethnic identity is largely self-evident, given the propensity of ethnic groups to conceive of group identity in terms of common descent and to speak about the group in familial terms.[259]

Appeals to a conception of Israel as a large extended family, united by a common shared history, appear in more than a dozen passages of deuteronomic legislation.[260] Appearances of this language in the law of the king (Deut. 17:14–17), in the law of the prophet (Deut. 18:15), in the list of those who might be most persuasive in encouraging non-Yahwistic worship (Deut. 13:7), in the law of levirate marriage (Deut. 25:5–8) and in the explanation for the admission of the Edomite into the Israelite community (Deut. 23:8–9) have already been discussed. As noted in several of these passages, the familial language seems to be used especially in cases in which the instruction might be considered particularly difficult; this is true also of a number of the other instances

---

258    In addition to the commentaries see the discussions in W. Houston, '"You Shall Open Your Hand to Your Needy Brother": Ideology and Moral Formation in Deut. 15,1–18', *The Bible in Ethics: The Second Sheffield Colloquium* (ed. J.W. Rogerson, M. Davies and M.D. Carroll R., JSOTSup 207, London, Continuum, 1995), 296–314; Perlitt, '"Ein einzig Volk von Brüdern"'; Sparks, *Ethnicity and Identity*, 225–267.

259    Cohen, *Custom and Politics*, 202; also Jones, *Archaeology of Ethnicity*, 84, with further references. As noted in Chapter Two, the reality of genetic cohesion is less significant for this purpose than the rhetoric of a common history and shared past. Note the determined rejection of this by C. Bultmann, *Der Fremde im antiken Juda: Eine Untersuchung zum sozialen Typenbegriff >ger< und seinem Bedeutungswandel in der alttestamentlichen Gesetzgebung* (FRLANT 153, Göttingen, Vandenhoeck & Ruprecht, 1992), 83, which likely at least partially explains his ability to include the גר among the Israelites: 'der Begriff *'aḥ* [hat] primär keine nationalen oder ethnischen Implikationen'.

260    Note Perlitt, '"Ein einzig Volk von Brüdern"', 59–60 regarding the non-legal origins of the usage.

of brother language, including the laws of debt remission (Deut. 15:1–11) and manumission (Deut. 15:12–18), the law concerning usury (Deut. 23:20–21) and the law mandating the return of lost property (Deut. 22:1–4).[261] Usage often seems intended to evoke an extra degree of responsibility or to imply a certain standard of behaviour as, for example, in the laws concerning false witness (Deut. 19:16–19), enslavement (Deut. 24:7), military exemptions (Deut. 20:5–9) and fraternal conflicts (Deut. 25:1–3, 11–12), sometimes almost invoking an element of shame upon the addressee(s) for even considering the betrayal of family ties which such behaviour constitutes.[262] The usury law (Deut. 23:20–21) will be discussed in more detail in the next section; here a few further comments regarding some of these other passages are warranted.

Probably the greatest concentration of deuteronomic family language occurs in the law of debt remission in Deut. 15:1–11 and the subsequent legislation of manumission (Deut. 15:12–18).[263] The twofold legislation in Deut. 15:1–11 addresses indebtedness, describing a system by which loans are remitted every seven years. Ignoring for the present purposes the practicalities of implementing such a system in an economically viable fashion, the point of note is that the law's applicability is determined by the community status of the debtor: for repayment the lender 'may not approach his neighbour, that is, his brother' (לא יגש את רעהו ואת אחיו, Deut. 15:2). This principle is elaborated in Deut. 15:3: 'The foreigner you may approach [to demand repayment], but for the one who

---

261 If deuteronomic, the use of the term in the context of provisions for the priests (and Levites?) in Deut. 18:1–8 would also fall in this category.

262 On the appeal to familial relations to evoke empathy in motivation of particular ethical behaviours in Deuteronomy see Kazen, *Emotions in Biblical Law*, 102–109; on its use as affective language see M.J. Williams, 'Taking Interest in Taking Interest', *Mishneh Todah: Studies in Deuteronomy and Its Cultural Environment in Honor of Jeffrey H. Tigay* (ed. N.S. Fox, D.A. Glatt-Gilad and M.J. Williams, Winona Lake, Ind., Eisenbrauns, 2009), 113–132; J.M. Hamilton, *Social Justice and Deuteronomy: The Case of Deuteronomy 15* (SBLDS 136, Atlanta, Ga., Scholars, 1992), 34–40.

263 Deuteronomy 15:1–3, 7–11 is the deuteronomic text usually identified (e.g., Nielsen, *Deuteronomium*, 158; Mayes, *Deuteronomy*, 243–244); alternately, Morrow sees both Deut. 15:7–11 and Deut. 15:12–18 as secondary because they are not part of his *mqwm*-sequence, with Deut. 15:4–6 constituting a separate addition drawing on Exodus 23 (Morrow, *Scribing the Center*, 20–22; W.S. Morrow, 'The Composition of Deut 15:1–3', *HAR* 12 [1990], 126–127). For arguments in favour of rhetorical unity see A.K. Mukenge, '"Toutefois, il n'y aura pas de nécessiteux chez toi": La stratégie argumentative de Deut. 15:1–11', *VT* 60 (2010), 69–86.

is yours as your brother you must remit the loans you hold' (אֶת הַנׇּכְרִי תִּגֹּשׂ וַאֲשֶׁר

יִהְיֶה לְךָ אֶת אָחִיךָ תַּשְׁמֵט יָדֶךָ).[264]

The change of person between Deut. 15:1, 3 and Deut. 15:2 and the associated change in legal style seems unlikely to be coincidental. As Nielsen and Veijola both suggest, Deut. 15:3 constitutes an explicit development of what is already implicit in Deut. 15:2, namely, that the category of persons meant by the term 'his neighbour' is in distinction to those who are more obviously outsiders.[265] The date of the more explicit rendering, however, is disputed: Nielsen contends that Deut. 15:1–2 are pre-deuteronomic and thus that the explicit exclusion of the foreigner in Deut. 15:3 is deuteronomic, while Veijola argues that the deuteronomic version only contained the implicit exclusion of Deut. 15:1–2 and that the explicit exclusion in Deut. 15:3 only came in with an exilic editor who was attempting to create an explicit 'brother ethic' ('Bruder-Ethik'). In terms of deuteronomic interests, however, preferential treatment in favour of members of the community is in keeping with the wider cultural project on which the deuteronomic law has embarked as well as the several laws discussed here. Veijola's assumption that an explicit sense of group identity only arose in the exilic period is typical of the scholarly tendency to view the exilic experience as the Israelites' first meaningful cultural encounter with non-Israelites and the first occasion on which a sense of community exclusiveness might have developed; we have already demonstrated that this is not the case. One may also note that both Deut. 15:1 and Deut. 15:3 are couched in the second person singular which tends to characterise the deuteronomic material (as opposed to the third singular of Deut. 15:2); it seems more likely that Deut. 15:1, 3 bracket and incorporate an existing law, elaborating it in line with deuteronomic interests.[266]

---

264   The reference to the foreigner will be addressed in 3.3.2. Differentiation between Israelites and Foreigners.

265   Nielsen, *Deuteronomium*, 158; Veijola, *Das 5. Buch Mose*, 310–311, 317.

266   Already Morrow, 'The Composition', with additional arguments; see also Christensen, *Deuteronomy 1:1–21:9*, 312 and Hamilton, *Social Justice*, 35 for the suggestion that 'his brother' in Deut. 15:2 is a deuteronomic gloss on 'his neighbour' as well as Morrow, 'The Composition', 116 on the possible LXX witness to the reverse. For discussions of the relationship of this chapter to laws in Exodus and Leviticus see B. Kilchör, 'Frei aber arm? Soziale Sicherheit als Schlüssel zum Verhältnis der Sklavenfreilassungsgesetze im Pentateuch', *VT* 62 (2012), 381–397; B.M. Levinson, 'The Case for Revision and Interpolation within the Biblical Legal Corpora', *Theory and Method in Biblical and Cuneiform Law: Revision, Interpolation, and Development* (Sheffield, Sheffield Phoenix, 2006), 37–59; G.C. Chirichigno, *Debt-*

The law instructs a specific and deliberate case of discrimination on the grounds of a persons' status as an Israelite. As Perlitt observes, the text makes clear that the brother language is not used as a broad appeal to the common lot of all human beings but specifically as a reference to those within the group; a person whose debts are remitted is not merely any fellow human ('der Mitmensch') but specifically a fellow Israelite ('der Mitisraelit'): 'Der Bruder ist demnach der Nicht-Ausländer, der Israelit.'[267] The law is thus a case of direct differentiation which favours the fellow Israelite.[268] In a law the practicality of which is notoriously problematic, the use of fraternal language simultaneously appeals to 'the strong sentiments and emotions that are associated with primary relations' and, in doing so, counteracts the potential for internal schism.[269] The text emphases that the Israelite division of persons must first and foremost be between Israelite and non-Israelite, not between creditor and debtor: 'Par là, l'indigent bénéficiaire de la bonté du créancier est défini par rapport à lui, il est son frère, son compatriot. Ce langage relationnel affecte le destinataire de la loi en créant une relation personnelle entre lui et le débiteur.'[270] The brother language is again employed in a case of especially difficult legislation.

With at least some of these difficulties in mind the passage goes on to address the potential hazards of this system for economically marginal Israelites in need of loans; the Israelite addressee must take care to act charitably toward the poor person who is also his brother by making loans available to him even as the date of remission draws near.[271] Again, the brother language, rather than

---

    *Slavery in Israel and the Ancient Near East* (JSOTSup 141, Sheffield, JSOT, 1993); and Fabry, 'Deuteronomium 15', 101 110, who also argues that the 'Geschwister-Ethik' is a post-exilic replacement for the state system, derived from priestly theology (similarly Nicholson, *Deuteronomy and the Judaean Diaspora*, 35–36, 52, 68–69).

267    Perlitt, '"Ein einzig Volk von Brüdern"', 56–57. He prefers, however, to see this as deriving 'nicht aus seiner ethnischen oder nationalistischen Intention' (Perlitt, '"Ein einzig Volk von Brüdern"', 64).

268    For discussion of the identity of the נכרי see 3.3.2. Differentiation between Israelites and Foreigners. As noted there, this favouritism is cleverly conceived, insofar as it provides preferential treatment for Israelites without prescribing anything out of the ordinary from the point of view of the non-Israelite.

269    Cohen, *Custom and Politics*, 209.

270    Mukenge, '"Toutefois, il n'y aura pas de nécessiteux chez toi"', 76–77, 84.

271    For discussion see Hamilton, *Social Justice and Deuteronomy*, 31–40; Houston, '"You Shall Open Your Hand"', 307–309. Hamilton has discussed the affective use of brother language here, contending that the phrase רעהו ואחיו includes 'all the financial relationships of the land' and therefore does not limit Israelite charitability to fellow Israelites (Hamilton, *Social Justice*, 37). However, his subsequent emphasis on both terms' connection to עברי undermines this, highlighting the way in which the passage's language is designed

extending the law, narrows its applicability. Though the text's disregard for the impoverished non-Israelite is not articulated explicitly, it constitutes an inevitable conclusion. The concern described here is not for just any economically marginal person whom the Israelite might encounter but for the marginal person who is also an Israelite.[272]

The law on remission of debts segues naturally into the subject of manumission of slaves, as perhaps the extreme example of indebtedness (Deut. 15:12–18). Again, the use of brother language indicates that the law should only be understood as pertaining to those slaves who, despite their economically subordinate status, are members of the Israelite community. Potentially complicating matters is the meaning of עברי/עברית.[273] The version of the law in Exod. 21:2–6 does not indicate the relationship between the עבד עברי and his owner; עברי may be interpreted simply as a term denoting the slave's social class, without indicating whether or not he is also considered 'Israelite'. Among the changes between this version and Deut. 15:12–18, however, is the explicit identification of the Hebrew as 'your brother' (אחיך, Deut. 15:12). While the debate over the

---

specifically as an appeal to a common Israelite identity: 'The I who is to be thought of as kin though now enslaved is also to be thought of as in a state with ties to one of the most evocative traditions in the nation's "internal history": that of slavery in Egypt when the whole of the national family was *'ibrîm'* (Hamilton, *Social Justice*, 39).

272   As the case of the גר attests, this disregard for the indigent non-Israelite is not absolute. The question of the גר will be revisited in greater detail in 3.3.3. The גר, but here it is worth observing his absence from both parts of this particular passage. One explanation is that the גר is a fellow Israelite, included in the category of the אח, but this is unlikely. The absence of the גר from the second section, especially, suggests that the גר is not considered at risk from the consequences legislated in the first part; as the fact of their economic marginality would put them at risk were they eligible for remission—and elsewhere their appearance is specifically related to the economic vulnerabilities, including the lending context, so the same might be reasonably expected here—it seems improbable that they are included among those eligible for remission, i.e., the Israelite brothers. Also a factor may be that the גר is simply not envisioned as a possible recipient of the type of long-term loan involved in this case (as opposed to the short-term loans address in Deut. 24:10–22) on account of his transient habits; this would be in contrast to the Israelite poor with permanent connections to the community which would make such loans possible. Contrast Houston, '"You Shall Open Your Hand"', 305, who assumes that the גר is classed alongside the brother here on the basis of Deut. 24:14, and Bultmann, *Der Fremde im antiken Juda*, 74–84, who explains his absence on the grounds that the גר is merely a landless Israelite.

273   Nelson, *Deuteronomy*, 198; see variously Chirichigno, *Debt-Slavery in Israel*, 277–282; N.P. Lemche, 'The Manumission of Slaves: The Fallow Year, the Sabbatical Year, the Jobel Year', *VT* 26 (1976), 38–59; Nielsen, *Deuteronomium*, 162–163; contra E. Lipiński, 'L'esclave hébreu', *VT* 26 (1976), 120–124, who argues that it does refer to an Israelite slave specifically.

term's earlier remit may be important for our understanding of the makeup of Israelite society, here it is sufficient to note that the deuteronomic text wishes to clearly identify both the עברי and the עברית as Israelites. Given this intent, the law is another case in which the deuteronomic author favours the members of the Israelite community, over and against those who are non-Israelites, as well as another case of the use of emotionally-laden familial language to encourage legislation which it was no doubt tempting to ignore.

The fate of the specifically Israelite slave is also the focus of Deut. 24:7, which declares that '[i]f a man is found stealing someone from his brothers, from the sons of Israel, and he treats him as a slave and sells him; then this thief will die and you will burn the evil from your midst' (כי ימצא איש גנב נפש מאחיו מבני ישראל והתעמר בו ומכרו ומת הגנב ההוא ובערת הרע מקרבך).

> This passage has certain peculiarities of phrasing which have attracted the interest of redactionally-minded commentators. In Deut. 24:7 the issue is the phrase 'from the sons of Israel' (מבני ישראל); the phrase turns up primarily in late parts of Deuteronomy (Deut. 1:3; 3:18; 4:44–45, etc.), although this is not exclusively the case (cf. Deut. 23:18).[274] If its presence here is an indication of an addition, it would represent a later, additional emphasis on the law's concern with community integrity, making it even more explicit that the problem is the theft of 'Israelites'. Although this emphasis is clear enough in the context of the deuteronomic material's language of brotherhood without the phrase identifying the brothers as the בני ישראל, it might have become subsequently desirable to make this explicit—perhaps in a context in which part of the interpretive audience was tending universal and inclined to understand 'brothers' as referring to all persons, Israelite or not. That the entire verse is not later is indicated by its cohesion with the surrounding deuteronomic material and the style in which it goes about revising the Exodus law for its own ends, which is characteristic of deuteronomic legislation.[275]

Both this and the preceding law indicate that the deuteronomic text has no immediate problem with the idea that an Israelite might be enslaved by a fellow Israelite but, here as with the preceding, there are clear parameters within which this is acceptable. Again, the points of difference between this and a similar law in Exodus are revealing. First, the target is specified as 'from among his brothers, from the sons of Israel', suggesting that there is something particular

---

274   Mayes, *Deuteronomy*, 324.
275   See Levinson, *Deuteronomy and the Hermeneutics of Legal Innovation*.

in the case of an Israelite slave thus captured which requires deuteronomic attention. Second, the deuteronomic text contains an additional motivation clause, explaining that the punishment of death is pronounced as a means of eradicating evil. Third, though every verb in the Exodus version appears in the deuteronomic revision (which also adds a fifth, עמר *hi.*, and sixth, בער *pi.*), the order and consequent meaning are changed.

In Exod. 21:16, the sequence of events is reported as steal, sell, find and die (גנב, מכר, מצא *ni.*, מות). The deuteronomic version begins with find, then proceeds to steal, treat as a slave, sell, die and burn (עמר *hi.*, מכר, מות, בער *pi.* מצא, גנב,). The change in sequence highlights a significant change in content and focus: whereas in Exodus the thief is to be put to death regardless of whether the person has already been sold or is still in the thief's possession, Deut. 24:7 eliminates the reference to the person being still in the thief's possession and focuses instead on situation in which the thief has already sold the person away into slavery.[276] Such an emphasis suggests that the crux of the offence, in the case of the Israelite slave, is in the sale of the 'stolen' person. As noted, the victim in Deut. 24:7 is explicitly identified as 'from among his brothers, from the sons of Israel'; although the target in the Exodus version might be assumed to be Israelite, the deuteronomic author makes this explicit.[277] The issue in the text is not enslavement itself but related to the fact that its victim is a fellow Israelite. The combined emphasis on the victim's status as an Israelite, a brother to the accused, and on the fact of the Israelite's having already been sold as a determining feature of the law suggests that the situation is perceived as a threat to the community: a case in which a member of the community is

---

276    עמר *hi.* might be interpretable as taking over the role of מצא *ni.* in Exod. 21:16 and thereby indicating that death is to ensue also if the thief has kept the person for himself and treated him as a slave without ever selling him on, but if such was the intent of the author it seems very strange that he altered his source text—which says precisely that and in far fewer words—in order to move the parallel verb into an essentially superfluous place at the start of the sentence. It seems more likely that עמר *hi.*—which only appears here and in Deut. 21:14—is intended to be read as a sort of hendiadys with מכר, making clear that the sale of the person stolen is into slavery.

277    This addition is particularly noted among commentators; e.g., Nelson, *Deuteronomy*, 289; Mayes, *Deuteronomy*, 324; Tigay, *Deuteronomy*, 224; also Weinfeld, *Deuteronomy 1–11*, 21. Tigay, *Deuteronomy*, 224 notes the addition with some consternation, pointing out that Deuteronomy 'devotes more attention to the welfare of resident aliens than any other biblical book' and that the restriction here seems incongruous with such concern. As Mayes, *Deuteronomy*, 324 observes, however, the limitation of other prohibitions to only Israelites occurs elsewhere also (e.g., Deut. 14:21; 15:3; 23:20).

removed and by his absence weakens the social fabric of the remaining group.[278] Rather like exogamy, the danger here is the loss of members of the community to outsiders.

### 3.3.2 Differentiation between Israelites and Foreigners

A foreigner is a person whose geographic origins are outside the land.[279] The foreigner is thus distinguished from the native inhabitants of the land, with whom the deuteronomic argument over Israelite identity is most concerned. This foreigner appears only rarely, in passages concerning the sale of carrion (Deut. 14:21a), the remission of debts (Deut. 15:1–3), the sort of king who is not allowed (Deut. 17:15) and the permission of loans at interest (Deut. 23:20–21). The rarity of the language, despite its rhetorical potential for an identity formation project, reiterates that something other than nationalistic, geographically- and politically-orientated xenophobia is at issue in the deuteronomic material.[280] Though present, the foreigner is not a significant part of the book's focus. In light of the widespread recognition that identity disputes tend to focus on those who are most similar rather than those who are quite different, this should come as little surprise.[281] This is not to say, however, that the deuteronomic legislation allows unfettered interaction between Israelites and foreigners. Like the local non-Israelites dealt with in other deuteronomic texts, interactions with these persons are minimised and differentiation between Israelites and foreigners is emphasised through differential treatment.

---

278   It is worth remembering how relatively small a population the audience for these laws would have been. Whether conservatively or generously estimated, the community in question would have been much smaller than the towns and cities the modern audience is accustomed to inhabit; the loss of even one individual—or many, if such a practice was very common—could pose a meaningful threat to the viability of the small community.

279   HALOT 2, s.v. נכרי; B. Lang, 'nkr; nēḵār; noḵrî', TDOT 9:423–431. נכרי may be used to denote someone or something which is 'other' more generally, rather than narrowly 'foreign', but its limited usage in Deuteronomy suggests a preference for אחר to denote 'non-Israelite' in this sense and נכרי to mean 'foreign' more specifically. N. Tan, The 'Foreignness' of the Foreign Woman in Proverbs 1–9 (BZAW 381, Berlin, de Gruyter, 2008) introduces the terminology of 'complete strangers' to convey this emphasis, though Tan's focus on the location in which Israelites encounter the נכרי, rather than the origin of the נכרי, obscures the term's geographical implications.

280   Contrast the use of foreigner terminology in the post-exilic arguments over whom Israelites may marry (see Southwood, Ethnicity, 191–211, with the theoretical discussion at 41–55).

281   Barth, 'Introduction', 16; Harrison, 'Identity'; Harrison, 'Cultural Difference'.

The principal means by which the deuteronomic material distinguishes between Israelites and foreigners is by taking advantage of the economic circumstances in which most foreigners are encountered, legislating differently for Israelites and foreigners.[282] Three cases of such discrimination appear in the deuteronomic text: the law dealing with the disposal of carrion (Deut. 14:21a), the law instructing the remission of Israelite debts (Deut. 15:1–3) and the law concerning lending at interest (Deut. 23:20–21). The usury law in Deut. 23:20–21 is the third of these: 'You will not charge interest to your brother ... to the foreigner you may charge interest but to your brother you may not charge interest' (לא תשיך לאחיך... לנכרי תשיך ולאחיך לא תשיך). This law is related to similar injunctions in Exod. 22:24–26 and Lev. 25:35–37 but marked in its deuteronomic rendering by its explicit permission of usury involving foreigners. Almost every attempt to explain the law concludes that the reason for the explicit permission of lending at interest to foreigners—and the reason for the distinction itself—lies in the association of foreigners with commerce, classifying it among the deuteronomic social laws exhibiting a particular concern for the economically marginal by ensuring that those in need of loans for non-commercial purposes are able to obtain them without the obligation to pay interest.[283] All assume that the natural audience for commercial loans is foreign tradesmen.[284]

A moment's reflection on commercial trading practices, however, calls this assumption into question. An individual in need of capital for a commercial trading endeavour requires it before setting out: to cover the costs of travel and to obtain goods from his own area to trade upon arrival at the foreign destination (goods which in turn are brought back and sold at home). A merchant in the midst of a trade mission—that is, the kind of merchant who would qualify as foreign—would have minimal need to obtain further capital upon arrival

---

282    The one other venue in which an Israelite might expect to encounter a non-Israelite is, of course, politics; on the rejection of the foreigner in the law of the king see 3.2.1. The King.

283    Thus N.M. Soss, 'Old Testament Law and Economic Society', *Journal of the History of Ideas* 34 (1973), 334; H. Gamoran, 'The Biblical Law against Loans on Interest', *JNES* 30 (1971), 127–134; B.J. Meislin and M.L. Cohen, 'Backgrounds of the Biblical Law against Usury', *CSSH* 6 (1964), 250–267. Note however Williams, 'Taking Interest', on the use of affective kinship language.

284    Thus Tigay, *Deuteronomy*, 218 writes that 'the foreigner is normally a businessman visiting the country for purposes of trade, and he borrows in order to invest in merchandise and make a profit, not to survive poverty'; Miller, *Deuteronomy*, 175 supposes that the distinction 'allow[s] the building of capital at the expense of those outside the community'; similarly Nielsen, *Deuteronomium*, 223; Christensen, *Deuteronomy 21:10–34:12*, 555; Nelson, *Deuteronomy*, 282.

at the foreign destination. If a foreign merchant did need capital, it is difficult to imagine what would persuade a lender to provide it—with or without interest—as the lender would have little guarantee that the merchant would return to repay the loan. While it is true that a very short term loan (that is, due before the merchant intended to leave) might be deemed sufficiently likely of repayment to be worth making, the means by which the merchant would have been expected to pay such a loan off remain problematic: if the merchant needs funds to obtain goods to sell, the only audience to which the sale of such items might occur at prices sufficient to cover the cost of the loan is an audience for whom such goods are exotic and valuable—in other words, his compatriots back home—and once the merchant set off home to sell those items there was no guarantee that he would return.

Without records of loans and commercial practices in the Levant it is difficult to categorically deny the possibility that lenders in Judah or Jerusalem might have found it financially viable to lend to foreign merchants, but it does seem implausible. Much more likely is that anyone in Judah intent on borrowing capital or soliciting investors for commercial ventures would have been residents. If this law was really a matter of ensuring interest-free social loans to impoverished kinsmen while permitting interest-bearing loans for commercial endeavours, the brother-foreigner dichotomy is not an appropriate cipher. In addition the law also differs from the Exodus and Leviticus laws in its failure to mention the economic status of the Israelite to whom loans at interest are forbidden, further reducing the likelihood of a specifically social justice motivation and further suggesting that the actual fact of foreignness is a more significant component of the law than usually recognised.[285] The deuteronomic law deliberately distinguishes between Israelite and foreigner,

---

285    Despite the designation of the persons to whom loans may be made at interest as being
       foreign, with its implication of distinct geographic origins, the practicalities indicate that
       the law should be understood with refererence to foreigners currently in the land; as
       already observed, lending to individuals not tied to the area would have been a high-risk
       enterprise. The inclusion of food as among the possibilities of what might be lent with
       or without interest also seems to suggest that the נכרי is resident. Perhaps the legisla-
       tion has in mind persons resident in Jerusalem or nearby for political purposes, perhaps
       those present as part of the local imperial governmental contingent or foreign adminis-
       trators resident at the local centre for tax and tribute collection; the excavators of Ramat
       Rahel, a few miles south of Jerusalem, argue that it served as one such venue (O. Lipschits,
       Y. Gadot, B. Arubas and M. Oeming, 'Palace and Village, Paradise and Oblivion: Unraveling
       the Riddles of Ramat Raḥel', *Near Eastern Archaeology* 74 [2011], 3, 16–20, 36; also
       O. Lipschits, O. Sergi and I. Koch, 'Judahite Stamped and Incised Jar Handles: A Tool for
       Studying the History of Late Monarchic Judah', *TA* 38 [2011], 5–41).

favouring the Israelite by legislating significantly advantageous terms in economic exchanges. By rendering intra-Israelite loans so favourable, the deuteronomic law also encourages Israelites engaged in the receiving of loans to do so with other Israelites; the law thus reiterates the encouragement elsewhere of social interactions within the group and discourages social interactions outside it.[286]

Likewise prejudicial in favour of the Israelite *vis-à-vis* the foreigner is Deut. 15:1–3, discussed already as one of the laws which provide for preferential treatment with reference to a familial relationship among Israelites. To recap, the applicability of the law is determined by the status of the debtor: for repayment the lender 'may not approach his neighbour, that is, his brother' (לא יגש את רעהו ואת אחיו, Deut. 15:2), but he may approach the foreigner (את הנכרי תגש, Deut. 15:3).[287] The text does not provide an explanation for this differentiation; as with the issue of interest in Deut. 23:20–21, the assumption is usually that loans to 'foreigners' means loans to merchants for commercial purposes rather than loans made to 'a poor brother or disadvantaged resident alien' for basic survival, with the law supposed to reflect a relationship which is in the latter case 'familial or neighborly' as opposed to commercial.[288] As with the

---

286  Cohen, *Custom and Politics*, 203. In fact, the legislation here is particularly clever, insofar as normal practice in the ancient Near East was both to charge interest and to charge it at exorbitant rates. As far as the foreigner was concerned his treatment would have been unremarkable. Those inside the community, however, would have seen the differentiation.

   The lending practices appropriate to interactions with the non-Israelite native population is not explicitly addressed by the deuteronomic text, and whether these are meant, by rhetorical extension, to be included in the category of 'foreigner' is not clear. Alternatively, these נכרי might be interpreted as a non-systematic application of 'foreigner' terminology to the native but non-Israelite inhabitants of the land, using language to drive a deeper wedge between Israelites and non-Israelites. If this latter is the case, the deuteronomic text is even less interested in the wider world than already observed.

287  On the redactional issues of these verses see 3.3.1. Preferential Treatment of the Israelite 'Brother'.

288  Nelson, *Deuteronomy*, 195. Similarly Mayes, *Deuteronomy*, 248: 'The foreigner is one who passes through Israel, perhaps on business; he is not integrated into the community, nor is he recommended to the charity of Israelites'. Tigay, *Deuteronomy*, 146 and Christensen, *Deuteronomy 1:1–21:9*, 312 also identify the foreigner here as a merchant or trader and point to a similar distinction in the Mesopotamian *mišarum* laws, presumably meaning that the identification of 'the Akkadians and the Amorites' in the seventeenth century edict of Ammisaduqa should be understood as exclusive; however, N.P. Lemche, '*Andurārum* and *Mišarum*: Comments on the Problem of Social Edicts and Their Application in the Ancient Near East', *JNES* 38 (1979), 11–22, 12 suggests that the phrase 'implies the whole

issue of loans at interest, this is unlikely; one need only realise that no foreign merchant is likely to be the subject of a six year loan while abroad. As in Deut. 23:20–21, the explanation for the disadvantageous treatment of the foreigner when it comes to repayment of a loan must be traced to a more fundamental desire to distinguish between Israelite and foreigner.[289]

This brings us to the final case of economic legislation relating to the foreigner. From the discussion of permissible foodstuffs in Deut. 14:3–20 (a large proportion of which is later elaboration) the text turns to a prohibition of the consumption of carrion (Deut. 14:21a). The law is made up of two parts: a categorical prohibition on consumption of carrion by the second person addressee and the presentation of two alternative uses to which the dead animal may be put: charitable donation to the גר or sale to the foreigner.[290] Concerning the alternative uses, two things are noteworthy. First, the text distinguishes between the גר and the נכרי and the addressee. The explicit prohibition of the consumption of carrion by Israelites, in combination with the law's admission that both the גר and the foreigner may consume carrion, explicitly eliminates

---

population' indiscriminately. See also J. Bottéro, 'Désordre économique et annulation des dettes en Mésopotamie à l'époque paléo-babylonienne', *JESHO* 4 (1961), 123.

289   Again, however, the ancient Near Eastern norm would have given the foreigner no cause for complaint: remission of debts is elsewhere associated only with changes in king (see Lemche, '*Andurārum* and *Mišarum*'). Contending that the law is not based on a principle of general solidarity with humanity (the idea that the laws in this chapter are essentially laws designed to ensure a certain basic level of social justice) but rather on the specific relationship between Yнwн and Israel (that is, the exodus), Braulik derives the differentiation in the treatment of the foreigner from the fact that the foreigner is not part of this special relationship (Braulik, *Deuteronomium 1–16,17*, 111–112); Nielsen similarly concludes that the foreigner is treated differently because he is not part of Yнwн's people (Nielsen, *Deuteronomium*, 160; cf. Veijola, *Das 5. Buch Mose*, 311, 314–315).

290   The opening plural address, which immediately changes to and continues in a consistent singular, appears to be a transitional mechanism from the plural of the material on clean and unclean animals, which almost certainly had some former existence before being added to a passage in the second singular; note the singular in the תועבה heading in Deut. 14:3 and the reversion to it after the first verb here. The location of a rationale for the prohibition in the addressees' identity as a holy people for Yнwн is probably connected to the preceding priestly expansions (כי עם קדוש אתה ליהוה אלהיך). Even if this reference to the holiness of the people is a late addition (thus Veijola, *Das 5. Buch Mose*, 300, on the grounds that holiness was an exilic means of articulating an identity opposed to enemies and foreigners; also Nielsen, *Deuteronomium*, 154), the elimination of Deut. 14:21aβ from the verse does no damage to the distinctions among the addressee(s), the גר and the foreigner.

the possibility that either the גר or the foreigner could be considered Israelites.[291] Second, the verse distinguishes between the גר and the נכרי. To the former the addressee(s) is to give the corpse as an act of charity, while to the latter he may sell it. The foreigner is not an object of charity; the foreigner is an individual for whom the purchase of carrion meat is viable both culturally and, apparently, financially. The text gives no further indications of the foreigners' identity.

The text's attitude in these laws represents an essentially neutral attitude regarding the foreigner: though the text favours fellow Israelites, it does so by treating the Israelite rather than the foreigner extraordinarily. The sale of meat to such individuals (Deut. 14:21a) is only notable in the context of the injunction against such a sale to members of the community and its gift to those in need. The charging of interest (Deut. 23:20–21) is remarkable only insofar as it is a practice not permitted within the community. The immutability of debt contracts (Deut. 15:2–3) is likewise entirely mundane; such contracts were assumed to be so barring the exceptional occurrence of a change in rulership and a declaration of debt remission in association. Each of these laws, as far as the foreigner is concerned, is perfectly in keeping with normal ancient Near Eastern practice; they are only unusual because of the extraordinary treatment they instruct with regard to Israelites. Such neutrality, it is worth note, contradicts the common claim that Deuteronomy works to undermine imperial authority: if anything, the author has devised an ingenious means of achieving the deuteronomic goal of Israelite differentiation without threatening the imperial status quo (cf. on Deut. 17:14–17).

In various subtle (and sometimes not-so-subtle) ways, these laws reflect the deuteronomic valuation of the Israelites' differentiation between themselves and non-Israelites, not only with regard to overall behaviour, but extending also to Israelites' actual treatment of non-Israelites. In differentiating between Israelites' relationships among themselves and relationships between Israelites and outsiders, these laws facilitate the development of an Israelite endoculture and discourage the prospect of dangerous exposure to non-Israelites.

### 3.3.3    The גר

Least straightforward of all Israelite interactions with non-Israelites is the case of the גר, whose identity has been the source of significant contention.

---

291    The reason that carrion is impermissible to the Israelite is usually assumed to be the danger of consuming its blood (cf. Exod. 22:30; Nelson, *Deuteronomy*, 180–181; Mayes, *Deuteronomy*, 243; Driver, *Deuteronomy*, 165; Christensen, *Deuteronomy 1:1–21:9*, 293; Braulik, *Deuteronomium 1–16,17*, 108; Nielsen, *Deuteronomium*, 154; Veijola, *Das 5. Buch Mose*, 299).

Although much debated, both noun (גר) and verb (גור) seem to indicate a
level of non-permanent residence; extra-biblical references also indicate
a category of non-native persons present for an indeterminate length of
time in the speaker's region, whose isolation from relatives contributes
to his social and economic marginality.[292] This appears to be the sense
in which the term is used in the deuteronomic material.[293] By contrast,
the post-deuteronomic material shows the development of the term into
a label for a proselyte (e.g., Deut. 29:10; 31:11–12); the Septuagint reflects
this in its propensity to translate גר as προσήλυτος.[294] Unfortunately, commentators frequently fail to distinguish between different uses of גר in
Deuteronomy, fuelled by appearances of the גר in the post-deuteronomic
material at the edges of the book and the temptation to see the charitable
treatment of the גר as reflecting a benevolent deuteronomic inclusiveness counterbalancing its emphasis on exclusiveness elsewhere. Veijola,
for example, concludes that 'brothers' in Deut. 1:16 includes 'foreigners',
noting the exceptional nature of this in ancient Near Eastern law but
neglecting to consider that at the time of writing גר no longer refers to a
true non-Israelite, according to the Yahwistic definition of an Israelite.[295]
Kellermann concludes that Deuteronomy's references to the גר have
in mind refugees from the former northern kingdom, but bases this
on texts from Chronicles in which the 'proselyte' transition seems
well under way.[296] Bultmann contends that the גר is an economically
marginal Israelite living in rural Judah, whose lack of property precludes
his involvement in the festivals and allows his disregard of the purity
issues which concern other Israelites (i.e., Deut. 14:21a), but this can
hardly be right, given the persistent differentiation between the גר and

---

292    Weinfeld, *Deuteronomy 1–11*, 308; D. Kellermann, '*gûr*; *gēr*; *gērûth*; *meghûrîm*', TDOT
       2:443–444.

293    HALOT 1, *s.v.* גר; C. van Houten, *The Alien in Israelite Law* [JSOTSup 107, Sheffield, JSOT,
       1991], 80–108; Kellermann, '*gûr*; *gēr*; *gērûth*; *meghûrîm*', 439–443; contrast Bultmann, *Der
       Fremde im antiken Juda*.

294    Kellermann, '*gûr*; *gēr*; *gērûth*; *meghûrîm*', 439–449; M. Greenberg, 'Mankind, Israel and
       the Nations in the Hebraic Heritage', *No Man Is Alien: Essays on the Unity of Mankind* (ed.
       J.R. Nelson, Leiden, Brill, 1971), 26–28; contra M. Cohen, 'Le "*Gēr*" biblique et son statut
       socio-religieux', *RHR* 207 (1990), 135–135.

295    Veijola, *Das 5. Buch Mose*, 26; cf. Braulik, *Deuteronomium II*, 182.

296    Kellermann, '*gûr*; *gēr*; *gērûth*; *meghûrîm*', 445; similarly Cohen, 'Le "*Gēr*"', who argues
       against either an exclusively ethnic or exclusively religious connotation for גר, following
       up Kellermann's argument in greater detail but ultimately still problematised by the deci-
       sion to begin with Chronicles and work backwards.

the Israelite addressed by the text: the way in which the text defines an Israelite—as a person who *acts* like an Israelite (not as someone who is Israelite by happenstance of birth)—precludes the inclusion of the גר in this category, excluded as he is from Israelite praxis.[297]

Part of the difficulty is the inconsistency of a deuteronomic agenda focused on defining and protecting Israelite identity and a deuteronomic law code which allows a non-Israelite regular, albeit limited, access to the Israelite community. It is not much of a surprise, therefore, to see a scholar like Bultmann conclude that 'die Beschreibung des *ger* [muss] als landbesitzloser Ortsfremder nicht um einen Aspekt nichtisraelitischer Herkunft erweitert werden … die Unterscheidung des *ger* vom *'aḥ* [führt] nicht auf eine Herkunft des *ger* von außerhalb Judas.'[298] The cause of such consternation is a general failure to recognise that, as reiterated from the beginning of this study, Israelite identity is a major, but not the only, focus of deuteronomic attention. One of the other concerns which characterises the deutcronomic material is an interest in the socially and economically marginal; it is the classification of the גר in this category which, despite his (or her) non-Israelite status, complicates the otherwise straightforward rejection and avoidance of non-Israelites.[299]

The role and status of the גר in deuteronomic texts is thus a curiously liminal one. On the one hand, the גר is of an economic status which prompts his inclusion among other poor and socially marginalised persons such as the widow and the orphan and allows him to receive various of the welfare provisions set out for the economically indigent (Deut. 14:29; 24:14–15, 17–22). At the same time, however, the גר remains outside the Israelite community, as indicated especially by his ability to benefit from charity unavailable to Israelites (Deut. 14:21a). Ramírez Kidd astutely observes that, while the term appears in the Covenant Code, the גר takes on a greater significance with the deuteronomic text in specific connection to the increased deuteronomic consciousness of Israelite identity: the use of the dyad גר-Israel, he notes, 'presupposes a certain consciousness of one's own "peoplehood", i.e., a particular notion of common origins and traditions'.[300]

---

297   Bultmann, *Der Fremde im antiken Juda*, 35–92, 121–132.

298   Bultmann, *Der Fremde im antiken Juda*, 83.

299   On the social and economic status of the גר, the widow and the orphan see also M. Sneed, 'Israelite Concern for the Alien, Orphan, and Widow: Altruism or Ideology?', ZAW 111 (1999), 498–507; Kellermann, *'gûr; gēr; gērûth; meghûrîm'*, 443–444.

300   Ramírez Kidd, *Alterity and Identity*, 32. Oddly, this contrasts with his own conclusions, in which he supposes that a heightened sense of nationalistic unity during the Josianic

While the presence of the גר is allowed by the deuteronomic text to the extent necessary to fulfil the charitable instructions arising from his poverty, he remains clearly distinguished from Israelites and is excluded from activities relating to Israelite self-definition. There are a number of passages which reflect this. Perhaps the clearest are the deuteronomic instructions for a tripartite pilgrimage calendar contained in Deut. 16:1–17, consisting of the feasts of Passover, Weeks and Tabernacles.[301] Though the exhortation to include various *personae miserae* in the festival meals might at first seem to emphasise social justice aspects of the deuteronomic legislation, this inclusion is not universal. In the descriptions of the festival meals of Weeks and Tabernacles, the גר is listed among a number of other people who are likewise to partake of the meal: children, servants, Levites, orphan and widow. This list, however, is absent from the instructions and exhortations regarding Passover.[302]

As others have noted, Passover revolves around Israel's mythology of origins: 'the story of the birth of God's people, who have come out of Egypt'.[303] It is the festival which celebrates the origins of Israel as a definable people and speaks of the events in leaving Egypt as the foundation of this transformation. The exodus tradition is a tradition about the origins of Israel as a distinctive and identifiable entity; the shared past represented by this event is a

---

period 'make[s] unlikely the possibility that the גר in Deuteronomy is a non-Israelite'; the awkwardness of this is reflected in the claim that the term 'functioned, on the one hand, as an internal boundary between the native members of the Israelite community and those newly accepted and, on the other hand, as a sort of external boundary of the community in relation to immigrants' (Ramírez Kidd, *Alterity and Identity*, 46). If rampant nationalist identity precluded the benevolence toward non-Israelites which is shown toward the גר, terminology which continued to distinguish these persons as not-really-quite-Israelites is difficult to conceive.

301    On the presence of deuteronomistic and post-deuteronomistic elements in these verses see Veijola, *Das 5. Buch Mose*, 327–328 and Nielsen, *Deuteronomium*, 166.

302    The relation of these laws to their counterparts in Exodus is notoriously problematic, especially due to the difficult conflation of Unleavened Bread and Passover: 'Few texts are more fractured in their syntax and more resistant to reading than the griffin-like combination of Passover and Unleavened Bread found in Deut 16:1–8' (B.M. Levinson, 'The Hermeneutics of Tradition in Deuteronomy: A Reply to J.G. McConville', *JBL* 119 [2000], 270–271). See also Levinson, *Deuteronomy and the Hermeneutics of Legal Innovation*, 53–97; J.G. McConville, 'Deuteronomy's Unification of Passover and *Maṣṣôt*: A Response to Bernard M. Levinson', *JBL* 119 (2000), 47–58; Levinson, 'The Hermeneutics of Tradition'; P.T. Vogt, 'The Passover in Exodus and Deuteronomy: An Introductory Examination', *A God of Faithfulness: Essays in Honour of J. Gordon McConville on His 60th Birthday* (ed. J.A. Grant, A. Lo and G.J. Wenham, LHBOTS 538, London, T&T Clark, 2011), 30–45.

303    Christensen, *Deuteronomy 1:1–21:9*, 336.

major source of the group's perceived commonality. The extraction of a group
of individuals from a given territorial space functions as an extraction of the
group in question from its previous existence as part of a larger society and its
formation into a differentiated group of its own, possessed now of its own distinct historical narrative in common with other members and—through the
legal efforts under discussion—soon to be possessed of a cultural tradition to
match. The exodus tradition, in other words, is the central tradition of identity
formation in the deuteronomic material; Passover is the community celebration and commemoration of that identity-forging event. It is significant, therefore, that the festival commemorating the exodus from Egypt, the foundational
story of Israel as a people, contains no mention of the גר.[304] The addressees of
the instructions for this festival are specified only as 'you', the Israelites (probably the male Israelites in particular).

This is in contrast with the two subsequent festivals, both of which contain
a list of persons who are to be included in the celebrations which includes the
גר: 'you and your son and your daughter and your servant and your maidser-
vant and the Levite who is in your gates and the גר and the orphan and the
widow who are in your midst' (אתה ובנך ובתך ועבדך ואמתך והלוי אשר בשעריך
והגר והיתום והאלמנה אשר בקרבך; Deut. 16:11, 14).[305] These two festivals, however, are not celebrations of Israel's origins: they are thanksgiving feasts for
successful harvests.[306] Everyone has an interest in the success of the crops;
accordingly everyone is included in the commandment of who is to celebrate.
The tenor of the celebrations are to be unmistakeably Yahwistic and the
commandments which follow on (Deut. 16:10, 11, 15) are emphatic that these
thanksgiving feasts for agricultural fertility and abundance must remain
wholly Yahwistic in character, with no room for theological ambiguity (Deut.

---

304    Note that he is also excluded from the instructions for sacrifice in Deut. 12:12, 18. He does
       materialise in the tithe law at Deut. 14:29, if that is not expansionary; his presence there,
       however, would seem to be in keeping with considerations of his economic marginality.

305    Even if parts of these two lists are deuteronomistic (so Nielsen, *Deuteronomium*, 166) it is
       notable that it is these two festivals in which these persons are specified, while no such
       wider scope is indicated for the Passover festival preceding.

306    Interestingly, the festivals legislation in Leviticus 23 does not include the גר in the
       Tabernacles legislation, at the same time as identifying the festival as a formative event in
       the genesis of Israelite identity through reference to the exodus (Lev. 23:43). The deutero-
       nomic text makes no such connection between Tabernacles and the exodus. The refer-
       ence to the audience having been a servant in Egypt (עבד היית במצרים) in Deut. 16:12 is
       among references to Egypt in which the audience's (ancestors') subordinated social status
       while there is put forth to motivate the fair treatment of those of similarly subordinate
       social status in the present.

16:20–21); nevertheless, the importance of the safe delivery of the harvests in ensuring the economic security of the marginalised is acknowledged by the inclusion of such persons in the celebrations. The גר may participate in the harvest festivals and celebrate with the community the successful gathering of the crops and the safe delivery of the livestock's offspring, but the גר is not a part of the group formed by the exodus experience and cannot therefore be included in the celebration of that event.[307]

The economic focus of the deuteronomic tolerance for the גר is evident also in Deut. 24:10–22, where he appears alongside the widow and the orphan in a series of laws designed, in part, to ensure the survival of economically marginal persons. The laws begin with instructions for securing the pledge of a person to whom the addressee has made a loan (Deut. 24:10–11); this is followed by the stipulation that possession of the pledge is not to interfere with the wellbeing of a person for whom the garment given in pledge is the only covering overnight (Deut. 24:12–13). The גר appears, in a continuation of this line of thought concerning protection of those for whom existence is a day-to-day affair, in an instruction that the wages of such persons must be paid daily (Deut. 24:14–15).[308] Having introduced the impoverished as the extremes which indicate the extent of this principle's applicability, the text continues this in its instruction of the just application of the law even unto those whose social power and influence is non-existent (Deut. 24:16–17), motivated by the

---

307   Tacitly affirming the exclusiveness of even the other festivals is also the summary statement at the end (Deut. 16:16), which requires 'every one of your males' to 'appear before Yhwh' three times each year. Kreuzer, 'Die Exodustradition im Deuteronomium', 87 (also Nielsen, *Deuteronomium*, 166) suggests that the inclusion of the *personae miserae* in Weeks and Tabernacles is secondary; if correct, this would entirely eliminate the presence of any non-Israelite from the central place. However, one of the few points to which the deuteronomic identity agenda seems regularly to give way is the preservation of the indigent. Though potentially at cross-purposes to the identity agenda, therefore, the allowance of the גר at those events facilitating his continued existence cannot be dismissed out of hand.

308   Note that the syntax in Deut. 24:14b is odd, both in the exceptional suffix already mentioned as well as in the double location of the גר as both 'in your land' (בארצך) and 'in your gates' (בשעריך), only the latter of which is usual idiom. The proliferation of the גר in this section makes his inclusion or exclusion in this verse of little consequence, but one does wonder whether the syntax reflects some later hand's efforts to render the point explicitly applicable to all hirelings. Solitary appearances of the גר are also usually in later deuteronomistic material, though there they also usually appear in connection with issues of religious integration which are absent here (Ramírez Kidd, *Alterity and Identity*, 35–36).

tradition of the Israelites' marginality in Egypt (Deut. 24:18).[309] Abandonment of the remnants of the harvests of the field, orchard and vineyard are similarly motivated (Deut. 24:19–22).

Though these laws are usually interpreted as constituting deuteronomic inclusiveness, the contents of these commands are solely legally and economically orientated: while the גר is not to be discriminated against in legal proceedings or deprived of the basic necessities for survival, these laws say nothing about the inclusion of the גר in the community itself. Due respect for the economically and socially marginal is motivated by the Israelites' own experience of being on the margins, but this implies nothing about the incorporation of the גר into the Israelite community.[310] If anything, the emphasis on the breadth of the principle speaks against any such inclusion; the גר is present to emphasise that these laws are predicated not on membership in the community but on a more universal principle. The presence of the גר in these texts functions as a rhetorical device, indicating the extent of the law's applicability. It is important to distinguish between a principle which safeguards the basics of existence and genuine inclusiveness: the גר is granted certain economic and legal protections, but he is not included in Israel.

Other appearances of the גר confirm his outsider status as well as his appearance in relation to economic concerns. The law concerning the uses to which an animal's corpse may be put has already been discussed in the context of its mention of the foreigner; the passage should also be noted with regard to the status of the גר. The text explicitly distinguishes between the גר and 'you', indicating that the גר is not included in the addressee; perhaps obvious in the case of the foreigner but worth noting explicitly with regard to the גר. However charitable the law encourages its Israelite audience to be with regard to the גר, the גר is not one of 'you' and is not an Israelite. Deuteronomy 24:14 similarly

---

309   On which see Kaiser, 'Von Ortsfremden', 47; Nielsen, *Deuteronomium*, 225. The motivation is not based on the Israelites having been non-Egyptians: note the use of עבדים, not גרים, in the motive clause (as also Deut. 15:15; 16:12; 24:22, cf. 6:12; 8:14; 13:5). Only in Deut. 10:19 and 23:8, both of which are probably later deuteronomistic additions, do motivations based on life in Egypt refer to the idea that the Israelites were גרים rather than to the issue of their social and economic status as עבדים. The social and economic rights granted the גר, in other words, are motivated by the memory of a specific social and economic experience, not by virtue of his inclusion in the community produced by that experience.

310   'This triad does not deal, properly, with "*the* גר in Israel", but specifically with the group of personae miserae in the late VII century BC' (Ramírez Kidd, *Alterity and Identity*, 14–42).

distinguishes between the hired labourer who is one 'of your brothers' (מאחיך)
and the hired labourer who is one 'of your גר' (מגרך).[311]

The deuteronomic tolerance of the non-Israelite גר remains somewhat curious in the context of the wider deuteronomic rejection of non-Israelites as
threats to Israelite identity. Indeed, there is no question but that the גר holds a
peculiar place in the deuteronomic cultural logic, caught awkwardly between
the desire to minimise Israelites' social interaction with outsiders and an interest in protecting the marginal arising from the tracing of Israel's origins to the
experience in Egypt.[312] It should come as no surprise that this liminal location
of the גר is carefully delineated, assuaging deuteronomic economic concerns
while facilitating the security of the community's ethnic identity, to which the
גר, as an outsider, poses a threat. The גר is carefully situated as a real element
of the social structure, provided with specific economic rights that must be
protected by the Israelite community, but not included as a member of that
community. The appearance of the גר in community celebrations is limited
to those in which agricultural success is celebrated and in these the Yahwistic
nature of the celebrations is especially emphasised, as if in counterpoint. He
is excluded from the definitively Israelite celebration of Passover, focused as
it is on the origins of Israelite identity in the exodus event. He is certainly not
brought into the Israelite fold by obligations of obedience to the various distinctively Israelite practices which the deuteronomic material enjoins on its
listeners. The dilemma of the גר is, perhaps, the paramount example of the
multiplicity of concerns facing the deuteronomic text, with his seemingly
contradictory presence a reflection of the fact that defining and safeguarding
Israelite identity is a major, but by no means the only, deuteronomic concern.


## 3      Conclusions

The wary toleration of the non-Israelite גר on the periphery of Israelite existence is a testament to the perceived strength of deuteronomic Israelite

---

311    Note the peculiarity of the possessive suffix. The double listing indicates that the גר would
       not be subsumed in the category of 'brother': the mention of the גר only after the identi-
       fication of the aforementioned impoverished as members of the community makes clear
       that the גר, though not to be oppressed, is not a member of the community. It has been
       suggested that Deut. 24:10–18 are dependent on Ezek. 18:5–20 (so Braulik, *Deuteronomium
       II*, 181), but this seems improbable (Nielsen, *Deuteronomium*, 227).

312    On additional motivations for protecting the גר especially see Sneed, 'Israelite Concern'.

identity.[313] Throughout the rest of the deuteronomic text Israelite identity is decisively formulated, enacted and protected using a diverse arsenal of identity formation mechanisms. These mechanisms reflect the range of ways in which identity may be formulated and expressed, going far beyond simple expressions of common genetic descent. Expressions of kinship are, of course, important in the deuteronomic project, most explicitly in the use of familial language to motivate particularly difficult points of legislation, where it '[e]xploit[s] the strong sentiments and emotions that are associated with primary relationship between members and the elementary family', but the relevance of genetic cohesion to Israelite identity is also evident elsewhere, especially in the variety of laws promoting endogamy and in the exclusion of the Ammonite and the Moabite from the community.[314] Family language is also used, of course, to explain the otherwise peculiar permission of entry for the Edomite. When 'genetic descent' is understood to reflect the broader notion of shared social descent, the particularly Israelite mythology of origins in Egypt may also be construed as an expression of a shared Israelite past.[315]

The mechanisms of the deuteronomic identity project are by no means, however, limited to expressions of Israelites' common descent. The importance of establishing the Israelites' spatial proximity is obvious in the prominent placement of the legislation of centralised worship, a phenomenon which contributes also to the peculiarity and distinctiveness of Israelite practice. Foremost among these practices is the establishment of an exclusively Yahwistic religious framework, with Israel defined in terms of an exclusive relationship with a single deity. This differentiation of Israelites from non-Israelites by virtue of their exclusive identification with YHWH is supported by the many ways in which the deuteronomic text works to differentiate Israelite practices, whether by reorganising the hierarchy of divinatory techniques or by the modification or elimination of culturally ambiguous officials and practices. These efforts at differentiation are complemented by efforts to isolate Israelites from non-Israelites. The imperatives regarding endogamy have already been mentioned; in this category are also the remarkable limitations placed on the Israelite king, the refusals to incorporate non-Israelites into the community and the legislation of differential treatment between Israelites and non-Israelites.

---

313   Perhaps even its perceived inevitability, to borrow a concept from P. Bourdieu, 'The Economics of Linguistic Exchanges', *Social Science Information* 16 (1977), 645–668 and Nestor, *Cognitive Perspectives*, especially 216–236.

314   Cohen, *Custom and Politics*, 208–109.

315   Keyes, 'The Dialectics of Ethnic Change', 5–7.

The identity thus formulated by the deuteronomic identity project is both ascribed and achieved. On the one hand, the reiteration of the community's shared past in Egypt and its emphatic use of familial language to motivate and explain difficult legislation indicate a deuteronomic conception of Israelite identity based on genetic descent. At the same time, however, the possibility of the eviction from the community of persons failing to enact key manifestations of Israelite identity, especially exclusive Yahwistic worship, and, conversely, the possibility of the admission to the community of outsiders without the relevant genetic credentials makes clear that Israelite identity is also based in the recognition and embodiment of Israelite cultural phenomena. As Eriksen pointed out, '[e]thnic identities are neither ascribed nor achieved: they are both'.[316]

The deuteronomic identity project is a complex undertaking, reflecting existing diversity in its attempts to homogenise Israelite practice as well as the intensity of debates over the appropriate parameters of Israelite identity in its virulent rhetoric towards those with competing claims. It deploys a remarkable range of techniques in corralling Israelite praxis according to the deuteronomic principles of Israelite identity and in identifying these mechanisms the anthropological studies of ethnic phenomena discussed in Chapter Two have been invaluable.

---

316  Eriksen, *Ethnicity*, 57.

# Cultural Diversity in the Southern Levant and the Formation of Ethnic Identity in Deuteronomy

The preceding has had three objectives. First, it sought to prove that the population of the southern Levant during the long seventh century experienced this period as an era of enhanced and intensified interaction with other cultural groups. This was undertaken through an extensive examination of the material culture remains which have been preserved from this period and which have been recovered archaeologically. This analysis, undertaken in Chapter One, began with a consideration of the Assyrian empire's involvement in the region and the implications of this involvement on the area's political, social and especially economic existence. The extensive evidence for an Assyrian presence in and influence on the region was noted, paying particular attention to the changes which the advent of imperial power wrought upon the area's political structures, its influence on material culture throughout the region and its effects on economic patterns. It was also noted that many of the Assyrian empire's effects on the southern Levant would have been felt by the region's inhabitants indirectly, especially as a result of the implications of Assyrian policies on the region's economic orientation, rather than through direct experiences with individual Assyrians.

The waning and waxing of Egyptian power was noted next, observing both its sometime availability as an outlet of southern Levantine political machinations as well as its persistent involvement as part of the region's trading networks. The involvement of the Phoenician cities in this network was also observed, acknowledging that Judah's direct experience of the Phoenicians was likely limited. By contrast, Judah's interactions with the Philistine cities were extensive. Philistia's major role in the trade routes originating in Arabia and Transjordan, passing via Judah's Beersheba and Arad valleys, is reflected in the preservation of substantial material remains transported from these locales in the Philistine cities. The Assyrian motivation behind the intensification of these routes was suggested by the varied indications of Assyrian presence and influence in Philistia, from the ceramic repertoire to architectural styles. In addition to the development of the trade routes culminating in Philistia, Judah's awareness of Philistia was enhanced by the transference of a large portion of the Shephelah to Philistine power after the defeat of Hezekiah by Sennacherib in 701. The substantial expansion of Ekron which occurred in conjunction with this shift, with its associated reorientation of the Shephelah's economic system, would have been particularly noticeable.

To the east, there was extensive evidence for major interactions between Judah and the Transjordan during the long seventh century. Again, this was substantially increased as a result of the development of trade routes originating there and in Arabia. Evidence of this interaction in the material culture is especially intense in the Beersheba and Arad valleys, at the heart of the east-west trade route, with the ceramic repertoire of some settlements witnessing to the substantial perpetuation of Transjordanian material culture in this area. Though substantial evidence of direct Assyrian material cultural influence in the Transjordan is lacking, it was noted that the development of an Edomite state during this period was probably the consequence of regional changes wrought by the advent of Assyrian power.

Chapter One culminated in an examination of the material remains from Judah. The importance of the trade routes between the Transjordan and Philistia to the cultural experience of Judahites was reiterated, with additional sites in the Negev, including Tel Beersheba, Tel 'Aroer and Tel Arad, attesting to a trading network connecting Judah with Philistia and the Transjordan as well as facilitating the arrival of goods and influences from as far afield as Phoenicia, Egypt and Assyria. The cultural shock of the reorientation of the Shephelah towards the coast was recapitulated, preceding an extensive discussion of the material remains preserved from Jerusalem and its environs which brought home the fact that cultural diversity in the long seventh century was not just an experience of the periphery but a phenomenon at Judah's very core. The economic and political changes to which the southern Levant was subjected during this period are concretely manifest in Jerusalem in the form of ceramics, luxury items, personal objects and economic instruments. For Judah as for its neighbours, the long seventh century was characterised by intensified interaction with the rest of the southern Levant.

Chapter Two considered the likely impact of this experience on Judah's inhabitants. Drawing on the anthropological literature concerning ethnic identity and ethnic phenomena, it argued that the experience of cultural alterity which characterised the southern Levant during this period provoked an identity crisis, arising from a heightened awareness of cultural difference and resulting in attempts to develop and reinforce ethnic boundaries. Making use of the work of Cohen in particular, the chapter drew attention to a number of mechanisms by which such boundaries might be articulated and enforced. Such mechanisms function as the means by which a community's common norms and beliefs are established; religious (ritual) phenomena have significant potential in this respect, as does a sense of shared kinship. In the latter category, specific mechanisms of ethnic identity formation include an emphasis on the genetic cohesiveness of the group's membership, especially in terms of lineal descent and focus on endogamy. Expressions of ethnic identity may also include the development of unique myths of origins or attempts to establish spatial proximity among group members, facilitating the development of an endo-culture to reinforce group norms by encouraging members' interactions with other members. Enforcement may include the discouragement of social interactions outside the group and a tendency to homogenise the group through the elimination of sub-cultures.

Chapter Three turned to the deuteronomic text with these identity phenomena in mind, exploring the possibility of reading this intensely disputed text in light of the conclusions drawn in Chapters One and Two. It came as little surprise to see both ritual identity ideologies and kinship identity ideologies at work: the book is widely recognised as a crucial document in the development of Yahwistic religion, while its use of familial language in many of its exhortations is one of its commonly remarked features. Manifestations of its ethnic identity concerns, however, went far beyond these. First, the role of exclusive Yahwism as an attempt to homogenise Israelite religious practice was noted, along with its importance as the foremost distinguishing characteristic of a deuteronomically-defined Israelite identity. Centralisation was noted as peculiarly Israelite as well as serving the critical function of bringing together Israelites at a single common site. The Israelites' shared past, accounted in a myth of Israel's origins in Egypt, is repeated throughout the deuteronomic text; the peculiarity of this to Israelites is reiterated through the integration of this myth with the identity of the peculiarly Israelite deity, Yhwh. Rounding out the ritual identity phenomena are laws which undertake to further differentiate Israelite practice, inverting the hierarchy of divination and banning cult officials and practices deemed insufficiently Israelite.

In the category of kinship ideology, Chapter Three observed several laws aimed at promoting and enforcing endogamous marriage as well as the brother language which occurs in nearly every chapter of the book, often in especially difficult cases or cases attempting to protect the community against outsiders. Efforts to isolate the Israelites from non-Israelites were witnessed also by laws discouraging interactions with outsiders, advocating their destruction and banning them from the community. More subtly, several laws differentiate between actions appropriate towards non-Israelites and actions appropriate toward Israelites. Throughout both the exhortation and the legislation the deuteronomic material demonstrated a complex understanding of Israelite ethnic identity, emphasising the relevance of descent principles while recognising the ultimate importance of cultural practice.

The ultimate goal of all of the preceding was to recognise the long seventh century as a period of significant possibility in discussions of Israelite ethnic identity. The panoply of archaeological evidence witnessing to the experience of material cultural diversity in the southern Levant, combined with anthropological evidence regarding the circumstances which provoke ethnic identity crises, raises the long seventh century as a period with major potential for scholars' efforts to understand the development of Israelite identity. The period between the emergence of Israel and the Babylonian exile does not comprise centuries of ethnic stagnation but, at least in its final stages, represents a turbulent period of dramatic change in understandings of what it meant to be an Israelite. Though by no means every expression of Israelite identity in the Hebrew Bible must or should be interpreted as arising in the long seventh century, it can no longer be assumed that such texts must derive from an exilic context in Babylonia or from the Persian period.

# Cited Works

Achenbach, R., 'Das sogenannte Königsgesetz in Deuteronomium 17,14–20', *ZABR* 15 (2009), 216–233.

———, 'Zur Systematik der Speisegebote in Leviticus 11 und in Deuteronomium 14', *ZABR* 17 (2011), 161–209.

Ackerman, S., 'The Personal is Political: Covenantal and Affectionate Love (*'āhēb, 'ahăbâ*) in the Hebrew Bible', *VT* 52 (2002), 437–458.

Aharoni, Y., 'The Use of Hieratic Numerals in Hebrew Ostraca and the Shekel Weights', *BASOR* 184 (1966), 13–19.

Ahn, J., *Exile as Forced Migrations: A Sociological, Literary, and Theological Approach on the Displacement and Resettlement of the Southern Kingdom of Judah* (BZAW 417, Berlin, de Gruyter, 2011).

Altmann, P., *Festive Meals in Ancient Israel: Deuteronomy's Identity Politics in Their Ancient Near Eastern Context* (BZAW 424, Berlin, de Gruyter, 2011).

Amzallag, N., 'Yahweh, the Canaanite God of Metallurgy?', *JSOT* 33 (2009), 387–404.

Ariel, D.T., and A. De Groot, eds., *Various Reports* (vol. 4 of *Excavations at the City of David 1978–1985 Directed by Yigal Shiloh*, Qedem 35, Jerusalem, Hebrew University of Jerusalem, 1996).

Ariel, D.T., ed., *Extramural Areas* (vol. 5 of *Excavations at the City of David 1978–1985 Directed by Yigal Shiloh*, Qedem 40, Jerusalem, Hebrew University of Jerusalem, 2000).

Armstrong, J.A., *Nations Before Nationalism* (Chapel Hill, N.C., University of North Carolina Press, 1982).

Arnold, B.T., 'The Love-Fear Antinomy in Deuteronomy 5–11', *VT* 61 (2011), 551–569.

Aspinen, M., 'Getting Sharper and Sharper: Comparing Deuteronomy 12–13 and 16:18–17:13', *Houses Full of All Good Things: Essays in Memory of Timo Veijola* (ed. J. Pakkala and M. Nissinen, Publications of the Finnish Exegetical Society 95, Göttingen, Vandenhoeck & Ruprecht, 2008), 42–61.

Assante, J., 'Bad Girls and Kinky Boys? The Modern Prostituting of Ishtar, Her Clergy and Her Cults', *Tempelprostitution im Altertum: Fakten und Fiktionen* (ed. T.S. Scheer, OikSAW 6, Berlin, Verlag Antike, 2009), 23–54.

Aubet, M.E., *The Phoenicians and the West: Politics, Colonies, and Trade* (2nd edn., Cambridge, Cambridge University Press, 2001).

Bagg, A.M. 'Palestine under Assyrian Rule: A New Look at Assyrian Policy in the West', *JAOS* 133 (2013), 119–144.

Bahrani, Z., 'Race and Ethnicity in Mesopotamian Antiquity', *World Archaeology* 38 (2006), 48–59.

Banks, M., *Ethnicity: Anthropological Constructions* (London, Routledge, 1996).

Barkay, G., 'Jerusalem of Old Testament Times: New Discoveries and New Approaches', *Strata* 6 (1985–1986), 32–43.

Barrett, R., *Disloyalty and Destruction: Religion and Politics in Deuteronomy and the Modern World* (LHBOTS 511, London, T&T Clark, 2009).

Barth, F., 'Introduction', *Ethnic Groups and Boundaries: The Social Organization of Cultural Difference* (ed. F. Barth, London, George Allen & Unwin, 1969), 9–38.

Bartlett, J.R., *Edom and the Edomites* (JSOTSup 77, Sheffield, JSOT, 1989).

Bartor, A., *Reading Law as Narrative: A Study in the Casuistic Laws of the Pentateuch* (Ancient Israel and Its Literature 5, Atlanta, Ga., SBL, 2010).

Bechmann, U., 'Die Kriegsgefangene Frau (Dtn 21,10–14)', *BK* 4 (2005), 200–204.

Beck, P., 'Ḥorvat Qitmit Revisited via 'Ën Ḥazeva', *TA* 23 (1996), 102–114.

————, 'Human Figurine with Tambourine', *Tel 'Ira: A Stronghold in the Biblical Negev* (ed. I. Beit-Arieh, MSIA 15, Tel Aviv, Tel Aviv University, 1999), 386–394.

————, 'A Neo-Assyrian Bulla', *Ḥorvat 'Uza and Ḥorvat Radum: Two Fortresses in the Biblical Negev* (ed. I. Beit-Arieh, MSIA 25, Tel Aviv, Tel Aviv University, 2007), 194–196.

Beit-Arieh, I., 'The Dead Sea Region: An Archaeological Perspective', *The Dead Sea: The Lake and Its Setting* (ed. T.M. Niemi, Z. Ben-Avraham and J.R. Gat, Oxford, Oxford University Press, 1997), 249–251.

————, 'The Edomites in Cisjordan', *You Shall Not Abhor an Edomite for He Is Your Brother: Edom and Seir in History and Tradition* (ed. D.V. Edelman, SBLABS 3, Atlanta, Ga., Scholars, 1995), 33–40.

————, 'Epigraphic Finds', *Ḥorvat 'Uza and Ḥorvat Radum: Two Fortresses in the Biblical Negev* (ed. I. Beit-Arieh, MSIA 25, Tel Aviv, Tel Aviv University, 2007), 122–187.

————, 'Excavations at Tel Malḥata: An Interim Report', *The Fire Signals of Lachish: Studies in the Archaeology and History of Israel in the Late Bronze Age, Iron Age, and Persian Period in Honor of David Ussishkin* (ed. I. Finkelstein and N. Na'aman, Winona Lake, Ind., Eisenbrauns, 2011), 17–32.

————, 'New Data on the Relationship between Judah and Edom toward the End of the Iron Age', *Recent Excavations in Israel: Studies in Iron Age Archaeology* (ed. S. Gitin and W.G. Dever, AASOR 49, Winona Lake, Ind., Eisenbrauns, 1989), 125–131.

————, 'Settlement in the Eastern Negev', *Tel 'Ira: A Stronghold in the Biblical Negev* (ed. I. Beit-Arieh, MSIA 15, Tel Aviv, Tel Aviv University, 1999), 1–8.

————, ed., *Ḥorvat Qitmit: An Edomite Shrine in the Biblical Negev* (MSIA 11, Tel Aviv, Tel Aviv University, 1995).

————, ed., *Ḥorvat 'Uza and Ḥorvat Radum: Two Fortresses in the Biblical Negev* (MSIA 25, Tel Aviv, Tel Aviv University, 2007).

————, ed., *Tel 'Ira: A Stronghold in the Biblical Negev* (MSIA 15, Tel Aviv, Tel Aviv University, 1999).

Beit-Arieh, I., and B. Cresson, 'An Edomite Ostracon from Ḥorvat 'Uza', *TA* 12 (1985), 96–101.

Bell, D., 'Ethnicity and Social Change', *Ethnicity: Theory and Experience* (ed. N. Glazer and D.P. Moynihan, London, Harvard University Press, 1975), 141–174.

Ben Zvi, E., 'Prelude to a Reconstruction of Historical Manassic Judah', *BN* 81 (1996), 31–44.

Bennett, C.M., 'Neo-Assyrian Influence in Transjordan', *Studies in the History and Archaeology of Jordan I* (ed. A. Hadidi, Amman, Department of Antiquities, 1982), 181–187.

———, 'Some Reflections on Neo-Assyrian Influence in Transjordan', *Archaeology in the Levant: Essays for Kathleen Kenyon* (ed. R. Moorey and P. Parr, Warminster, Aris & Phillips, 1978), 164–171.

Ben-Schlomo, D., 'Material Culture', *Ashdod VI: The Excavations of Areas H and K (1968–1969)* (ed. M. Dothan and D. Ben-Schlomo, IAA Reports 24, Jerusalem, Israel Antiquities Authority, 2005), 63–246.

Bentley, G.C., 'Ethnicity and Practice', *CSSH* 29 (1987), 24–55.

Bienkowski, P., 'Architecture of Edom', *Studies in the History and Archaeology of Jordan V* (ed. K. 'Amr, F. Zayadine and M. Zaghloul, Amman, Department of Antiquities, 1995), 135–143.

———, 'The Edomites: The Archaeological Evidence from Transjordan', *You Shall Not Abhor an Edomite for He Is Your Brother: Edom and Seir in History and Tradition* (ed. D.V. Edelman, Archaeological and Biblical Studies 3, Atlanta, Ga., Scholars, 1995), 41–92.

———, 'Transjordan and Assyria', *The Archaeology of Jordan and Beyond: Essays in Honor of James A. Sauer* (ed. M.D. Coogan, J.A. Greene, and L.E. Stager, SAHL 5, Winona Lake, Ind., Eisenbrauns, 2000), 44–58.

———, '"Tribalism" and "Segmentary Society" in Iron Age Transjordan', *Studies on Iron Age Moab and Neighbouring Areas in Honour of Michèle Daviau* (ed. P. Bienkowski, ANESupS 29, Leuven, Peeters, 2009), 7–26.

Bienkowski, P., and E. Van der Steen, 'Tribes, Trade, and Towns: A New Framework for the Late Iron Age in Southern Jordan and the Negev', *BASOR* 323 (2001), 21–47.

Bird, P., 'The End of the Male Cult Prostitute: A Literary-Historical and Sociological Analysis of Hebrew *qādēš-qĕdēšîm*', *Congress Volume: Cambridge 1995* (ed. J.A. Emerton, VTSup 66, Leiden, Brill, 1997), 37–80.

Blenkinsopp, J., 'Deuteronomy and the Politics of Post-Mortem Existence', *VT* 45 (1995), 1–16.

Bloch-Smith, E., '*Maṣṣēbôt* in the Israelite Cult: Argument for Rendering Implicit Cultic Criteria Explicit', *Temple and Worship in Biblical Israel* (ed. J. Day, LHBOTS 422, London, T&T Clark, 2005), 28–39.

Boehm, O., 'Child Sacrifice, Ethical Responsibility and the Existence of the People of Israel', *VT* 54 (2004), 145–156.

Bord, L.-J., and D. Hamidović, 'Écoute Israël (Deut. vi 4)', *VT* 52 (2002), 13–29.

Borger, R., with A. Fuchs, *Beiträge zum Inschriftenwerk Assurbanipals: Die Prismenklassen A, B, C = K, D, E, F, G, H, J und T sowie andere Inschriften* (Wiesbaden, Harrassowitz, 1996).

Bosman, H.L., 'Redefined Prophecy as Deuteronomic Alternative to Divination in Deut. 18:9–22', *Acta Theologica* 16 (1996), 1–23.

Bottéro, J., 'Désordre économique et annulation des dettes en Mésopotamie à l'époque paléo-babylonienne', *JESHO* 4 (1961), 113–164.

Bourdieu, P., 'The Economics of Linguistic Exchanges', *Social Science Information* 16 (1977), 645–668.

———, *Outline of a Theory of Practice* (Cambridge Studies in Social Anthropology 16, transl. R. Nice, Cambridge, Cambridge University Press, 1977).

Brandl, B., 'A Scarab, a Bulla and an Amulet from Stratum II', *The Finds from the First Millennium BCE: Text* (vol. 2 of *Timnah (Tel Batash) Final Reports*, ed. A. Mazar and N. Panitz-Cohen, Qedem 42, Jerusalem, Hebrew University of Jerusalem, 2001), 266–272.

———, 'Scarabs, Scaraboids, Other Stamp Seals, and Seal Impressions', *Area E: The Finds* (vol. 7B of *Excavations at the City of David 1978–1985 Directed by Yigal Shiloh*, ed. A. De Groot and H. Bernick Greenberg, Qedem 54, Jerusalem, Hebrew University of Jerusalem, 2012), 377–396.

———, 'A Seventh Century B.C.E. Scarab', *Tel 'Ira: A Stronghold in the Biblical Negev* (ed. I. Beit-Arieh, MSIA 15, Tel Aviv, Tel Aviv University, 1999), 414–420.

Braulik, G., *Deuteronomium 1–16, 17* (NEchtB 15, Würzburg, Echter, 1986).

———, *Deuteronomium II: 16,18–34,12* (NEchtB 28, Würzburg, Echter, 1992).

———, 'The Rejection of the Goddess Asherah in Israel: Was the Rejection as Late as Deuteronomistic and Did it Further the Oppression of Women in Israel?', *The Theology of Deuteronomy: Collected Essays of Georg Braulik, O.S.B.* (BIBAL Collected Essays 2, North Richland Hills, Tex., BIBAL, 1994), 165–182.

Brett, M.G., 'Nationalism and the Hebrew Bible', *The Bible in Ethics: The Second Sheffield Colloquium* (ed. J. Rogerson, M. Davies and M.D. Carroll R., JSOTSup 207, Sheffield, Sheffield Academic, 1995), 136–163.

Bromley, Y., 'The Term Ethnos and Its Definition', *Soviet Ethnology and Anthropology Today* (ed. Y. Bromley, The Hague, Mouton, 1974), 55–72.

Broshi, M., 'The Expansion of Jerusalem in the Reigns of Hezekiah and Manasseh', *IEJ* 24 (1974), 21–26.

———, 'Naṣbeh, Tell en-', *The New Encyclopedia of Archaeological Excavations in the Holy Land* (ed. E. Stern, Jerusalem, Israel Exploration Society, 1993), 912–918.

Broshi, M., and I. Finkelstein, 'The Population of Palestine in Iron Age II', BASOR 287 (1992), 47–60.

Bultmann, C., *Der Fremde im antiken Juda: Eine Untersuchung zum sozialen Typenbegriff >ger< und seinem Bedeutungswandel in der alttestamentlichen Gesetzgebung* (FRLANT 153, Göttingen, Vandenhoeck & Ruprecht, 1992).

Bunimovitz, S., and Z. Lederman, 'Close Yet Apart: Diverse Cultural Dynamics at Iron Age Beth-Shemesh and Lachish', *The Fire Signals of Lachish: Studies in the Archaeology and History of Israel in the Late Bronze Age, Iron Age, and Persian Period in Honor of David Ussishkin* (ed. I. Finkelstein and N. Na'aman, Winona Lake, Ind., Eisenbrauns, 2011), 33–53.

———, 'The Final Destruction of Beth-Shemesh and the *Pax Assyriaca* in the Judean Shephelah', TA 30 (2003), 1–26.

Cahill, J.M., '"Horus Eye" Amulets', *Various Reports* (vol. 4 of *Excavations at the City of David 1978–1985 Directed by Yigal Shiloh*, ed. D.T. Ariel and A. De Groot, Qedem 35, Jerusalem, Hebrew University of Jerusalem, 1996), 291–297.

Calhoun, C., 'Nationalism and Ethnicity', *Annual Review of Sociology* 19 (1993), 211–239.

Canby, J.V., 'The Stelenreihen at Aššur, Tell Halaf, and *Maṣṣēbôt*', *Iraq* 38 (1976), 113–128.

Carmichael, C.M., *The Laws of Deuteronomy* (London, Cornell University Press, 1974).

Chavel, S., 'The Literary Development of Deuteronomy 12: Between Religious Ideal and Social Reality', *The Pentateuch: International Perspectives on Current Research* (ed. T.B. Dozeman, K. Schmid and B.J. Schwartz, FAT 78, Tübingen, Mohr Siebeck, 2011), 303–326.

Childs, B.S., 'Deuteronomic Formulae of the Exodus Traditions', *Hebräische Wortforschung, Festschrift zum 80. Geburtstag von Walter Baumgartner* (ed. B. Hartmann, E. Jenni, E.Y. Kutscher, V. Maag, I.L. Seeligmann and R. Smend, VTSup 16, Leiden, Brill, 1967), 30–39.

Chirichigno, G.C., *Debt-Slavery in Israel and the Ancient Near East* (JSOTSup 141, Sheffield, JSOT, 1993).

Christensen, D.L., *Deuteronomy 1:1–21:9, revised* (2nd edn., WBC 6A, Nashville, Tenn., Thomas Nelson, 2001).

———, *Deuteronomy 21:10–34:12* (WBC 6B, Nashville, Tenn., Thomas Nelson, 2002).

Ciasca, A., 'Some Particular Aspects of the Israelitic Miniature Statuary at Ramat Raḥel', *Excavations at Ramat Raḥel (Seasons 1961 and 1962)* (ed. Y. Aharoni and A. Ciasca, Jerusalem, Hebrew University of Jerusalem, 1964), 95–100.

Clements, R.E., 'The Concept of Abomination in the Book of Proverbs', *Texts, Temples, and Traditions: A Tribute to Menahem Haran* (ed. M.V. Fox, V.A. Hurowitz, A. Hurvitz, M.L. Klein, B.J. Schwartz and N. Shupak, Winona Lake, Ind., Eisenbrauns, 1996), 211–225.

———, 'The Deuteronomic Law of Centralization and the Catastrophe of 587 B.C.E.', *After the Exile: Essays in Honour of Rex Mason* (ed. J. Barton and D.J. Reimer, Macon, Ga, Mercer University Press, 1996), 5–25.

Cogan, M.D., *Imperialism and Religion: Assyria, Judah and Israel in the Eighth and Seventh Centuries B.C.E.* (SBLMS 19, Missoula, Mont., Scholars, 1974).

———, 'Judah under Assyrian Hegemony: A Reexamination of Imperialism and Religion', *JBL* 112 (1993), 403–412.

———, 'The Other Egypt: A Welcome Asylum', *Texts, Temples, and Traditions: A Tribute to Menahem Haran* (ed. M.V. Fox, V.A. Hurowitz, A. Hurvitz, M.L. Klein, B.J. Schwartz and N. Shupak, Winona Lake, Ind., Eisenbrauns, 1996), 65–70.

Cohen, A., *Custom and Politics in Urban Africa: A Study of Hausa Migrants in Yoruba Towns* (London, Routledge, 1969).

———, 'Variables in Ethnicity', *Ethnic Change* (ed. C.F. Keyes, London, University of Washington Press, 1981), 306–331.

Cohen, A.P., *The Symbolic Construction of Community* (London, Tavistock, 1985).

Cohen, M., 'Le "*Gēr*" biblique et son statut socio-religieux', *RHR* 207 (1990), 131–158.

Cohen, R., 'The Excavations at Kadesh Barnea (1976–78)', *BA* 44 (1981), 93–107.

———, 'The Iron Age Fortresses in the Central Negev', *BASOR* 236 (1979), 61–79.

Collins, B.J., 'The Bible, The Hittites, and the Construction of the "Other"', *Tabularia Hethaeorum: Hethitologische Beiträge Silvin Košak zum 65. Geburtstag* (ed. D. Groddek and M. Zorman, Dresdner Beiträge zur Hethitologie 25, Wiesbaden, Harrassowitz, 2007), 153–161.

Collon, D., 'Examples of Ethnic Diversity on Assyrian Reliefs', *Ethnicity in Ancient Mesopotamia: Papers Read at the 48th Rencontre Assyriologique Internationale: Leiden, 1–4 July 2005* (ed. W.H. Van Soldt, Leiden, Netherlands Institute for the Near East, 2005), 66–77.

Cornelius, S., '"*Eunuchs*"? The Ancient Background of *Eunouchos* in the Septuagint', *Septuagint and Reception: Essays Prepared for the Association for the Study of the Septuagint in South Africa* (ed. J. Cook, VTSup 127, Leiden, Brill, 2009), 321–333.

Craigie, P.C., *The Book of Deuteronomy* (NICOT, Grand Rapids, Mich., Eerdmans, 1976).

Cross, F.M., 'Two Offering Dishes with Phoenician Inscriptions from the Sanctuary of Arad', *BASOR* 235 (1979), 75–78.

Cross, F.M., and D.N. Freedman, 'Josiah's Revolt against Assyria', *JNES* 12 (1953), 56–58.

Crouch, C.L., 'The Threat to Israel's Identity in Deuteronomy: Mesopotamian or Levantine?', *ZAW* 124 (2012), 541–554.

———, *War and Ethics in the Ancient Near East: Military Violence in Light of Cosmology and History* (BZAW 407, Berlin, de Gruyter, 2009).

Cryer, F.H., *Divination in Israel and Its Ancient Near Eastern Environment: A Socio-Historical Investigation* (JSOTSup 142, Sheffield, JSOT, 1994).

Daube, D., 'One from among Your Brethren Shall You Set King over You', *JBL* 90 (1971), 480–481.

Davidson, R.M., 'Divorce and Remarriage in the Old Testament: A Fresh Look at Deuteronomy 24:1–4', *Journal of the Adventist Theological Society* 10 (1999), 2–22.

Davies, E.W., 'Inheritance Rights and the Hebrew Levirate Marriage: Part 1', *VT* 31 (1981), 138–144.

———, 'Inheritance Rights and the Hebrew Levirate Marriage: Part 2', *VT* 31 (1981), 259–268.

Davies, P.R., *In Search of 'Ancient Israel'* (2nd edn., JSOTSup 148, Sheffield, Sheffield Academic Press, 1992).

———, 'Josiah and the Law Book', *Good Kings and Bad Kings: The Kingdom of Judah in the Seventh Century B.C.E.* (ed. L.L. Grabbe, LHBOTS 393, London, T&T Clark, 2005), 65–77.

Day, J., 'Asherah in the Hebrew Bible and Northwest Semitic Literature', *JBL* 105 (1986), 385–408.

———, *Yahweh and the Gods and Goddesses of Canaan* (JSOTSup 265, Sheffield, Sheffield Academic Press, 2002).

De Bernardi, C., 'Methodological Problems in the Approach to Ethnicity in Ancient Mesopotamia', *Ethnicity in Ancient Mesopotamia: Papers Read at the 48th Rencontre Assyriologique Internationale: Leiden, 1–4 July 2004* (ed. W.H. Van Soldt, Leiden, Netherlands Institute for the Near East, 2005), 78–89.

De Boer, P.A.H., 'Egypt in the Old Testament: Some Aspects of an Ambivalent Assessment', *Selected Studies in Old Testament Exegesis* (ed. C. van Duin, OTS 27, Leiden, Brill, 1991), 152–167.

De Groot, A., and D.T. Ariel, eds., *Stratigraphical, Environmental, and Other Reports* (vol. 3 of *Excavations in the City of David 1978–1985 Directed by Yigal Shiloh*, Qedem 33, Jerusalem, Hebrew University of Jerusalem, 1992).

De Groot, A., and H. Bernick-Greenberg, 'The Pottery of Strata 12–10 (Iron Age IIB)', *Area E: The Finds* (vol. 7B of *Excavations at the City of David 1978–1985 Directed by Yigal Shiloh*, ed. A. De Groot and H. Bernick Greenberg, Qedem 54, Jerusalem, Hebrew University of Jerusalem, 2012), 57–198.

———, eds., *Area E: The Finds* (vol. 7B of *Excavations at the City of David 1978–1985 Directed by Yigal Shiloh*, Qedem 54, Jerusalem, Hebrew University of Jerusalem, 2012).

De Groot, A., H. Geva and I. Yezerski, 'Iron Age II Pottery', *The Finds from Areas A, W and X-2: Final Report* (vol. 2 of *Jewish Quarter Excavations in the Old City of Jerusalem: Conducted by Nahman Avigad, 1969–1982*, ed. H. Geva, Jerusalem, Israel Exploration Society, 2003), 1–49.

de Jong Ellis, M., 'Observations on Mesopotamian Oracles and Prophetic Texts: Literary and Historiographic Considerations', *JCS* 41 (1989), 127–186.

De Moor, J.C., 'Standing Stones and Ancestor Worship', *UF* 27 (1995), 1–20.

De Wette, W.M.L., *Beiträge zur Einleitung in das Alte Testament* (2 vols., Hildesheim, Olms, 1806–1807).

Dempster, S., 'The Deuteronomic Formula *kî yimmāṣē'* in the Light of Biblical and Ancient Near Eastern Law', *RB* 91 (1984), 188–211.

Dever, W.G., *Did God Have a Wife? Archaeology and Folk Religion in Ancient Israel* (Grand Rapids, Mich., Eerdmans, 2005).

Dicou, B., *Edom, Israel's Brother and Antagonist: The Role of Edom in Biblical Prophecy and Story* (JSOTSup 169, Sheffield, JSOT, 1994).

Dietler, M., and I. Herbich, 'Habitus, Techniques, Style: An Integrated Approach to the Social Understanding of Material Culture and Boundaries', *The Archaeology of Social Boundaries* (ed. M.T. Stark, London, Smithsonian Institute, 1998), 232–263.

Dion, P.E., 'Deuteronomy 13: The Suppression of Alien Religious Propaganda in Israel during the Late Monarchical Era', *Law and Ideology in Monarchic Israel* (ed. B. Halpern and D.W. Hobson, JSOTSup 124, Sheffield, JSOT, 1991), 147–216.

Dothan, M., and D. Ben Schlomo, eds., *Ashdod VI: The Excavations of Areas H and K (1968–1969)* (IAA Reports 24, Jerusalem, Israel Antiquities Authority, 2005).

Dothan, T.K., and S. Gitin, 'Tell Miqne, 1984', *IEJ* 35 (1985), 67–71.

———, 'Tell Miqne, 1985', *IEJ* 36 (1986), 104–107.

Douglas, M.T., *Purity and Danger: An Analysis of Concepts of Pollution and Taboo* (London, Routledge, 1969).

Driver, S.R., *Deuteronomy* (ICC, Edinburgh, Charles Scribner, 1895).

Dutcher-Walls, P., 'The Circumscription of the King: Deuteronomy 17:16–17 in Its Ancient Social Context', *JBL* 121 (2002), 601–616.

Edelman, D.V., ed., *You Shall Not Abhor an Edomite for He Is Your Brother: Edom and Seir in History and Tradition* (Archaeological and Biblical Studies 3, Atlanta, Ga., Scholars, 1995).

Ehrlich, C.S., *The Philistines in Transition: A History from ca. 1000–730 BCE* (SHANE 10, Leiden, Brill, 1996).

Elat, M., 'The Economic Relations of the Neo-Assyrian Empire with Egypt', *JAOS* 98 (1978), 20–34.

———, 'Monarchy and Development of Trade in Ancient Israel', *State and Temple Economy in the Ancient Near East II: Proceedings of the International Conference Organized by the Katholieke Universiteit Leuven from the 10th to the 14th of April 1978* (ed. E. Lipiński, OLA 6, Leuven, Departement Oriëntalistiek, 1979), 527–546.

———, 'Phoenician Overland Trade within the Mesopotamian Empire', *Ah, Assyria . . . Studies in Assyrian History and Ancient Near Eastern Historiography Presented to Hayim Tadmor* (ed. M. Cogan and I. Eph'al, ScrHier 23, Jerusalem, Magnes, 1991), 21–35.

Elayi, J., 'Les relations entre les cités phéniciennes et l'empire Assyrien sous le règne de Sennachérib', *Semitica* 35 (1985), 19–26.

Emberling, G., 'Ethnicity in Complex Societies: Archaeological Perspectives', *Journal of Archaeological Research* 5 (1997), 295–344.

Emberling, G., and N. Yoffee, 'Thinking about Ethnicity in Mesopotamian Archaeology and History', *Fluchtpunkt Uruk: Archaeologische Einheit aus methodologischer Vielfalt: Schriften für Hans J. Nissen* (ed. H. Kuehne, R. Bernbeck and K. Bartl, Rahden, Marie Leidorf Verlag, 1999), 272–281.

Emerton, J., 'New Light on Israelite Religion: The Implications of the Inscriptions from Kuntillet 'Ajrud', *ZAW* 94 (1982), 2–20.

Eran, A., 'Stone Weights', *The Finds from the First Millennium BCE: Text* (vol. 2 of *Timnah (Tel Batash) Final Reports*, ed. A. Mazar and N. Panitz-Cohen, Qedem 42, Jerusalem, Hebrew University of Jerusalem, 2001), 238–243.

————, 'Weights and Weighing in the City of David: The Early Weights from the Bronze Age to the Persian Period', *Various Reports* (vol. 4 of *Excavations at the City of David 1978–1985 Directed by Yigal Shiloh*, ed. D.T. Ariel and A. De Groot, Qedem 35, Jerusalem, Hebrew University of Jerusalem, 1996), 204–256.

Eriksen, T.H., *Ethnicity and Nationalism: Anthropological Perspectives* (Anthropology, Culture and Society 1, London, Pluto, 1993).

Eshel, I., 'Two Pottery Groups from Kenyon's Excavations on the Eastern Slope of Ancient Jerusalem', *The Iron Age Cave Deposits on the South-east Hill and Isolated Burials and Cemeteries Elsewhere* (vol. 4 of *Excavations in Jerusalem 1961–1967*, ed. I. Eshel and K. Prag, BAMA 6, Oxford, Oxford University Press, 1995), 1–158.

Eshel, I., and K. Prag, eds., *The Iron Age Cave Deposits on the South-east Hill and Isolated Burials and Cemeteries Elsewhere* (vol. 4 of *Excavations in Jerusalem 1961–1967*, BAMA 6, Oxford, Oxford University Press, 1995).

Fabry, H.-J., 'Deuteronomium 15: Gedanken zur Geschwister-Ethik im Alten Testament', *ZABR* 3 (1997), 92–111.

Fahn, A., and E. Werker, 'Macrobotanical Remains', *Stratigraphical, Environmental, and Other Reports* (vol. 3 of *Excavations in the City of David 1978–1985 Directed by Yigal Shiloh*, ed. A. De Groot and D.T. Ariel, Qedem 33, Jerusalem, Hebrew University of Jerusalem, 1992), 106–115.

Fales, F.M., *Guerre et paix en Assyrie: Religion et impérialisme* (Paris, Editions du CERF, 2010).

Fantalkin, A., 'The Final Destruction of Beth-Shemesh and the *Pax Assyriaca* in the Judean Shephelah: An Alternative View', *TA* 31 (2004), 245–261.

————, 'Identity in the Making: Greeks in the Eastern Mediterranean during the Iron Age', *Naukratis: Greek Diversity in Egypt: Studies on East Greek Pottery and Exchange in the Eastern Mediterranean* (ed. A. Villing and U. Schlotzhauer, The British

Museum Research Publication Number 162, London, The British Museum, 2006), 199–208.

———, 'Meẓad Ḥashavyahu: Its Material Culture and Historical Background', *TA* 28 (2001), 3–165.

———, 'Why Did Nebuchadnezzar II Destroy Ashkelon in Kislev 604 B.C.E.?', *The Fire Signals of Lachish: Studies in the Archaeology and History of Israel in the Late Bronze Age, Iron Age, and Persian Period in Honor of David Ussishkin* (ed. I. Finkelstein and N. Na'aman, Winona Lake, Ind., Eisenbrauns, 2011), 87–111.

Fantalkin, A., and O. Tal, 'Re-Discovering the Iron Age Fortress at Tell Qudadi in the Context of Neo-Assyrian Imperialistic Policies', *PEQ* 141 (2009), 188–206.

Faust, A., 'The Interests of the Assyrian Empire in the West: Olive Oil Production as a Test-Case', *JESHO* 54 (2011), 62–86.

———, 'Settlement and Demography in Seventh Century Judah and the Extent and Intensity of Sennacherib's Campaign', *PEQ* 140 (2008), 168–194.

———, 'The Settlement of Jerusalem's Western Hill and the City's Status in Iron Age II Revisited', *ZDPV* 121 (2005), 97–118.

Faust, A., and E. Weiss, 'Judah, Philistia, and the Mediterranean World: Reconstructing the Economic System of the Seventh Century BCE', *BASOR* 338 (2005), 71–92.

Finkelstein, I., 'The Archaeology of the Days of Manasseh', *Scripture and Other Artifacts: Essays on the Bible and Archaeology in Honor of Philip J. King* (ed. M.D. Coogan, J.C. Exum and L.E. Stager, Louisville, Ky., Westminster John Knox, 1994), 169–187.

———, 'Environmental Archaeology and Social History: Demographic and Economic Aspects of the Monarchic Period', *Biblical Archaeology Today 1990* (ed. A. Biran and J. Aviram, Jerusalem, Israel Exploration Society, 1993), 55–66.

———, 'Gezer Revisited and Revised', *TA* 29 (2002), 262–296.

———, 'Ḥorvat Qitmīt and the Southern Trade in the Late Iron Age II', *ZDPV* 108 (1992), 156–170.

———, 'Is the Philistine Paradigm Still Viable?', *The Synchronisation of Civilisations in the Eastern Mediterranean in the Second Millennium B.C. III: Proceedings of the SCIEM 2000—2nd EuroConference, Vienna, 28th of May–1st of June 2003* (ed. M. Bietak and H. Hunger, Contributions to the Chronology of the Eastern Mediterranean 9, Vienna, Österreichische Akademie der Wissenschaften, 2007), 517–523.

———, 'Kadesh Barnea: A Reevaluation of Its Archaeology and History', *TA* 37 (2010), 111–125.

———, 'Khirbet en-Nahas, Edom and Biblical History', *TA* 32 (2005), 119–125.

———, *Living on the Fringe: The Archaeology and History of the Negev, Sinai and Neighbouring Regions in the Bronze and Iron Ages* (Monographs in Mediterranean Archaeology 6, Sheffield, Sheffield Academic Press, 1995).

———, 'The Rise of Jerusalem and Judah: The Missing Link', *Jerusalem in Bible and Archaeology: The First Temple Period* (ed. A.G. Vaughn and A.E. Killebrew, SBLSymS, Atlanta, Ga., Society of Biblical Literature, 2003), 81–101.

————, 'The Settlement History of Jerusalem in the Eighth and Seventh Century BCE', *RB* 115 (2008), 499–515.

Finkelstein, I., and L. Singer-Avitz, 'The Pottery of Edom: A Correction', *Antiguo Oriente* 6 (2008), 13–24.

Finkelstein, I., and N. Na'aman, 'The Judahite Shephelah in the Late 8th and Early 7th Centuries BCE', *TA* 31 (2004), 60–79.

Finkelstein, I., and N.A. Silberman, 'Temple and Dynasty: Hezekiah, the Remaking of Judah and the Rise of the Pan-Israelite Ideology', *JSOT* 30 (2006), 259–285.

Fox, N.S., 'Gender Transformation and Transgression: Contextualizing the Prohibition of Cross-Dressing in Deuteronomy 22:5', *Mishneh Todah: Studies in Deuteronomy and Its Cultural Environment in Honor of Jeffrey H. Tigay* (ed. N.S. Fox, D.A. Glatt-Gilad and M.J. Williams, Winona Lake, Ind., Eisenbrauns, 2009), 49–71.

————, *In the Service of the King: Officialdom in Ancient Israel and Judah* (HUCM 23, Cincinnati, Ohio, Hebrew Union College Press, 2000).

Frahm, E., 'Rezensionen. H. Tadmor, The Inscriptions of Tiglath-pileser III, King of Assyria', *AfO* 44–45 (1997/1998), 399–404.

Franken, H.J., and M.L. Steiner, eds., *The Iron Age Extramural Quarter on the South-East Hill* (vol. 2 of *Excavations in Jerusalem 1961–1967*, BAMA 2, London, Oxford University Press, 1990).

Frankena, R., 'The Vassal-Treaties of Esarhaddon and the Dating of Deuteronomy', *OTS* 14 (1965), 122–154.

Frankenstein, S., 'The Phoenicians in the Far West: A Function of Neo-Assyrian Imperialism', *Power and Propaganda: A Symposium on Ancient Empires* (ed. M.T. Larsen, Mesopotamia 7, Copenhagen, Akademisk Forlag, 1979), 263–293.

Freud, L., 'Pottery: Iron Age', *Tel 'Ira: A Stronghold in the Biblical Negev* (ed. I. Beit-Arieh, MSIA 15, Tel Aviv, Tel Aviv University, 1999), 189–289.

Fried, L.S., 'The High Places (*Bāmôt*) and the Reforms of Hezekiah and Josiah: An Archaeological Investigation', *JAOS* 122 (2002), 437–465.

Friedman, J., 'Notes on Culture and Identity in Imperial Worlds', *Religion and Religious Practice in the Seleucid Kingdom* (ed. P. Bilde, T. Engberg-Pedersen, L. Hannestad and J. Zahle, Studies in Hellenistic Civilization 1, Aarhus, Aarhus University Press, 1990), 14–39.

Fuchs, A., *Die Inschriften Sargons II. aus Khorsabad* (Göttingen, Cuvillier, 1994).

Gamoran, H., 'The Biblical Law against Loans on Interest', *JNES* 30 (1971), 127–134.

Garrett, A.J.M., 'A New Understanding of the Divorce and Remarriage Legislation in Deuteronomy 24:104', *JBQ* 39 (2011), 245–250.

Geertz, C., *The Interpretation of Cultures: Selected Essays* (London, Fontana, 1973).

Gellner, E., *Nations and Nationalism* (Oxford, Blackwell, 1983).

Gerstenberger, E., 'בעת *t'b* pi. to abhor', *Theological Lexicon of the Old Testament* (3 vols., ed. E. Jenni and C. Westermann, transl. M.E. Biddle; Peabody, Mass., Hendrickson, 2004), 1428–1431.

Geva, H., 'Western Jerusalem at the End of the First Temple Period in Light of the Excavations in the Jewish Quarter', *Jerusalem in Bible and Archaeology: The First Temple Period* (ed. A.G. Vaughn and A.E. Killebrew, SBLSymS, Atlanta, Ga., Society of Biblical Literature, 2003), 183–208.

————, ed., *Architecture and Stratigraphy: Areas A, W and X-2: Final Report* (vol. 1 of *Jewish Quarter Excavations in the Old City of Jerusalem: Conducted by Nahman Avigad, 1969–1982*, Jerusalem, Israel Exploration Society, 2000).

————, ed., *The Finds from Areas A, W and X-2: Final Report* (vol. 2 of *Jewish Quarter Excavations in the Old City of Jerusalem: Conducted by Nahman Avigad, 1969–1982*, Jerusalem, Israel Exploration Society, 2003).

Geva, S., 'The Painted Sherd of Ramat Raḥel', *IEJ* 31 (1981), 186–189.

Gibson, S., and G. Edelstein, 'Investigating Jerusalem's Rural Landscape', *Levant* 17 (1985), 139–155.

Gieselmann, B., 'Die sogenannten josianische Reform in der gegenwärtigen Forschung', *ZAW* 106 (1994), 223–242.

Gilmour, G., 'An Iron Age II Pictorial Representation from Jerusalem Illustrating Yahweh and Asherah', *PEQ* 141 (2009), 87–103.

Gitin, S., 'Israelite and Philistine Culture and the Archaeological Record in Iron Age II: The "Smoking Gun" Phenomenon', *Symbiosis, Symbolism, and the Power of the Past: Canaan, Ancient Israel, and Their Neighbors From the Late Bronze Age through Roman Palaestina* (ed. W.G. Dever and S. Gitin, Winona Lake, Ind., Eisenbrauns, 2003), 279–295.

————, 'The Neo-Assyrian Empire and its Western Periphery: The Levant, with a Focus on Philistine Ekron', *Assyria 1995* (ed. S. Parpola and R.M. Whiting, Helsinki, Neo-Assyrian Text Corpus Project, 1997), 77–103.

————, 'Seventh Century B.C.E. Cultic Elements at Ekron', *Biblical Archaeology Today 1990* (ed. A. Biran and J. Aviram, Jerusalem, Israel Exploration Society, 1993), 248–258.

————, 'Tel Miqne-Ekron in the 7th Century B.C.E.: The Impact of Economic Innovation and Foreign Cultural Influences on a Neo-Assyrian Vassal City-State', *Recent Excavations in Israel: A View to the West* (ed. S. Gitin, Archaeological Institute of America, Colloquia and Conference Papers 1, Dubuque, Ia., Kendall/Hunt, 1995), 61–79.

————, 'Tel Miqne-Ekron: A Type Site for the Inner Coastal Plain in the Iron Age II Period', *Recent Excavations in Israel: Studies in Iron Age Archaeology* (ed. S. Gitin and W.G. Dever, AASOR 49, Winona Lake, Ind., Eisenbrauns, 1989), 23–58.

Gitin, S., T.K. Dothan and J. Naveh, 'A Royal Dedicatory Inscription from Ekron', *IEJ* 47 (1997), 1–16.

Glassner, J.-J., *Mesopotamian Chronicles* (SBLWAW 19, Atlanta, Ga., Society of Biblical Literature, 2004).

Glazer, N., and D.P. Moynihan, eds., *Ethnicity: Theory and Experience* (London, Harvard University Press, 1975).

Goodblatt, D., *Elements of Ancient Jewish Nationalism* (Cambridge, Cambridge University Press, 2006).

Goodfriend, E.A., 'Prostitution (Old Testament)', *Anchor Bible Dictionary* (6 vols., ed. D.N. Freedman, New York, N.Y., Doubleday, 1992), 507–510.

Grabbe, L.L., ed., *'Like a Bird in a Cage': The Invasion of Sennacherib in 701 BCE* (JSOTSup 363 / European Seminar in Historical Methodology 4, London: Sheffield Academic, 2003).

Graesser, C.F., 'Standing Stones in Ancient Palestine', *BA* 35 (1972), 33–63.

Gray, J., 'The Book of Job in the Context of Near Eastern Literature', *ZAW* 82 (1972), 251–269.

Grayson, A.K., *Assyrian and Babylonian Chronicles* (Texts from Cuneiform Sources 5, Locust Valley, N.Y., Augustin, 1975).

Grayson, A.K., and J. Novotny, *The Royal Inscriptions of Sennacherib, King of Assyria (704–681 BC), Part 1* (RINAP 3/1, Winona Lake, Ind., Eisenbrauns, 2012).

Greenberg, M., 'Mankind, Israel and the Nations in the Hebraic Heritage', *No Man Is Alien: Essays on the Unity of Mankind* (ed. J.R. Nelson, Leiden, Brill, 1971), 15–40.

Greenhut, A., and A. De Groot, 'The Pottery', *Salvage Excavations at Tel Moza: The Bronze and Iron Age Settlements and Later Occupations* (ed. Z. Greenhut and A. De Groot, IAA Reports 39, Jerusalem, Israel Antiquities Authority, 2009), 61–110.

Greenhut, Z., 'The Egyptian-Blue Scepter Head', *Salvage Excavations at Tel Moza: The Bronze and Iron Age Settlements and Later Occupations* (ed. Z. Greenhut and A. De Groot, IAA Reports 39, Jerusalem, Israel Antiquities Authority, 2009), 149–152.

Greenhut, Z., and A. De Groot, eds., *Salvage Excavations at Tel Moza: The Bronze and Iron Age Settlements and Later Occupations* (IAA Reports 39, Jerusalem, Israel Antiquities Authority, 2009).

Greifenhagen, F.V., *Egypt on the Pentateuch's Ideological Map: Constructing Biblical Israel's Identity* (JSOTSup 361, Sheffield, Sheffield Academic Press, 2002).

Grosby, S., *Biblical Ideas of Nationality: Ancient and Modern* (Winona Lake, Ind., Eisenbrauns, 2002).

Gruber, M.I., 'Hebrew *qĕdēšāh* and Her Canaanite and Akkadian Cognates', *UF* 18 (1986), 133–148.

Guillaume, P., 'Binding "Sucks": A Response to Stefan Schorch', *VT* 61 (2011), 335–337.

———, 'Thou Shalt Not Curdle Milk with Rennet', *UF* 34 (2002), 213–215.

Hackett, J.A., 'Religious Traditions in Israelite Transjordan', *Ancient Israelite Religion: Essays in Honor of Frank Moore Cross* (ed. P.D. Miller Jr., P.D. Hanson and S.D. McBride, Philadelphia, Pa., Fortress, 1987), 125–136.

Hadley, J.M., *The Cult of Asherah in Ancient Israel and Judah: Evidence for a Hebrew Goddess* (University of Cambridge Oriental Publications 57, Cambridge, University of Cambridge, 2000).

Hagedorn, A.C., *Between Moses and Plato: Individual and Society in Deuteronomy and Ancient Greek Law* (FRLANT 204, Göttingen, Vandenhoeck & Ruprecht, 2004).

———, 'Edom in the Book of Amos and Beyond', *Aspects of Amos: Exegesis and Interpretation* (ed. A.C. Hagedorn and A. Mein, LHBOTS 536, London, T&T Clark, 2011), 41–57.

———, 'Looking at Foreigners in Biblical and Greek Prophecy', *VT* 57 (2007), 432–448.

———, 'Placing (A) God: Central Place Theory in Deuteronomy 12 and at Delphi', *Temple and Worship in Biblical Israel* (ed. J. Day, LHBOTS 422, London, T&T Clark, 2005), 188–211.

Hallo, W.W., 'Biblical Abominations and Sumerian Taboos', *JQR* 76 (1985), 21–40.

Halpern, B., 'The Canine Conundrum of Ashkelon: A Classical Connection?', *The Archaeology of Jordan and Beyond: Essays in Honor of James A. Sauer* (ed. M.D. Coogan, J.A. Greene and L.E. Stager, SAHL 1, Winona Lake, Ind., Eisenbrauns, 2000), 133–144.

———, 'The Centralization Formula in Deuteronomy', *VT* 31 (1981), 10–38.

———, 'Jerusalem and the Lineages in the Seventh Century BCE: Kinship and the Rise of Individual Moral Liability', *Law and Ideology in Monarchic Israel* (ed. B. Halpern and D.W. Hobson, JSOTSup 124, Sheffield, JSOT, 1991), 11–107.

Hamilton, J.M., *Social Justice and Deuteronomy: The Case of Deuteronomy 15* (SBLDS 136, Atlanta, Ga., Scholars, 1992).

Hamilton, M.W., 'The Past as Destiny: Historical Visions in Sam'al and Judah under Assyrian Hegemony', *HTR* 91 (1998), 215–250.

Hammond, P.E., 'Religion and the Persistence of Identity', *Journal for the Scientific Study of Religion* 27 (1988), 1–11.

Hamori, E.J., 'Echoes of Gilgamesh in the Jacob Story', *JBL* 130 (2011), 625–642.

Haran, M., 'Das Böcklein in der Milch seiner Mutter und das Säugende Muttertier', *TZ* 41 (1985), 135–159.

———, 'Seething a Kid in Its Mother's Milk', *JJS* 30 (1979), 23–35.

Harland, P.J., 'Menswear and Womenswear: A Study of Deuteronomy 22:5', *ExpTim* 110 (1998), 73–76.

Harrison, S., 'Cultural Difference as Denied Resemblance: Reconsidering Nationalism and Ethnicity', *CSSH* 45 (2003), 343–361.

———, 'Identity as a Scarce Resource', *Social Anthropology* 7 (1999), 239–251.

Hart, S., 'The Edom Survey Project 1984–85: The Iron Age', *Studies in the History and Archaeology of Jordan III* (ed. A. Hadidi, Amman, Department of Antiquities, 1987), 287–290.

Hastings, A., *The Construction of Nationhood: Ethnicity, Religion and Nationalism* (Cambridge, Cambridge University Press, 1997).

Hayes, C., *Gentile Impurities and Jewish Identities: Intermarriage and Conversion from the Bible to the Talmud* (Oxford, Oxford University Press, 2002).

———, 'Intermarriage and Impurity in Ancient Jewish Sources', *HTR* 92 (1999), 3–36.

Hegmon, M., 'Technology, Style, and Social Practices: Archaeological Approaches', *The Archaeology of Social Boundaries* (ed. M.T. Stark, London, Smithsonian Institute, 1998), 264–279.

Herr, L.G., 'Archaeological Sources for the History of Palestine: The Iron Age II Period: Emerging Nations', *BA* 60 (1997), 114–183.

Herrmann, W., 'Jahwe und des Menschen Liebe zu Ihm: Zu Dtn. vi 5', *VT* 50 (2000), 47–54.

Herzog, Z., 'The Fortress Mound at Tel Arad: An Interim Report', *TA* 29 (2002), 3–109.

———, 'Perspectives on Southern Israel's Cult Centralization: Arad and Beer-scheba', *One God—One Cult—One Nation: Archaeological and Biblical Perspectives* (ed. R.G. Kratz and H. Spieckermann in collaboration with B. Corzilius and T. Pilger, BZAW 405, Berlin, de Gruyter, 2010), 169–200.

Herzog, Z., M. Aharoni, A.F. Rainey and S. Moshkovitz, 'The Israelite Fortress at Arad', *BASOR* 254 (1984), 1–34.

Hesse, B., 'Animal Use at Tel Miqne-Ekron in the Bronze Age and Iron Age', *BASOR* 264 (1986), 17–27.

———, 'Pig Lovers and Pig Haters: Patterns of Palestinian Pork Production', *Journal of Ethnobiology* 10 (1990), 195–225.

Hesse, B., and P. Wapnish, 'Can Pig Bones Be Used for Ethnic Diagnosis in the Ancient Near East?', *The Archaeology of Israel: Constructing the Past, Interpreting the Present* (ed. N.A. Silberman and D. Small, JSOTSup 237, Sheffield, Sheffield Academic, 1997), 238–270.

Hodder, I., 'Economic and Social Stress and Material Culture Patterning', *American Antiquity* 44 (1979), 446–454.

———, *Reading the Past: Current Approaches to Interpretation in Archaeology* (2nd edn., Cambridge, Cambridge University Press, 1991).

———, 'Social Organisation and Human Interaction: The Development of Some Tentative Hypotheses in Terms of Material Culture', *The Spatial Organisation of Culture* (ed. I. Hodder, London, Duckworth, 1978), 199–269.

———, *Symbols in Action: Ethnoarchaeological Studies of Material Culture* (New Studies in Archaeology, Cambridge, Cambridge University Press, 1982).

Hoffman, Y., 'The Deuteronomistic Concept of the Herem', *ZAW* 111 (1999), 196–209.

Hoffmeier, J.K., 'Egypt's Role in the Events of 701 B.C. in Jerusalem', *Jerusalem in Bible and Archaeology: The First Temple Period* (ed. A.G. Vaughn and A.E. Killebrew, SBLSymS, Leiden, Brill, 2003), 219–234.

————, 'Egypt's Role in the Events of 701 B.C.: A Rejoinder to J.J.M. Roberts', *Jerusalem in Bible and Archaeology: The First Temple Period* (ed. A.G. Vaughn and A.E. Killebrew, SBLSymS, Leiden, Brill, 2003), 285–289.

Hoffner, H.A., 'Symbols for Masculinity and Femininity: Their Use in Ancient Near Eastern Sympathetic Magic Rituals', *JBL* 85 (1966), 326–334.

Holloway, S.W., *Aššur is King! Aššur is King!: Religion in the Exercise of Power in the Neo-Assyrian Empire* (CHANE 10, Leiden, Brill, 2001).

Horowitz, D.L., 'Ethnic Identity', *Ethnicity: Theory and Experience* (ed. N. Glazer and D.P. Moynihan, London, Harvard University Press, 1975), 111–140.

Hossfeld, F.-L., 'Volk Gottes als "Versammlung"', *Unterwegs zu Kirche: Alttestamentliche Konzeptionen* (ed. J. Schreiner, QD 110, Freiburg, Herder, 1987), 123–142.

Houston, W., '"You Shall Open Your Hand to Your Needy Brother": Ideology and Moral Formation in Deut. 15,1–18', *The Bible in Ethics: The Second Sheffield Colloquium* (ed. J.W. Rogerson, M. Davies and M.D. Carroll R., JSOTSup 207, London, Continuum, 1995), 296–314.

Houtman, C., 'Die ursprünglichen Bewohner des Landes Kanaan im Deuteronomium: Sinn und Absicht der Beschreibung ihrer Identität und ihres Charakters', *VT* 52 (2002), 51–65.

Hulst, A.R., 'Der Name "Israel" im Deuteronomium', *OTS* 9 (1951), 65–106.

Humbert, P., 'Le substantif *to'ēbā* et le verbe *t'b* dans l'Ancien Testament', *ZAW* 72 (1960), 217–237.

Hutchinson, J., 'Ethnicity and Modern Nations', *Ethnic and Racial Studies* 23 (2000), 651–670.

Hutton, J.M., 'Southern, Northern and Transjordanian Perspectives', *Religious Diversity in Ancient Israel and Judah* (ed. F. Stavrakopoulou and J. Barton, London, T&T Clark, 2010), 149–174.

Isaacs, H.R., 'Basic Group Identity: The Idols of the Tribe', *Ethnicity: Theory and Experience* (ed. N. Glazer and D.P. Moynihan, London, Harvard University Press, 1975), 29–52.

Jackson, B.S., 'The "Institutions" of Marriage and Divorce in the Hebrew Bible', *JSS* 56 (2011), 221–251.

Janzen, J.G., 'On the Most Important Word in the Shema (Deuteronomy VI 4–5)', *VT* 37 (1987), 280–300.

Jeffers, A., *Magic and Divination in Ancient Palestine and Syria* (SHANE 8, Leiden, Brill, 1996).

Joffe, A.H., 'The Rise of Secondary States in the Iron Age Levant', *JESHO* 45 (2002), 425–467.

Jones, S., *The Archaeology of Ethnicity: Constructing Identities in the Past and Present* (London, Routledge, 1997).

Kahn, D., 'The Assyrian Invasions of Egypt (673–663 B.C.) and the Final Expulsion of the Kushites', *Studien zur Altägyptischen Kultur* 34 (2006), 251–267.

Kaiser, O., 'Von Ortsfremden, Ausländern und Proselyten—Vom Umgang mit den Fremden im Alten Testament', *Gott, Mensch und Geschichte: Studien zum Verständnis des Menschen und seiner Geschichte in der klassischen, biblischen und nachbiblischen Literatur* (BZAW 413, Berlin, de Gruyter, 2010), 41–62.

Kamp, K.A., and N. Yoffee, 'Ethnicity in Ancient Western Asia: Archaeological Assessments and Ethnoarchaeological Prospectives', *BASOR* 237 (1980), 85–104.

Katzenstein, H.J., *The History of Tyre: From the Beginning of the Second Millennium B.C.E. until the Fall of the Neo-Babylonian Empire in 538 B.C.E.* (Jerusalem, The Schocken Institute for Jewish Research of the Jewish Theological Seminary of America, 1973).

Kazen, T., *Emotions in Biblical Law: A Cognitive Science Approach to Some Moral and Ritual Issues in Pentateuchal Legal Collections* (Sheffield, Sheffield Phoenix, 2011).

Kedourie, E., *Nationalism* (Oxford, Blackwell, 1993).

Keel, O., *Das Böcklein in der Milch seiner Mutter und Verwandtes: Im Lichte eines altorientalischen Bildmotivs* (OBO 33, Freiburg, Universitätsverlag, 1980).

Keel, O., and C. Uehlinger, *Gods, Goddesses, and Images of God in Ancient Israel* (transl. T.H. Trapp, Minneapolis, Minn., Fortress, 1998).

Kellermann, D., '*gûr; gēr; gērûth; meghûrîm*', *Theological Dictionary of the Old Testament* (15 vols., ed. G.J. Botterweck and H. Ringgren, transl. J.T. Willis, Grand Rapids, Mich., Eerdmans, 1975), 439–449.

Kelley, J., 'Toward a New Synthesis of the God of Edom and Yahweh', *Antiguo Oriente* 7 (2009), 255–280.

Kelm, G.L., and A. Mazar, *Timnah: A Biblical City in the Sorek Valley* (Winona Lake, Ind., Eisenbrauns, 1995).

Keyes, C.F., 'The Dialectics of Ethnic Change', *Ethnic Change* (ed. C.F. Keyes, London, University of Washington Press, 1981), 3–30.

———, ed., *Ethnic Change* (London, University of Washington Press, 1981).

Kilchör, B., 'Frei aber arm? Soziale Sicherheit als Schlüssel zum Verhältnis der Sklavenfreilassungsgesetze im Pentateuch', *VT* 62 (2012), 381–397.

Killebrew, A.E., *Biblical Peoples and Ethnicity: An Archaeological Study of Egyptians, Canaanites, Philistines, and Early Israel, 1300–1100 B.C.E.* (Archaeology and Biblical Studies 9, Leiden, Brill, 2005).

Kletter, R., 'Clay Figurines: Human and Animal Clay Figurines', *Tel 'Ira: A Stronghold in the Biblical Negev* (ed. I. Beit-Arieh, MSIA 15, Tel Aviv, Tel Aviv University, 1999), 374–385.

———, *Economic Keystones: The Weight System of the Kingdom of Judah* (JSOTSup 276, Sheffield, Sheffield Academic Press, 1998).

———, 'The Inscribed Weights of the Kingdom of Judah', *TA* 18 (1991), 121–163.

———, 'Pots and Polities: Material Remains of Late Iron Age Judah in Relation to Its Political Borders', *BASOR* 314 (1999), 19–54.

Knauf, E.A., 'The Cultural Impact of Secondary State Formation: The Cases of the Edomites and the Moabites', *Early Edom and Moab: The Beginning of the Iron Age in Southern Jordan* (ed. P. Bienkowski, Sheffield Archaeological Monographs 7, Sheffield, Collis, 1992), 47–54.

———, 'The Glorious Days of Manasseh', *Good Kings and Bad Kings: The Kingdom of Judah in the Seventh Century B.C.E.* (ed. L.L. Grabbe, LHBOTS 393, London, T&T Clark, 2005), 164–188.

———, 'Zur Herkunft und Sozialgeschichte Israels: "Das Böckchen in der Milch seiner Mutter"', *Bib* 69 (1988), 153–169.

Knauf, E.A., and C.J. Lenzen, 'Edomite Copper Industry', *Studies in the History and Archaeology of Jordan III* (ed. A. Hadidi, Amman, Department of Antiquities, 1987), 83–88.

Knoppers, G.N., 'The Deuteronomist and the Deuteronomic Law of the King: A Reexamination of a Relationship', *ZAW* 108 (1996), 329–346.

Koch, C., *Vertrag, Treueid und Bund: Studien zur Rezeption des altorientalischen Vertragsrechts im Deuteronomium und zur Ausbildung der Bundestheologie im alten Testament* (BZAW 383, Berlin, de Gruyter, 2008).

Kochavi, M., 'Malḥata, Tel', *Encyclopedia of Archaeological Excavations in the Holy Land* (ed. M. Avi-Yonah and E. Stern, Oxford, Oxford University Press, 1977), 771–775.

Kosmala, H., 'The Term *geber* in the Old Testament and in the Scrolls', *Congress Volume: Rome 1968* (ed., VTSup 17, Leiden, Brill, 1969), 159–169.

Kratz, R.G., *Die Komposition der erzählenden Bücher des Alten Testaments* (Göttingen, Vandenhoeck & Ruprecht, 2000).

———, 'The Idea of Cultic Centralization and Its Supposed Ancient Near Eastern Analogies', *One God—One Cult—One Nation: Archaeological and Biblical Perspectives* (ed. R.G. Kratz and H. Spieckermann in collaboration with B. Corzilius and T. Pilger, BZAW 405, Berlin, de Gruyter, 2010), 121–144.

Kreuzer, S., 'Die Exodustradition im Deuteronomium', *Das Deuteronomium und seine Querbeziehungen* (ed. T. Veijola, Schriften der Finnischen Exegetischen Gesellschaft 62, Göttingen, Vandenhoeck & Ruprecht, 1996), 81–106.

Kuhrt, A., *The Ancient Near East: c.3000–330 B.C.* (vol. 2., 2nd edn., Routledge History of the Ancient World, London, Routledge, 1997).

Labuschagne, C.J., 'Divine Speech in Deuteronomy', *Das Deuteronomium: Entstehung, Gestalt und Botschaft* (ed. N. Lohfink, BETL 68, Leuven, Leuven University Press, 1985), 111–126.

Laney, J.C., 'Deuteronomy 24,1–4 and the Issue of Divorce', *Bibliotheca Sacra* 149 (1992), 3–15.

Lang, B., '*nkr; nēḵār; noḵrî*', *Theological Dictionary of the Old Testament* (15 vols., ed. G.J. Botterweck, H. Ringgren and H.-J. Fabry, transl. D.E. Green, Cambridge, Eerdmans, 1998), 423–431.

Lapp, N.L., *The Third Campaign at Tell el-Ful: The Excavations of 1964* (AASOR 45, Cambridge, Mass., ASOR, 1981).

Leahy, A., 'Ethnic Diversity in Ancient Egypt', *Civilizations of the Ancient Near East* (ed. J.M. Sasson, New York, N.Y., Charles Scribner, 1995), 225–234.

Lehmann, G., 'Reconstructing the Social Landscape of Early Israel: Rural Marriage Alliances in the Central Hill Country', *TA* 31 (2004), 141–193.

Leichty, E., *The Royal Inscriptions of Esarhaddon, King of Assyria (680–669 BC)* (RINAP 4, Winona Lake, Ind., Eisenbrauns, 2011).

Lemaire, A., 'Ostraca and Incised Inscriptions', *The Iron Age and Post-Iron Age Pottery and Artefacts* (vol. 4 of *The Renewed Archaeological Excavations at Lachish (1973–1994)*, ed. D. Ussishkin, PIA 22, Tel Aviv, Emery and Claire Yass Publications in Archaeology, 2004), 2099–2132.

Lemche, N.P., '*Andurārum* and *Mīšarum*: Comments on the Problem of Social Edicts and Their Application in the Ancient Near East', *JNES* 38 (1979), 11–22.

———, 'The Manumission of Slaves: The Fallow Year, the Sabbatical Year, the Jobel Year', *VT* 26 (1976), 38–59.

Lemos, T.M., 'Shame and Mutilation of Enemies in the Hebrew Bible', *JBL* 125 (2006), 225–241.

Lernau, H., and O. Lernau, 'Fish Bone Remains', *Excavations in the South of the Temple Mount: The Ophel of Biblical Jerusalem* (ed. E. Mazar and B. Mazar, Qedem 29, Jerusalem, Institute of Archaeology, Hebrew University of Jerusalem, 1989), 155–161.

———, 'Fish Remains', *Stratigraphical, Environmental, and Other Reports* (vol. 3 of *Excavations in the City of David 1978–1985 Directed by Yigal Shiloh*, ed. A. De Groot and D.T. Ariel, Qedem 33, Jerusalem, Hebrew University of Jerusalem, 1992), 131–148.

Leuchter, M., 'A King Like All The Nations: The Composition of I Sam 8,11–18', *ZAW* 118 (2005), 543–558.

Levinson, B.M., '"But You Shall Surely Kill Him!": The Text-Critical and Neo-Assyrian Evidence for MT Deuteronomy 13:10', *Bundesdokument und Gesetz: Studien zum Deuteronomium* (ed. G. Braulik, HBS 4, Freiburg, Herder, 1995), 37–63.

———, 'The Case for Revision and Interpolation within the Biblical Legal Corpora', *Theory and Method in Biblical and Cuneiform Law: Revision, Interpolation, and Development* (ed. B.M. Levinson, Sheffield, Sheffield Phoenix, 2006), 37–59.

———, *Deuteronomy and the Hermeneutics of Legal Innovation* (Oxford, Oxford University Press, 1997).

———, 'Esarhaddon's Succession Treaty as the Source for the Canon Formula in Deuteronomy 13:1', *JAOS* 130 (2010), 337–348.

———, 'The Hermeneutics of Tradition in Deuteronomy: A Reply to J.G. McConville', *JBL* 119 (2000), 269–286.

————, 'The Reconceptualization of Kingship in Deuteronomy and the Deuteronomistic History's Transformation of Torah', *VT* 51 (2001), 511–534.

————, '*The Right Chorale*': *Studies in Biblical Law and Interpretation* (Winona Lake,
Ind., Eisenbrauns, 2011).

————, 'Textual Criticism, Assyriology, and the History of Interpretation: Deuteronomy
13:7a as a Test Case in Method', *JBL* 120 (2001), 211–243.

Levtow, N., *Images of Others: Iconic Politics in Ancient Israel* (Biblical and Judaic Studies
11, Winona Lake, Ind., Eisenbrauns, 2008).

Levy, T.E., R.B. Adams, M. Najjar, A. Hauptmann, J.D. Anderson, B. Brandl, M.A.
Robinson and T. Higham, 'Reassessing the Chronology of Biblical Edom: New
Excavations and 14C Dates from Khirbat en-Nahas (Jordan)', *Antiquity* 78 (2004),
865–879.

Levy, T.E., T. Higham and M. Najjar, 'Response to van der Steen & Bienkowski', *Antiquity*
80 (2006), n.p.

Lewis, T.J., *Cults of the Dead in Ancient Israel and Ugarit* (HSM 39, Atlanta, Ga., Scholars,
1989).

L'Hour, J., 'Les interdits *to'eba* dans le Deutéronome', *RB* 71 (1964), 481–503.

Liphshitz, N., 'Dendroarchaeological Studies 150: The Ophel (Jerusalem) 1986',
*Excavations in the South of the Temple Mount: The Ophel of Biblical Jerusalem* (ed.
E. Mazar and B. Mazar, Qedem 29, Jerusalem, Hebrew University of Jerusalem,
1989), 142–143.

Lipiński, E., 'L'esclave hébreu', *VT* 26 (1976), 120–124.

Lipschits, O., 'The Date of the "Assyrian Residence" at Ayyelet ha-Shaḥar', *TA* 17 (1990),
96–99.

————, *The Fall and Rise of Jerusalem: Judah under Babylonian Rule* (Winona Lake,
Ind., Eisenbrauns, 2005).

————, 'The Origin and Date of the Volute Capitals from the Levant', *The Fire Signals
of Lachish: Studies in the Archaeology and History of Israel in the Late Bronze Age,
Iron Age, and Persian Period in Honor of David Ussishkin* (ed. I. Finkelstein and
N. Na'aman, Winona Lake, Ind., Eisenbrauns, 2011), 203–225.

Lipschits, O., O. Sergi and I. Koch, 'Judahite Stamped and Incised Jar Handles: A Tool
for Studying the History of Late Monarchic Judah', *TA* 38 (2011), 5–41.

————, 'Royal Judahite Jar Handles: Reconsidering the Chronology of the *lmlk* Stamp
Impressions', *TA* 37 (2010), 3–32.

Lipschits, O., Y. Gadot, B. Arubas and M. Oeming, 'Palace and Village, Paradise and
Oblivion: Unraveling the Riddles of Ramat Raḥel', *Near Eastern Archaeology* 74
(2011), 2–49.

Liverani, M., 'The Ideology of the Assyrian Empire', *Power and Propaganda: A
Symposium on Ancient Empires* (ed. M.T. Larsen, Mesopotamia 7, Copenhagen,
Akademisk Forlag, 1979), 297–318.

———, 'Memorandum on the Approach to Historiographic Texts', *Or* 42 (1973), 178–194.

Lohfink, N., 'Culture Shock and Theology', *BTB* 7 (1977), 12–22.

———, 'Distribution of the Functions of Power: The Laws Concerning Public Offices in Deuteronomy 16:18–18:22', *A Song of Power and the Power of Song: Essays on the Book of Deuteronomy* (ed. D.L. Christensen, transl. R. Walls, Sources for Biblical and Theological Study 3, Winona Lake, Ind., Eisenbrauns, 1993), 336–352.

Lowery, R.H., *The Reforming Kings: Cults and Society in First Temple Judah* (JSOTSup 210, Sheffield, JSOT, 1991).

Machinist, P.B., 'Assyria and Its Image in the First Isaiah', *JAOS* 103 (1983), 719–737.

———, 'The Rab Saqeh at the Wall of Jerusalem: Israelite Identity in the Face of the Assyrian "Other"', *HS* 41 (2000), 151–168.

Magen, I., and M. Dadon, 'Nebi Samwel', *One Land—Many Cultures: Archaeological Studies in Honour of Stanislao Loffreda OFM* (ed. G. Bottini, L. Di Segni and L.D. Chrupcala, Studium Biblicum Franciscanum, Collectio Maior 41, Jerusalem, Franciscan, 2003), 123–138.

Magness, J., 'Early Archaic Greek Pottery', *The Finds from the First Millennium BCE: Text* (vol. 2 of *Timnah (Tel Batash) Final Reports*, ed. A. Mazar and N. Panitz-Cohen, Qedem 42, Jerusalem, Hebrew University of Jerusalem, 2001), 141–144.

Malamat, A., 'Josiah's Bid for Armageddon: The Background of the Judean-Egyptian Encounter in 609 B.C.', *JANESCU* 5 (1973), 267–279.

———, 'The Kingdom of Judah between Egypt and Babylon: A Small State within a Great Power Confrontation', *Text and Context: Old Testament and Semitic Studies for F.C. Fensham* (ed. W. Classen, JSOTSup 48, Sheffield, JSOT, 1988), 117–129.

———, 'The Last Years of the Kingdom of Judah', *The Age of the Monarchies: Political History* (vol. 4 of *A World History of the Jewish People*, ed. A. Malamat, Jerusalem, Massada, 1979), 205–221.

———, 'The Twilight of Judah: In the Egyptian-Babylonian Maelstrom', *Congress Volume: Edinburgh 1974* (ed. J. Emerton, VTSup 28, Leiden, Brill, 1975), 123–145.

Margalit, B., 'The Meaning and Significance of Asherah', *VT* 40 (1990), 264–297.

Master, D.M., 'Trade and Politics: Ashkelon's Balancing Act in the Seventh Century B.C.E.', *BASOR* 330 (2003), 47–64.

Matthiae, P., 'The Painted Sherd of Ramat Raḥel', *Excavations at Ramat Raḥel (Seasons 1961 and 1962)* (ed. Y. Aharoni and A. Ciasca, Jerusalem, Hebrew University of Jerusalem, 1964), 85–94.

Maul, S.M., '*kurgarrû* und *assinnu* und ihr Stand in der babylonischen Gesellschaft', *Außenseiter und Randgruppen: Beiträge zu einer Sozialgeschichte des Alten Orients* (ed. V. Haas, Xenia 32, Konstanz, Universitätsverlag Konstanz, 1992), 159–171.

Mayes, A.D.H., *Deuteronomy* (NCB, London, Marshall, Morgan & Scott, 1981).

———, 'Deuteronomy 14 and the Deuteronomic World View', *Studies in Deuteronomy in Honour of C.J. Labuschagne on the Occasion of his 65th Birthday* (ed. F. García

Martínez, A. Hilhorst, J.T.A.G.M. van Ruiten and A.S. van der Woude, VTSup 53, Leiden, Brill, 1994), 165–181.

Mazar, A., and N. Panitz-Cohen, eds., *The Finds from the First Millennium BCE: Text* (vol. 2 of *Timnah (Tel Batash) Final Reports*, Qedem 42, Jerusalem, Hebrew University of Jerusalem, 2001).

Mazar, B., T.K. Dothan and I. Dunayevsky, *En-Gedi: The First and Second Seasons of Excavations, 1961–1962* (Atiqot 5, Jerusalem, Hebrew University of Jerusalem, 1966).

Mazar, E., and B. Mazar, eds., *Excavations in the South of the Temple Mount: The Ophel of Biblical Jerusalem* (Qedem 29, Jerusalem, Hebrew University of Jerusalem, 1989).

McBride, Jr., S.D., 'Polity of the Covenant People: The Book of Deuteronomy', *Int* 41 (1987), 229–244.

McCarthy, D.J., 'Notes on the Love of God in Deuteronomy and the Father-Son Relationship between Yahweh and Israel', *CBQ* 27 (1965), 144–147.

McConville, J.G., 'Deuteronomy's Unification of Passover and *Maṣṣôt*: A Response to Bernard M. Levinson', *JBL* 119 (2000), 47–58.

———, *God and Earthly Power: An Old Testament Political Theology, Genesis-Kings* (JSOTSup 454, London, T&T Clark, 2007).

McKane, W., *Proverbs: A New Approach* (OTL, London, SCM, 1970).

McKay, J.W., *Religion in Judah under the Assyrians, 732–609 B.C.* (SBT 26, London, SCM, 1973).

Meislin, B.J., and M.L. Cohen, 'Backgrounds of the Biblical Law against Usury', *CSSH* 6 (1964), 250–267.

Meskell, L.M., 'The Intersections of Identity and Politics in Archaeology', *ARA* 31 (2002), 279–301.

Mettinger, T.N.D., *No Graven Image? Israelite Aniconism in Its Ancient Near Eastern Context* (ConBOT 42, Stockholm, Almqvist & Wiksell, 1995).

Mienes, H.K., 'Molluscs', *Stratigraphical, Environmental, and Other Reports* (vol. 3 of *Excavations at the City of David 1978–1985 Directed by Yigal Shiloh*, ed. A. De Groot and D.T. Ariel, Qedem 33, Jerusalem, Hebrew University of Jerusalem, 1992), 122–130.

Milgrom, J., *Leviticus 1–16: A New Translation with Introduction and Commentary* (AB 3, New York, N.Y., Yale University Press, 1991).

Millard, A.R., 'Assyrian Involvement in Edom', *Early Edom and Moab: The Beginning of the Iron Age in Southern Jordan* (ed. P. Bienkowski, Sheffield Archaeological Monographs 7, Sheffield, Collis, 1992), 35–39.

Miller, D.R. 'The Shadow of the Overlord: Revisiting the Question of Neo-Assyrian Imposition on the Judaean Cult during the Eighth–Seventh Centuries BCE', *From Babel to Babylon: Essays in Biblical History and Literature in Honor of Brian Peckham* (ed. J.R. Wood, J.E. Harvey and M. Leuchter, LHBOTS 455, London, T&T Clark, 2006), 146–168.

Miller, J.B., *The Ethics of Deuteronomy: An Exegetical and Theological Study of the Book of Deuteronomy* (D.Phil. diss., University of Oxford, 1995).

Miller, P.D., *Deuteronomy* (IBC, Louisville, Ky., John Knox, 1990).

Mittmann, S., 'Hiskia und die Philister', *JNSL* 16 (1991), 91–106.

Moberly, R.W.L., '"Yahweh is One": The Translation of the Shema', *Studies in the Pentateuch* (ed. J.A. Emerton, VTSup 41, Leiden, Brill, 1990), 209–215.

Monroe, L.A.S., 'Israelite, Moabite and Sabaean War-*herem* Traditions and the Forging of National Identity: Reconsidering the Sabaean Text RES 3945 in Light of Biblical and Moabite Evidence', *VT* 57 (2007), 318–341.

———, *Josiah's Reform and the Dynamics of Defilement: Israelite Rites of Violence and the Making of a Biblical Text* (Oxford, Oxford University Press, 2011).

Moran, W.L., 'The Ancient Near Eastern Background of the Love of God in Deuteronomy', *CBQ* 25 (1963), 77–87.

———, 'The Literary Connection between Lv. 11:13–19 and Dt. 14:12–18', *CBQ* 28 (1966), 271–277.

Morrow, W.S., 'The Composition of Deut 15:1–3', *HAR* 12 (1990), 115–131.

———, *Scribing the Center: Organization and Redaction in Deuteronomy 14:1–17:13* (SBLMS 49, Atlanta, Ga., Scholars, 1995).

Mukenge, A.K., '«Toutefois, il n'y aura pas de nécessiteux chez toi»: La stratégie argumentative de Deut. 15:1–11', *VT* 60 (2010), 69–86.

Mullen, Jr, E.T., *Narrative History and Ethnic Boundaries: The Deuteronomistic History and the Creation of Israelite National Identity* (SBLSymS, Atlanta, Ga., Scholars, 1993).

Na'aman, N., 'An Assyrian Residence at Ramat Raḥel?', *TA* 28 (2001), 260–280.

———, 'The Debated Historicity of Hezekiah's Reform in the Light of Historical and Archaeological Research', *ZAW* 107 (1995), 179–195.

———, 'Ekron under the Assyrian and Egyptian Empires', *BASOR* 332 (2003), 81–91.

———, 'Hezekiah and the Kings of Assyria', *Ancient Israel and Its Neighbors: Interaction and Counteraction* (vol. 1 of *Collected Essays*, Winona Lake, Ind., Eisenbrauns, 2005), 98–117.

———, 'The Israelite-Judahite Struggle for the Patrimony of Ancient Israel', *Bib* 91 (2010), 1–23.

———, 'The Kingdom of Judah under Josiah', *Ancient Israel and Its Neighbors: Interaction and Counteraction* (vol. 1 of Collected Essays, Winona Lake, Ind., Eisenbrauns, 2005), 329–398.

———, 'Nebuchadrezzar's Campaign in the Year 603 BCE', *Ancient Israel and Its Neighbors: Interaction and Counteraction* (vol. 1 of *Collected Essays*, Winona Lake, Ind., Eisenbrauns, 2005), 399–402.

———, 'No Anthropomorphic Graven Image? Notes on the Assumed Anthropomorphic Cult Statues in the Temples of YHWH in the Pre-exilic Period', *UF* 31 (1999), 391–415.

———, 'Population Changes in Palestine following Assyrian Deportations', *Ancient Israel and Its Neighbors: Interaction and Counteraction* (vol. 1 of *Collected Essays*, Winona Lake, Ind., Eisenbrauns, 2005), 200–219.

———, 'Province System and Settlement Pattern in Southern Syria and Palestine in the Neo-Assyrian Period', *Neo-Assyrian Geography* (ed. M. Liverani, Quaderni di geografia storica 5, Rome, University of Rome, 1995), 103–115.

———, 'Sennacherib's "Letter to God" on his Campaign to Judah', *Ancient Israel and Its Neighbors: Interaction and Counteraction* (vol. 1 of *Collected Essays*, Winona Lake, Ind., Eisenbrauns, 2005), 135–152.

———, 'Sennacherib's Campaign to Judah and the Date of the *lmlk* Stamps', *VT* 29 (1979), 61–86.

———, 'Textual and Historical Notes on the Eliashib Archive from Arad', *TA* 38 (2011), 83–93.

———, 'Two Notes on the History of Ashkelon and Ekron in the Late Eighth-Seventh Centuries BCE', *Ancient Israel and Its Neighbors: Interaction and Counteraction* (vol. 1 of *Collected Essays*, Winona Lake, Ind., Eisenbrauns, 2005), 68–75.

———, 'When and How did Jerusalem Become a Great City? The Rise of Jerusalem as Judah's Premier City in the Eighth-Seventh Centuries B.C.E.', *BASOR* 347 (2007), 21–56.

Na'aman, N., and R. Zadok, 'Assyrian Deportations to the Province of Samerina in the Light of Two Cuneiform Tablets from Tel Hadid', *TA* 27 (2000), 159–188.

———, 'Sargon II's Deportations to Israel and Philistia (716–708 B.C.)', *JCS* 40 (1988), 36–46.

Na'aman, N., and Y. Thareani-Sussely, 'Dating the Appearance of Imitations of Assyrian Ware in Southern Palestine', *TA* 33 (2006), 61–82.

Naveh, J., 'A Hebrew Letter from the Seventh Century B.C.', *IEJ* 10 (1960), 129–139.

———, 'The Excavations of Meṣad Ḥashavyahu: Preliminary Report', *IEJ* 12 (1962), 89–113.

———, 'More Hebrew Inscriptions from Meṣad Ḥashavyahu', *IEJ* 12 (1962), 27–32.

———, 'Writing and Scripts in Seventh-Century BCE Philistia: The New Evidence from Tell Jemmeh', *IEJ* 35 (1985), 8–21.

Nelson, R.D., *Deuteronomy* (OTL, London, Westminster John Knox, 2004).

———, '*Ḥerem* and the Deuteronomic Social Conscience', *Deuteronomy and the Deuteronomic Literature: Festschrift C.H.W. Brekelmans* (ed. M. Vervenne and J. Lust, BETL 133, Leuven, Leuven University Press, 1997), 39–54.

———, 'Realpolitik in Judah (687–609 BCE)', *Scripture in Context II: More Essays on the Comparative Method* (ed. W.W. Hallo, J.C. Moyer and L.G. Perdue, Winona Lake, Ind., Eisenbrauns, 1983), 177–189.

Nestor, D.A., *Cognitive Perspectives on Israelite Identity* (LHBOTS 519, London, T&T Clark, 2010).

Nevader, M., *Yahweh versus David: The Monarchic Debate of Deuteronomy and Ezekiel* (OTM; Oxford: Oxford University Press, 2014).

Nicholson, E.W., 'Deuteronomy 18.9–22: The Prophets and Scripture', *Prophecy and Prophets in Ancient Israel: Proceedings of the Oxford Old Testament Seminar* (ed. J. Day, LHBOTS 531, London, T&T Clark, 2010), 151–171.

———, *Deuteronomy and the Judean Diaspora* (Oxford, Oxford University Press, 2014).

———, *Deuteronomy and Tradition* (Oxford, Basil Blackwell, 1967).

———, '"Do Not Dare to Set a Foreigner over You": The King in Deuteronomy and "The Great King"', *ZAW* 118 (2006), 46–61.

———, '*Traditum* and *traditio*: The Case of Deuteronomy 17:14–20', *Scriptural Exegesis: The Shapes of Culture and the Religious Imagination: Essays in Honour of Michael Fishbane* (ed. D.A. Green and L.S. Lieber, Oxford, Oxford University Press, 2009), 46–61.

Nielsen, E., *Deuteronomium* (HAT I/6, Tübingen, Mohr Siebeck, 1995).

Niemann, H.M., 'Das Ende des Volkes der Perizziter: Über soziale Wandlungen Israels im Spiegel einer Begriffsgruppe', *ZAW* 105 (1993), 233–257.

Nissinen, M., 'The Dubious Image of Prophecy', *Prophets, Prophecy and Prophetic Texts in Second Temple Judaism* (ed. M.H. Floyd and R.D. Haak, LHBOTS 427, London, T&T Clark, 2006), 26–41.

Nyberg, K., 'Sacred Prostitution in the Biblical World?', *Sacred Marriages: The Divine-Human Sexual Metaphor from Sumer to Early Christianity* (ed. M. Nissinen and R. Uro, Winona Lake, Ind., Eisenbrauns, 2008), 305–320.

Oded, B., *Mass Deportations and Deportees in the Neo-Assyrian Empire* (Weisbaden, Reichert, 1979).

———, 'Observations on Methods of Assyrian Rule in Transjordan after the Palestinian Campaigns of Tiglath-pileser III', *JNES* 29 (1970), 177–186.

———, 'The Phoenician Cities and the Assyrian Empire in the Time of Tiglath-pileser III', *ZDPV* 90 (1974), 38–49.

Ofer, A., '"All the Hill Country of Judah": From A Settlement Fringe to a Prosperous Monarchy', *From Nomadism to Monarchy: Archaeological and Historical Aspects of Early Israel* (ed. I. Finkelstein and N. Na'aman, Jerusalem, Israel Exploration Society, 1994), 92–121.

Olyan, S.M., '"Anyone Blind or Lame Shall Not Enter the House": On the Interpretation of Second Samuel 5:8b', *CBQ* 60 (1998), 218–227.

———, *Asherah and the Cult of Yahweh in Israel* (SBLMS 34, Atlanta, Ga., Scholars, 1988).

———, *Disability in the Hebrew Bible: Interpreting Mental and Physical Differences* (Cambridge, Cambridge University Press, 2008).

———, 'Equality and Inequality in the Socio-Political Visions of the Pentateuchal Sources', *JHS* 10 (2010), n.p.

————, 'Honor, Shame, and Covenant Relations in Ancient Israel and Its Environment', *JBL* 115 (1996), 201–218.

Oren, E.D., 'Ethnicity and Regional Archaeology: The Western Negev under Assyrian Rule', *Biblical Archaeology Today 1990* (ed. A. Biran and J. Aviram, Jerusalem, Israel Exploration Society, 1993), 102–105.

Ornan, T., 'The Mesopotamian Influence on West Semitic Inscribed Seals: A Preference for the Depiction of Mortals', *Studies in the Iconography of Northwest Semitic Inscribed Seals* (ed. B. Sass and C. Uehlinger, OBO 125, Freiburg, Universität Freiburg, 1993), 52–73.

————, 'A Rediscovered Lost Seal from Gezer', *PEQ* 145 (2013), 53–60.

Otto, E., *Das Deuteronomium: Politische Theologie und Rechtsreform in Juda und Assyrien* (BZAW 284, Berlin, de Gruyter, 1999).

————, 'False Weights in the Scales of Biblical Justice? Different Views of Women from Patriarchal Hierarchy to Religious Equality in the Book of Deuteronomy', *Gender and Law in the Hebrew Bible and the Ancient Near East* (ed. V.H. Matthews, B.M. Levinson and T. Frymer-Kensky, London, T&T Clark, 1998), 128–146.

————, 'Town and Rural Countryside in Ancient Israelite Law: Reception and Redaction in Cuneiform and Israelite Law', *JSOT* 57 (1993), 3–22.

————, 'Treueid und Gesetz: Die Ursprünge des Deuteronomiums im Horizont neuassyrischen Vertragsrechts', *ZABR* 2 (1996), 1–52.

————, 'Das Verbot der Wiederherstellung einer geschiedenen Ehe: Deuteronomium 24,1–4 im Kontext des israelitischen und judäischen Eherechts', *UF* 24 (1992), 301–310.

Otzen, B., 'Israel under the Assyrians', *Power and Propaganda: A Symposium on Ancient Empires* (ed. M.T. Larsen, Mesopotamia 7, Copenhagen, Akademisk Forlag, 1979), 251–261.

Pakkala, J., 'The Date of the Oldest Edition of Deuteronomy', *ZAW* 121 (2009), 388–401.

————, 'Der literar- und religionsgeschichtliche Ort von Deuteronomium 13', *Die deuteronomistischen Geschichtswerke: redaktions- und religionsgeschichtliche Perspektiven zur 'Deuteronomismus'-Diskussion in Tora und Vorderen Propheten* (ed. M. Witte, K. Schmid, D. Prechel and J.C. Gertz, BZAW 365, Berlin, de Gruyter, 2006), 125–137.

————, 'Why the Cult Reforms in Judah Probably Did Not Happen', *One God—One Cult—One Nation: Archaeological and Biblical Perspectives* (ed. R.G. Kratz and H. Spieckermann in collaboration with B. Corzilius and T. Pilger, BZAW 405, Berlin, de Gruyter, 2010), 201–235.

Panitz-Cohen, N., and A. Mazar, eds., *The Finds from the Second Millennium BCE* (vol. 3 of *Timnah (Tel Batash) Final Reports*, Qedem 45, Jerusalem, Hebrew University of Jerusalem, 2006).

Parpola, S., *Assyrian Prophecies* (SAA 9, Helsinki, The Neo-Assyrian Text Corpus Project, 1997).

————, *Letters from Assyrian and Babylonian Scholars* (SAA 10, Helsinki, The Neo-Assyrian Text Corpus Project, 1993).

Parpola, S., and K. Watanabe, *Neo-Assyrian Treaties and Loyalty Oaths* (SAA 2, Helsinki, Helsinki University Press, 1988).

Parsons, T., 'Some Theoretical Considerations on the Nature and Trends of Change in Ethnicity', *Ethnicity: Theory and Experience* (ed. N. Glazer and D.P. Moynihan, London, Harvard University Press, 1975), 53–83.

Peckham, B., 'Phoenicians and Aramaeans: The Literary and Epigraphic Evidence', *The World of the Arameans: Studies in Language and Literature in Honour of Paul-Eugéne Dion* (ed. P.M.M. Daviau, J.W. Wevers and M. Weigl, JSOTSup 324, Sheffield, Sheffield Academic, 2001), 19–44.

Peek, L., 'Becoming Muslim: The Development of a Religious Identity', *Sociology of Religion* 66 (2005), 215–242.

Peel, J.D.Y., 'The Cultural Work of Yoruba Ethnogenesis', *History and Ethnicity* (ed. E. Tonkin, M. McDonald and M. Chapman, ASA Monographs 27, London, Routledge, 1989), 198–215.

Perlitt, L., *Deuteronomium* (BKAT 5, Neukirchen-Vluyn, Neukirchener Verlag, 1990–).

————, '"Ein einzig Volk von Brüdern": Zur deuteronomischen Herkunft der biblischen Bezeichnung "Bruder"', *Deuteronomium-Studien* (FAT 8, Tübingen, Mohr, 1994), 50–73.

Petersson-Solimany, M., and R. Kletter, 'The Iron Age Clay Figurines and a Possible Scale Weight', *Salvage Excavations at Tel Moza: The Bronze and Iron Age Settlements and Later Occupations* (ed. Z. Greenhut and A. De Groot, IAA Reports 39, Jerusalem, Israel Antiquities Authority, 2009), 115–124.

Phillips, A., 'Some Aspects of Family Law in Pre-exilic Israel', *JSOT* 23 (1973), 349–361.

Postgate, J.N., 'The Economic Structure of the Assyrian Empire', *The Land of Assur and the Yoke of Assur: Studies on Assyria 1971–2005* (J.N. Postgate, Oxford, Oxbow, 2007), 71–100.

Pressler, C., *The View of Women Found in the Deuteronomic Family Laws* (BZAW 216, Berlin, de Gruyter, 1993).

Preuss, H.D., *Deuteronomium* (EdF 164, Darmstadt, Wissenschaftliche Buchgesellschaft, 1982).

————, 'תּוֹעֵבָה *tôʿēḇâ*; תעב *tʿb*', *Theological Dictionary of the Old Testament* (15 vols., ed. G.J. Botterweck, H. Ringgren and H.-J. Fabry, transl. D.E. Green, Cambridge, Eerdmans, 2006), 591–604.

Rainey, A.F., 'Manasseh, King of Judah, in the Whirlpool of the Seventh Century B.C.E.', *Kinattūtu ša dārâti: Raphael Kutscher Memorial Volume* (ed. A.F. Rainey, Tel Aviv Occasional Publications 1, Tel Aviv, Tel Aviv University, 1993), 147–164.

Ramírez Kidd, J.E., *Alterity and Identity in Israel: The גר in the Old Testament* (BZAW 283, Berlin, de Gruyter, 1999).

Ratner, R., and B. Zuckerman, 'A Kid in Milk? New Photographs of KTU 1.23, Line 14', *HUCA* 57 (1986), 15–60.

Reeder, C.A., *The Enemy in the Household: Family Violence in Deuteronomy and Beyond* (Grand Rapids, Mich., Baker, 2012).

Reese, D.S., 'Marine Invertebrates and Other Shells from Jerusalem (Sites A, C and L)', *The Iron Age Cave Deposits on the South-east Hill and Isolated Burials and Cemeteries Elsewhere* (vol. 4 of *Excavations in Jerusalem 1961–1967*, ed. I. Eshel and K. Prag, BAMA 6, Oxford, Oxford University Press, 1995), 265–278.

Reich, R., 'On the Assyrian Presence at Ramat Raḥel', *TA* 30 (2003), 124–129.

———, 'The Persian Building at Ayyelet ha-Shaḥar: The Assyrian Palace at Hazor?', *IEJ* 25 (1975), 233–237.

Reich, R., and B. Brandl, 'Gezer under Assyrian Rule', *PEQ* 117 (1985), 41–54.

Reich, R., and E. Shukron, 'The Urban Development of Jerusalem in the Late Eighth Century B.C.E.', *Jerusalem in Bible and Archaeology: The First Temple Period* (ed. A.G. Vaughn and A.E. Killebrew, SBLSymS, Leiden, Brill, 2003), 209–218.

Reimer, D.J., 'Concerning Return to Egypt: Deuteronomy XVII 16 and XXVIII 68 Reconsidered', *Studies in the Pentateuch* (ed. J.A. Emerton, VTSup 41, Leiden, Brill, 1990), 217–229.

Reuter, E., *Kultzentralisation: Entstehung und Theologie von Dtn 12* (BBB 87, Frankfurt, Anton Hain, 1993).

Riegner, I.E., *The Vanishing Hebrew Harlot: The Adventures of the Hebrew Stem ZNH* (Studies in Biblical Literature 73, Oxford, Peter Lang, 2009).

Roaf, M., 'Ethnicity and Near Eastern Archaeology: The Limits of Inference', *Ethnicity in Ancient Mesopotamia: Papers Read at the 48th Rencontre Assyriologique Internationale: Leiden, 1–4 July 2002* (ed. W.H. Van Soldt, Leiden, Netherlands Institute for the Near East, 2005), 306–315.

Roberts, J.J.M., 'Egypt, Assyria, Isaiah, and the Ashdod Affair: An Alternative Proposal', *Jerusalem in Bible and Archaeology: The First Temple Period* (ed. A.G. Vaughn and A.E. Killebrew, SBLSymS, Leiden, Brill, 2003), 265–283.

Rofé, A., 'The Laws of Warfare in the Book of Deuteronomy: Their Origins, Intent and Positivity', *Deuteronomy: Issues and Interpretation* (OTS, London, T&T Clark, 2002), 149–168.

———, 'The Strata of the Law about the Centralization of Worship in Deuteronomy and the History of the Deuteronomic Movement', *Deuteronomy: Issues and Interpretation* (OTS, London, T&T Clark, 2002), 97–102.

Römer, T.C., *The So-Called Deuteronomistic History: A Sociological, Historical and Literary Introduction* (London, T&T Clark, 2007).

Römer, W.H.P., 'Randbemerkungen zur Travestie von Deut. 22,5', *Travels in the World of the Old Testament: Studies Presented to Professor M.A. Beek on the Occasion of His 65th Birthday* (ed. M.S.H.G. Heerma van Voss, Ph. H.J. Houwink ten Cate and N.A. van Uchelen, SSN 16, Assen, Van Gorcum, 1974), 217–222.

Roscoe, W., 'Priests of the Goddess: Gender Transgression in Ancient Religion', *HR* 35 (1996), 195–230.

Rose, M., 'Yahweh in Israel, Qaus in Edom?', *JSOT* 4 (1977), 28–34.

Sade, M., 'Faunal Remains', *Ḥorvat ʿUza and Ḥorvat Radum: Two Fortresses in the Biblical Negev* (ed. I. Beit-Arieh, MSIA 25, Tel Aviv, Tel Aviv University, 2007), 289–297.

Sadler, Jr., R.S., *Can A Cushite Change His Skin? An Examination of Race, Ethnicity, and Othering in the Hebrew Bible* (LHBOTS 425, London, T&T Clark, 2005).

Sanders, S.L., *The Invention of Hebrew* (Traditions, Chicago, Ill., University of Illinois, 2011).

Sass, B., 'Arabs and Greeks in Late First Temple Jerusalem', *PEQ* 122 (1990), 59–61.

———, 'The Pre-Exilic Hebrew Seals: Iconism vs. Aniconism', *Studies in the Iconography of Northwest Semitic Inscribed Seals* (ed. B. Sass and C. Uehlinger, OBO 125, Freiburg, Universität Freiburg, 1993), 194–256.

Sasson, J.M., 'Ritual Wisdom? On "Seething a Kid in Its Mother's Milk"', *Kein Land für sich allein: Studien zum Kulturkontakt in Kanaan, Israel/Palaestina und Ebirnâri für Manfred Weippert zum 65. Geburtstag* (ed. U. Hübner and E.A. Knauf, OBO 186, Göttingen, Vandenhoeck & Ruprecht, 2002), 294–308.

Scacewater, T., 'Divorce and Remarriage in Deuteronomy 24:1–4', *JESOT* 1 (2012), 63–79.

Schäfer-Lichtenberger, C., 'The Goddess of Ekron and the Religious-Cultural Background of the Philistines', *IEJ* 50 (2000), 82–91.

Schaudig, H., 'Cult Centralization in the Ancient Near East? Conceptions of the Ideal Capital in the Ancient Near East', *One God—One Cult—One Nation: Archaeological and Biblical Perspectives* (ed. R.G. Kratz and H. Spieckermann in collaboration with B. Corzilius and T. Pilger, BZAW 405, Berlin, de Gruyter, 2010), 145–168.

Schipper, B.U., 'Egypt and the Kingdom of Judah under Josiah and Jehoiakim', *TA* 37 (2010), 200–226.

Schmid, K., *Genesis and the Moses Story: Israel's Dual Origins in the Hebrew Bible* (transl. J. Nogalski, Siphrut 3, Winona Lake, Ind., Eisenbrauns, 2010).

Schorch, S., '"A Young Goat in Its Mother's Milk"? Understanding an Ancient Prohibition', *VT* 60 (2010), 116–130.

Schroer, S., 'Die Problematik der Verkleidung im Alten Israel', *Diasynchron: Beiträge zur Exegese, Theologie und Rezeption der hebräischen Bibel: Walter Dietrich zum 65. Geburtstag* (ed. T. Naumann and R. Hunziker-Rodewald, Stuttgart, Kohlhammer, 2009), 329–344.

Schulmeister, I., *Israels Befreiung aus Ägypten: Eine Formeluntersuchung zur Theologie des Deuteronomiums* (Österreichische Biblische Studien 36; Frankfurt: Peter Lang, 2010).

Schwartz, S., 'Language, Power and Identity in Ancient Palestine', *Past and Present* 148 (1995), 3–47.

Scott, R.B.Y., 'The N-Ṣ-P Weights from Judah', *BASOR* 200 (1970), 62–66.

———, 'Weights from Jerusalem', *Excavations in Jerusalem 1961–1967* (ed. A.D. Tushingham, Toronto, Royal Ontario Museum, 1985), 195–212.

Segal, I., 'Analysis of a Blue Sample from the Scepter Head', *Salvage Excavations at Tel Moza: The Bronze and Iron Age Settlements and Later Occupations* (ed. Z. Greenhut and A. De Groot, IAA Reports 39, Jerusalem, Israel Antiquities Authority, 2009), 152–153.

Shamir, O., 'Loomweights and Textile Production at Tel Miqne-Ekron: A Prelimary Report', *'Up to the Gates of Ekron': Essays on the Archaeology and History of the Eastern Mediterranean in Honor of Seymour Gitin* (ed. S.W. Crawford, A. Ben-Tor, J.P. Dessel, W.G. Dever, A. Mazar and J. Aviram, Jerusalem, W.F. Albright Institute of Archaeological Research and Israel Exploration Society, 2007), 43–49.

Shennan, S., 'Introduction: Archaeological Approaches to Cultural Identity', *Archaeological Approaches to Cultural Identity* (ed. S. Shennan, London, Routledge, 1994), 1–32.

Shiloh, Y., 'Judah and Jerusalem in the Eighth-Sixth Centuries B.C.E.', *Recent Excavations in Israel: Studies in Iron Age Archaeology* (ed. S. Gitin and W.G. Dever, AASOR 49, Winona Lake, Ind., Eisenbrauns, 1989), 97–105.

———, 'South Arabian Inscriptions from the City of David, Jerusalem', *PEQ* 119 (1987), 9–18.

Simon-Shoshan, M., 'Ain't Nothing but a Hound Dog? The Meaning of the Noun *klb* in Northwest Semitic Languages in Light of Bt Rosh Hashanah 4a', *A Common Cultural Heritage: Studies on Mesopotamia and the Biblical World in Honor of Barry L. Eichler* (ed. G. Frame, E. Leichty, K. Sonik, J.H. Tigay and S. Tinney, Bethesda, Md., CDL, 2011), 177–194.

Singer-Avitz, L., 'Arad: The Iron Age Pottery Assemblages', *TA* 29 (2002), 110–214.

———, 'Beersheba—A Gateway Community in Southern Arabian Long-Distance Trade in the Eighth Century B.C.E.', *TA* 26 (1999), 3–75.

———, '"Busayra Painted Ware" at Tel Beersheba', *TA* 31 (2004), 80–89.

———, 'A Group of Phoenician Vessels from Tel Beersheba', *TA* 37 (2010), 188–199.

———, 'On Pottery in Assyrian Style: A Rejoinder', *TA* 34 (2007), 182–203.

Smith, A.D., *The Nation in History: Historiographic Debates about Ethnicity and Nationalism* (Menahem Stern Jerusalem Lectures, Hanover, N.H., University Press of New England, 2000).

Smith, M., 'A Note on Burning Babies', *JAOS* 95 (1975), 477–479.

Smith, M.S., *The Early History of God: Yahweh and the Other Deities in Ancient Israel* (2nd edn., Grand Rapids, Mich., Eerdmans, 2002).

Sneed, M., 'Israelite Concern for the Alien, Orphan, and Widow: Altruism or Ideology?', *ZAW* 111 (1999), 498–507.

Soss, N.M., 'Old Testament Law and Economic Society', *Journal of the History of Ideas* 34 (1973), 323–344.

Southwood, K.E., *Ethnicity and the Mixed Marriage Crisis in Ezra 9–10: An Anthropological Approach* (OTM, Oxford, Oxford University Press, 2012).

Spalinger, A., 'Assurbanipal and Egypt: A Source Study', *JAOS* 94 (1974), 316–328.

———, 'Esarhaddon and Egypt: An Analysis of the First Invasion of Egypt', *Or* 13 (1976), 295–326.

Sparks, K.L., *Ethnicity and Identity in Ancient Israel: Prolegomena to the Study of Ethnic Sentiments and Their Expression in the Hebrew Bible* (Winona Lake, Ind., Eisenbrauns, 1998).

Speiser, E.A., '"People" and "Nation" of Israel', *JBL* 79 (1960), 157–163.

Spieckermann, H., *Juda unter Assur in der Sargonidenzeit* (FRLANT 129, Göttingen, Vandenhoeck & Ruprecht, 1982).

Stackert, J., 'Mosaic Prophecy and the Deuteronomic Source of the Torah', *Deuteronomy in the Pentateuch, Hexateuch, and the Deuteronomistic History* (ed. R.F. Person, Jr. and K. Schmid, FAT II 56, Tübingen, Mohr Siebeck, 2012), 47–63.

———, 'The Syntax of Deuteronomy 13:2–3 and the Conventions of Ancient Near Eastern Prophecy', *JANER* 10 (2010), 159–175.

Stager, L.E., 'Farming in the Judean Desert during the Iron Age', *BASOR* 221 (1976), 145–158.

———, 'Why Were Hundreds of Dogs Buried at Ashkelon?', *BAR* 17 (1991), 27–42.

Stager, L.E., D.M. Master and J.D. Schloen, *Ashkelon 3: The Seventh Century B.C.* (Winona Lake, Ind., Eisenbrauns, 2011).

Stark, M.T., ed., *The Archaeology of Social Boundaries* (London, Smithsonian Institute, 1998).

Stavrakopoulou, F., *King Manasseh and Child Sacrifice: Biblical Distortions of Historical Realities* (BZAW 338, Berlin, de Gruyter, 2004).

———, *Land of Our Fathers: The Roles of Ancestor Veneration in Biblical Land Claims* (LHBOTS 473, London, T&T Clark, 2010).

Stavrakopoulou, F., and J. Barton, eds., *Religious Diversity in Ancient Israel and Judah* (London, T&T Clark, 2010).

Steinberg, N., 'The Deuteronomic Law Code and the Politics of State Centralization', *The Bible and Liberation: Political and Social Hermeneutics* (ed. N.K. Gottwald and R.A. Horsley, Maryknoll, N.Y., Orbis, 1993), 365–375.

Steiner, M.L., *The Settlement in the Bronze and Iron Ages* (vol. 3 of *Excavations in Jerusalem 1961–1967* (Copenhagen International Seminar, London, Oxford University Press, 2001).

Stern, E., 'Stratum V: The Late Judean Period', *En-Gedi Excavations I: Final Report* (ed. E. Stern, Jerusalem, Israel Exploration Society, 2007), 77–192.

——, ed., *En-Gedi Excavations I: Final Report* (Jerusalem, Israel Exploration Society, 2007).

Steymans, H.U., *Deuteronomium 28 und die Adê zur Thronfolgeregelung Asarhaddons: Segen und Fluch im Alten Orient und in Israel* (OBO 145, Göttingen, Vandenhoeck & Ruprecht, 1995).

——, 'Eine assyrische Vorlage für Deuteronomium 28:20–44', *Bundesdokument und Gesetz: Studien zum Deuteronomium* (ed. G. Braulik, HBS 4, Freiburg, Herder, 1995), 119–141.

Stipp, H.-J., 'Die *Qedešen* im Alten Testament', *Die Erzväter in der biblischen Tradition: Festschrift für Matthias Köckert* (ed. A. Hagedorn and H. Pfeiffer, BZAW 400, Berlin, de Gruyter, 2009), 209–240.

Stökl, J., 'Ištar's Women, YHWH's Men? A Curious Gender-Bias in Neo-Assyrian and Biblical Prophecy', *ZAW* 121 (2009), 87–100.

——, *Prophecy in the Ancient Near East: A Philological and Sociological Comparison* (CHANE 56, Leiden, Brill, 2012).

Stulman, L., 'Encroachment in Deuteronomy: An Analysis of the Social World of the D Code', *JBL* 109 (1990), 613–632.

Sweeney, M.A., 'The Critique of Solomon in the Josianic Edition of the Deuteronomistic History', *JBL* 114 (1995), 607–622.

Swersky, A., 'Gemstones', *Various Reports* (vol. 4 of *Excavations at the City of David 1978– 1985 Directed by Yigal Shiloh*, ed. D.T. Ariel and A. De Groot, Qedem 35, Jerusalem, Hebrew University of Jerusalem, 1996), 268–275.

Tadmor, H., 'Philistia under Assyrian Rule', *BA* 29 (1966), 86–102.

——, 'Rab-saris and Rab-shakeh in 2 Kings 18', *The Word of the Lord Shall Go Forth: Essays in Honor of David Noel Freedman in Celebration of His Sixtieth Birthday* (ed. C.L. Meyers and M. O'Connor, Special Volume Series (American Schools of Oriental Research) 1, Winona Lake, Ind., Eisenbrauns, 1983), 279–285.

——, 'Was the Biblical *saris* a Eunuch?', *Solving Riddles and Untying Knots: Biblical, Epigraphic, and Semitic Studies in Honor of Jonas C. Greenfield* (ed. Z. Zevit, S. Gitin and M. Sokoloff, Winona Lake, Ind., Eisenbrauns, 1995), 317–325.

Tan, N., *The 'Foreignness' of the Foreign Woman in Proverbs 1–9* (BZAW 381, Berlin, de Gruyter, 2008).

Tatum, L., 'Jerusalem in Conflict: The Evidence for the Seventh-Century B.C.E. Religious Struggle over Jerusalem', *Jerusalem in Bible and Archaeology: The First Temple Period* (ed. A.G. Vaughn and A.E. Killebrew, SBLSymS, Leiden, Brill, 2003), 291–306.

——, 'King Manasseh and the Royal Fortress at Ḥorvat 'Uza', *BA* 54 (1991), 136–145.

Tebes, J.M., 'Trade and Nomads: The Commercial Relations between the Negev, Edom, and the Mediterranean in the Late Iron Age', *Journal of the Serbian Archaeological Society* 22 (2006), 45–62.

———, '"You Shall Not Abhor an Edomite, for He is Your Brother": The Tradition of Esau and the Edomite Genealogies from an Anthropological Perspective', *JHS* 6 (2006), n.p.

Thareani, Y., 'The Spirit of Clay: "Edomite Pottery" and Social Awareness in the Late Iron Age', *BASOR* 359 (2010), 35–56.

Thareani-Sussely, Y., 'The "Archaeology of the Days of Manasseh" Reconsidered in the Light of Evidence from the Beersheba Valley', *PEQ* 139 (2007), 69–77.

———, 'Desert Outsiders: Extramural Neighborhoods in the Iron Age Negev', *Bene Israel: Studies in the Archaeology of the Israel and the Levant during the Bronze and Iron Ages in Honour of Israel Finkelstein* (ed. A. Fantalkin and A. Yasur-Landau, CHANE 31, Leiden, Brill, 2008), 197–212, 288–302.

Thistlethwaite, S.B., '"You May Enjoy the Spoils of Your Enemies": Rape as Biblical Metaphor for War', *Semeia* 61 (1993), 59–75.

Thompson, C.J.S., *Mysteries of Sex: Women Who Posed as Men and Men Who Impersonated Women* (London, Hutchinson, 1974).

Thompson, R.H., *Theories of Ethnicity: A Critical Appraisal* (New York, N.Y., Greenwood, 1989).

Tigay, J.H., *Deuteronomy* (JPS Torah Commentary, Philadelphia, Pa., JPS, 1996).

Turner, V.W., *The Ritual Process: Structure and Anti-Structure* (New York, N.Y., Aldine, 1969).

Uehlinger, C., 'Arad, Qiṭmīt—Judahite Aniconism vs. Edomite Iconic Cult?', *Text, Artifact, and Image: Revealing Ancient Israelite Religion* (ed. G.M. Beckman and T.J. Lewis, BJS 346, Providence, R.I., Brown Judaic Studies, 2006), 80–112.

Ussishkin, D., 'Appendix: Asymmetrical Bowls and Bowls in Assyrian Style', *The Iron Age and Post-Iron Age Pottery and Artefacts* (vol. 4 of *The Renewed Archaeological Excavations at Lachish (1973–1994)*, ed. D. Ussishkin, PIA 22, Tel Aviv, Emery and Claire Yass Publications in Archaeology, 2004), 1900–1906.

———, 'The Date of the Judean Shrine at Arad', *IEJ* 38 (1988), 142–157.

———, 'The Destruction of Lachish by Sennacherib and the Dating of the Royal Judean Storage Jars', *TA* 4 (1977), 28–60.

———, 'The Fortifications of Philistine Ekron', *IEJ* 55 (2005), 35–65.

———, ed., *The Iron Age and Post-Iron Age Pottery and Artefacts* (vol. 4 of *The Renewed Archaeological Excavations at Lachish (1973–1994)*, PIA 22, Tel Aviv, Emery and Claire Yass Publications in Archaeology, 2004).

Van Beek, G.W., 'Digging up Tell Jemmeh: Smithsonian Archaeologists Unlock a Mound's Secrets', *Archaeology* 36 (1983), 12–19.

———, 'Jemmeh, Tell', *The New Encyclopedia of Archaeological Excavations in the Holy Land* (ed. E. Stern, Jerusalem, Israel Exploration Society, 1993), 667–674.

Van De Mieroop, M., *A History of the Ancient Near East: ca. 3000–323 BC* (2nd edn., Oxford, Blackwell, 2007).

Van Der Steen, E., 'Nelson Glueck's "String of Fortresses" Revisited', *Studies on Iron Age Moab and Neighbouring Areas in Honour of Michèle Daviau* (ed. P. Bienkowski, ANESupS 29, Leuven, Peeters, 2009), 117–128.

Van Der Steen, E., and P. Bienkowski, 'Radiocarbon Dates from Khirbat en-Nahas: A Methodological Critique', *Antiquity* 80 (2006), n.p.

van Driel, G., 'Ethnicity, How to Cope with the Subject', *Ethnicity in Ancient Mesopotamia: Papers Read at the 48th Rencontre Assyriologique Internationale: Leiden, 1–4 July 2006* (ed. W.H. Van Soldt, Leiden, Netherlands Institute for the Near East, 2005), 1–9.

Van Gennep, A., *Les rites de passage* (Paris, Picard, 1981).

van Houten, C., *The Alien in Israelite Law* (JSOTSup 107, Sheffield, JSOT, 1991).

Van Seters, J., 'The Terms "Amorite" and "Hittite" in the Old Testament', *VT* 22 (1972), 64–81.

Van Soldt, W.H., ed., *Ethnicity in Ancient Mesopotamia: Papers Read at the 48th Rencontre Assyriologique Internationale: Leiden, 1–4 July 2002* (Leiden, Netherlands Institute for the Near East, 2005).

Vanderhooft, D., 'The Edomite Dialect and Script: A Review of Evidence', *You Shall Not Abhor an Edomite for He Is Your Brother: Edom and Seir in History and Tradition* (ed. D.V. Edelman, SBLABS 3, Atlanta, Ga., Scholars, 1995), 137–158.

Varšo, M., 'Abomination in the Legal Code of Deuteronomy: Can an Abomination Motivate?', *ZABR* 13 (2007), 249–260.

Vaughn, A.G., and A.E. Killebrew, eds., *Jerusalem in Bible and Archaeology: The First Temple Period* (Atlanta, Ga., Society of Biblical Literature, 2003).

Vedeler, H.T., 'Reconstructing Meaning in Deuteronomy 22:5: Gender, Society, and Transvestitism in Israel and the Ancient Near East', *JBL* 127 (2008), 459–476.

Veijola, T., *Das 5. Buch Mose: Deuteronomium: Kapitel 1,1–16,17* (ATD 8,1, Göttingen, Vandenhoeck & Ruprecht, 2004).

Vogt, P.T., 'The Passover in Exodus and Deuteronomy: An Introductory Examination', *A God of Faithfulness: Essays in Honour of J. Gordon McConville on His 60th Birthday* (ed. J.A. Grant, A. Lo and G.J. Wenham, LHBOTS 538, London, T&T Clark, 2011), 30–45.

von Rad, G., *Das fünfte Buch Mose: Deuteronomium* (ATD 8, Göttingen, Vandenhoeck & Ruprecht, 1964).

Wacker, M.-T., '"Kultprostitution" im Alten Israel? Forschungsmythen, Spuren, Thesen', *Tempelprostitution im Altertum: Fakten und Fiktionen* (ed. T.S. Scheer, OikSAW 6, Berlin, Verlag Antike, 2009), 55–84.

Wallerstein, I., *The Capitalist World-Economy* (Cambridge, Cambridge University Press, 1979).

Wapnish, P., 'Camel Caravans and Camel Pastoralists at Tell Jemmeh', *JANESCU* 13 (1981), 101–121.

————, 'The Dromedary and Bactrian Camel in Levantine Historical Settings: The Evidence from Tell Jemmeh', *Animals and Archaeology* (ed. J. Clutton-Brock and C. Grigson, BAR International Series 202, Oxford, BAR, 1984), 171–200.

Wapnish, P., and B. Hesse, 'Pampered Pooches or Plain Pariahs? The Ashkelon Dog Burials', *BA* 56 (1993), 55–80.

Warner, R.S., 'Work in Progress Toward a New Paradigm for the Sociological Study of Religion in the United States', *American Journal of Sociology* 98 (1993), 1044–1093.

Washington, H.C., ' "Lest He Die in the Battle and Another Man Take Her": Violence and the Construction of Gender in the Laws of Deuteronomy 20–22', *Gender and Law in the Hebrew Bible and the Ancient Near East* (ed. V.H. Matthews, B.M. Levinson and T. Frymer-Kensky, London, T&T Clark, 1998), 185–213.

————, 'Violence and the Construction of Gender in the Hebrew Bible: A New Historicist Approach', *BibInt* 5 (1997), 324–363.

Weeks, S.D.E., 'Biblical Literature and the Emergence of Ancient Jewish Nationalism', *BibInt* 10 (2002), 144–157.

Weinfeld, M., 'Burning Babies in Ancient Israel: A Rejoinder to Morton Smith's Article in *JAOS* 95 (1975), 477–79', *UF* 10 (1978), 411–413.

————, 'Cult Centralization in Israel in the Light of a Neo-Babylonian Analogy', *JNES* 23 (1964), 202–212.

————, *Deuteronomy 1–11: A New Translation with Introduction and Commentary* (AB 5, London, Doubleday, 1991).

————, *Deuteronomy and the Deuteronomic School* (Oxford, Clarendon, 1972).

————, 'Traces of Assyrian Treaty Formulae in Deuteronomy', *Bib* 46 (1965), 417–427.

Weippert, M., 'The Relations of the States East of the Jordan with the Mesopotamian Powers During the First Millennium BC', *Studies in the History and Archaeology of Jordan III* (ed. A. Hadidi, Amman, Department of Antiquities, 1987), 97–105.

Weisberg, D.E., 'The Widow of Our Discontent: Levirate Marriage in the Bible and Ancient Israel', *JSOT* 28 (2004), 403–429.

Weiss, E., and M.E. Kislev, 'Plant Remains as Indicators of Economic Activity: A Case Study from Iron Age Ashkelon', *Journal of Archaeological Science* 31 (2004), 1–13.

Wenham, G.J., and J.G. McConville, 'Drafting Techniques in Some Deuteronomic Laws', *VT* 30 (1980), 248–252.

Westbrook, R., 'The Prohibition on Restoration of Marriage in Deuteronomy 24:1–4', *Studies in Bible, 1986* (ed. S. Japhet, ScrHier 31, Jerusalem, Magnes, 1986), 387–406.

————, *Property and the Family in Biblical Law* (JSOTSup 113, Sheffield, JSOT, 1991).

Westenholz, J.G., 'Tamar, *Qĕdēša*, *Qadištu*, and Sacred Prostitution in Mesopotamia', *HTR* 82 (1989), 245–265.

Williams, M.J., 'Taking Interest in Taking Interest', *Mishneh Todah: Studies in Deuteronomy and Its Cultural Environment in Honor of Jeffrey H. Tigay* (ed. N.S. Fox, D.A. Glatt-Gilad and M.J. Williams, Winona Lake, Ind., Eisenbrauns, 2009), 113–132.

Wilson, I.D., 'Judean Pillar Figurines and Ethnic Identity in the Shadow of Assyria', *JSOT* 36 (2012), 259–278.

Winter, U., *Frau und Göttin: Exegetische und Ikonographische Studien zum Weiblichen Gottesbild im Alten Israel und in dessen Umwelt* (OBO 53, Göttingen, Vandenhoeck & Ruprecht, 1983).

Wright, J.L., 'The Commemoration of Defeat and the Formation of a Nation in the Hebrew Bible', *Prooftexts* 29 (2009), 433–473.

———, 'Warfare and Wanton Destruction: A Reexamination of Deuteronomy 20: 19–20 in Relation to Ancient Siegecraft', *JBL* 127 (2008), 423–458.

Wright, J.L., and M.J. Chan, 'King and Eunuch: Isaiah 56:1–8 in Light of Honorific Royal Burial Practices', *JBL* 131 (2012), 99–119.

Wylie, A., *Thinking from Things: Essays in the Philosophy of Archaeology* (Berkeley, Ca., University of California Press, 2002).

Younger, Jr., K.L., 'Assyrian Involvement in the Southern Levant at the End of the Eighth Century B.C.E.', *Jerusalem in Bible and Archaeology: The First Temple Period* (ed. A.G. Vaughn and A.E. Killebrew, SBLSymS, Leiden, Brill, 2003), 235–263.

Zalcman, L., 'Shield of Abraham, Fear of Isaac, Dread of Esau', *ZAW* 117 (2005), 405–410.

Zehnder, M., 'Anstösse aus Dtn 23,2–9 zur Frage nach dem Umgang mit Fremden', *FZPhTh* 52 (2005), 300–314.

Zevit, Z., 'Text Traditions, Archaeology, and Anthropology: Uncertainties in Determining the Populations of Judah and Yehud from ca. 734 to ca. 400 BCE', *'Up to the Gates of Ekron': Essays on the Archaeology and History of the Eastern Mediterranean in Honor of Seymour Gitin* (ed. S.W. Crawford, A. Ben-Tor, J.P. Dessel, W.G. Dever, A. Mazar and J. Aviram, Jerusalem, W.F. Albright Institute of Archaeological Research and Israel Exploration Society, 2007), 436–443.

Ziffer, I., 'Stamps and Stamp Seals: I. The Iron Age', *Ḥorvat 'Uza and Ḥorvat Radum: Two Fortresses in the Biblical Negev* (ed. I. Beit-Arieh, MSIA 25, Tel Aviv, Tel Aviv University, 2007), 197–200.

Zimhoni, O., 'Two Ceramic Assemblages from Lachish Levels III and II', *TA* 17 (1990), 3–52.

Zorn, J., 'Naṣbeh, Tell en-', *New Archaeological Encyclopedia of the Holy Land* (ed. A. Negev and S. Gibson, New York, N.Y., Continuum, 2001), 912–918.

Zsolnay, I., 'The Misconstrued Role of the Assinnu in Ancient Near Eastern Prophecy', *Prophets Male and Female: Gender and Prophecy in the Hebrew Bible, the Eastern Mediterranean and the Ancient Near East* (ed. C. Carvalho and J. Stökl, Ancient Israel and its Literature 15, Atlanta, Ga., Society for Biblical Literature, 2013), 81–99.

Zuckerman, S., 'Beads and Pendants', *Various Reports* (vol. 4 of *Excavations at the City of David 1978–1985 Directed by Yigal Shiloh*, ed. D.T. Ariel and A. De Groot, Qedem 35, Jerusalem, Hebrew University of Jerusalem, 1996), 276–290.

# Archaeological Sites Index

# Author Index

# Biblical Index

# Subject Index